Gardening with Hardy Heathers

The garden of Beverly and James Thompson in Manchester, California, demonstrates how soil mounds and creative planting can turn a flat site into billows of heather.

Gardening with Hardy Heathers

David Small and Ella May T. Wulff

Timber Press
Portland | London

To Alice Knight, a founder of the North American Heather Society, who in both official and unofficial capacities has helped to guide the North American Heather Society since its inception in 1977,

and

to Anne Small, former administrator of The Heather Society, who managed the day-to-day affairs of the Society with quiet attention to detail for more than two decades,

this book is dedicated with gratitude.

Photographs by David Small, Barry L. Wulff, and Ella May T. Wulff, unless otherwise credited. Species distribution maps © Tasha L. Wulff.

Copyright © 2008 by David Small and Ella May T. Wulff.
All rights reserved.

Published in 2008 by Timber Press, Inc.

The Haseltine Building
133 S.W. Second Avenue, Suite 450
Portland, Oregon 97204-3527
timberpress.com

2 The Quadrant
135 Salusbury Road
London NW6 6RJ
timberpress.co.uk

ISBN: 978-1-60469-470-3

Designed by Dick Malt
Printed in the United States of America

The Library of Congress has previously cataloged the hardcover edition as follows:

Small, David.
 Gardening with hardy heathers / David Small and Ella May T. Wulff.
   p. cm.
 Includes bibliographical references and index.

 ISBN-13: 978-0-88192-782-5
 1. Heather. 2. Heather gardens. I. Wulff, Ella May T. II. Title.
 SB413.H42S63 2008
 635.9'3366--dc22
                    2007038816

A catalog record for this book is also available from the British Library.

Contents

Preface 7
Acknowledgments 8

1. Why Grow Heathers? 11
   What Is a Heather? 12
   Heathers in the Wild 14
   Natural History 16
   Human Uses for Heather 20
   The Future of Heathers 23
   The Language of Heather Growers 24

2. Care and Cultivation 26
   Climate 26
   Soils 32
   Mycorrhizae 36
   Fertilizing 39
   Buying Heather Plants 40
   Planting 43
   Transplanting 46
   Mulch 47
   Watering 48
   Pruning 49
   Pests and Diseases 59

3. Propagation 68
   Layering 69
   Dropping 70
   Cuttings 70
   Seed 78

4. Designing a Heather Garden 81
   Site Selection 84
   Getting Started 88
   Design Ideas 93
   Designing with Color 104

5. Companion Plants 113
   Trees 114
   Shrubs and Vines 119
   Grasses and Grasslike Plants 129
   Herbaceous Perennials 135
   Spring-Flowering "Bulbous" Plants 140
   Heathers in the Mixed Border 143
   Annuals 145
   Heathers as Companions or Foils for Other Plants 147
   Winning Combinations 149

6. Heather Breeding 152
   Rights and Patents 153
   Three Outstanding Modern Heather Breeders 155
   The Direction of Future Heather Breeding 166
   Basic Genetics for Plant Breeders 168
   Guide for Novice Heather Breeders 170
   How to Register a Heather Name 173

7. The Cultivated Hardy
   Heathers 176
   Calluna 176
   Daboecia 188
   Erica 192
   A Caution about Heather Names 230

8. Heathers as Cut Flowers 232
   Flower Arrangements 232
   Nosegays and Other Bouquets 236
   Drying Heathers 237
   Preserving Heathers 238
   Showing Heathers 239
   Species and Cultivars for Cutting 243

9. Heathers for Special Uses 245
   Alkaline Soil Tolerant 245
   Amenable to Hard Pruning 246
   Bud Bloomers 146
   Cape Heaths 247
   Cold Tolerant 249
   Drought Tolerant 250
   Early Bloomers among the
     Summer-Flowering Heathers 250
   Edgers 251

Fragrant 251
Ground Covers, Low Carpeters, and
  Heather Lawns 253
Heat Tolerant 253
Heat and Humidity Tolerant 253
Hedges 254
Late Bloomers among the
  Summer-Flowering Heathers 254
Long Blooming 255
Novelty Flowers with Garden Value 255
Rock Gardens, Sinks, and Troughs 255
Saint Kilda Heathers 256
Shade Tolerant 257
Trailing 257
Tree Heaths 258
Unusual Foliage 258
Winter Foliage Color 259

Heather Societies 260
Plant Sources 261
Garden Designers 266
Gardens with Heather Interest 268
Glossary 276
Bibliography 279
Index 289

Preface

The sight of wild heathers in full bloom has captivated people for millennia. Inevitably, heather plants were brought into gardens, where they sometimes performed less admirably than their undomesticated relatives living nearby. Just as inevitably, garden writers began to give advice about heather cultivation, which eventually led to the creation of many lovely heather gardens.

An updated treatment of the hardy heathers has long been needed. With the exception of Karla Lortz's beautiful, self-published book, *Heaths & Heathers: Color for All Seasons*, which features photographs of heathers in gardens on the west coast of the United States and makes no pretense of being a comprehensive work, there is in English no other large format heather book in print. Out-of-print heather books, while still useful aids to planning a heather garden, contain outdated species, hybrid, and even generic names. Many excellent cultivars have been introduced since the last of these books was published, and DNA research has shed new light upon relationships within the vast heather family.

When we were approached by Timber Press to write a new heather book, we decided that we could not, in good conscience, turn the offer down. Little did we know what the project would entail, or how long it would take!

As we traveled the long road from initial contact to final proofs, we were encouraged and assisted by many people, whose help we acknowledge elsewhere. We hope that this book will repay the favor, encouraging and assisting gardeners all over the world to plant hardy (and some not-so-hardy) heathers.

David Small, Creeting Saint Mary, Suffolk, UK
Ella May T. Wulff, Philomath, Oregon, USA

Acknowledgments

This book would not have been possible without the assistance and encouragement of many people, especially the wonderful international network of heather enthusiasts. The following individuals have answered questions, contributed ideas or illustrations, made suggestions for additions or improvements, proofread the manuscript, and cheered us on when the task threatened to overwhelm us; some have done all of the above.

We wish to thank:
In Australia: Nancye Cowan, John Sandham, Ian Small.
In Canada: Marjorie Mason, John and Joyce Prothero, Linda Smith, Bryan and Joan Taylor, Willa Wick, David Wilson.
In England: Peter Bingham, Carolyn Burraston, Joshua Burrill, David Edge, Daphne and Maurice Everett, Maria Green, John Griffiths, Allen Hall, Jean Julian, Anna Mumford (our long-suffering London editor), Charles Nelson, Ralph Noble, David and Rita Plumridge, Barry Sellers, Anne Small, Alison Stein, Mick Waring.
In Germany: Kurt Kramer, Jürgen Schröder.
In Ireland: Susan Kay.
In the Netherlands: Jos Flecken.
In New Zealand: Simon V. Fowler.
In Norway: Eileen Bonner Petterssen.
In Scotland: Marion Davie, John Grieve, David Lambie.
In South Africa: E. G. H. Oliver.
In Sweden: Brita Johansson.
In the United States: Mario Abreu, Greg Bennett, George and Elizabeth Bernard, Mark and Val Bloom, Ramona Bloomingdale, Ed and Kay Chapman, Janet Christie, Christina Coffey, Stacie Crooks, Glennda Couch-Carlberg, Dee Daneri, Edith Davis, Paul Dickey, Nancy Doubrava, Judith Doyle, Susan Ewalt, J. A. Fagerstrom, Stephenson and Susan Ford, the Forest Heights Homeowners Association, Ben Gardner, Cleo Hall, Sharon Hardy, Floyd Hutchins, Cynthia Janes, Rom Kim (our Portland editor), Alice Knight, Kathleen Kron, Berndt Lautenschlaeger, Janice Leinwebber, Kathy Lewis, Karla Lortz, Cathi Love, Donald A. M. Mackay, Stefani McRae-Dickey, Vivagean Merz, Elaine Miller, Robert S. Moreland, Donna Mummery, Judith Neher, Ernie and Marietta O'Byrne, Shirley Pierce, Kym Pokorny, Richard Poruban, Barbara and Ralph Reed, Lily Ricardi, Gail Safstrom, Carolyn Scagel, Gary Schuldt, Monika Shepherd, Kathy Slack, Alexa St. Clair, Steven Trudell, Katherine H. Udall, Berberie vanValey, Alan Williams, Priscilla H. Williams, Beverly Witchner, Barry Wulff, Tasha Wulff.

We are grateful for the help received from the colleagues, friends, neighbors, and relatives listed here. To others who helped with the book but whose names have been inadvertently omitted, we apologize and offer thanks, nonetheless. Special thanks go to John Griffiths, Kurt Kramer, and David Wilson for completing long questionnaires about their heather breeding activities—and for helping with other aspects of the book, as well. A huge debt of gratitude is owed to Charles Nelson, who has critiqued parts of the manuscript throughout their many incarnations, giving freely of his time and knowledge. Any errors that remain are the authors'.

1 Why Grow Heathers?

Few plants exhibit such diversity of size, form, and color of flower and foliage as do the heathers. The apparent uniformity of the magnificent purple vistas of the heather moorlands of Britain and Ireland is deceiving. Most gardeners are overwhelmed when presented for the first time with the infinite variation of the many garden selections of heather.

In moderate climates, it is possible to have heathers in flower every month of the year, in an enticing range of colors from white through the palest of pinks and lilacs to glowing crimson and purple. As if that were not enough, these small shrubs retain their leaves all year and are available with foliage colored yellow, gold, orange, red, gray, and, of course, many shades of green. The combination of brilliant colors in flowers and in foliage is hard to find in any other group of garden plants, and some of the easiest heathers to grow are at their colorful best in the drabbest months of the year.

The diversity of flower and foliage colors is enhanced by a vast range of growth habits. There are many prostrate forms reaching no taller than a few inches; at the other extreme, tree heaths can grow to a height of 6 ft. (2 m) or more. Some kinds are further enhanced by delightful floral fragrances.

Most of the color in this late-summer photograph of young heather plants produced by the Hachmann Nursery in Barmstedt, Germany, is foliage rather than flower color.

In most temperate areas of the world, the European heathers are among the easiest plants to cultivate. Although some species are tender, most are tough. If their few simple cultural requirements are met, within a few years they will cover the ground with a carpet of color. They can soon provide a weed-free garden that needs little maintenance.

Heathers are nearly carefree and thrive on quite poor soils, including those near the sea, many of them in windy places. They are easy to propagate and are also relatively free from diseases and pests, so upkeep costs are low. Many heathers make excellent cut flowers and also dry well. In short, heaths and heathers are the perfect, long-lasting plants for busy (or lazy) gardeners.

With more than 700 cultivated varieties available in the genus *Calluna* alone, heather growers truly have a wealth of choices. This book describes the variety of ways in which heathers can be grown: as hedges, in rock gardens, on gently sloping hillsides, in island beds, in raised beds, in containers, or with other plants in mixed borders.

What Is a Heather?

To most people living in the Northern Hemisphere, heather is the plant that in some parts of Scotland turns the hillsides purple when it flowers in late summer—*Calluna vulgaris*. Heather enthusiasts also welcome other plants as heathers. There are, for example, bell heather, *Erica cinerea*, which also colors the Scottish hills, and the many plants called heath: Saint Dabeoc's heath (*Daboecia*), Cornish heath (*E. vagans*), and cross-leaved heath (*E. tetralix*), to name a few. Traditional names for these plants vary with location: *Calluna*, *E. cinerea*, and *E. tetralix* are each called "cat heather" in some parts of Scotland (Nelson 2003).

The grouping of plants commonly called heathers, or heaths and heathers (the monospecific genus *Calluna* having the honor of being the "true heather" in the eyes of North American enthusiasts), is based upon a number of shared characteristics. All are members of the Ericaceae, the heather family; and the majority of European plants called heaths or heathers are in the genus *Erica*, from which the family takes its name. DNA sequence data suggest that "*Erica* species form a single well-defined group and...their closest living relative is *Calluna vulgaris*" (Small and Kron 2001). Slightly more distant but still closely related to both *Calluna* and *Erica* is *Daboecia*. These three genera constitute the tribe Ericeae. *Calluna*, *Daboecia*, and non-African *Erica* species are all native to the heathlands of Europe at various elevations. Some species also form part of *maquis* or *garigue* ecosystems.

All heathers of the Northern Hemisphere are small-leaved, evergreen shrubs with a tendency to smother themselves with flowers when in bloom. Most have low, mounding shapes—the tree heaths being a notable exception to this last characteristic.

Plants not in the Ericeae are sometimes called heather. The so-called mountain

At the higher elevations on Pico, Azores, *Daboecia azorica* replaces *Erica scoparia* subsp. *azorica* as the dominant heather. Here, part way up the volcano, the two species coexist, along with *Calluna vulgaris*.

heathers, in the genera *Cassiope* and *Phyllodoce*, found throughout the Northern Hemisphere at high latitudes and altitudes, certainly fit the description of heather in the preceding paragraph. However, they are only distantly related to heathers. They also have different cultivation requirements from those of heathers and are more often raised by specialist alpine gardeners than by heather growers.

Andromeda, commonly called bog rosemary, has sometimes been considered a heather because of a quirk of the organization that attempts to regulate the naming of plants. The International Commission for the Nomenclature of Cultivated Plants has placed the genus *Andromeda* within the purview of The Heather Society (United Kingdom), along with *Calluna*, *Daboecia*, and *Erica*. Because The Heather Society is the designated International Cultivar Registration Authority for *Andromeda*, some authors have included this genus in their books about heather. Botanically and horticulturally, this makes little sense.

Although it is a member of the Ericaceae, *Andromeda* does not fit comfortably into the common perception of heather. A casual observer who compared it with *Calluna*, *Daboecia*, and *Erica* would not call it heather. It is not a rosemary, either, or even distantly related to the culinary herb rosemary—a member of the mint family (Lamiaceae), which shows how misleading common names can be. In their review of both DNA and morphological evidence for the Ericaceae, Kron et al. (2002) placed *Andromeda* far from the heather tribe on their new family tree. It is no more closely related to heathers than are cranberries (*Vaccinium* species).

One additional "heather" bears mention here, another victim of its common English names. Mexican heather, also called false heather or Hawaiian heather, is not even in the Ericaceae. The plant laboring under this burden of mistaken nomenclature is *Cuphea hyssopifolia*, a tender subshrub belonging to the Lythraceae, native from Mexico to Guatemala. Despite its multitude of tiny, lavender-colored flowers—and three common names that insist otherwise—this plant is definitely not a heather.

The focus of this book is the cultivation, uses, and descriptions of the European species of the closely related genera *Calluna*, *Daboecia*, and *Erica*, and their hybrids. The shared characteristics and similar cultural requirements of these plants called heather make it easy to plant an entire garden of heathers or to use the different kinds of heather interchangeably in a variety of garden situations.

Heathers in the Wild

Heathers are primarily associated with or even sometimes define two closely related ecosystems in western Europe: heaths and moorlands, where they grow mixed with other shrubs, forbs, grasses, and, occasionally, trees. Heathers are so closely associated with heathlands that, in some languages, the word for the plant is the same as the word for the ecosystem in which it predominates. According to James Parry (2003), the root of the modern word heather is the Old English *hæð*, which was used for both the place and the plant. The modern English word *heath* also is used for both. In the *Concise Oxford English Dictionary* (Soanes and Stevenson 2004), a heath is described as "an area of open uncultivated land, typically on acid sandy soil and covered with heather, gorse, and coarse grasses." A heath also is "a dwarf shrub with small leathery leaves and small pink or purple flowers, characteristic of heathland and moorland." The German word *Heide* also means both heathland and heather.

Heather colors Germany's Lüneberg Heath mauve in late August.

The *Concise Oxford English Dictionary* defines *moor* as "a tract of open uncultivated upland, typically covered with heather." Both heathland and moorland are often thought of as open, rolling, infertile, or boggy wasteland. Parry elucidated a simple way to distinguish between heathland and moorland: moorlands are based on peaty soils, whereas heaths are not. Heaths are, Parry says, "manufactured landscapes.... Without continued intervention by man... heaths would revert to forest." Only maritime heaths, where tree cover was never common, exist without human intervention.

Heaths

Heathland is characterized by the low incidence of trees and the prevalence of dwarf shrubs such as heather and gorse (*Ulex* species). According to Parry, they are "usually found on nutrient-poor acidic soils that have developed on freely draining sands and gravels." Humic acid produced by plant decomposition is washed by rain through the top layers of soil, where it activates iron oxides, which are then leached down to form a layer of iron compounds called a *pan*. Most plant roots cannot penetrate this layer, so they are confined to the shallow soil layer above it. Therefore, most heathland vegetation is very shallow rooted, spreading wide but not deep.

There are many kinds of heath, but with the exception of lichen or sphagnum-dominated heaths (very dry or very wet, respectively), "on most heaths, heathers form the framework for the entire heathland community" (Parry 2003).

Moorlands

Occurring primarily in the British Isles, moorlands usually are "uplands... botanically analogous to the lowland heaths... but high, wet, and cold," although they are not truly mountainous (Smout 2004). They are dominated by heather and coarse grasses.

Some authorities consider moorland to be, like heathland, not wilderness but an artifact of human modification dating back to Mesolithic times, at least, when forests were opened up by hunters for easy stalking of wild grazing animals (Simmons 2003). Many moorlands are the result of early and continued human activity after glaciers retreated in the last ice age (Rees 1996). People cleared trees and scrub for firewood and, as they domesticated the wild grazing animals, cleared even more land for the animals to graze. In turn, the grazing by livestock prevented re-invasion by scrub and trees in many places.

This view of moorland as analogous to heathland, in having strictly human origins, is not shared by everyone. Oliver Rackham (2003) states that climate is the primary determinant, the overriding reason that moorland is confined to high-rainfall areas of high latitudes and high altitudes. "Where the ground is forever wet, plant remains do not rot but compress... into... peat," and "high rainfall also leaches minerals out of the soil." Plants such as sphagnum and heathers, which are adapted to soils low in fertility, become dominant under such conditions.

In support of his argument for mixed origins of moorland, Rackham points out that in some parts of western Scotland, moorlands are expanding without human intervention as ancient pine trees die and spreading peat prevents the establishment of tree seedlings. Human activities, such as tree felling, merely accelerate the transition from woodland to moorland in high-rainfall areas. "Drier, less peaty moorland, like heathland, would still be wildwood but for human intervention" (Rackham 2003).

Only the area trampled by visitors to the standing stones of the Ring of Brodgar, Orkney, Scotland, is uncarpeted by heather.

Maquis

Unlike the heathlands and moorlands of northern and western Europe and the British Isles, heather habitats in southern Europe and around the shores of the Mediterranean are primarily of natural origin, though they, too, have been affected by human activity for millennia. Their heather inhabitants differ from those of heath and moorland in being considerably more drought tolerant.

Maquis is the French term for a drought-resistant Mediterranean scrub ecosystem composed of evergreen shrubs and small trees (usually 1 to 3 yd. [1 to 3 m] tall), with thick, leathery leaves or needle-like foliage, adapted for survival during long summer droughts. Common *maquis* species are *Erica arborea*, *E. lusitanica*, and *E. scoparia*.

In an examination of root depth in *Erica*-dominated *maquis* in Portugal, Joaquim S. Silva and Francisco C. Rego (2003) found that the average maximum rooting depth for the 28 deepest *Erica* roots was 87 in. (220 cm). The deepest root was estimated to be about 130 in. (330 cm) long. This is in sharp contrast to the shallow-rooted ericas of heath and moorland, which are far less tolerant of drought.

Garigue (also spelled *garrigue*)

This is another French term for another ecosystem found near the Mediterranean coast. It may be naturally occurring or the result of degradation of forest or *maquis* by human (and their associated domesticated animals') activity. This shrub community develops on rocky ground, often over large expanses of limestone (karst topography). There are high *garigues*, characterized by shrubs up to about a yard (1 m) high, and there are also low garigues, with shrubs less than ½ yard (0.5 m) high. *Erica multiflora* is a typical garigue heather.

Natural History

Heathers serve as sources of food and shelter for many kinds of animals. *Calluna* plants can live for up to 40 years, and many other heather species are also quite long-lived. A heathland in which all stages in the life cycle of the heather are present, even collapsed dead plants, contains a diversity of microhabitats in which many other organisms can thrive. Some of the more conspicuous animals associated with heathers are discussed here.

Birds

Birds are among the easily seen residents of heather-dominated landscapes, nesting among the heathers and feeding on the abundant insect life that heathlands support. Many migratory birds nest in the heather: curlew, plover, lapwing, merlin, and others (Rees 1996).

Heathers are well known as habitat and a source of food for grouse in the British

Small, carefully controlled fires are set every year on heath and moorland managed as grouse habitat. Each area is burned approximately once every 10 years here on Waskerley Moor, County Durham, England. Photo by David Plumridge.

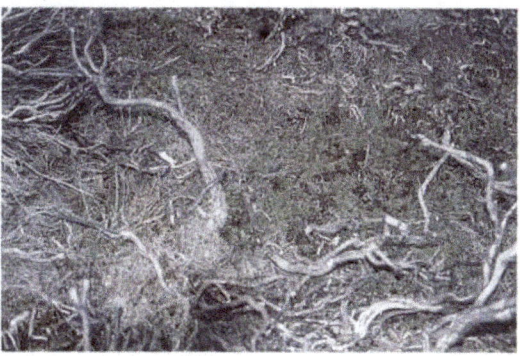

Heather regenerates from both seeds and roots after a burn. Photo by David Plumridge.

Three stages of heather growth on a moor managed as grouse habitat: soon after a burn (right), young growth beginning to flower (left foreground), and mature growth (rear). Photo by David Plumridge.

Sheep graze on heather near the reservoir on Waskerley Moor, County Durham, England. The number of sheep on the moor must be strictly limited to prevent their grazing from making the moor unsuitable for grouse habitat. The band of bleached *Calluna* skeletons crossing the picture resulted from a recent moor burn.

Isles. Red grouse (*Lagopus lagopus* subsp. *scoticus*) are year-round residents of moorlands and heaths. Throughout much of Britain, controlled moor burns and the regular cutting of heather are used to ensure a continuous supply of the young heather shoots relished as food by young grouse and also by sheep (Mackay 2005a). (Rees [1996] notes that the preference of sheep for *Calluna* over *Erica tetralix* has led to the dominance of *E. tetralix* in some areas.)

Grouse hunting has become a considerable source of income for holders of large land parcels suitable for maintaining as heather moorland. A failed attempt to establish grouse for hunting in New Zealand led to that country's present problem with introduced *Calluna vulgaris* crowding out the native tussock grasses on the North Island.

In their native South Africa, the large-flowered Cape heaths (*Erica* species) are sources of nectar for sunbirds (Nectariniidae), which return the favor by pollinating the ericas. Several species of hummingbirds (Trochilidae), which occupy a similar ecological niche in the Americas, regularly visit the Cape heaths planted in the arboretum of the University of California at Santa Cruz. According to the curator of the South African Collections at the arboretum, Ron Arruda (2005), a "tiny forest of [Erica] seedlings" springing up "on every hand" indicates that the hummingbirds have taken over the pollinating function of the sunbirds.

Farther north, in Mendocino County, California, and in Benton County, Oregon, rufous hummingbirds (*Selasphorus rufus*) have been observed visiting the flowers of *Daboecia cantabrica* 'Waley's Red', *D.* ×*scotica* 'Tabramhill' and 'William Buchanan', *Erica cinerea* 'Purple Beauty' (Somer 2005), and *E. umbellata* 'David Small'. Whether they also can serve as pollinators for these European heaths has not been determined.

Insects

Heathers are important food sources for the caterpillars of two moths, *Saturnia pavonia* and *Lasiocampa quercus* subsp. *callunae*, that feed on heather foliage (Rees 1996). Heathlands provide a home for a multitude of insects, but heathers of the *maquis* and *garigue* also shelter many arthropods. According to David McClintock (1990), the rough bark of old trunks of *Erica scoparia* and *E. terminalis* provides habitat for numerous kinds of insects.

Many kinds of butterflies visit heather flowers for their nectar. In North American gardens, spring heather flowers, for example, *Erica carnea*, are a good early source of nectar for butterflies that overwinter as adults, such as Milbert's Tortoiseshell (*Nymphalis milberti*) and Mourning Cloak (*N. antiopa*). Many other heathers also attract butterflies, with *E. vagans* being especially good for this purpose (Jackson 2006). During a recent banner year for Painted Lady (*Vanessa* species) in the Pacific Northwest, blooming plants of *E. arborea* 'Estrella Gold' and *E. tetralix* 'Alba Mollis' were at times covered with these butterflies, the insects seeming to be especially attracted to heathers with white flowers. They visited nearby blue and red flowers (including *E. cinerea*) in lesser numbers.

Heather flowers are superb food sources for many kinds of bees, which gather from them both nectar and pollen. Although honeybees (*Apis mellifera*) may be seen visiting heather flowers, they are nectar robbers rather than pollinators. Ericaceous plants have developed a specialized method of pollen release to insect visitors. The anthers are formed as tubes, with pollen grains released inside the tubes, which have pores to the outside. A visiting insect must be able to shake the anthers in order to gather the pollen (an action known as "buzz-pollination"), which honeybees are not able to do (Edwards 1996).

In the British Isles, two heather-pollinating bee species, *Colletes succinctus* and *Andrena fuscipes*, are ground-nesting solitary bees that require bare ground among the heathers for their nests. This bare ground is normally provided by the collapse of senescing heather plants, which opens areas that are then colonized by heather seedlings. Mike Edwards (1996) warns that human activity resulting in dense ground coverage jeopardizes the survival of these pollinators.

Daboecia cantabrica 'Cupido', photographed in Scotland, shows evidence of visitation by bumblebees. Note the irregular holes near the bases of two flowers.

Some bumblebees, *Bombus* species, and also other bees, have developed a behavior that allows them to obtain food from flowers with fused corollas whose openings are too small to admit the foraging bees, such as daboecias and *Erica ciliaris*. They bite holes near the bases of the corollas in order to gather pollen from the flowers. Such behavior is thought to lessen the chance that flowers will be pollinated with pollen from other flowers on the same plant. It forces pollinating bees to fly farther and thus increases genetic diversity (a positive effect) within the species targeted by pollen robbers (Maloof 2001).

Of course, some heather flowers are not pollinated by bees at all but by much smaller insects often unnoticed by the casual observer. Else and Olaf Hagerup (1953) determined that *Erica tetralix* flowers are both self-pollinated and pollinated by thrips (*Ceratothrips ericae*, formerly known as *Taeniothrips ericae*), which lay their eggs inside the corollas. Because male thrips are rare and wingless, the female thrips must visit many flowers to find mates. In so doing, they carry pollen from flower to flower. Hagerup and Hagerup found scars produced by thrips on herbarium specimens of plants collected from northern Spain to southern Norway and Sweden, the entire natural range of *E. tetralix*. These thrips are often found in *Calluna* flowers, in which they also lay eggs, but they do not visit *E. cinerea*.

Human Uses for Heather

Today, the uses of heathers are primarily ornamental: as garden plants and cut flowers. It is hard to imagine that as late as the eighteenth century, heathers had not yet become popular for gardens. Early uses of heather were much more closely associated with human survival, especially for dwellers of the heaths and moorlands.

Heather has been put to practical purposes for millennia. Heather rope, for example, is "one of the strongest and toughest ropes in the world and was used for tying up boats" on the Isle of Man (Chapple 1967) and for many other purposes.

Baskets, doormats, and pot scrubbers were all made from heather (Lambie 1994), and it was woven into fences (Chapple 1952). The 1969 *Yearbook of The Heather Society* contains a photograph by P. J. O'Hare (Plate 3) of a lobster trap from County Mayo, Ireland, that was made of an osier frame interlaced with heather. As far back as Roman times, old, woody heather stems were used in Britain for road and track foundations (Rees 1996).

Heather was used in traditional medicines, as were many other plants, to treat a variety of ailments. *Calluna*, *Daboecia*, and *Erica erigena* are noted by Manuel Pardo de Santayana et al. (2002) as having been used in Spain for their astringent and antiseptic properties. In Britain, young heather shoots were boiled in water, and the decoction was then used to cleanse and bathe wounds (Parry 2003).

Basket made from heather, photographed at the Corrigall Farm Museum, Orkney, Scotland.

Heather for Shelter

The use of heather for thatching is well known, although heather is too woody to compress closely enough to be watertight. A roof thatched solely with heather is no match for heavy or continuous rain. Heather is still occasionally used for thatching because of its appealing color when the thatch has aged, but modern heather thatch is usually laid over a watertight roofing material (Chapple 1952).

Stems of *Erica arborea* and *E. australis* are used in Spain to make huts and the bases of roofs for stables and grain stores. The heather stems are then overlaid with an impermeable layer such as rye straw (Pardo de Santayana et al. 2002).

Early heathland houses were built of cut sods or turves, especially in Scandinavia. Many Danish words for soil types refer to their consistency. The Danish words for heather, *lyng* and *lung*, are references to how light in weight heather turves are when compared to the weight of grass sods. The word for the turf came to be the word for the area where the turf was cut. It eventually became the word for the plants that grew in that area (Lange 1999). In English, the corresponding word is *ling*, used in some parts of Britain as the common name for *Calluna*.

Other Uses for Heather

Danish heathland farmers also used heather for bedding (for example, as mattress stuffing), and for litter and winter forage for livestock, as well as for dyeing cloth. Heather produces brown-red, lemon-yellow, or green dyes, depending upon what mordant is used. Pieces carved from the woody heather stems were used to make rake pegs and shoe plugs (to hold shoes together, instead of gluing them) (Lange 1999).

In Norway, too, heather enjoyed widespread use as animal fodder. As was customary in the British Isles, the heaths of western Norway were burned every few years to increase the production of nutritious new shoots for forage. Norwegian children eat the sweet flowers of *Calluna* (Alm 1999).

One of the first uses of heather was, of course, as fuel. In many countries, the old, woody stems of *Calluna* were gathered for firewood. In Spain, *Calluna*, *Erica multiflora*, and *E. vagans* were used as firewood, whereas the wood of *E. arborea*, *E. australis*, and *E. umbellata* was used to make charcoal. *Erica australis* was best for this purpose (Pardo de Santayana et al. 2002) and was used primarily in forges.

Another ancient and long-standing use for heather is to make brooms and besoms. In Britain, *Calluna* is cut for brushes and brooms after the sap has risen but before the flowers are formed, beginning about the end of June (Chapple 1952). *Erica scoparia* is considered the best species for brooms in Spain (Pardo de Santayana et al. 2002), although *Calluna*, *E. multiflora*, and *E. tetralix* are also used there for that purpose.

Heather besom, Corrigall Farm Museum, Orkney, Scotland.

Erica arborea roots are the source of wood for briar pipes. In Spain, they are also carved into necklaces, jewel cases, and musical instruments (Pardo de Santayana et al. 2002). The very hard wood is boiled for 12 hours, then left to dry, after which it can be carved into bell clappers, cowbells, heels for clogs, eating utensils, and many other household items.

Cut heather branches make good packing material, and in the early twentieth century, they were used for packing earthenware and iron pipes. Later in the century, cut *Calluna* stems were employed for another purpose. In a walk on the North Yorkshire

A technique originally developed to produce floor tiles during World War II now is used in making heather jewelry, such as this necklace photographed against the winter foliage of *Calluna vulgaris* 'Soay'.

(England) moors in 1990, Jean Sharpe and Albert Julian (1992) discovered neatly baled heather that had just been cut from the moorland and was destined for export to the Netherlands, where it would be used in sewage filter beds.

During World War II, the use of timber for flooring was restricted in Britain, but a suitable substitute was soon found. *Calluna* stems were bundled, tightly compressed, held together with a bonding agent, then sliced transversely to make floor tiles that were resilient, hard wearing, and long lasting (Lambie 1994). When the easing of timber restrictions after the war made heather tiles uneconomical to produce, the technique was converted to the making of heather jewelry. The stems are now dyed before bundling, and the slices are cut into cabochons and polished, so that they resemble semiprecious stones.

Heather Honey

A traditional heather use that persists into the present time is as a source of nectar for honey. Honey and beeswax have been valued for thousands of years and were very important economically until the last few centuries (Parry 2003), when sugar and paraffin became widely available.

Heather gardens offer double value to beekeepers. Nectar from winter- and spring-blooming heathers may be the only source of food for honeybees taking winter cleansing flights, thus helping to keep a hive alive through the winter. Summer-blooming heathers are excellent honey plants.

Many heather species are useful in the production of honey. *Calluna* honey, in particular, has excellent flavor and a fragrance that recalls the fragrance of moorland and heathland in full bloom.

A Caution

Gardeners who take up beekeeping in order to enjoy the bonus of heather honey from their gardens should be careful in their selection of companion plants. Although many other members of the Ericaceae make excellent heather companions, some have toxic nectar whose honey produces the symptoms of heather intoxication or "mad honey disease" when eaten by humans and other animals.

The offending toxin is grayanotoxin, formerly called andromedotoxin, acetylandromedol, or rhodotoxin (U. S. Food and Drug Administration 2006). Some plants notable for containing this toxin are *Rhododendron albiflorum*, *R. macrophyllum*, *R. occidentale*, and *R. ponticum*. The former three species are native to North America, while the last is found in Mediterranean regions and naturalized throughout much of Britain and Ireland. Some other *Rhododendron* species also produce grayanotoxin. *Andromeda*, *Leucothoe*, and *Kalmia* species (one of which bears the common name "lambkill"!) contain grayanotoxin, as do *Pieris* species (University of Pennsylvania 2002).

Most ornamental ericaceous plants that contain grayanotoxin flower in the spring, although summer-flowering or re-blooming *Rhododendron* hybrids are now becoming available. Avoid planting late-blooming toxic companions if honey production is an important reason for planting a heather garden. After the above-mentioned toxic species have finished flowering, beekeepers should remove the honey produced from them so that it does not contaminate the late-summer-to-autumn heather honey crop (Honey Health.com). This precaution is necessary only when there are large numbers of toxic nectar-producing plants in the garden or the surrounding area. Nectar from only a few toxic plants will be sufficiently diluted by that collected from other plants so as not to cause problems with the honey.

Religious Associations of Heathers

Heather has not been associated with religion as an object of veneration in itself, as were, for example, certain kinds of trees worshiped by the druids, and other trees that are still treated with respect by some Asian peoples as the residences of spirits. Heather is, instead, venerated indirectly through its association with historic visions of the Virgin Mary in some primarily Catholic countries.

In Spain, according to Ramón Morales et al. (2003), there are two Castilian sanctuaries where the Virgin Mary is venerated with allusions to heaths. The shrine for Nuestra Señora del Brezo (Our Lady of the Heather), in the province of Palencia, was built high in the Sierra del Brezo (Heather Mountains) in the eighteenth century, although according to local tradition, the veneration has a history tracing back to 1478. The shrine, nearly 4600 ft. (1400 m) above sea level, was constructed exactly on a line of contact between limestone and siliceous rocks. The surrounding shrub vegetation that gives its name to the region includes *Calluna vulgaris*, *Erica arborea*, *E. australis*, *E. cinerea*, and *E. vagans*.

Nuestra Señora de los Brezales (Our Lady of the Heather Moors), in the province of Soria, is at about 3500 ft. (1060 m) above sea level. The local river is Río Brezales (River of Heaths), named after the heathers that are the main component of the local vegetation and also give their name to the Virgin of the local hermitage. Here may be found *Calluna vulgaris*, *Erica arborea*, *E. cinerea*, *E. scoparia*, *E. tetralix*, and *E. vagans*.

The Future of Heathers

Many of the traditional uses of heather have been superseded by modern substitutes, just as the automobile replaced the horse and buggy. Some heather products, such as brooms and besoms, are still superior to those made from other materials, and there will always be a market for heather honey.

An old peat cut in Birsay Moor Nature Reserve, Orkney, Scotland, is now completely regrown with heather.

There will also be a need to preserve the wild places, even those resulting from human intervention, such as heaths. Heathers will survive as long as there is moorland and heathland, for they are superbly suited to such environments. New practical uses may be found for these versatile shrubs, such as the reclamation of wasteland and mine spoils (see "Mycorrhizae" in chapter 2).

Heather's glorious future lies in cultivation, as more and more gardeners discover its virtues. The heather plants now growing in gardens are a small fraction of those that could—and would—be grown if their ease of cultivation and many potential uses were more widely known. Despite their antiquity in the wild, heathers are practically newborn babes in the garden. Come explore with us some of the ways that heather can make gardening both easier and more exciting.

The flowers of the bud bloomer *Calluna vulgaris* 'Alexandra' never open, giving this attractive cultivar an extended "blooming" period that makes it valuable for autumn and winter garden color.

The Language of Heather Growers

Every specialist field of study or interest group has its own peculiar jargon. Heather specialists are not immune to this affliction and use a few exclusive descriptive terms that you will find repeated throughout this book. The glossary at the back of the book contains explanations of terms not discussed here.

Bud-blooming Heathers

Bud bloomers are cultivars of *Calluna vulgaris* whose flowers color but never open. These are also called *bud flowerers*. (For further explanation, see "Bud Bloomers" in chapter 9.)

Cultivar

Short for "cultivated variety," cultivars are named, cultivated plants all of which have been propagated asexually from a single plant that may have been either a seedling or a mutation (sport) on another plant. All plants of a cultivar are genetically identical, clones of the original plant. The cultivar name is properly written after the species or hybrid name and enclosed within single quotation marks: for example, *Calluna vulgaris* 'Colette'.

When a hybrid name has not been assigned, the cultivar name is written after the genus name, for example, *Erica* 'Winter Fire'. Sometimes a name is written this way to save space when the species name has been mentioned earlier in a paragraph. A cultivar name may be used only once for each genus of heathers, so the species name may be omitted without its omission causing confusion.

Hardy Heathers

Hardiness is relative. Most gardeners would say that if a plant is "hardy," it is able to withstand below freezing temperatures. How far below freezing and for how long that cold lasts determines how hardy the plant is. Although other factors such as heat, sunlight, precipitation, and humidity also influence plant survival, heathers are generally considered hardy if they can tolerate (with or without winter protection) temperature regimes as cold as those in United States Department of Agriculture (USDA) Hardiness Zone 8 or colder. Obviously, a plant that will tolerate only the cold experienced in Zone 8 is far less winter hardy than one that can survive in Zone 4. Hardiness zone ratings have not yet been determined for some of the newer hybrids.

Spring-tipped Heathers

Spring tips are new spring growth that is a color other than green. It is not the individual leaves that are tipped with color but rather the entire growing tip of each shoot. The phenomenon is found frequently in hybrids between heather species. According to Ian Small and Hazel Alanine (1994), it is thought to be due to genetic incompatibility between the parent species causing delayed chlorophyll and carotenoid development in new growth. Other pigments in the new growth are responsible for the color seen in spring tips before chlorophyll finally develops and hides it.

Spring tips also occur in *Calluna* cultivars of garden origin but have never been found in wild *Calluna* plants. Because plants brought together in gardens may have been collected from opposite ends of the extensive geographic range of *C. vulgaris*, genetic incompatibility could explain the appearance of spring tips in their offspring.

Although the colored new growth phenomenon usually occurs only in spring (whence the term "spring tips"), a few cultivars have colored tips whenever they make new growth. These cultivars, for example, *Calluna vulgaris* 'Mrs Pat', are less cold tolerant than the average plant of the species and need to be planted in locations sheltered from cold winter winds.

Calluna vulgaris 'Mrs Pat' takes the spring tip phenomenon to extremes, producing colored tips whenever new growth is made throughout the year, not only in spring. The bright pink foliage tips are far more impressive than the pale lavender, late summer flowers.

2 Care and Cultivation

Heathers may be grown in many temperate climate regions if their few specific cultural needs are met. With knowledge and implementation of these requisites for survival, and of additional beneficial cultural practices, they may be grown well and become valuable garden assets.

Climate

Heathers useful for planting in temperate zone gardens are often termed "hardy." This term emanates from Great Britain and Ireland, whose climates are strongly maritime-influenced. It provides little guidance to gardeners in countries with harsher, continental climates.

Years ago, botanists and horticulturists gathered weather records throughout North America to compile a database that would show the average annual minimum temperature for each region. These records were condensed into a range of temperature bands that became known as plant hardiness zones. The United States Department of Agriculture Plant Hardiness Zone Map (1990) is generally considered the standard measure of plant hardiness throughout much of the United States and Canada. (A revised USDA map will soon be published that reflects recent changes in regional climates resulting from global warming.) A similar map is available for Europe. Although far from perfect, especially since weather and climates appear to be undergoing considerable fluctuations, the USDA plant hardiness zone ratings are useful predictors of winter survival potential.

USDA Hardiness Zone Temperatures

Zone 1:	below −50°F	(below −46°C)
Zone 2:	−50 to −40°F	(−46 to −40°C)
Zone 3:	−40 to −30°F	(−40 to −34°C)
Zone 4:	−30 to −20°F	(−34 to −29°C)
Zone 5:	−20 to −10°F	(−29 to −23°C)
Zone 6:	−10 to 0°F	(−23 to −18°C)
Zone 7:	0 to 10°F	(−18 to −12°C)
Zone 8:	10 to 20°F	(−12 to −7°C)
Zone 9:	20 to 30°F	(−7 to −1°C)
Zone 10:	30 to 40°F	(−1 to 4°C)
Zone 11:	above 40°F	(above 4°C)

Average annual minimum temperature is insufficient information for determining if a certain plant could survive in a certain zone. The total number of days that the plant will be subjected to such temperatures is important, as are large temperature fluctuations above and below freezing.

Akira Sakai and Satoshi Miwa (1979) conducted freezing experiments on 12 European heather species and hybrids, and on 26 South African *Erica* species. They confirmed that, in general, European species are much more resistant to freezing than are the South African Cape heaths. Of the European species tested, *Erica lusitanica* foliage showed the least resistance to freezing. *Calluna* cultivars were, as expected, tolerant of more degrees of frost than other heathers; but even among *Calluna* cultivars, there was considerable variation in tolerance. *Calluna vulgaris* 'Joy Vanstone', for example, showed foliage damage at 1°F (−17°C), whereas the foliage of 'Gold Haze' was not damaged until the temperature dropped to −22°F (−30°C), the temperature at which xylem damage occurred in all other *Calluna* cultivars tested.

The foliage of *Erica carnea* sustained frost damage at a higher temperature than did *Calluna* foliage, but the xylem of *E. carnea* could tolerate lower temperatures than that of any other heather, down to −40°F (−40°C) in the cultivar 'Snow Queen'. In contrast, many Cape heaths showed foliage damage at 23°F (−5°C), with the hardiest tested (*E. canaliculata*, *E. cerinthoides*, and *E. speciosa*) showing foliage damage at 18°F (−8°C) and xylem damage at 14°F (−10°C).

The flowers of this *Erica carnea* 'Bell's Extra Special' emerged undamaged from beneath a heavy snow load.

Cold tolerance is only one factor that determines where a particular plant can grow. Heat tolerance is also important, as are humidity, exposure to wind, and the amount and timing of rainfall. It is the combination of these factors acting together that will ultimately decide what plant may survive where. Therefore, when considering the suitability of a species for a particular region, it is advisable to take these additional factors into account.

USDA plant hardiness zones should be used only as rough guidelines when choosing heather species for the garden. For example, most heathers that do well in Zone 8 in Great Britain and along the northern Pacific coast of North America will not thrive in Zone 8 regions of the American Southeast because of the high humidity that accompanies summer heat there. Gardeners in the extremely dry American Great Basin states and Southwest and much of the Iberian Peninsula are required to choose different heathers and provide them with different garden habitats than would gardeners living in the same cold-tolerance zones in wetter regions, for example, Ireland.

Knowing your climate and your garden's microclimates—which could enable you to grow plants not normally hardy in your area—is essential to the planning of a successful garden. Most gardeners suffer to some degree from what has been called "zonal denial," the refusal to recognize that some plants just cannot be grown in their gardens.

So they push the limits, planting Zone 8 plants in a Zone 7 garden, for instance. Sometimes they get away with it, because the zone ratings for many cultivars are based upon the limited experiences of a few people who have grown the plants, or because they have Zone 8 microclimates in their gardens. If you really like a heather species that is rated as marginally hardy where you garden, try to grow a few plants of it. Within a given species, there may be cultivars that are more tolerant of heat or cold or drought than others of the same species. Your chance of success will increase if you can obtain a cultivar whose climate of origin closely approximates that of your garden. That information may be available in the *Handy Guide to Heathers* (Small and Small 2001) or the *International Register of Heather Names, Vol. 1* (Nelson and Small 2000).

Hardiness is relative. Cape heaths and fuchsias thrive in the sheltered microclimate of this private garden near Dublin, Ireland.

Unusually strong winter winds can seriously challenge heathers that normally would be safe to grow in a particular zone. The possibility of such damage should be considered when siting heather plantings. Heather protected from the full force of the wind during below-freezing temperatures by a winter mulch or a shelter belt may survive undamaged, although the same kind of heather without protection will be severely damaged or even killed by prolonged exposure to cold winds. When plant roots are frozen, they cannot take up water. The wind will take all available moisture out of the plant (through transpiration), but the roots will not be able to replace it from the frozen ground. Affected plant parts die from desiccation, not from freezing.

Plants that are normally hardy in a particular region can be wiped out by a disastrously abnormal season. Such a winter occurred in 2003–04 along nearly the entire Atlantic coast of North America. It killed plants that had done well there for decades, including mature trees. A sudden, extreme temperature drop with no snow cover, which followed a long, warm autumn that had prevented plants from undergoing their normal, gradual slide into winter dormancy, was more than most plants could take, many heathers among them.

Although the survivors of such a winter are to be cataloged and promoted, the cultivars that succumbed to the anomaly may be perfectly good choices for a new garden. Such an event may not happen again for decades, if ever—or it could happen next year. Climate and weather are among the many challenges that make gardening interesting.

Climate affects not just survival but growth rate and ultimate size of the plant. Plants growing in a climate where the growing season is cut short by cold, snow, or drought will naturally grow much more slowly than those in a climate where they can grow throughout much of the year. Cultivar heights and widths given in this book are average for plants grown in the southeast of England and the west coast of Europe. Plants growing in the benevolent climates of western Ireland, southwestern England, and the maritime Pacific Northwest region of North America will grow larger than these dimensions. Those growing in continental climates that experience many months of freezing temperatures will be smaller than the given sizes. Such climatic influences upon growth should be taken into account when designing a garden.

Cultivars should be carefully chosen for their suitability for the climate where they are to grow. The huge natural latitudinal range of *Calluna vulgaris* in western Europe means that its cultivars differ greatly in their heat and cold tolerance, depending upon where they grew in the wild. Knowing the provenance of a cultivar before you buy it will help to ensure that it is a match for your garden's climate.

Drought tolerance is another consideration that may be influenced by provenance. *Erica mackayana*, found in the wild in Ireland and northern Spain, is normally thought of as drought intolerant because most of the early cultivars originated from rather wet environments in Ireland. Cultivars of Spanish origin, such as 'Shining Light', may have been subjected to seasonal drought stress in their native habitats and should be more tolerant of occasional drying than those from Ireland, although no cultivar of this species does well under dry conditions.

What is often not considered is that cultivars also vary in their humidity and sun tolerance. These factors mean that some of the most attractive cultivars grown for foliage color will not do well in some places where they would be perfectly at home temperature-wise.

Heathers with silvery gray leaves will not tolerate the combination of high heat with high humidity. They can also suffer during extended periods of very cold and wet weather. The tiny hairs on the leaves and stem, which give them their desirable color, trap too much water vapor; and they quickly succumb to disease organisms encouraged by those conditions. Silver-leaved heathers will, however, do fairly well in hot areas with relatively low humidity.

Golden-foliaged heathers with white flowers have a tendency to sunburn in hot summer sun and are practically impossible to grow in very hot, dry places like the California Central Valley (which is inhospitable to heathers, golden-foliaged or otherwise). Where summers are hot and dry, but not as hot and dry as in the Central Valley, it is possible to grow some white-flowered golds, but they must be carefully chosen for the location. For instance, in the Wulff garden in Oregon's Willamette Valley, *Calluna vulgaris* 'Carole Chapman' and 'Lemon Gem' burn in full sun exposures, but 'Christina' and 'Marion Blum' do not. Sunburn will not kill susceptible cultivars outright in these intermediate climates, but it will make them unattractive.

Some heather cultivars with golden foliage and colored flowers also can sunburn, for example, *Calluna vulgaris* 'Fire King'. This is particularly unfortunate, because many in this category are valuable for the beautiful shades of orange and red that their foliage assumes in winter. Usually, those that retain a bit of orange in the foliage in summer, such as 'Firefly', are not likely to sunburn, because they have enough anthocyanin pigment to protect them. Also fairly sun resistant are the white-flowered cultivars whose foliage is not quite yellow, such as 'Lime Glade'. The leaves of this cultivar have more chlorophyll than those of the completely yellow or golden heathers but not as much chlorophyll as normal heather foliage.

Other heather species with cultivars selected for unusual foliage color will react to the combination of light, temperature, and humidity in the same way as does *Calluna vulgaris*. For example, *Erica carnea* 'Golden Starlet' and 'Westwood Yellow' can sunburn in hot summer climates, as can *E. tetralix* 'Swedish Yellow'. Most *E. tetralix* cultivars are finely hairy, so they are not good choices for hot summer regions with high humidity.

Gardeners who are uncertain whether a particular heather species can survive in their climate should try planting cultivars of that species with plain, dark green foliage. If those survive, then they can experiment with the colored-foliage varieties.

Heat Amelioration

Although most guides for growing heather recommend full sun exposure or at least a half-day of sunlight, shade may be just what is needed to allow heathers to survive in hot summer climates. In regions with very hot summer days, plant heathers where they will receive morning sun, then shade from noon until evening.

Alternatively, site heathers where they will receive dappled shade or bright, indirect light for most of the day. This is most easily achieved by planting them under the canopies of tall deciduous trees that have had their lower branches removed, a process known as "limbing up." When planting under trees, remember that tree roots will remove significant amounts of water from the soil in their root zones. Heathers grown under trees will need extra watering to compensate for what the trees use.

Either shading method will reduce flowering somewhat as compared to plants growing in full sun in a cool climate. They will also reduce the intensity of gold and winter-red foliage colors. Shade with fewer heather flowers and less intense foliage color is infinitely preferable to full sun and dead or badly burned heather plants.

Winter Protection

Heathers can be grown in zones colder than their rated tolerance if they receive winter protection. Without question, the best winter protection is reliable snow cover that begins early and stays late. Where snow can be counted upon, heathers need no other protection. However, where snow rarely falls but temperatures can drop well below freezing for extended periods, the hardier heather species can often be brought through the winter if they are given a protective covering that will moderate extremes of temperature and prevent the ground from freezing deeply.

Such covers can be cut conifer boughs laid over the beds, floating fabric row covers, oak leaves, salt marsh hay, or pine needles. Do not use hay from cereal crops as winter mulch unless you plan to convert the heather garden to a cornfield. Even straw can introduce unwanted seeds to the garden.

When grown in semi-shade, *Erica* ×*griffithsii* 'Valerie Griffiths' has light green foliage instead of the golden foliage it will produce when grown in sunny situations. Photo by Joyce Prothero.

The primary consideration in choosing winter mulch is that it not pack down and smother the heathers. Surprisingly, Ontario gardener Willa Wick (personal communication) found that she could effectively use a thick mulch of shredded maple leaves (*Acer negundo* and *A. saccharum*) mixed with a few grass clippings as winter protection on her heathers. The plants emerged from under their winter blanket, which was gradually removed in early spring, appearing fresh and green.

In very cold climates, heather enthusiasts have sheltered individual plants under the polystyrene foam insulating covers sold as "rose cones," with some success (Gail Safstrom, personal communication). Pine needles can be a problematic choice for winter cover, because they also provide winter shelter for mice, which quite naturally will nibble on the readily available heather foliage. Mice and voles are not normally a problem in heather gardens, but they may become one when they are provided with such a comfortable winter bed. Their damage can be minimized if the upper layer of soil is allowed to freeze before the mulch is applied.

Do not be in a hurry to remove winter cover in the spring. Severe cold damage is most likely to occur if a late freeze occurs after the plants have begun to come out of winter dormancy. This is a serious problem for *Erica* ×*darleyensis*, which is particularly vulnerable to stem splitting caused by freezing. Sometimes such late freezes will kill the tops of heather plants, but when the roots are unaffected, the plants will produce new growth from the roots. If winter damage occurs, cut off the dead top growth and wait a month or two to see if the plant will sprout new growth.

Soils

The ideal soil for all hardy heather species is the same as is favored by most members of the Ericaceae. If you can grow rhododendrons easily, you probably have good soil for heathers. It should be slightly acidic, high in organic matter, freely draining yet moisture retentive. An acidic sandy loam with lots of humus is excellent. If your soil does not quite fit this description, adding organic matter to it is the best start toward making it heather friendly. Some soils will benefit from other amendments, as well.

Heathers can be quite happy for many years growing in nothing but a deep pile of aged conifer bark or other organic matter that will decompose slowly. They also can live in very sandy soil to which a large quantity of organic matter has been added. Mycorrhizal fungal associations enable them to survive in soils that are otherwise low in nutrients. In their natural environments, heathers grow in nutrient-poor soils.

Ben Gardner, of Pistol River, Oregon, planted a heather garden on an ancient sand dune to which he had added considerable organic matter and which he waters regularly. (Do not try this on a primary dune exposed directly to the ocean.) The original heathers have thrived, and they have seeded around very happily, probably aided by the frequent coastal fog in that mild-winter region. Ben also gave up pruning long ago, and his garden now has a distinctly wild appearance. With his addition of *Watsonia* plants to one hillside, the garden could be mistaken from a distance for South African *fynbos*; some of Ben's European heathers have achieved the stature of the larger Cape heaths.

In Pistol River, Oregon, Ben Gardner's heathers thrive on an old sand dune to which he added copious amounts of organic matter.

Drainage

Although heathers need to have at least some moisture available at all times—*Erica mackayana* having perhaps the greatest need for moisture—heathers cannot stand water-logged soil and will quickly die if planted where water stands for long periods. Freely draining soil is essential, one reason why planting heathers on a slope is advisable.

Heathers cannot survive if planted in clay. Not only is it difficult for their fine roots to penetrate; it holds too much water. If the gooey stuff came with your property, you have several options. Grow something other than heather; seriously amend the clay with large amounts of organic matter and sand or grit; or plant above the clay in raised beds filled with a soil mix specially formulated for ericaceous plants.

When amending clay soils with sand, unless you add more sand to the upper layers of soil than there is clay, you get something closely resembling concrete. This is not what heathers need. If you add only organic matter to the clay, the heathers will be happy for a few years, until all the organic matter has decomposed and nothing is left but the original clay. They will then expire or put on such a sulk that you'll wish they had.

The secret to amending clay soils, which by definition have the smallest size soil particles, is to add large quantities of variously sized larger soil particles such as sand and grit. (Adding grit to heavy soils is particularly important for success in growing *Erica cinerea*, which resents being planted in heavy soils that remain wet in the winter.) A mixture of particle sizes is sometimes sold as "builders' sand." Because the particles are considerably larger than clay particles and are of varying dimensions, they cannot pack as closely together as can clay particles, so there will be room for water and air to move through the soil.

Use only sharp, quarried sand for amending clay soils. Do not use beach sand. The water-rounded particles will not promote drainage well, and the heathers will not appreciate the salt content of sand from ocean beaches.

In addition to adding the sand and grit mix, it is absolutely essential to add as much organic matter as possible. You cannot add too much, unless you are adding freshly ground wood, whose decomposition will deplete the soil of nitrogen. Although heathers naturally grow on nutrient-deficient soils, even they will have difficulty surviving in fresh wood chips. Choose, instead, finely chopped aged conifer bark (whose very slow decomposition does not deplete the soil as does that of chopped wood), chopped leaves, and aged compost. If you purchase commercially prepared compost such as that sold by many municipalities from their recycling stations, be sure that lime has not been added to the compost.

Unless you plan to plant lime-tolerant species, avoid the use of sedge peat and spent mushroom compost, which usually contains lime and other unwanted goodies. Most sphagnum peat substrates, unless they have been sterilized, contain ericoid mycorrhizal fungi that will potentially improve heather growth (Gorman and Starrett 2003).

Should you choose to amend clay soil, your greatest chance of success comes with adding amendments to the clay gradually, so that there is not a sharp demarcation between pure clay and amended soil. Where such a line exists, the heather roots (and other plant roots, as well) will simply stop at the line and then travel along the boundary between the layers, not through it. This situation can be prevented by creating a gradient, so that the upper soil layers are mostly sand and organic matter, the amount of clay gradually increasing as the soil gets deeper.

The Wulff heather garden in western Oregon was made on a slope of pure clay, the kind that will coat your boots with so much mud during the winter rainy season that you can barely lift your feet. During the dry summers of this cool Mediterranean climate region, the same clay will repel a pickaxe. To prepare the clay slope for the heather garden, we began by removing or killing all weeds with a herbicide containing glyphosate. A 6-inch (15-cm) layer of builders' sand was spread on the designated garden area and thoroughly mixed into the clay with a large rototiller. Then a 6-inch layer of rotted conifer bark, well-aged waste from a sawmill, was spread and tilled in. Another 6-inch layer of sand followed, also tilled in. A few large rocks were strategically placed to stabilize the steepest parts of the slope. Then the paths were laid out

After all grass and weeds were killed, several alternating layers of sand and rotted conifer bark were spread over the heather garden site and tilled into the Philomath clay.

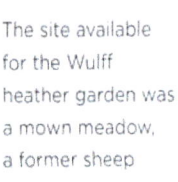

The site available for the Wulff heather garden was a mown meadow, a former sheep pasture.

Once the soil had been amended and the larger rocks placed, Ella May used garden hoses to outline future heather beds.

and the amended soil removed from the paths was used to build up the soil in the new garden beds.

After the paths were excavated, the entire garden area was topped with a 6-inch (15-cm) layer of finish mix composed of three parts builders' sand, three parts rotted bark, and one part sandy loam dredged from a local river bottom. The mix was thrown onto the garden from a gravel truck and raked into place. Any finish mix that landed on a path was removed and used where needed to build up the beds. Finally, all beds were topped with a 4-inch (10-cm) mulch of partly decomposed ground hemlock bark, the large companion plants were planted, and the paths were lined with landscape cloth and covered with 4 in. of medium grade freshly chopped Douglas fir bark. All garden preparation was done in autumn.

Planting of the heathers did not begin until the following spring, thus allowing plenty of time for the amended soil to settle with the winter rains. The heathers have thrived in this garden, with one exception. In one small spot, the initial *Erica cinerea* planting died, as did several adjacent *E. carnea* plants. A different cultivar of *E. carnea* was planted in place of the dead *E. cinerea*. *Daboecia* replaced the entire *E. carnea* grouping when it became obvious that the surviving *E. carnea* plants were going to crowd into adjacent plants rather than fill in the gap remaining where the others had died.

The replacement plants also died, except for the *Daboecia* plants that were replacing the *Erica carnea* survivors. Obviously, something was not right in that spot. Digging in the area disclosed that unamended clay was only about 6 in. (15 cm) below the surface of the bed—too far down to have been discovered when the plants from 4-inch (10-cm) pots were put in but close enough to provide a serious challenge to their roots as they tried to grow into the soil. Heathers really cannot stand clay.

Planting in raised beds is probably more practical than amending clay soil if the garden is not large. The beds should be at least 18 in. (45 cm) deep, although 24 in. (60 cm) would be preferable. Simply fill the beds with freely draining acidic compost high in organic matter, and plant the heather. If you choose to garden in raised beds, be sure that the plants receive adequate rainfall or supplemental watering, especially in summer. Raised beds naturally will dry out fairly rapidly. They will also warm up sooner in the spring than will the surrounding soil. The raised-bed method will also solve the problem of growing lime-hating heathers in a garden with naturally alkaline soil.

pH

Some species of heather absolutely must have acidic soil conditions to thrive. Others will tolerate neutral or even slightly alkaline soils. The degree of alkalinity or acidity of soil is measured on a scale of 0 to 14 known as the pH scale. Each number increase on the pH scale represents a ten-fold decrease in the concentration of hydrogen ions in a solution. A pH of 7 is considered neutral.

Soils vary from very acidic, with a pH of 3.5, to very alkaline, with a pH above 8. A pH between 5.5 and 6.5 is excellent for heathers. Most ericaceous plants require significant quantities of iron, which in soils with a pH above 6.5 is rendered virtually insoluble in water and therefore not available for plant absorption. Hence iron deficiency sets in, causing the plants to yellow and then die.

Before you can decide which heathers to grow, you need to know the pH of your soil. If you do not know your soil pH, purchase a soil testing kit. Kits are available at most garden centers. Try to obtain the type containing test tubes already filled with the testing liquid. Dry the soil very slowly (overnight) before testing, to get the most accurate result. Avoid using pH probes that require no battery, also widely available in garden centers, as these do not produce sufficiently accurate results. Alternatively, if you would rather not do the test yourself, contact the nearest agricultural college, which will run the test for you for a small fee.

Where unpredictable or inadequate rainfall makes gardening in raised beds impractical without considerable supplemental watering, it is possible to acidify the soil (if necessary) by treating it with sulfur, providing that the water table is not close to the soil surface. On heavy clay soils, first amend with organic compost and sand, then treat with elemental sulfur in the amount of approximately 4 oz./yd.^{2} (113 g/m^2). On lighter soils, less sulfur will be needed. Before treating your soil, test soil samples from several places in the garden to determine how much sulfur your particular soil needs to lower its pH to neutral or slightly acidic.

The best kind of sulfur to add is sold as "flowers-of-sulfur," a powder best applied on calm days when the wind will not blow it onto the applicator. Flowers-of-sulfur is not harmful to humans, but it can harm woolen clothing. Heathers can be safely planted immediately after flowers-of-sulfur has been incorporated into the soil.

Sulfur in chip form may also be used to reduce soil pH, but it takes longer to take effect than does the powdered form. Iron sulfate, added in the same proportion as flowers-of-sulfur, will reduce soil alkalinity, but it is harmful to plants and must be used only on new beds that will not be planted for six months.

Yet another option for growing heathers on alkaline soil is to fertilize each year with a commercial fertilizer made especially for ericaceous plants. This does not change the soil pH but makes nutrients immediately available to the plants. It will need to be applied twice: in spring and again in early summer. This is the least desirable option.

The best option is to choose species that will tolerate neutral or slightly alkaline soils. Among these is *Erica vagans*. This species will tolerate many kinds of soil if they are not deficient in magnesium. To grow *E. vagans* in magnesium-deficient soil, you will need to add magnesium sulfate (sold as Epsom salts) to the soil. In this case, too, you are advised to test your soil to be sure that it is really magnesium deficient before adding Epsom salts. The best way to add magnesium to alkaline soils is by drenching the soil with a solution of Epsom salts, which has the advantage of making the magnesium immediately available to the plants. Seek advice from professional soil scientists as to the strength of Epsom salts solution needed to correct your particular soil's magnesium deficiency.

Soil testing and amending may seem like a lot of work, but it needs to be done only once. The initial effort and expense will pay for itself many times over in the beauty and longevity of a garden planted in soil that meets the needs of the plants growing in it.

Mycorrhizae

Heathers and other members of the heath family occupy a unique ecological niche, a consequence of their having evolved beneficial root associations with specific kinds of fungi that enable them to thrive where few other plants can live. Plants of the Ericaceae have "characteristic structural uniformity of their root systems" (Read 1981). They have "hair roots" to help absorb nutrients, instead of the root hairs that perform this function in other plants. The outer cells of the hair roots are normally filled with the coiled hyphae (microscopic filaments) of the soil fungi that grow in mutualistic association with members of the family. The combined root and fungal structure is known as an *ericoid mycorrhiza*. Mycorrhiza literally translates as "fungus root." Ericoid mycorrhizae constitute one of seven currently recognized kinds of mycorrhizae (Trudell 2000). Two other kinds of mycorrhizal associations can be found in the

Ericaceae—arbutoid and monotropoid. However, only ericoid mycorrhizae have been reported on heathers from the Northern Hemisphere.

According to David J. Read (1981), most northern European plants with ericoid mycorrhizae are restricted to soils with "low pH, low levels of available nutrients and high organic content," which suggests that the association between fungus and plant developed in response to the stress of living in low-nutrient environments. Fungal hyphae extend from the plant roots out into the surrounding soil, facilitating the exploitation of nutrients in the soil. These fungi transfer nutrients to their plant hosts and, in exchange, receive carbohydrates from the plant.

In the native heathlands of the European heather species, the essential nutrients nitrogen and phosphorus are almost completely tied up in soil organic material (plant and microbial detritus) and are thus unavailable to most plants. However, members of the Ericaceae are able, through their symbiotic relationship with ericoid mycorrhizal fungi, to utilize the nitrogen and phosphorus in organic residues. David J. Read and Jesús Pérez-Moreno (2003) noted that the mycorrhizal fungus most commonly associated with heathers, the ascomycete *Hymenoscyphus ericae*, produces enzymes that have the ability to break down the chemical bonds that bind nitrogen and phosphorus within organic matter, thus making those elements accessible to its ericoid mycorrhizal plant partners. Interestingly, these enzymes work optimally at very low pH (3 to 5) (Cairney and Burke 1998). Thus, both the fungi and the plants need a low pH environment to function and grow best.

The ascomycete fungi *Hymenoscyphus ericae* and *Oidiodendron maius* are commonly reported mycorrhizal partners of plants forming ericoid mycorrhizae. Although the most common ericoid mycorrhizal fungi are ascomycetes, some basidiomycetes have also been known to form ericoid mycorrhizae. Richard Poruban (2006) has been working with the basidiomycetes *Clavaria argillacea* and *C. acuta* as potential growth enhancers for nursery crop production. He discovered that the former species will form ericoid mycorrhizae with *Calluna vulgaris* and the latter with *Vaccinium macrocarpon*.

A fascinating literature review of host and fungus relationships by Colin Straker (1996) pointed out that the structure of the hair root cell walls found in the Ericaceae may be conducive to colonization by fungi. The different structure of root cell walls in non-host plants may result in their degradation by the fungi (instead of colonization and symbiosis), as occurs with fungal diseases that cause root rot. The results of a recent study support this observation about the relationship of fungal colonization to root structure, although from a different perspective.

Luis Villarreal-Ruiz et al. (2004) isolated a fungus (*Cadophora finlandia*) related to *Hymenoscyphus ericae* from pine trees (a plant type that most commonly forms ectomycorrhizae) in a 160-year-old Scottish woodland. When the fungus was grown in an aseptic culture with Scots pine (*Pinus sylvestris*) seedlings, it formed ectomycorrhizae with the tree seedlings. When, however, seedlings of *Vaccinium myrtillus* (bilberry) were exposed to fungal derivatives from these ectomycorrhizae, the fungal hyphae entered the cells of the *Vaccinium* hair roots and formed coils within the cells typical of ericoid mycorrhizae. Villarreal-Ruiz et al. also reported that the presence of the fungus stimulated *Vaccinium* root growth and altered root architecture. Similarly, Bergero et al. (2000) reported species of *Oidiodendron* fungi were found in roots of *Erica arborea* and the nearby *Quercus ilex*.

The fungus *Hymenoscyphus* has also been reported to form associations with the root-like structures (rhizoids) on leafy liverworts in the families Adelanthaceae, Calypogeiaceae, Cephaloziaceae, Cephaloziellaceae, and Lepidoziaceae (Duckett and Read 1995). Since many of these liverworts also form mats in bogs, it is possible that there are complex interactions among liverworts, ericaceous plants, and conifers that are mediated by the fungus.

Research in Ireland (Gibson and Mitchell 2006) has demonstrated yet another way that the ericoid mycorrhizal relationship is beneficial to plants of the Ericaceae. Inoculation of *Calluna vulgaris* with *Hymenoscyphus ericae* helped promote the heather's growth on abandoned copper mine spoil. Plants from the mine site inoculated with *H. ericae* performed better than uninoculated plants. There was also a reduction of copper accumulation in the shoots of *Calluna* plants inoculated with an ericoid mycorrhizal fungus from the mine site, although there was no corresponding reduction of zinc accumulation in the shoots and no change in the growth of these plants. Elena Martino et al. (2003) have found that *Oidiodendron maius* from *Vaccinium myrtillus* on metal-contaminated soils was less sensitive to high concentrations of toxic metals (including zinc) than *O. maius* from non-contaminated soil.

Several researchers have reported that the ericoid mycorrhizal association is capable of protecting plants at metal contaminated sites; however, few studies explain how this protection is achieved. Some researchers have hypothesized that the mechanisms of tolerance may include the production of mucilage and extracellular pigments by the fungi. Tolerance of ericoid mycorrhizal fungi to copper and zinc is influenced by pH. Brian R. Gibson and Derek T. Mitchell (2006) found that the sensitivity of ericoid mycorrhizal fungi to metals increases when the pH rises. This finding highlights the importance of low soil pH in enhancing the benefits that plants may derive from an ericoid mycorrhizal partner.

The study of ericoid mycorrhizae is ongoing in research facilities around the world. To date, most research on the ericoid mycorrhizal relationship has focused upon the fungus *Hymenoscyphus ericae*. Thus, we have poor understanding of physiological variation in natural populations of ericoid mycorrhizal fungi.

Species and cultivars of ericaceous plants can exhibit different levels of colonization when inoculated with the same fungus under the same cultural conditions, and inoculation can cause different plant responses (Scagel 2005). Although many economically and ecologically important plants form associations with ericoid mycorrhizal fungi, there is almost no information concerning how these fungi influence the physiology of their host plants in horticultural production systems or in the landscape.

As more is learned about how the mycorrhizal relationship functions, how many different fungi can enter into the relationship, and the ways in which the relationship benefits plants of the Ericaceae, the potential uses for this knowledge will also increase. Certainly among the first of these will be the development of methods for growth enhancement of plants, such as heathers, that are capable of entering into ericoid mycorrhizal relationships.

Fertilizing

Because heathers naturally live in and are adapted to nutrient-poor soils, heathers planted in gardens rarely need fertilizing. The incorporation of organic matter into the soil before planting is usually sufficient for them. Old, rotted cow manure worked well into the soil at least six months before planting will both add nutrients and improve soil tilth.

Be especially careful not to add fresh manure to the soil, as it can burn the heather roots. Fertilizers are, generally, salts, and the fine hair roots of ericaceous plants are more susceptible to salt injury than are the larger roots of other plants. High nutrient levels tend to prevent the formation of mycorrhizae and to kill off existing mycorrhizal relationships. Mycorrhizal relationships with specific roots are transient, and highly available nutrition makes mycorrhizal relationships irrelevant to the plant (Richard Poruban, personal communication).

A small amount of bone meal added to the soil at the bottom of each individual planting hole should carry the plants through their first few years in the garden. After planting, fertilize the plants only if they are growing very poorly or are showing signs of nutrient deficiency, such as yellowing foliage in normally green cultivars—first being sure to test the soil to determine what is lacking. Instead of needing the nitrogen, potassium, and phosphorus that are the primary ingredients in synthetic fertilizers, the soil may be deficient in a trace element such as iron or magnesium.

A light application of fertilizer specially formulated for acid-loving plants (rhododendron and camellia fertilizer), or a weak general-purpose fertilizer such as 6-8-6, may be used to improve vigor. Annual renewal of an organic mulch can greatly reduce or eliminate the need for supplemental fertilizers.

Container-grown heathers will require regular fertilizing because of their limited root balls and lack of mycorrhizal fungi. Pelletized, slow-release fertilizer in a 14-14-14 formulation added to the potting soil when the heathers are planted will keep them supplied with nutrients for months. Once that is exhausted, they may be given regular applications of liquid fertilizer.

Compost tea, a microbial brew sometimes touted as the miracle food for all plants, can be beneficial for container-grown heathers. Liquid fish fertilizers or seaweed extracts can also supply nutrients to potted plants. Fertilizers formulated for orchids also are suitable for heathers. All fertilizers are better applied in weak solutions at frequent intervals rather than as strong solutions applied occasionally.

Buying Heather Plants

You have done your homework, visited well-established public and private heather gardens and made lists of those cultivars that caught your eye. You know your soil type and have amended the soil and improved its tilth and drainage, if necessary. All weeds in the area to be planted have been completely removed (including persistent tap roots) or killed with a fast-degrading herbicide such as glyphosate. The garden paths are in place and provision made for watering and garden lighting. You even have a planting plan based upon what heathers should thrive under the conditions you can offer them. You are finally ready to plant your garden.

Begin planting a new garden with the trees, tree heaths, or other shrubs that will anchor the garden or serve as accent plants. Once they are in place, it will be easy to plant the heathers around them.

Choosing a Heather at the Garden Center

Purchase your heathers either from specialist heather nurseries, the best choice, or from reliable garden centers that can be depended upon to keep the potted plants properly watered from the time they are received from the grower until the time they are sold. A heather that appears to die soon after planting may actually have been dead before it left the garden center. Once a pot has been allowed to go completely dry, it may take a few days before the plant shows its displeasure by dropping all its leaves. Desiccated heathers, particularly those in bloom, may appear to be healthy when they are actually beyond redemption.

Large chain stores with garden departments that are only a small part of their business are the most likely to sell plants that have been inadequately watered at the store. Because proprietary composts used by many commercial heather growers are formulated to produce maximum growth in minimum time, the plants may be overgrown for their pot sizes. Consequently, during casual watering by inexperienced store employees, water may roll off the foliage instead of penetrating to the roots.

Be particularly suspicious of "bargain priced" heathers. Take the time to examine marked down heathers carefully. Gently stroke the foliage, and reject the plant if any part of the foliage feels crisp to the touch. Examine the soil surface under the foliage. The presence

The excellent signage at Garland Nursery, an Oregon garden center, is an indication that the proprietors are knowledgeable about heathers and will care for them properly. Note that the plants being offered for sale in early summer are well proportioned to the sizes of their containers. Note also that *Calluna vulgaris* 'Tib' is already showing bud color.

of many dropped heather leaves indicates that the plant has been allowed to dry out at some point and will probably not survive long.

To determine the health of a potential purchase, knock the plant out of its pot and examine the roots. Badly root-bound plants will have brown roots tightly packed and encircling the pot. Regretfully, plants in this condition are sometimes received from mail-order nurseries. As long as they have not been allowed to go dry, these plants can be salvaged by slicing through the outside of the root ball in several places, spreading the root ball apart (a process known as "butterflying") and working soil between the spread halves or spreading them over a cone of soil in the center of the planting hole. This process encourages the roots to grow outward instead of continuing in the circular path established in the pot.

Sometimes root-bound plants do not survive despite being butterflied, although they may live for months after planting. When they finally die and are dug up, the gardener will discover that the roots never spread beyond the original potting medium. They never had a chance.

Rather than trying to rescue root-bound heathers, purchase plants that have many new white roots visible when the plants are knocked out of their pots. These do not need to be butterflied but can be planted intact. Those new roots will quickly spread out into the surrounding soil. A plant with many new roots will establish much more quickly than one that has been root-bound.

Although the roots are, without question, the most important part of the plant, also be sure that the plant you select is full and well branched. The number of flowers or buds on the plant at time of purchase is inconsequential unless it is destined for a short-term planter arrangement or a gift. The shape of the plant is more important for long-term garden performance. It is better to purchase a well-shaped, bushy plant than to have to compensate for nursery neglect with drastic pruning.

The *Erica* plant on the left has new white roots showing. It is in ideal condition for planting. The remaining plants are badly root-bound, with tightly tangled roots forming a brown mat against all pot surfaces. These plants will need to be "butterflied" if they are to survive in the garden more than a year or two. Note that the root ball of the plant on the right has been sliced through so that it may be spread apart during planting.

Color

The winter- and spring-flowering heather species, in particular, have flowers that increase in color saturation as they age. White buds that open to pale pink flowers in January may have turned magenta by March. Consider this when making color selections based upon plants in the nursery or garden center.

Erica ×*darleyensis* 'Kramer's Rote' beginning to bloom in midautumn. Note the more intense color of the flowers on the right, which have been open longer than the flowers on the left.

Where color seriously matters, it is better to buy named cultivars according to their descriptions in this book, in the *Handy Guide to Heathers* (Small and Small 2001), or in a nursery catalog, than to depend upon the plant color you see at a nursery or garden center. Growing conditions (soil type, light, and temperature) influence heather flower and foliage color. Cultivars described in the *Handy Guide to Heathers* have been carefully observed, the color given being the average for the cultivar. If possible, purchase the single sheet official color chart from The Heather Society that was based upon the 1966 *RHS Colour Chart*. Its colors are more accurate than those printed in the 2001 *Handy Guide to Heathers*.

Winter foliage color is primarily dependent upon light and temperature and the combination of the two. The brightest winter foliage will occur when bright sunlight combines with low temperatures. A region with low winter temperature but frequent fog or cloud cover will have less colorful heather foliage than a region of similar temperature but many clear days. The same plant can look different in the garden during different winters. Some cultivars, for example, *Calluna vulgaris* 'Fraser's Old Gold', require colder weather than do others to develop their brightest winter colors. If the winter is exceptionally warm or overcast, this heather may stay gold instead of acquiring the flame tones it usually has in winter.

This same dependence upon bright light and cold temperature means that heathers grown outside will have brighter winter foliage color than the same variety raised in a glasshouse or polyethylene growing tunnel. Likewise, flower colors of shelter-grown heathers will not be nearly as bright as they would be in the open garden. Again, the plant description or seeing the variety growing in several gardens will give you a more accurate idea of how the cultivar can perform than just seeing a potted plant at the garden center.

Choosing Size

Smaller is better. When buying heathers, choose young plants in small pots well proportioned to the size of the plants. Usually, the foliage in a well-grown plant will hide most of the potting compost. A plant that spills too far over the side of the pot probably should have been moved into a larger pot and may be root-bound.

Small plants a year or, at most, two years from cuttings will establish quickly in the garden. If you have a lot of ground to cover and a small budget, you may want to start with plugs, known in the United States as "liners," essentially rooted cuttings. These will take a bit more fussing over than plants that have had a full growing season in pots, but if they are carefully planted, mulched, and given adequate water, they should survive and prosper and may even catch up to plants that spent a year in pots.

When Planting Must Be Delayed

When you have purchased heather plants before you have a garden spot prepared for them, you may need to move them to the next pot size to avoid their becoming root-bound while they wait. When moving a plant into a larger pot, be sure to treat its roots just as you would when planting it in the ground. If the plant is root-bound, cut through and spread apart the root ball, then fill in below and around it in the new pot with potting compost formulated for ericaceous plants. A plant with new white roots showing may need only to have new compost added around it to fill the larger pot. Always pack compost firmly around the roots, and water thoroughly after repotting to remove any air pockets. After watering, you may need to add more compost and water again, until the plant is secure in its new pot and does not wobble if the pot is gently shaken.

Be sure that all potted heathers are watered frequently and thoroughly. Potted plants will dry out much more quickly than those in the ground. In hot weather, this can mean watering them every day.

Planting

Heathers to be planted in Zone 6 or colder are best planted in spring after the weather has settled, to ensure that there is plenty of time for root growth before the onset of cold weather. Newly planted heathers are susceptible to the stress of sudden freezes, which may heave the root balls out of the ground, causing death by dehydration, if not from the cold.

Early autumn planting is preferable in Zone 7 and warmer. Although these zones can have cold winters, there is usually a long period in autumn warm enough for substantial root growth. In Mediterranean-type climates, where most of the annual precipitation occurs as winter rain, fall planting is particularly important. Spring planting may not allow enough time for the plants to become established before they are stressed by summer's heat and drought.

Spacing of Plants

Height and width measurements given for heather cultivars described in this book are for plants that have received annual pruning and are three to five years old from cuttings. They are approximations only, based upon conditions in southeastern England, and actual plant size will vary considerably from one growing region to another. Plants grown where the climate is rigorous, particularly those with relatively short growing seasons, such as Ontario, Canada, will grow more slowly and be smaller at five years than the given sizes. Those in mild weather areas where growth can occur much of the year, such as coastal northern California, will be larger than the given sizes when they are five years old. That region is known as the "Redwood Empire" for a reason!

Spacing of plants should take growing conditions into account. Some gardeners plant all their heathers the same distance apart and hope for the best, no matter what the predicted size of the cultivar. That arbitrary spacing usually ranges from 14 in.

(35 cm) to 24 in. (60 cm). The occasional landscape gardener has been known to space heathers 36 in. (90 cm) apart.

Rather than pick a set distance and stick with it, think about the growth propensities of the different cultivars. Consider not only the given width but also the growth habit. Creeping heathers may be able to increase in width for many years, because the stems will often root where they touch the ground, giving extra strength to the plant. These plants can safely be planted much farther apart than the given width at age five. Conversely, small plants with naturally compact upright growth are more likely to remain within the range of the predicted width for many years, especially if they are pruned carefully.

Most people do not want to look at bare earth for years. They would prefer that the plants begin to touch each other when they are four or five years old. If you have

Heathers in the Wulff garden were planted as far apart as each cultivar's predicted width in the Handy Guide to Heathers (Small and Small 2001). Note the gray-foliaged plants of Erica tetralix 'Alba Mollis' to the right of the dry streambed, photographed in late spring.

Three years later, the plants have already met, and Erica tetralix 'Alba Mollis' is in full bloom (upper right). Obviously, heathers in western Oregon gardens should be spaced farther apart than the widths given on labels and in catalogs (which are usually derived from the Handy Guide to Heathers).

chosen a cultivar with upright growth habit whose predicted width at five years after planting is 12 in. (30 cm), and you space the plants 36 in. (90 cm) apart, the plants may never meet. However, spacing plants on 36-inch (90-cm) centers may work well when the predicted five-year width for a plant of open and vigorous habit is 24 in. (60 cm) and the growing conditions favor heathers.

It may take a few trials and errors to determine how well your growing conditions match the predicted sizes. Unless your garden conditions are extremely challenging for heathers, plants of a given cultivar should be spaced at least as far apart from each other as the width given in this book. You probably should give a cultivar described as "vigorous" a few more inches . If you live in redwood country, you probably should give it an extra foot (30 cm).

Calluna cultivars are the least tolerant of being crowded. They are much more likely to succumb to disease when crowded than are *Erica* or *Daboecia* plants. They also have the widest range of growth habits. Careful attention to the cultivar descriptions when spacing *Calluna* plants will reward you with healthy plants for many years.

Should you find that you have planted your heathers too close together, you can relieve the crowding when they begin to impinge upon their neighbors simply by removing plants here and there. Gardeners impatient for instant effect have been known to deliberately place plants so close together that they meet within two years. They then remove half the plants, and the garden matures to a healthy old age.

Planting Process

Before planting your new heathers, soak them thoroughly in a container of water to saturate the growing medium. Pots that float when you drop them into the water were perilously close to being too dry for the plants' survival. Wait for the potted plant to sink to the bottom of the bucket, an indication that the planting medium is saturated with water, before planting the heather.

While the plants are soaking, dig their planting holes. Push away any mulch that covers the planting area, reserving it for replacement after the heathers are planted. If the soil in the planting bed has been thoroughly prepared, the planting holes need be only a few inches larger than the root balls of the plants. Leave a little extra room at the bottom of each planting hole so that you can incorporate about a half trowelful of bone meal into the soil. Once that is mixed in, fill the hole with water. When soil preparation has been adequate, the water will be absorbed into the surrounding soil fairly rapidly—but not immediately.

Knock each plant out of its pot and check for pot-bound roots, slicing through the sides of the root ball and butterflying it when necessary. Hold the plant in the planting hole so that the top of the root ball is level with the surrounding soil, and fill in around the plant with the soil removed from the hole, firming it under and around the plant well and working it into the root ball if slicing was necessary. Water each plant thoroughly, and add more soil to bring the soil level even with the rest of the bed. Water again, then replace any shoved aside mulch, bringing it close to the stem of each plant. If there was no mulch on the bed, now is the time to add mulch. Finally, water once more so that the mulch is wet through. Check to be sure that the soil under the mulch is wet, because some mulches repel or shed water when first applied.

Water new plants every few days to ensure that they do not dry out, making certain that the water penetrates the mulch if you are watering from overhead. If there is no substantial rain, water at least twice per week for the first month. After that, once per week should suffice unless the weather is extremely hot and dry. Regular watering during the first summer after planting is extremely important. Even during the second summer, be sure that the plants get regular watering. By their third summer, the plants should need less frequent watering. Well-established plants may be able to get by with no supplemental watering at all, depending upon climate and weather conditions.

Transplanting

Transplanting heathers is not recommended except for very young plants. They are not good candidates for the game of "musical plants," as they strongly resent being moved once they are established. It is far better to plan carefully for their permanent locations than to move them after they have had a chance to send their roots well into the soil and establish a hyphal weft. Rather than trying to transplant a heather that is growing in the wrong place, dig and discard the plant and buy a new young plant right for the place.

That having been said, if you must transplant a precious one-of-a-kind cultivar that cannot be replaced (by all means, take cuttings from it first!), or if you cannot resist a challenge, begin digging far enough from the plant to be moved to ensure that most of its roots remain intact. Carefully transport it with soil attached into an already prepared generous planting hole, firm additional soil around it, water it well, mulch around it, and hope for the best. Be sure that the transplant is never allowed to go dry during the first year or two of its life after transplanting—assuming that it does, indeed, live.

Erica cinerea, the most persnickety of the hardy heathers in cultivation—although the showiest when it is happy—is very resentful of root disturbance. At the opposite extreme is *E. arborea*, which can be moved successfully when it is several years old and has already developed the long, woody roots that enable the species to survive periodic drought conditions in its native *maquis* habitat near the shores of the Mediterranean. The strong regenerative properties that make drastic pruning of this tree heath possible also come to its aid after transplantation.

Heathers that produce roots along stems in contact with the ground, a process known as "self-layering," can have the rooted stems severed from the mother plant and gently lifted, with as much attached soil as possible, for moving to a new location. This is an easy way of gaining more plants and is usually successful. The severed rooted stems can be planted as you would any new plant, although they may need to be babied more than plants with a larger root system. Heathers that root in this manner include some *Calluna* cultivars, *Daboecia*, *Erica carnea*, *E. cinerea*, *E. mackayana*, and even *E. ciliaris*.

Mulch

Mulch is the finishing touch on a garden, the blanket that reduces extremes of temperature and moisture levels. It can be spread on the prepared garden site after the larger companion plants and tree heaths are planted but before the heathers are planted, with the mulch being shoved aside to plant the heathers, then pulled back around them after planting. Alternatively, all mulching can be done after planting is completed.

An organic mulch spread several inches deep around heather plants will minimize weed growth and help to retain soil moisture while the plants are getting established. Four to six inches (10 to 15 cm) of mulch is usually adequate for weed suppression, and an additional inch or two (3 to 5 cm) should be spread around the plants every year until the heathers completely cover the ground.

The ideal mulch is composed of different sized particles, to allow water to easily pass through the mulch to the soil beneath it. Avoid using peat as mulch, not only to conserve peat bog habitat, but also because finely ground peat will form an impermeable crust on top that sheds water rather than absorbing it. Plants mulched with peat will actually suffer from moisture deprivation. Better choices are aged compost, partially decomposed conifer bark in a mixture of medium and small sizes, pine needles, or chopped oak leaves, which do not mat down as do leaves from other deciduous trees.

In a rock garden, the small crushed rocks normally used to mulch alpine plants are also suitable around heathers, except for light colored rocks that would reflect too much heat onto the heathers, and alkaline rocks such as limestone. Even heathers tolerant of alkaline soils will have difficulty if they are subjected to the excessive alkalinity of such mulch. Crushed rock is also not as good at suppressing the germination of weed seeds as are other mulches. In fact, some weeds find it the perfect seedbed.

Mulch should be drawn up close to the crowns of the plants but should not cover the foliage. In regions where summers are very hot and humid, or where there is considerable summer fog, such as in coastal northern California, leave a little "breathing space" around the plants, particularly *Calluna*, to discourage the development of fungal diseases caused by such pathogens as *Botrytis cinerea*, *Phytophthora cinnamomi*, and *Rhizoctonia solani*, that thrive on heat and moisture.

A good time to renew the mulch each year is just after pruning. The new layer of mulch will cover the bits of heather clippings not easily removed from the beds. If a new heather bed is thoroughly cleared of all weeds, including tap-rooted perennials, before planting and is mulched immediately after planting, then this yearly refreshment of mulch should be sufficient to keep the garden weed-free with little effort. The few weed seedlings that manage to germinate in the mulch will be easy to remove, and after the heathers completely cover the garden, their dense shade should be sufficient to prevent most seeds from germinating, making further mulching unnecessary.

Watering

Gardeners in regions where frequent and adequate rainfall cannot be relied upon must make provision to water their heathers. Regular watering is absolutely essential in the first few years after planting, until the plants have had a chance to get established and send their roots well into the soil. Although most heather species are fairly drought tolerant once well established, they need some summer water even after those critical first years. They may, in fact, need winter watering should an extended winter drought occur.

Some heathers are more susceptible to drought than are others. (See the list of drought-tolerant species in chapter 9.) According to Karla Lortz (2004), heathers with gold, orange, or red foliage are more susceptible to drought than are those with green foliage.

Overhead watering is the least practical way to water heathers. It wastes water to evaporation, and it also can encourage diseases by wetting the heather foliage when what is needed is water for the heather roots.

Soaker hoses and drip irrigation deliver water to the root zone without wetting the foliage. Neither method is perfect, although both are preferable to overhead sprinklers. Soaker hoses are more difficult to install and will, when working properly, shed water all along the length of the hose, whether the hose is near its target plants or crossing a paved walkway. Sometimes the tiny holes in a soaker hose become clogged, so that the hose waters unevenly, missing some spots.

When installing soaker hoses on a slope, take care to lay them across the slope, just as you would do contour plowing. This will lessen the problem of having water pool at the end of the hose. If you must run the hose parallel to the slope, start it at the bottom of the slope, so that the hose end is near the top.

Soaker hoses should be covered with a layer of soil or mulch, or both. This greatly increases their efficiency, as water seeping from the hose goes directly into the soil, not into the air. It also extends their effective life by blocking their exposure to sunlight, which can degrade the hoses.

Drip irrigation has its own problems. Although it is designed to individually water each plant, with no water wasted, the tiny emitters are easily clogged and must be examined frequently. Some plants require more than one emitter. Pay attention to how well your drip irrigation is functioning. Unless it is adjusted properly, the plants may receive either too much or too little water.

Heathers in containers may be watered with drip irrigation or by careful hand watering. They will dry out much faster than heathers planted in the ground, and it is essential that the container planting mix remain moist (not soggy) at all times. The smaller the container, the faster it will dry out. Letting a container go dry for one day may be fatal to its heathers.

Pruning

Because the importance of proper pruning is the least understood aspect of heather culture, Oregon Heather Society presentations to general gardening audiences invariably end with a pruning demonstration. Just as invariably, there is a collective gasp from the audience as the demonstrator grabs a generous handful of stems from an overgrown potted *Calluna* and proceeds to cut off the lot with a pair of sheep shears. Much heather is planted in Oregon, but few gardeners, even professional landscapers, follow through with the pruning needed to keep the plants performing and looking their best.

Heathers benefit from annual pruning that removes the spent flowering stems. Pruning not only removes the dead flowers and winter-damaged stems and foliage but also encourages the plants to branch at the site of the cut. Pruned heathers produce more flowering stems than unpruned plants, and pruning has a rejuvenating effect upon the plants. They usually live longer than unpruned plants, which may eventually develop holes in the center and fall apart.

Pruning *Calluna*

The group of heathers for which pruning is most critical are the *Calluna* cultivars. With few exceptions, callunas should be pruned annually. These heathers do not produce leaves on the parts of stem that carry the flowers. Most unpruned callunas soon become gangly and awkward-looking, if not downright ugly. Each stem will have long bare patches where the dead flowers fell off, interspersed with sections bearing foliage. Unless the gardener was trying to achieve the appearance of an old heather moor, this is probably not the look envisioned when the heather was planted.

When a heather is pruned can affect the quality and timing of its flowering and even its survival. In cold winter areas where temperatures regularly fall well below freezing and snow cover cannot be guaranteed, *Calluna* cultivars should not be pruned until spring. The old flowering stems help to protect the plants from the cold. Wait to prune in the spring until the weather has settled enough that a sudden extreme temperature drop is unlikely. Do not, however, wait so long that new growth is well underway. Cutting off too much new growth late in the spring may stress the plant so much that it dies, particularly if the plant is already stressed in other ways, such as not being well established or having an inadequate root run.

Where winters are reliably mild, with the temperature rarely dropping much below freezing for very long, the timing of *Calluna* pruning is much less critical. They can be pruned safely any time between fall and spring, whenever the gardener has a few moments to spare.

Members of the California North Coast Chapter of the North American Heather Society (now the Mendocino Coast Heather Society) conducted an experiment at the Mendocino Coast Botanical Gardens in Fort Bragg, California, to compare the effects of spring and autumn pruning on the genus *Calluna* and its various cultivars. Some plants of each cultivar were pruned in the autumn, while others planted within the same grouping were not pruned until the following spring. Fall pruning was begun in October, and spring pruning was carried out between March and May (the very late pruning being caused by the wetness of the ground at the Gardens). *Calluna vulgaris* 'Bradford' was so vigorous that it was pruned both spring and fall to keep it tidy.

When the plants were evaluated in late July, the evaluators noted a difference between the plants pruned in March and those pruned in May. The plants pruned in March showed better growth than those trimmed in May. Cultivars pruned in the fall had the greatest foliage growth.

According to Beverly Witchner (2001), the pruning project investigators determined that in the mild coastal climate of Fort Bragg, the timing of pruning of callunas made only a small difference. Although slightly more foliage growth was produced with the fall pruning, its effect upon flower production was neutral. They concluded that the timing of pruning heathers in this type of climate is a matter of personal preference.

Although timing of pruning in mild winter areas does not affect plant survival or quality of flowering, it is best done in a logical sequence dependent upon the garden effects for which the *Calluna* cultivars were chosen. Pruning of cultivars with colorful winter foliage is best left until last, so that there is a maximum amount of foliage on the plant to brighten the winter and early spring garden. Prune these just as new growth commences in the spring.

Cultivars grown primarily for their colorful spring new growth should be pruned

The plant of *Calluna vulgaris* 'Fire Star' on the right has been properly pruned, with stems cut off evenly over the entire plant below the level of the spent flowers. The unpruned plant on the left, however, displays the full intensity of winter color that this cultivar can achieve. Pruning of cultivars grown for their winter foliage color should be delayed until just before new growth begins in spring.

before new growth begins, so that pruning does not remove the new growth. Delay autumn pruning of spring-tip cultivars until late autumn. Early autumn pruning may encourage vigorous cultivars such as *Calluna vulgaris* 'Spring Torch' to flower again—and again—that autumn, as a Seattle area gardener discovered (Janet Christie, personal communication). The pruning of such cultivars will need to be done only once a year if pruning is delayed until the onset of cold weather.

Standard advice has always been that when pruning *Calluna* cultivars, the stems should be cut just below the spent flowers. Novice heather growers who take this advice to heart sometimes make the mistake of thinking that each stem must be cut off individually right below the flowers, no matter where that spot is in relation to the corresponding spots on the other stems of the plant. They painstakingly cut each stem individually. The following year, they are faced with many more stems to cut, all at different levels on the plant. If they have also acquired more heather plants, they eventually realize that they cannot continue this tedious attention.

Yes, callunas should be pruned to remove the parts of the stems that bore flowers, but unless the gardener has only a few plants to tend and wishes to achieve an uneven "artistic" effect, cuts should be made evenly over the entire plant. Some authorities (for example, van de Laar 1978) recommend pruning different stems at different heights to achieve a "natural," graceful appearance. This is certainly an option, and such pruning will have no deleterious effect upon the health of the plants; but if you have more than a few heathers, you soon will discover that such careful attention to detail is inordinately time-consuming and not worth the effort, as the new growth on many *Calluna* cultivars is naturally graceful. The few dead flowers that remain low inside the plant will be hidden by the new season's growth.

When plants are young, their sides should be cut back as well as their tops. As they age and the plants grow together, a grouping of plants of one cultivar may be pruned as if it were a single large plant, trimmed only on the top and on the outside edge of the group. Not only is this less tedious than pruning each plant separately, but it avoids having the garden appear to be composed of a lot of balls, thus ruining the graceful interwoven tapestry effect that a well-designed heather garden can achieve.

Pruning may be done with sharp secateurs (by-pass rather than anvil types, which smash the stems), sheep shears, electric hedge trimmers or even, horrors, a strimmer (string trimmer) or power brush cutter if acres of heathers are to be pruned. Non-flowering stems should be cut off to the same level as those that flowered. They, too, will branch to produce a fuller plant with more flowers. When nurserymen are rearing young heathers from seed or cuttings, they are constantly pinching off the growing tips so that by the time the plants are of marketable size, they will be full and well shaped. Regular pruning of heathers after they are planted in the garden will maintain this full appearance.

If a year's pruning has been missed, or maybe even two years, callunas can still be pruned to remove the year or two's worth of bare stems, providing that they are not cut back to leafless old wood. In general, woody *Calluna* stems older than three years will not produce new growth when cut but will remain bare stubs.

A few *Calluna* cultivars make so little growth each year, with few or no flowers, that they require no pruning to keep them compact. These are the "bun" formers beloved of rock gardeners, for example, *Calluna vulgaris* 'The Pygmy'. Carpeting heathers may also require no pruning, not because they do not flower but because their horizontal new growth can be counted upon to cover up the bare old flower stems from previous years.

Calluna vulgaris 'The Pygmy' grows naturally as a compact "bun" with only an occasional flower. It requires virtually no pruning.

Pruning *Daboecia*

The half-hardy *Daboecia azorica* has a short blooming season in early summer. Its spent flowering stems should be cut off shortly after all the flowers drop. Other pruning should be confined to removal of winter-killed foliage and gentle shaping of the plants in the spring. If damaged or dead foliage is removed in early spring, the plant may produce new growth from the roots.

Daboecia cantabrica and *D.* ×*scotica* cultivars can produce flowers from early summer through autumn. Because the spent flowers drop cleanly from the stems of all daboecias except the double-flowered 'Charles Nelson' and *D. cantabrica* f. *blumii* cultivars such as 'White Blum', busy gardeners may choose to prune these heaths only once a year, in spring. At that time, in addition to cutting off the old flowering tips, part of the previous year's growth should be removed to encourage branching and a fuller plant.

During the growing season, a flowering stem that is cut off after its last flower falls will branch and make new flowers. Daboecias bloom in flushes. Rather than trying to cut individual stems as they finish blooming, it is better to cut the entire plant back after a flush. This encourages the plant to continue flower production right up until a hard frost. Late-season flowering stems should be allowed to remain on the plant as winter protection and should be removed during spring pruning. Prune off any winter-killed foliage. Where die-back is severe, prune off the dead wood nearly to the ground. These species often resprout from the roots after top growth has been killed by winter cold.

Pruning *Erica*

Although *Daboecia* and *Erica* species are, in general, less fussy about their pruning needs than is *Calluna vulgaris*, timing is important for some of these, too. The winter-flowering heathers, *Erica carnea*, *E. erigena*, and the hybrid between them, *E.* ×*darleyensis*, must be pruned very soon after the last flowers have faded, because they make buds for the next year's bloom very early. If pruning is delayed into early summer, the new buds may be removed and an entire year's bloom missed.

Pruning of these species is especially important when they are young and should be done annually for the first few years after planting to ensure full plants. After that, pruning does not absolutely need to be done annually, as it does for *Calluna*. The plants will, nevertheless, be fuller and have longer flower spikes if they are pruned regularly to shape them and remove spent flowers.

Young *Erica carnea* and *E.* ×*darleyensis* plants may be pruned in the same manner as callunas, cutting stems evenly below the dead flowers. Older plants may be pruned slightly differently. To maintain the habit of the plant, the "skirt" of the plant can be lifted and the underlying stems cut away, leaving the top intact.

A variation of this method was used by Bryan and Joan Taylor (personal communication) to reduce the size of a long border of *Erica* ×*darleyensis* 'Margaret Porter' that had badly overgrown the adjacent main pathway in the Abkhazi Garden, Victoria, British Columbia. The heaths, about 30 years old, had grown freely during the seven years before the Taylors began caring for them. Someone working in the garden a year earlier had made a crude attempt to reduce the size of a few plants by cutting them back to old wood with probably no green on it at all. The old wood had sprouted new growth with healthy green leaves.

Taking their cue from this successful regrowth, Bryan and Joan undertook drastic pruning of the old border. Because the garden had to look good for the visiting public at all times, they needed to have the tops of the plants remain green. So they shortened the tops somewhat but reached underneath to drastically shorten the lower branches, reducing the width of the plants by about 10 in. (25 cm) and cutting in such a way that all the cut ends pointed downwards and were not visible to anyone standing above the plant. After this pruning, which yielded 12 overflowing wheelbarrow

During years of neglect following the death of the garden's creators, a border of *Erica* ×*darleyensis* 'Margaret Porter' overgrew much of the adjacent path in the Abkhazi Garden, Victoria, British Columbia.

Joan Taylor with the magnificent result of the renovation pruning that she and her husband, Bryan, did on the overgrown border of *Erica* ×*darleyensis* 'Margaret Porter' in the Abkhazi Garden (viewed from the opposite direction as in the previous photo). Photo by Bryan Taylor.

loads of clippings, the plants would have appeared somewhat mushroom-shaped if viewed in cross-section.

During the following year, the cut ends produced new growth, and the new flower spikes were about four times longer than had been the ones from the old wood. The renovation was so successful that the old heathers were allowed to remain in the garden for several more years. However, they have now been replaced with the Kurt Kramer introduction *Erica* ×*darleyensis* 'Spring Surprise'. The flowers of the long-blooming 'Margaret Porter' plants had begun to fade by the time the garden opened to the public each spring. 'Spring Surprise', selected for its later flowering season and deeper flower color, provides a better show for garden visitors. The plants are pruned annually to keep them floriferous and within their allotted border.

Most heather growers do not prune *Erica erigena* severely enough. If the old flowers are cut off and several inches of foliage removed all over the plant following its natural shape, this heath will respond with a spectacular display of flowers the following year. This species will sprout from the base when winter-damaged, a good indicator that the plants will tolerate hard pruning into old wood. *Erica erigena* plants

Plants of *Erica erigena* pruned into cone shapes not only make handsome potted specimens but resist snow splitting. Cultivars shown here at Forest Edge Nursery, Dorset, England, are 'Brian Proudley' (left foreground), 'Irish Dusk' (right foreground), and 'Superba' (rear). Photo by David Edge.

may be pruned into low hedges, but the larger-growing cultivars can also stand alone as architectural specimens. Pruning these larger cultivars into cone shapes will help to minimize their splitting under heavy snow loads.

The flowers of *Erica ciliaris* turn a beautiful russet brown as they age and are best left on the plants until spring, both to give winter protection to this somewhat tender species and to add winter interest to the garden. In spring, cut off all the old flower stems and also any of the foliage that has suffered winter damage, shaping the plant as you cut. This species tolerates fairly rigorous pruning.

Erica cinerea should be pruned every spring just as new growth begins, removing some of the old flowers and shaping the plants evenly as you would callunas. The plants do not need to be cut back as far as do callunas. A light pruning all over the plant will suffice to encourage good growth and flowering. The stems of *E. cinerea* are too tough to prune with sheep shears but will require by-pass pruners or sharp hedge shears.

Although some *Erica cinerea* cultivars grown for their colored foliage produce few flowers, most should nevertheless have the previous year's growth cut part way back each spring to encourage branching and produce a full, shapely plant. In her legacy book *Hardy Heather Species*, Dorothy Metheny (1991) recommended that 'Golden Hue' be left unpruned. This cultivar is so unlike all the others in growth habit, being both the tallest and the most erect, that such advice should be seriously considered. Left to its own devices, it makes an interesting contrast with the mound form of the other cultivars.

Cutting off the initial flowering stems when most, but not all, flowers have gone by can induce some cultivars of *Erica cinerea* to produce a second flush of flowers. Commercial heather growers who depend upon selling plants in bloom are currently experimenting to determine which cultivars will rebloom after summer pruning (Floyd Hutchins, personal communication).

Erica ×*griffithsii* tolerates quite hard pruning and is useful for low hedges. It should be pruned in early spring, with the old flowering stems and any unwanted growth removed at that time.

Erica mackayana, *E. tetralix*, and the *E. tetralix* hybrids *E.* ×*stuartii*, *E.* ×*watsonii* and *E.* ×*williamsii* can have their flowers removed throughout the growing season as they turn brown. Many cultivars of these species produce flowers all summer and autumn, and the removal of spent flowers will encourage further flower production, in addition to giving the garden a tidier appearance. Busy gardeners can delay pruning until spring, when the plants should receive their annual pruning. In spring, shear the plants back far enough to remove most of the previous year's remaining dead flowers and remove any winter-killed foliage.

Because *Erica manipuliflora* has very long flowering stems, it should be pruned early in the spring to allow plenty of time for the plant to generate new ones. As with *E. cinerea*, there is no need to remove all of the previous season's growth, although the plants tolerate hard pruning well and some cultivars are suitable for low hedging.

Erica spiculifolia should be pruned in early spring to remove the previous year's spent flowers. After its early bloom flush, it may be pruned again to encourage the development of new buds. The *E. spiculifolia* hybrid *E.* ×*gaudificans* should be pruned once a year in early spring, even though this may mean cutting off flowers and buds. Plants more than a few years old can tolerate having at least 6 in. (15 cm) of growth cut off, possibly more. Such annual pruning will keep the plants full and well shaped, and they will resume flowering a few months after pruning.

Erica umbellata may be given a light pruning after flowering to remove dead flowers and encourage branching. If pruning this species in spring, do not delay too long, as it is an early summer bloomer.

Erica vagans is another species whose spent flowers may be left on the plants to add winter interest. The species will tolerate severe pruning back to bare wood, although it will die if cut all the way to ground level. Bare stubs a few inches tall will soon sprout new green growth that will flower the same season if pruning is done early enough in spring. When pruning is delayed until early summer, the cut stems will sprout new growth, but there will be no flowers that year.

Erica vagans 'Mrs D. F. Maxwell' in late spring, pruned back to bare wood where it had grown over a stepping stone. Note the few unpruned branches against the wall, left to show how large the plant had been.

The same plant in late summer, with no bare wood visible after excellent regrowth of the pruned area

Pruning Tree Heaths

True to its name "tree heath," *Erica arborea* produces sturdy wooden stems that with time can reach 10 ft. (3 m) in height in some garden cultivars (taller in the wild). The species should be pruned well when young, removing a third to a half of the new growth each year to promote branching and full, shapely plants. After the first few years, pruning is optional, but the occasional over-exuberant branch should be shortened so that it does not make the plant appear unbalanced.

Both *Erica arborea* var. *alpina* and *E. arborea* 'Estrella Gold' produce abundant flowers that some people may not consider attractive after they turn conspicuously brown in late spring. Whether or not to prune off the dead flowers is a matter of personal taste. The "tree" will be taller sooner if they are not removed, but it will be fuller if pruned each spring to remove the dead flowers.

Well-budded *Erica arborea* stems make attractive fillers in early spring bouquets. Some "pruning" can be accomplished by cutting budded branches for the house. An *E. arborea* that has not been pruned for several years and has become awkward in shape can be safely cut off at ground level in early spring or just after flowering. It will sprout from the base.

The other spring-flowering tree heaths, *Erica australis*, *E. lusitanica*, *E.* ×*oldenburgensis*, *E. scoparia*, and *E.* ×*veitchii*, also benefit from rigorous pruning after flowering the first few years after they are planted. Older plants may be left unpruned to reach "tree" dimensions or be cut back lightly after flowering to maintain the desired shape and encourage more flower production.

An unusual container planting at Dancing Oaks Nursery in Monmouth, Oregon, takes advantage of the special attributes of the tree heath *Erica arborea* 'Estrella Gold'. Its drought tolerance suits the species for planting with succulents, as shown here. Its ability to withstand severe pruning enables it to survive in a confined space, such as in this hypertufa trough, where it has lived for four years. Design by Leonard Foltz.

Erica terminalis, the only summer-flowering and the hardiest tree heath, is a pruning puzzle. It bears its terminal flowers at several levels on the plant, making removal of all the spent flowers impossible unless hours are devoted to pruning a single plant. Rather than attempt such a task, trim back the entire plant evenly in early spring for the first few years after planting, at the same time shaping it into the desired form. This shrub can sprawl widely as well as grow tall, so where growing space is limited, you may prefer to prune more on the sides than on the top. It will tolerate being pruned severely for use as a low hedge.

If specimen plants of *Erica terminalis* are desired, light pruning to shape and encouraging branching should be all that is required after the first three years to keep this long-flowering species attractive. Mature plants that were not shaped during their younger years may be improved by cutting the oldest stems back hard in the spring to encourage fresh young growth from the base.

A Pruning Experiment

When you must choose between cutting an overgrown heather way back or removing the plant, you have nothing to lose by severe pruning. Berndt Lautenschlaeger (personal communication), whose 1½ acre (0.6 ha) garden in Otis, Oregon, contains thousands of heathers, decided to experiment with mowing beds of old heather in early spring. He first used a brush cutter to shorten the heathers to a few inches high, then ran his motorized lawn mower over them, reducing the plants to stubs with no green showing at all. To his delight, many of the old plants produced new green sprouts from the base.

Erica cinerea 'Atropurpurea' came back fast and was blooming in October. Both *E.* ×*watsonii* 'Dawn' and *Daboecia cantabrica* f. *alba* came back beautifully. *Calluna vulgaris* 'Alba Erecta' and 'County Wicklow' died. *Calluna vulgaris* 'Silver Knight' made a little growth on two of the eight mowed plants. *Erica* ×*darleyensis* cultivars came back sparsely and did not amount to anything even five months after mowing. A very dry summer, during which the heathers were given no supplemental watering, probably contributed to the loss of some plants.

This technique is definitely not recommended as a general practice, even by Berndt, who regularly prunes with a brush cutter; but it was an interesting experiment with results that may prove useful to other gardeners. Obviously, some heather species regenerate after severe pruning. Others do not.

Pruning to Maintain Order in the Garden

Correct pruning of the plants that edge a path needs to be undertaken from their first season, when the plants are still well back from the path. The aim is to avoid having a "wall" of brown cut twigs showing where edging plants have grown over the path and been cut back.

A way to achieve this is by constantly pruning as far back as possible ("hard" pruning but never to bare stems) on the path side of the edging plants. Gradually taper up from the ground toward the center of each plant, so that the cut surface is sloped away from the path, not vertical to the ground.

Plants whose stems arch in fountain shape or grow nearly parallel to the ground so that new stems lie over older ones may have the lowest stems along the path cut way back and the newer ones overlying them shortened considerably. This technique, akin to the "mushroom" pruning done to rejuvenate *Erica* ×*darleyensis* 'Margaret Porter' in the Abkhazi Garden, keeps the plants in bounds while retaining their naturally graceful shape. It may be used with many of the low edging plants listed in chapter 9.

Although the rules for pruning the various kinds of heather are fairly straightforward, what do you do when adjacent plants of different cultivars begin to touch each other? The answer to this question depends upon the style of the garden and the inclinations of the gardener. If the aim in planting heathers has been to cover the ground with an attractive, varied assortment of low-maintenance plants, then it will not matter if the cultivars grow into each other and intertwine. In fact, such intermingled growth can be very beautiful. The entire bed can then be pruned only as much around the edges as is required to keep pathways clear, and the tops of the plants should be shortened enough to encourage good flowering every year.

This approach to pruning falls into the "naturalistic" style of gardening and does, indeed, mimic the way plants grow in the wild. However, the more vigorous, sprawling cultivars will inevitably overwhelm the weaker or more compact growers or those growing near the limits of their hardiness zones. Donald Mackay (2005b) observed that in northern Vermont (Zone 3), unless callunas are restrained, they will crowd out the various ericas planted with them. Five hundred miles (800 km) to the south, in the Washington, D.C. area (Zone 7), the situation is reversed. Gardens that had started out with a mixture of callunas and ericas ended up containing mostly ericas, especially *Erica* ×*darleyensis*, which does well in that climate, whereas *Calluna vulgaris* falters because of the high summer humidity. Intermediate between these extremes is New York City, where neither genus appears to dominate.

If the gardener wants to retain all cultivars as discreet entities, then all growth impinging upon that of neighboring cultivars will need to be removed annually. When this is done carefully, the year's new growth will quickly hide the cuts, and the cultivars will appear to merge into each other without physically intermingling.

The task of keeping cultivars discreet can be made much easier, of course, if cultivars of similar vigor are planted next to each other. When a particular planting scheme dictates otherwise, then judicious pruning will have to compensate for the inequities of growth.

Sometimes the only way compatibility of cultivars can be determined is through trial and error. Reading cultivar descriptions, although it is a good starting point, cannot replace the knowledge gained by seeing the cultivars actually growing in various gardens under differing conditions. Ultimately, the way plants perform depends upon both their natural, genetically determined propensities and the conditions under which they are grown. When an inordinate amount of pruning is required to keep a cultivar from mugging its neighbor, the best remedy may be to remove that cultivar and replace it with a more congenial companion.

Pests and Diseases

Heathers are relatively free from both pests and diseases. When talking about heather gardens, the term "pests" usually refers to rabbits and deer and not to the parasites that you might normally associate with garden plants. Damage caused to heather by insects is trifling compared with that caused to many other types of plant.

Four-Legged Pests

Rabbits and Hares

In certain areas, rabbits can be a problem in heather gardens, particularly recently planted heather gardens. They tend to nibble from the top down, rarely attacking heathers once the plants are more than 12 in. (30 cm) tall.

Because of its low stature and tendency to set its flower buds very early, *Erica carnea* is the heather most likely to suffer rabbit damage. Those sweet juicy buds are irresistible, and, for some unknown reason, the rabbits seem to prefer the darker colored cultivars to the paler or white varieties.

In general, rabbits will nibble around the edge of a bed. They rarely leap into a clump and nibble within it. Therefore, rabbits can actually be useful for keeping your *Erica carnea* plants from straying outside their allotted space, as long as you do not mind a green band with no flowers around the edge of the planting.

European rabbits, unlike their North American cousins, are great diggers and will disrupt and nibble heather roots when they burrow into a bed. This burrowing habit, in a way, makes European rabbit populations self-limiting. Living and breeding underground, the rabbits are liable to contract the insect-transmitted myxoma virus, most likely spread by fleas and fur mites that overwinter in the burrows. The myxomatosis disease caused by the myxoma virus is fatal in approximately 90 percent of European rabbits that contract it and has been introduced to Australia to control the introduced rabbit population there (Burrill 2003). (In other species of rabbits, it may produce only mild disease symptoms.) Periodic outbreaks of the disease, about every seven years, tend to keep the European rabbit population in check.

The most effective way of controlling rabbits in the garden is undoubtedly to shoot them when they are first detected. However, the neighbors and civil authorities may frown upon this method. Very often, the only positive solution is to erect small-mesh wire netting fences around the beds.

A way to stop winter predation by rabbits was discovered accidentally by Willa Wick of Ontario, Canada (personal communication) when she covered her heather garden for protection against the cold. Her uncovered *Erica carnea* plants had been getting smaller by the day (she observed their rabbit "pruner" from her house window) until she dumped several inches of shredded leaves over the plants in late fall. When she uncovered the plants the following spring, they were in excellent condition. Willa also discovered that the molded screen covers sold to protect food served outdoors from insects can be used to protect small budding heather plants from rabbit damage.

Natural predation by larger mammals and by raptors helps to control rabbit populations. Rabbits prefer to live within a short distance of cover, to which they can quickly flee to escape predators. Placing a heather garden far from such significant rabbit havens as bramble patches can reduce the likelihood that rabbits will bother the garden.

Hares, non-burrowing rabbit relatives that are unaffected by myxomatosis, are occasionally pests of heather gardens but are much less a problem in Great Britain than are rabbits. Their presence can be detected through the presence of heather tops strewn around the site.

Rats and Mice

Other pests that leave similar telltale signs are rats. These also tend to create small digs, like rabbits. Rats seem to be particularly interested in the hardier Cape heaths when those are grown in the garden. Mice are usually a problem in the heather garden only in cold climates where a thick layer of pine needles is being used as winter protection.

Deer

In areas where deer are significant garden pests, as they are in much of North America, heathers can be planted with little fear of predation. In general, North American deer leave *Calluna*, *Erica cinerea*, and *E. tetralix* alone. They do eat *E.* ×*griffithsii*,

Because the golden foliage of *Erica carnea* 'Aurea' takes on reddish tints in winter, this plant remains a garden asset even though deer have eaten its flowers.

E. manipuliflora, and *E. vagans* flowers occasionally and may browse regularly on *Daboecia* flowers, removing one-third to one-half of them at a meal. However, the *Daboecia* plants quickly produce more flowers; in fact, they may produce even greater quantities of flowers for having been "pruned."

Winter- and spring-flowering heathers, such as *Erica carnea*, *E.* ×*darleyensis*, and *E. erigena* and other tree heaths (except the summer-blooming *E. terminalis*), are more susceptible to deer browsing than are the summer bloomers, because they provide tender buds and flowers at a time when there is little else for the deer to eat. Because only the bud-bearing shoots are eaten, the utility of cultivars chosen for their foliage rather than their flowers will be little affected. *Erica carnea* 'Sherwood Creeping' appears to be particularly attractive to deer; they will walk across *E.* ×*darleyensis* cultivars to get to the *E. carnea* 'Sherwood Creeping' (Barbara Reed, personal communication).

Deer usually prefer to eat plants with high nitrogen content, and most heathers growing on nitrogen-poor soils, such as those found in their native habitats, are not attractive to deer. However, heathers that have been fertilized regularly, such as potted plants being grown for market, have high nitrogen content and will be eaten even though unfertilized heathers in nearby gardens are left untouched (Lortz 2002a). For this reason, it may be necessary to give newly planted heathers protection from deer until they have exhausted the excess nitrogen acquired during commercial cultivation.

Deer are creatures of habit and are basically lazy. They follow regular paths, making a wide circuit of their territory, a practice that allows time between visits for the growth of tender new shoots on their favorite browse. If a garden is created along a deer trail, the plants next to the trail will be sampled, especially by the fawns, which try everything. Deer can be rerouted around the heather garden by the placing of inexpensive low wire fences (sold in short, connectible lengths in garden centers) across their trails until they get out of the habit of going across the garden. They can easily jump low fences, but unless a particularly toothsome plant is on the other side of the fence, the deer find it easier to just go around them.

If you have a heather that deer might find somewhat attractive were it along their regular route, for example, a tree heath, putting it in the middle of a bed of callunas may be enough to save it from the deer. They will not take the trouble to pick their way across the uninteresting shrubs to get to the slightly more interesting one.

On the other hand, planting a heather garden near a landscape feature beloved of deer, such as an apple tree, is sheer folly. Only a very strong, very high fence can prevent the deer from visiting such an attraction, and heathers planted near the deer's favorite food may be browsed upon—simply because they are there. Care also should be exercised in the choice of companion plants for heather gardens located in deer territory. Otherwise excellent heather companions, for example, *Ophiopogon planiscapus* var. *nigrescens*, can serve as deer "magnets," attracting them to heather gardens that they would not ordinarily visit. Even if the deer do not eat the heathers near a magnet plant, they will probably trample them to death.

Deer are very curious and will taste unfamiliar plants they encounter, so they may give newly planted heathers, even unfertilized ones, unwelcome attention. In the process of sampling a newly planted heather, a deer will pull the entire plant out of the ground, then drop it as uninteresting. Gardeners in deer territory need to patrol their newly planted beds (and reset pulled up plants) for several weeks, until the plants have become established and the deer have lost interest.

Newly planted gardens also need protection from deer that are looking for a cool place to take a summer nap. Freshly dug soil, even when covered with mulch, is very attractive to deer; they will scoop out comfy little hollows in it for their beds. The deer may not eat the heathers, but they may squash or bury them! Strategically spaced sticks, rocks, or bricks temporarily placed among the young plants, with bird netting or poultry wire fencing laid over them if some extreme discouragement is necessary, can keep the deer off the heather beds during their first summer, after which the deer will usually leave them alone. These suggestions apply to any kind of new planting in deer-challenged areas.

Arthropods

Heather Beetle (*Lochmaea suturalis*)

The heather beetle is rarely found in heather gardens, but it can have severe implications for moorland and heathland and can affect *Calluna vulgaris* plants in gardens close to these natural habitats. Beetle outbreaks are sporadic, occurring approximately every 10 years, possibly because the beetles are themselves commonly infected with a debilitating protozoan parasite that limits their numbers. During these outbreaks, great damage is done to heathers, although wild heathers invariably recover and regrow after the beetle outbreak subsides.

Both larvae and mature beetles feed on the terminal buds and young heather leaves, causing the shoots to die off. A large beetle outbreak will result in severe heather defoliation. Adults lay eggs in the spring, and the larvae start feeding in late spring and feed throughout the summer. Initially they are pale green but later on grayish brown. The young beetles appear in late summer and feed through autumn until they go into hibernation for the winter. They are about ¼ in. (6 mm) long and olive brown in color with a black head, and they drop to the ground when disturbed so are not easy to see. The best garden control for these beetles is to cut back the infested plants.

Although generally considered to be a pest in Europe, the heather beetle is quite specific to *Calluna vulgaris*. It was deliberately introduced to New Zealand in 1996, sans parasite, as a potential biological control for the introduced *Calluna* that is replacing native vegetation in Tongariro National Park, on the North Island. Since heather's 1912 introduction to the park, *Calluna vulgaris* has spread to cover more than 124,000 acres (50,000 ha), and its sale within New Zealand is now banned.

Heather beetles have so far caused only limited damage to a few patches of *Calluna* in New Zealand, and there was a large beetle population collapse at the original release site in 2002. Field studies and laboratory research into the possible causes of the beetle's generally low establishment rate in New Zealand, and the population collapse in the main established colony, did not show either disease or predation by native insects and arachnids as cause of the beetles' general failure to thrive. Researchers speculate that "the poor establishment and success of heather beetle around Tongariro National Park to date is most likely caused by adverse weather conditions" (Peterson et al. 2004).

Red Spider Mite (*Tetranychus urticae*)

These very small mites form a web from a tissue of threads, mainly on the lower surface of the leaves, and suck sap from the leaves. The mites are scarcely visible to the unaided eye, but the web can often be seen. Affected leaves turn a rusty color, and later whole shoots turn brown. This pest is most likely to spread in dry, warm weather in late summer. It affects heathers much less than many other plants.

One of the simplest ways of stopping spider mite attacks is to spray the plants with a fine mist of water two or three times a day. The mites will not thrive in high humidity, and their numbers will soon start to drop.

Hygiene is important for control. All old bits of plant material, straw, and the like that could harbor hibernating mites need to be removed. Thorough washing and sterilizing of glasshouses, tunnels, frames, and other winter shelters is of great benefit to reduce the number of overwintering females.

Vine Weevil (*Otiorhynchus sulcatus*)

Vine weevils have been increasing in significance to gardeners over the past few decades due to the increased use of ornamental containers and container-grown plants from nurseries. The larvae, small white grubs with brown heads, live around heather roots and can eat almost all the roots before foliar damage is noticed. By that time, it is, of course, too late for effective treatment.

Notched leaves on rhododendrons (the result of night feeding by adult weevils) indicate the presence of vine weevils, and immediate steps should be taken to control them. Once established, vine weevils are difficult to eradicate, particularly for amateur gardeners, as some of the pesticides used by commercial growers to control weevils are unavailable for home use.

Some nontoxic measures that can be used are traps made from corrugated cardboard, rolled into tubes for the adult beetles to hide in during the day. Alternatively, some moist sacking provides dark, daytime hiding places for the adults, which can be collected from both kinds of trap during the day, when they are relatively inactive. Another approach is to use sacrificial, container-grown plants such as primulas, polyanthus, and cyclamen, which are favored plants for adult weevils to lay their eggs by. These should be left near your treasured heathers to attract the weevils away from the heathers.

Finally, there is biological control available in the form of parasitic nematodes (*Steinernema kraussei*) that must be applied in late summer when the soil temperature is warm enough for the nematodes to be active (41 to 68°F [5 to 20°C]) but before the weevil larvae are large enough to cause damage. The Royal Horticultural Society (2006a) warns that gardeners should continue to monitor for vine weevils on a regular basis, because "stopping treatment after the apparent disappearance of the pest can allow numbers to build up again."

Fungal Diseases

In general, diseases are far more likely to affect container-grown heather plants than plants growing in the garden. Naturally occurring beneficial microorganisms in soil usually are sufficient to protect garden plants from disease-causing microorganisms, unless environmental conditions favor the growth of the latter. Container-grown plants must contend with wide temperature and moisture fluctuations, which make them more susceptible to disease than are garden-grown plants, and they are highly dependent upon the composition of the potting media in which they are grown.

Ralph Noble and Emma Coventry (2005) conducted an extensive review of research into the disease-suppressive effects of compost (partially decomposed organic matter resulting from aerobic decomposition of the raw feedstock) in potting media. Although none of the research included in their review specifically targeted heather (most was on food crops), their observations may be applicable to many plants grown in containers, including heathers. Disease suppression varied widely depending upon the crop, the disease being studied, and the feedstock for the compost (for example: animal manures, garden trimmings, ground bark, and municipal waste).

Most research reviewed by Noble and Coventry concluded that a positive correlation exists between the presence of compost in potting media and the suppression of diseases caused by *Phytophthora cinnamomi*, *Rhizoctonia solani*, and several species of *Pythium*. The review showed that, in general, the disease-suppressive effect of compost increased with the rate of application. Significant disease suppression occurred if compost constituted at least 20 percent of the growing medium, particularly a peat-based medium. (Lower amounts of compost showed disease-suppressive effects in soil-based media.) Disease suppression did not occur if the composted materials were sterilized or pasteurized. This latter observation indicates that the disease-suppressive effect is primarily the result of biological activity.

Heather growers troubled by any of the diseases described below may wish to experiment with the addition of compost to their container media or their gardens. The chemical properties of the various available composts should be a factor in compost selection. Avoid composts that increase the pH of the growing medium.

Root Rot (*Phytophthora cinnamomi*)

Phytophthora cinnamomi is a root fungus that causes serious disease and death of a wide variety of plant species, including heathers. High nutrient levels, especially of potassium and nitrogen, encourage growth of the fungus (Richard Poruban, personal communication). Saturated soils not favorable to plant growth can predispose plants to infection by the fungus (Pscheidt 2005). *Phytophthora cinnamomi* thrives in moist conditions and feeds on the roots and basal stem tissues of the plants, weakening or killing them by hindering the movement of water and nutrients within the plant. The fungus forms thick-walled resting spores that can survive in the soil for many years.

Plants are particularly vulnerable to *Phytophthora cinnamomi* during the summer months, when the soil is moist and the temperature high. Rapid spread of the infection tends to occur after a very warm period that is followed within a few days by a great deal of rain. Overwatering of heathers during very hot dry weather mimics the natural conditions that favor the spread of the fungus.

The symptoms appear about a month later. The leaves of the attacked plants, or of a few shoots, turn an ashen green. On *Calluna vulgaris*, the bases of the shoots frequently become reddish brown. The tips of the shoots droop, and within a few weeks the plants are dead. In cool, damp weather the disease progression is slower. The root systems of diseased plants become wholly or partially brown and rotten.

Although there are fungicides for controlling this pathogen, these generally are not available to the home gardener. Fortunately, most fungal problems occur with heathers that are growing in containers, as all of these pathogens require high soil temperatures and moist conditions. (In most regions where heather is cultivated, garden soil rarely reaches the critical temperatures.) Regulating watering, for instance by decreasing the amount and duration, is an important way to control *Phytophthora* diseases. Plants in which the disease is detected should always be quickly removed, then burned to prevent its spread.

Research has shown that the fungus can be killed in the soil by low temperatures. If the soil temperature in winter—presumably for a period of several weeks—is low enough, and the frost can penetrate the ground deeply enough, infection by this fungus is highly unlikely. A hard winter is thus good for the control or suppression of the disease.

Sudden Oak Death (*Phytophthora ramorum*)

The symptoms of sudden oak death were first recognized in California in 1994–1995 (Rizzo and Garbelotto 2003), but it was not until 2001 that Sabine Werres et al. published a description of the pathogen, which was infecting rhododendrons and viburnums in European nurseries. According to David Rizzo and Matteo Garbelotto, this species of *Phytophthora* appears to infect only the above-ground plant parts, unlike other members of the genus, such as *P. cinnamomi*, which are root fungi.

This fungus infects a wide range of plant species in many families, including the Ericaceae, but the infection is fatal in only some of the affected plants. A survey by the Plant Health Risk Assessment Unit of the Canadian Food Inspection Agency (2003) found that in hosts other than oaks, symptoms are "often restricted to leaf spots, stem and twig blight or occasionally seedling blight or tip dieback."

In *Calluna vulgaris*, the symptoms are that the shoot apices turn brown to dark brown for 1 to 2 in. (2 to 5 cm). The heather itself is not badly damaged by the pathogen, but it is significant as a carrier (host) of the disease. In assays of susceptibility to *Phytophthora ramorum* (using both European and North American strains of the disease), leaf inoculation studies indicated the potential for *Calluna* to be "virtually immune" to the disease and for *Erica cinerea* to be resistant (UK PRA 2003).

Because of the potential for forest destruction through the spread of *Phytophthora ramorum*, nurseries growing host plants such as *Calluna vulgaris* are now being inspected and regulated throughout much of North America and are being closely watched in Europe. The danger from this organism is not to heathers directly but to susceptible plants growing near infected heathers.

Thread Mold (*Rhizoctonia solani*)

This is another fungus that prefers warm, wet conditions. Although not as serious as *Phytophthora cinnamomi*, it is more widespread. It is a common cause of the death of cuttings, particularly those propagated under polyethylene.

The symptoms are a general browning of the lower foliage, often in an even manner for about 1 in. (3 cm) above the soil. *Calluna vulgaris* is particularly susceptible. *Rhizoctonia* will rarely cause problems in a garden unless conditions are unfavorable for good plant growth.

Root Rot (*Pythium* species)

Pythium is a very common fungus found in garden and nursery soils, composts, ground water, and water tanks. Although it grows happily on dead organic material, it is an opportunistic pathogen; that is, it will attack heathers when they are under any sort of stress.

Pythium tends to attack specific stems and is normally characterized by a reddening of the foliage. In severe cases, *Pythium* will kill the plant. Where only part of the plant is affected, trim off the damaged foliage and then boost the plant with a foliar feed to promote recovery. (Some foliar feeds are specially formulated for weakened plants.) If the whole plant is affected, dig it up and burn it. Also remove from the garden, bag, and discard any soil that was in contact with the infected plant's root system. You will need to replace this soil with fresh soil from another part of the garden before replanting. Nurserymen can use fungicides against *Pythium*, but such chemicals are not available to home gardeners.

Gray Mold (*Botrytis cinerea*)

Botrytis cinerea is one of the most damaging pathogens for both amateur gardeners and commercial heather nurseries. It grows on both dead and live material and is most damaging during heather propagation, when cuttings are being rooted in a warm, humid environment. Older plants can also be severely affected if conditions are suitable for infection.

Foliage turns brown on affected areas and may become covered in gray-brown spore masses, just barely visible to the unaided eye. Cuttings can be killed and a large number of plants rendered unfit to sell.

Botrytis is a ubiquitous pathogen that spreads by means of tiny, airborne spores. Good hygiene, such as the removal of any dead, dying or unhealthy plant material, will help to reduce the number of spores. Successful control depends upon the manipulation of growing conditions to favor heather growth rather than fungal growth.

Commercial nurseries use a combination of fungicidal sprays to prevent *Botrytis* infection, and amateur gardeners may also find it beneficial to drench or spray cuttings with a suitable fungicide. If the amateur grower can reduce the temperature and humidity immediately after heather cuttings have rooted, and free air movement is then allowed, *Botrytis* should present few problems.

Older heathers grown in very close proximity, either in pots (for example, commercial stock plants) or in gardens may suffer from *Botrytis*. This fungus normally causes problems in gardens on susceptible cultivars when weather conditions are warm and humid. *Calluna vulgaris* is particularly affected, with the growing tips turning brown—just as though someone has waved a blowtorch close to the plant.

One of the best ways to get rid of *Botrytis* on garden heathers is simply to remove the infected plants and burn them. However, a thorough pruning of affected branches and a thinning of plants in affected beds may help to solve the problem. Fungicidal sprays or drenches may also help. *Botrytis* rarely kills mature plants.

3 Propagation

Heathers frequently manage to propagate themselves without help from gardeners: through seeding into the garden and lawn, through self-layering where branches touch the ground, or even by sprouting roots on prunings or on branch tips that were sampled by deer, then dropped onto the ground. It is only when gardeners want to propagate specific heathers that the plants sometimes appear reluctant to cooperate in their own perpetuation. Many gardeners trying to propagate heathers for the first time seem to have difficulty, and so the subject is presented here in some depth.

Despite receiving no care and no supplemental watering in a cool Mediterranean climate that receives little summer rainfall, self-sown heather seedlings (including *Calluna*, *Daboecia*, *Erica cinerea*, *E. tetralix*, *E. vagans*, and *E.* ×*watsonii*) thrive in the meadow next to the former nursery stock plant area at Alice Knight's Heather Acres in Elma, Washington. At least two commercially viable cultivars originated in this meadow.

Heather cultivars can be reproduced only vegetatively (asexually). Seed collected from cultivars may germinate and grow into plants similar to the parents but will be genetically different and, therefore, may not be called by the same cultivar name. Many "chance" seedlings are found in nurseries specializing in the growing of ornamental heathers. Most, however, are of little garden value.

There are two predominant ways in which heathers are propagated vegetatively: by layering and by cuttings.

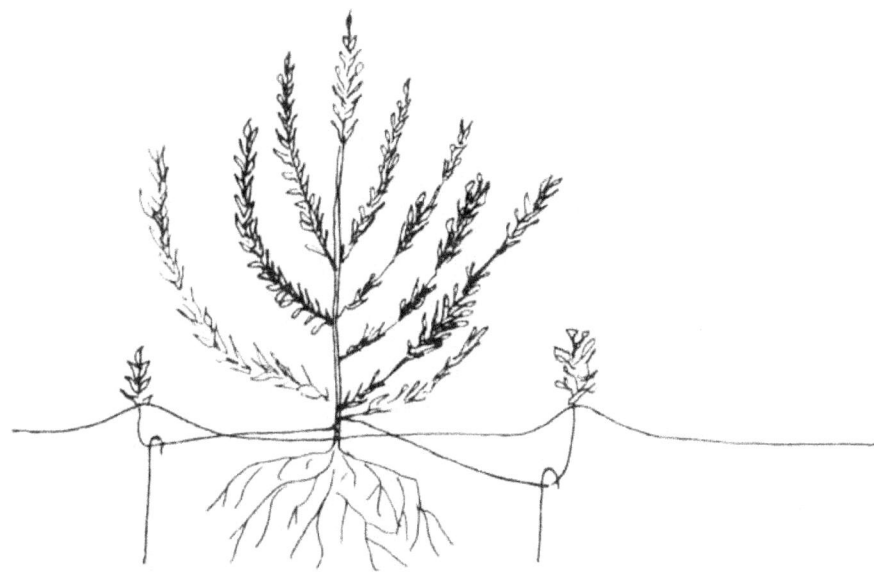

When layering heathers, strip the lowest outer branches of their lower leaves, peg the branches down into soil or ericaceous compost, and bury the pegged stems, mounding up the compost so that the leafy branch tips point upward.

Layering

Layering is the simplest and most reliable method for the gardener who wants just a few plants of a particular variety. Select a branch or several branches on the outside of the plant. Then, with a trowel, make a shallow trench into which each selected branch, stripped of its lower leaves, can be drawn. Fill the trench with a 1:1 mixture of sphagnum moss peat (or other well-composted organic matter) and gritty sand. Draw the selected branch down into the trench, taking care not to break it. Peg it down firmly with wire hooks about 6 in. (15 cm) long, and be sure that the tip of the branch is protruding and turned upwards. Instead of pegs, stones may be used to hold the layer in position. Cover the branch with the peat and sand mixture, and mound it up around the now-upright tip. Water the layer well. It is important to keep the layered area moist at all times.

A layer can be made at any time of year, but during the spring growing season is, perhaps, the best time. Nine to ten months later, a root system will have formed at the bend in the stem where it was pegged. When the layered portion shows signs of good new growth, it then can be severed from the parent plant and moved to its final growing position. Several such layers can be made around the plant without affecting its appearance.

Although layering is the easiest propagation method, it tends to produce rather lopsided plants that will need several seasons of pruning to achieve the good shape that plants grown from cuttings have almost from the beginning.

Self-Layering

Many heather cultivars will produce roots on stems that touch the ground. These rooted stems can be carefully severed from the mother plant and moved elsewhere in the garden or potted up and given away.

Dropping

An alternative to layering when more plantlets are required is to dig up the plant, create a larger hole, and bury the plant so that only the growing tips are exposed. This technique, known as "dropping," is best practiced in the dormant season and primarily on heathers that have become woody at the base. The stems should have formed roots by the following autumn, at which time they can be detached from the old plant.

On an especially large, well-established specimen, you can practice "upward dropping," or mounding (Wick 2005). Instead of digging out the plant to put it into a deeper hole, simply pile up around the plant the same peat and sand mixture that you would use to fill a layering trench. This practice can resurrect a neglected old plant that has developed a hole in its center. Fill the hole with soil, and mound up around all the branches, so that you have only a circle of growing tips showing, just as you would for normal dropping. Water it well. By the following year, each buried stem will have developed roots and can be severed from the mother plant.

An overgrown, potted *Calluna vulgaris* 'Spring Torch', "dropped" in the autumn, was beginning to show its characteristic spring tip color when this photograph was taken in early spring. Each buried branch of a dropped plant will form roots. Rooted branches may be detached from the parent plant and moved where needed in the garden.

Cuttings

The most common method of producing heathers is from cuttings. Many gardeners have trouble rooting heathers from cuttings, but if a number of simple rules are followed, a high success rate can be achieved.

What happens when a cutting roots? Why do some species root more easily than others? Why do cuttings root more easily at certain times? These questions and many others like them arise irrespective of the form of propagation used.

Rooting depends upon many interrelated factors. Some are beyond our control, but an understanding of these factors can be helpful in determining the type of material to select. In general, cuttings should be taken from healthy, vigorous plants, preferably not more than three years old. Other criteria are species-dependent, as will be discussed later in this chapter.

Composts for Propagation

A compost into which rooting can take place can be prepared from three parts sphagnum moss peat (do *not* use sedge peat, as this can often have a high pH and poor aeration) and one part of horticultural perlite. Acidic gritty sand, where it is available, can be used instead of perlite, but it *must* be acidic. This applies even for the propagation of heathers that would normally grow in any soil, as an acidic medium will improve the rooting yield.

Cuttings will also root well in a mixture that is half peat and half sand or perlite. In fact, they will root in pure sand, pure perlite, vermiculite, or in commercial potting mix that is not alkaline. The only requirement is that the mixture and growing containers drain freely and have been sterilized (to prevent the loss of cuttings to fungi or damping-off organisms).

There is no need to add fertilizer at this stage. In fact, the yield is likely to be higher if none is added. There is also no need to add rooting hormones. Most heathers root quite freely without added hormones.

If horticultural perlite is being used, add water to the perlite as instructed by the manufacturer. If you are using commercial peat, be sure that your propagation mix is thoroughly wet, as dry peat is extremely difficult to moisten.

Methods of Propagation

A cutting severed from the parent plant will continue to lose moisture through transpiration from its leaves. The two basic ways of rooting heather cuttings attempt to keep this moisture loss to a minimum. The first, open to all amateur growers and described below, relies on keeping the cuttings humid. The second is more sophisticated: mist propagation.

Closed Polyethylene Method

This method relies on keeping cuttings humid to minimize transpiration and is suitable for rooting most of the widely grown hardy species of heather. There are many adaptations of this method, depending on whether small or large quantities of rooted cuttings are being produced. The main danger with this approach is the risk of fungal attack. If small numbers are required, the following method minimizes that risk.

Fill a 4-inch (10-cm) clay pot with sand. Then put a small amount of rooting compost into the bottom of a 6-inch (15-cm) plastic pot. Place the sand-filled pot on top of the compost in the plastic pot; the top of the clay pot should be level with the top of the plastic pot. Then fill the space between pots with more compost, firm the compost, water to remove any air pockets in the compost, and let it drain thoroughly.

Using a nail or sharpened pencil, make holes in the compost about ¾ in. (2 cm) apart, close to both pot edges. (Alternate between holes close to the clay pot and holes close to the plastic pot.) Place cuttings in the prepared holes but do not firm them in. Once the pot has been filled with cuttings, water it heavily so that compost seals the dibbed holes. Let the pot sit for about 20 minutes, making sure that all excess water has drained away. Be sure to label each pot with the name of the cultivar(s) and the date the cuttings were stuck.

Cut two 12-inch (30-cm) lengths of thin, flexible wire and insert their ends a short distance into the compost on opposite sides of the plastic pot, crossing the wires at 90-degree angles to form arches over the cuttings. Then slip a polyethylene bag (such as those used for fresh produce at the grocery store—one without holes in it) over the wire arches and the plastic cuttings pot, tucking the bag ends under the pot. The wire arches will help to insure that the polyethylene does not touch the cuttings, allowing air to circulate around them.

When only a few cuttings are needed, they may be rooted using the "twin pots" approach. Wire arches keep the polyethylene bag covering the pot on the left from lying directly upon the cuttings to be rooted. Note that the inside of the bag is fogged, indicating that there is adequate moisture inside the bag. The twin pot on the right contains rooted *Daboecia* cuttings ready for transplanting to individual pots or directly into the garden.

If slightly larger numbers of cuttings are required, the twin pots approach can be replaced with a plastic seed tray. Lightly firm compost into the tray and dib holes ¾ in. (2 cm) apart. As described above, water the cuttings into place, allow the tray to drain thoroughly, then cover it with a tightly fitting raised plastic lid or seal it inside a large polyethylene bag held away from the cuttings.

Place the pot (or tray) against the shady side of a wall or in light shade under a bush—any place where no direct sunlight will hit the bag. Never place the pot in a greenhouse, because the temperature variation is too great. In cold climates, the pot can be buried to its rim in soil or mulch to minimize the risk of freezing if it is to be left over the winter. In very cold climates, cuttings pots can be placed in cold frames, with mulch tucked around the pots; but be sure that these frames are not in direct sunlight. Another option for gardeners in climates with very cold winters is to root cuttings in an unheated basement under cool fluorescent lights.

Leave the pot for several months, checking it occasionally to be sure that the polyethylene bag is fogged, an indication that the compost is still moist. If the bag is not fogged, heavily water the sand in the clay pot, allow the pots to drain, and then reseal the bag. Water will slowly percolate through the clay to the rooting compost without dislodging the cuttings or wetting their foliage. Any cuttings that die should be removed to minimize the risk of disease in the surviving cuttings.

After several months, you can check for rooting by *gently* pulling on a cutting. If it resists your gentle tug, you can be sure that rooting is taking place. If not, the cutting will come out easily and can be replaced just as easily.

Once most of the cuttings have rooted and begun new top growth, and if the weather is expected to remain above freezing, they can be carefully weaned from the humid atmosphere in which they rooted. On cloudy days, partially lift the polyethylene cover for a short time each day, gradually increasing the period until the cover can be completely removed.

Allow the cuttings to "harden off" in the place where they rooted, while watering them carefully as necessary. Watering the sand pot minimizes the risk that watering will dislodge the cuttings and break their fragile new roots. During the course of several weeks after the cover has been removed, the cuttings pot can gradually be moved out of the shade, until it finally is in full sunlight. The cuttings are now ready to be separated and either planted directly into the garden or moved into individual pots full of a compost suitable for ericaceous plants.

Mist Propagation

This technique relies upon chilling the leaves of the cuttings by intermittently misting the cuttings with very fine droplets of water and encouraging the water to evaporate off the cuttings between mistings. It minimizes transpiration by closing the stomata on the undersides of the leaves, but it allows the portions of the cuttings below the soil surface to remain at a much higher temperature than the leaves.

Misting is not done, as is often believed, to keep the cuttings wet. Some cheap mist systems produce constantly wet cuttings that consequently root poorly. When cuttings are kept constantly wet, rooting is confined to the soil surface. This effect can happen with the "closed polyethylene" technique, as well, if the cuttings are over-watered.

Because mist propagation is not carried out in such humid conditions as with the closed polyethylene method, weaning is not necessary. Although this technique can be used for the more easily rooted species, such as *Calluna vulgaris*, *Erica tetralix*, and *E. ×darleyensis*, it comes into its own when rooting the more difficult European species such as *E. arborea* and *E. multiflora*. It is by far the best method to root South African species.

There are several types of mist propagation systems on the market for both amateur and professional growers. These include electronic leaf systems, light integration systems, and multi-sensing systems.

Timing of Cuttings

Although cuttings taken in the seasons given here for the different species and hybrids have the greatest likelihood of rooting success, most commercial growers will admit that the best time to make cuttings is when the gardener has the time to do so. Some heathers, for example, *Calluna vulgaris*, *Erica carnea*, *E. ciliaris*, *E. cinerea*, and *E. tetralix*, will produce a reasonable percentage of rooted cuttings whenever they are made. The odds for successful rooting definitely improve for other species, for example, *E. lusitanica*, if cuttings are made in the right season. Only about 30 percent of 'George Hunt' cuttings taken in midspring successfully rooted. However, when cuttings of that cultivar were taken in late summer, successful rooting increased to more than 90 percent.

If your only access to cuttings of a long-sought cultivar happens to occur at the "wrong" season, try to root them anyway. You may beat the odds.

Choice and Preparation of Cutting Material, by Species

Calluna vulgaris

Cuttings can be taken from *Calluna vulgaris* in midspring using the leafy growth appearing above last year's flowers. In this case, select stems where the leafy growth is at least ½ in. (1 cm) long. Cut the stem with a sharp knife or scissors ¾ in. (2 cm) below the leafy growth. Remove any dead flowers by rubbing your finger and thumb down the stem.

Calluna vulgaris cuttings can also be taken during mid- to late summer from the growth just below the flowering stem. Select stems that are semi-ripe—firm and just turning straw-brown. Do not use stems where the leaf nodes are more than 1/10 in. (2.5 mm) apart, as these will be more difficult to root and will make a less shapely plant. Cut a suitable stem immediately below the flowers and discard this top cutting. Then cut again immediately below the first cut to create a cutting 1½ to 2 in. (4 to 5 cm) long. Remove (strip) the leaves from the lower ¾ in. (2 cm) of the cutting by rubbing your finger and thumb up and down the stem.

Calluna vulgaris cuttings ready for sticking. The tip cutting (left), taken in midspring, has had the leaves or dead flowers removed from the lower part of the stem. The cutting taken in midsummer (right) has had its tip removed and the leaves stripped from the lower part of the stem.

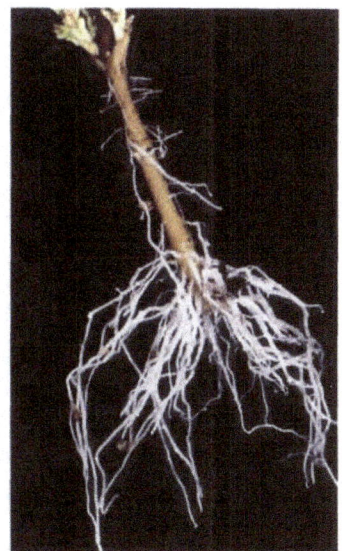

The winter colors of *Calluna vulgaris* 'Skone'. Green and gold in summer, this cultivar is valued more for its unusual foliage than for its impact in the landscape. To perpetuate the combination of leaf colors in 'Skone' and other chimaeras, such as 'Goldsworth Crimson Variegated', cuttings must be taken only from stems that have both green and gold leaves. This makes them more expensive to produce commercially.

Unlike some other heathers that root primarily or exclusively from the bases of cuttings, callunas can produce roots along the entire length of below-ground stems.

About two weeks after the cuttings are taken, a gradual swelling of the whole stem is observed. After three to four weeks, roots start to form above a leaf nodule. After about 10 weeks, more roots can be observed coming through the calluses formed over the nodules. These tend to be rather weak compared to the other roots, which are well developed by this time.

Because the hairy foliage of gray-leaved *Calluna* cultivars traps moisture, cuttings from these plants are particularly susceptible to rotting before rooting occurs (and sometimes even after rooting). When caring for cuttings with gray foliage, ensure that the foliage does not remain wet. To minimize the loss of gray-leaved cultivars when using the closed polyethylene method, wean these cuttings as soon as possible after they have rooted.

Daboecia

Cuttings from *Daboecia* are best taken in midsummer. Select side shoots about 1½ to 2 in. (4 to 5 cm) long that are firm and just turning to straw-brown. Pull a shoot down carefully to tear the cutting from the main stem so as to leave a small "heel" at the base of the cutting. Strip the leaves from the lower half of the cutting by pulling downward on them. Sometimes this type of cutting is not readily available, in which case prepare *Daboecia* cuttings in a manner similar to a midsummer *Calluna* cutting.

Stems of *Erica carnea* suitable for cuttings have leaf nodes very closely spaced (right). Stems with leaf nodes farther than 1/10 in. (2.5 mm) apart (left) are poor candidates for rooting.

Erica carnea

Take cuttings from *Erica carnea* in mid- to late summer by selecting stems that do not have buds forming on them. Ideally, heel cuttings about 1½ to 2 in. (4 to 5 cm) long are best; but if these are in short supply, a tip cutting can be prepared. If making tip cuttings, cut off and discard the top 2 in. (5 cm) of growth. Avoid stems where the leaf nodes are more than 1/10 in. (2.5 mm) apart.

Strip off the leaves on the lower half of a tip cutting. In the case of a heel cutting, pinch out the growing tip. Because *Erica carnea* flowers profusely, it may be difficult to find cutting material without buds. In this case, budded stems will have to be used. Prepare them as you would stems without buds, but remove all flower buds by rubbing a finger and thumb upwards along the stem. Some commercial propagators do not take the time to remove flower buds, but the cuttings root, anyway. It is great fun to see rooted cuttings in full bloom in their misting beds in early spring.

Erica carnea cuttings can also be taken in early to midspring. At this time of year, use the top 2 in. (5 cm) of growth but do *not* pinch out the growing tip. Nature has already provided a number of buds: more, in fact, than you can create by pinching out the tip.

Erica cinerea

Cuttings of *Erica cinerea* are best taken during mid- to late summer using non-flowering heel cuttings. Often, heel cuttings of this type are difficult to find. If available, these are likely to be quite small, ½ to ¾ in. (1 to 2 cm) long. Strip the leaves from the lower half of the cutting by gently rubbing finger and thumb down the stem.

Stems below flowering shoots can be used for cuttings, provided that the spacing between the tufts of leaves does not exceed 1/10 in. (2.5 mm). Cut these from the plant in a similar way to that described for midsummer *Calluna* cuttings. Because roots usually appear from only the base of the cutting, make sure the lower cut is made immediately below a tuft of leaves. Remove the leaves from the lower half of the cutting.

Erica cinerea roots by producing a large swelling at the base of the cutting (it does not matter whether it is a stem or heel cutting). The

This sprig of *Erica cinerea* 'Iberian Beauty' has an abundance of the non-flowering side shoots that are best for making mid- to late-summer heel cuttings, such as the one to its right.

time it takes to do this varies considerably. Roots appear two to three weeks later. It rarely roots around leaf nodes, which may account for the difficulty that many propagators have with this species.

Erica ciliaris, *E. mackayana*, and *E. tetralix*

Cuttings of these species are best taken during mid- to late summer using non-flowering heel cuttings about ½ to ¾ in. (1 to 2 cm) long, which are usually plentiful. These species root in a similar manner to *Erica cinerea*; that is, roots generally appear only near the base of the cutting.

Instead of branching, some shoots of *Erica ciliaris*, *E. mackayana*, and *E. tetralix* continue to grow on the previous year's growth (note the slight angle where the conspicuously larger-leaved new growth emerged from that of the preceding year). Avoid such shoots when making cuttings.

Erica tetralix cutting producing roots near its base.

Remove the leaves from the lower half of the cutting as described above. Incidentally, the removal of leaves from the cutting does not improve the rooting response, but it does make it much easier to test whether the cutting is rooted. These species have a tendency to continue growing on the previous year's growth instead of branching. Shoots like this should be avoided for taking cuttings.

Erica ×*darleyensis*, *E. erigena*, and *E. vagans*

These species root in a similar way to *Erica carnea*. Interestingly, the hybrid between *E. tetralix* and *E. vagans*, *E.* ×*williamsii*, generally behaves similarly to *E. tetralix* (basal rooting) despite its leaf attachment being more like that of *E. vagans*. Cuttings are best taken in late summer, making particularly sure in the case of *E. erigena* that the stem is semi-ripe: firm and turning to straw-brown. Take cuttings that are 1 to 2 in. (3 to 5 cm) long, and prepare as described for *E. ciliaris*.

Other *Erica* Species

Prepare cuttings as you would those of *Erica* ×*darleyensis*.

Seed

Most gardeners enjoy the challenge of growing plants from seed. Plants with very small seeds, such as heathers, present a somewhat greater challenge than do most plants with larger seeds, but the satisfaction of having successfully germinated such seeds is correspondingly greater.

Collecting

European heathers begin to set seeds shortly after flowering, and the seeds ripen over a period of months, the length of time from pollination to ripe seed depending upon the species. Because ripe seed capsules can open suddenly on a dry day and release all their seed (Sellers 1999), if you intend to gather heather seed, begin inspecting the plants a few weeks after flowering. The swollen brown seed capsules should be gathered when they are nearly ready to open, to avoid losing valuable seed. (See "Guide for Novice Heather Breeders" in chapter 6 for instructions on collecting and storing heather seed.)

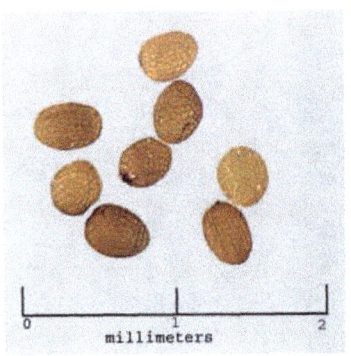

These tiny seeds of *Erica mackayana* 'Shining Light' were photographed through a microscope. Photo by Allen Hall.

The flowering and seed-collecting seasons of long-blooming species and cultivars will, of necessity, overlap. For example, collection of *Daboecia cantabrica* seeds may begin about six weeks after flowering (Kurt Kramer, personal communication), so it may be possible to collect *Daboecia* seeds from midsummer through midwinter. Additionally, seed capsules may remain on heather plants for extended periods without shedding all their seeds, so if you have missed the main seed-collecting season, it may be worthwhile to examine the plants for retained seed during the rest of the year.

Most interspecific hybrids are sterile, but this is not invariably so. Although they may not be capable of setting seed, they may produce viable pollen. Fully double flowers, whose reproductive parts have been converted into petal-like structures, are also sterile. Some semi-double flowers may be capable of setting seed and would warrant careful examination if double-flowered seedlings are desired.

Sowing

Whether you have made your own heather cross or collected seeds from garden or wild plants, you will want to ensure good seed germination and survival rates for the resulting seedlings. Heather breeder David Wilson offers this seed-sowing advice for achieving those goals.

Be sure that your containers are clean, preferably sterilized, and that the germina-

	midwinter	late winter	early spring	midspring	late spring	early summer	midsummer	late summer	early autumn	midautumn	late autumn	early winter
Calluna vulgaris		S				F	F	F	F	F	F	F
Daboecia azorica					F	F	F	F	F	S	S	
Daboecia cantabrica	S					F	F	F	F	F	F	S
Erica arborea				F	F	F	S	S	S			
Erica australis				F	F	F		S	S	S		
Erica carnea	F	F	F	F	S	S					F	F
Erica ciliaris	S	S				F	F	F	F	F	F	S
Erica cinerea						F	F	F	F	F	S	S
Erica erigena	F	F	F	F	F	S	S				F	F
Erica lusitanica	F	F	F	F	F	S	S	S			F	F
Erica mackayana						F	F	F	F	F	S	S
Erica manipuliflora	S						F	F	F	F	S	
Erica multiflora	S	S	S	S					F	F	F	F
Erica scoparia					F	F		S	S			
Erica spiculifolia						F	F	F	S	S		
Erica terminalis	S	S					F	F	F	F	S	S
Erica tetralix					F	F	F	F	F	F	F	S
Erica umbellata				F	F	F			S	S		
Erica vagans	S	S					F	F	F	F		S

Months when seed can be collected from European heather species (after Sellers 1999). Long-blooming heathers may have ripe seed and flowers simultaneously.

F = flowering period

S = seed collecting period

tion medium is also sterile. You may use a commercial seed starting mix or a simple homemade seed mix of equal parts fine peat, perlite, and sand, sieved to remove lumps. Fill your growing container to a depth of 2 to 3 in. (5 to 8 cm), and press the mix firmly into the container. You may wish to screen a thin layer of peat over the surface and firm it, then sow the seeds directly onto that. Alternatively, you could sprinkle a bit of fine grit onto the surface to help prevent fungal growth. Do not cover the seeds, but allow them to fall down into the spaces in the grit.

Water by soaking from below, until the surface of the starting mix has become damp. Then let the container drain for about 20 minutes, so that there is no chance of excess water remaining in it. This thorough watering needs to be done only once. Cover the container with plastic or a sheet of glass to retain moisture. If you are using a commercial seed starting kit, the cover will come with it. If the surface begins to dry out before germination, use a very fine mist to wet it so as not to dislodge and damage any seeds that may be just starting to germinate.

Provide gentle bottom heat, no more than 55 to 60°F (13 to 16°C), and place the container in a cool spot out of direct sunlight. Warmer temperatures will encourage the growth of molds. Check in two to three weeks for any problems, although these should be minimal if all your materials were clean to begin with.

Germination may occur within four to six weeks, but it is better to wait until you are satisfied with the number of seedlings before removing the cover. Even though the early germinators may stretch for the light and fall over, they can still make good garden plants if they are given extra care during transplanting. When transplanting floppy seedlings, plant them a little deeper than normal, enough to support the seedlings and encourage them to grow upright.

Once the seedlings are up and growing, you can gently screen some of the mix over them to help anchor them. Put the containers into a well-ventilated area where they will be kept from extremes of temperature until they have developed eight to ten sets of true leaves.

Adding artificial light will help to develop strong, stocky seedlings, but allowing the seedlings to go dry is the quickest way to kill them. They are happier too wet than too dry. They will require no feeding until they are well-branched little plants.

Transplant the seedlings into individual pots when they are large enough to be handled. They may be left to grow in the seed flat or pot for quite some time if they are not crowded.

4 Designing a Heather Garden

The design of a garden is personal and should reflect both the creativity of its owner and the surroundings of the garden. There are many reasons for making a garden: to showcase a collection of plants (often the main reason for making a garden that contains primarily one kind of plant); to provide a pleasant view from within the house; to create an outdoor living area or a beautiful setting for the house; or simply to indulge one's artistic impulses. A well-designed heather garden can do any of these.

The Heather Society's stand (winner of a Flora Silver Medal) at the Royal Horticultural Society's London show in August of 1983 featured cultivar groupings of young heather plants, dwarf conifers, and rocks: a heather garden in miniature. Photo by Maurice Everett.

Go look at gardens, lots of gardens. Notice how heathers are used in these gardens and whether the effect is pleasing or the heathers seem out of place. If possible, go into the natural landscape where the various heather species grow wild. Look around you—at the rocks and the water. Look at the natural companions of heathers. A Scottish hillside may have three species of heather mixed with *Festuca*, *Thymus*, and *Campanula rotundifolia*.

Where heathers are not native but where they have naturalized somewhat (preferably not to the detriment of the native plants, as happened on the North Island of New Zealand), what are the growing conditions? You do not need to recreate wild moorland or a peat bog, but seeing these environments can give you ideas for creating a place hospitable to heathers, where they will look at home.

Ideally, a heather garden should be laid out in a natural fashion that mimics, at least minimally, the distribution and spacing of plants in the wild. Such a garden best displays heather species and cultivars. This usually means designing in an informal style with the avoidance of straight lines, which are rarely seen in nature. However, massed heathers have been used to good effect in modernistic plantings full of straight lines!

An award-winning public landscape design in Forest Heights, Oregon. "The Wave," composed of hundreds of plants of a single *Calluna* cultivar, swoops across a green background criss-crossed with lines of golden *Euonymus*. Design by Michihiro Kosuge, for MCM Architects, PC, Portland, Oregon.

In a small garden, heathers can, with advantage, occupy the greater part of the space. With careful planning, a new heather garden can give a colorful display in three to four years, requires little maintenance, and will last 15 to 25 years or longer.

There are so many heather cultivars available, with so many different flowering times, growth habits, and foliage colors, that a garden planted only with heathers can be interesting and colorful throughout the year. These versatile shrubs can be ground covers, edgers, background, middle interest, and specimen plants. In fact, *Calluna vulgaris* cultivars alone can fill most of these functions, so that effective heather gardens are possible even in areas with severely cold winters. Where the climate is more benign, other heather species can extend the season of bloom throughout the year.

A well-designed heather garden will be beautiful in all seasons, unlike many other specialty gardens devoted to one kind of plant (sometimes called plant ghettos) that usually have only a few weeks of glory annually and can be distinctly boring, or even downright ugly, the rest of the year. The various—and changeable—foliage colors of the different heather cultivars make it possible to have a garden that looks good all the time.

Conifers, rhododendrons, tree heaths, and a fence form the backdrop for lower growing heathers in the Plumridge garden, County Durham, England. The bright pink heath in the center back of this photo, taken in late spring, is *Erica australis* 'Holehird'.

Although late spring and early summer are often considered "low season" for bloom in the heather garden, this can be a time of particular beauty and tranquillity. It is the season when most heathers are making new growth, and the garden is a subtle blend of soft, muted foliage tones. Most of the reds and oranges of winter have changed back to gold, but in many cultivars with golden foliage, early summer color is a greenish gold, not the strong yellow gold it will become as the foliage matures.

In late spring and early summer, there is still yellow or red visible on the plants with spring tips, although these colors are now faint and blended into the emerging greens and grays. It is also in late spring and early summer that the differing growth habits of the cultivars are most apparent, as the new growth gracefully curves or strongly ascends or droops, depending upon its inherited inclination.

The heather garden is at its most tranquil in late spring and early summer, when there are few flowers blooming and the foliage colors are muted.

Site Selection

The first thing to do is to choose a suitable site for the heather garden. How large an area is it to be? Is it flat or sloping? Is the soil heavy clay or light and sandy? Is it acidic, alkaline, or neutral? Is it in full sun or partly shaded?

A slope filled with heathers and dwarf conifers makes this Walterville, Oregon, garden an inviting place to stroll. Design by Val Bloom.

In winter, the foliage of *Calluna vulgaris* 'Highland Rose' exposed to sunlight becomes reddish orange, while shaded leaves remain green or gold.

The Ideal Site

Let's go roamin' through the heather on the hill.
Lerner 1947

The ideal site for a heather garden is a sunny, gently sloping hillside, where the garden can be viewed from the bottom of the slope and winding paths invite the garden visitor to wander among the heathers. Heather flowers, forms, and colors show to best advantage when seen from below, especially the cultivars that turn orange or red in the winter on the side of the plant facing the sun. It is the sunny side of each plant that will exhibit strong winter color. In fact, it is the sunny side of each sun-facing leaf that will turn orange or red (Rogers 2006). The rest of the leaf will remain green or yellow, depending on the cultivar, as will interior leaves shaded by outer ones.

Dealing with Steep Slopes

Gentle slopes provide the necessary good drainage required by all heathers, and the fibrous heather roots are excellent for stabilizing the soil on slopes once the plants are established. Unfortunately, very steep slopes may encourage so much runoff that newly planted heathers do not receive sufficient water to survive their first summer. Steep slopes can be terraced, so that planting areas are only slightly inclined. On a large slope, tree trunks laid horizontally across the slope can slow or block the flow of water—and mulch—down the slope. If partially rotted logs are used this way, heathers can even be planted in the hollows of the logs, which will eventually decompose completely. Long before that happens, the heathers will have spread to hide most of the logs.

Another option is to create individual planting pockets for the young heathers, using anything available to slow the flow of water downhill for the first year or two after planting, to allow time for it to be absorbed by the plants. Groupings of small rocks can create such pockets, as can shingles or short lengths of cut saplings stood on end in a U-shape immediately below each plant.

The plump, pyramidal shoots of *Calluna vulgaris* 'Tom Thumb' make this dwarf cultivar, a rock garden favorite, easy to recognize.

A very steep slope can be turned into a rock garden, a substantial undertaking that will be a great garden asset if well done. (Many books have been written about rock gardening and are worth consulting before you begin such an enterprise.) Heathers of all sizes can be accommodated in large rock gardens; there are tiny heather cultivars that can join alpine treasures in smaller-scaled rock gardens; and cultivars with prostrate growth seem to have been designed to spill over rocks. Conversely, rocks are never out of place in a heather garden—although they can be poorly positioned, whether they are used for the practical purpose of slope stabilization or purely as decorative elements.

Erica cinerea 'Kerry Cherry' sprawls over rocks in the Wulff garden.

Creating a Slope Where None Exists

Lack of a natural slope is no reason to abandon the designing of a heather garden. Very successful heather gardens have been made on flat or only slightly sloping ground. Various means can be employed to create slopes or the appearance of slopes on level ground.

A simple way to create a gentle slope for planting heathers is to sculpt the existing soil into mounds or berms. Once garden pathways have been laid out, soil removed from the pathways to make room for paving materials can be piled onto the adjacent garden beds. Even a small change in height will create a more freely draining planting area, and the planting will slope slightly up from the paths. Planting taller growing cultivars on the top of such mounds and lower growing ones near the bottom accentuates the underlying topography, giving the illusion of greater grade change than actually exists. The famous heather garden of Beverly and James Thompson in Manchester, California, is built on level ground, but cleverly sculpted low mounds of soil planted with large sweeps of heather give it the billowing wave effect for which it is known.

Another, even easier, way to create heather beds is to simply dump truckloads of suitable soil or special ericaceous planting mix onto the places where you want your heather beds. This avoids digging entirely and has been the favored method of Berndt Lautenschlaeger, who has completely surrounded his house with heathers. When he is ready to extend a bed or create a new one, he simply buys and dumps another truckload of soil, which he spreads to a depth of at least 18 in. (45 cm). This labor-saving technique would allow the planting of acid-loving species in areas where the soil is alkaline, such as on chalk.

Berndt Lautenschlaeger chats with late summer visitors to his heather garden in Otis, Oregon.

A more ambitious undertaking involves the creation of hills where none exist. Using a technique employed for decades by keen rock gardeners who own flat land, the hill is constructed upon a foundation of discarded tires. The tires are laid flat in the desired shape of the hill footprint but slightly within the planned outside boundary. The tires are then filled with gravel, thus ensuring excellent drainage for the new hill. Successive layers of tires, each smaller in extent than the layer beneath and each filled with a mixture of soil and gravel in about equal parts, are added until the hill is nearly the desired height. The tires are then covered top and sides with about 18 to 24 in. (45 to 60 cm) of soil or prepared planting mix, with rocks used to stabilize the soil just as they would be on a natural hillside. The new hill can then be planted just as a natural hill would be.

Such a created hill has one big advantage over a natural landform. As it is built, irrigation pipes can be run up through the tires (or, rather, the tires and gravel can be stacked around the pipes, which have been installed first) so that the irrigation system is in place by the time the hill is finished, no digging required.

Getting Started

Once you have determined where you will create your new heather garden, draw a rough map to scale, showing existing trees or shrubs you wish to keep and utilitarian fixtures you wish to hide. You will need to keep these in mind as you decide upon your garden layout.

Next, decide whether to have a heather bed designed to peak at a particular time of year or whether to have a bed that has something in flower for most of the year. The "peaked" bed will give a spectacular floral display for six to ten weeks, and then judiciously chosen foliage varieties can give it a subdued but still colorful display for the rest of the year.

When James Thompson designed his garden, he decided that the garden should be at its peak of bloom in late summer. However, not wanting to be without winter flowers, he decided to plant the winter bloomers around the edges of the garden (Daneri 1998). In this way, they serve as a green frame for the summer flower colors. In the winter, they provide the color attraction against the foliage backdrop of the summer bloomers.

If you have chosen to make a peaked garden and space permits, you could make several planting beds, each peaked for a different season. It is a good idea to place winter-flowering beds close to the house, where they can be seen easily from the house. The summer-flowering beds can be placed farther away, where they can be viewed by a leisurely stroll around the garden in fine weather.

Site Preparation

Be sure that *all* unwanted vegetation is removed from the area that will be your new heather garden. Pay particular attention to removing deep-rooted perennial weeds such as thistle, bindweed, and ground elder. If even a tiny bit of their roots remain, they can continue to grow and make all your design efforts futile. Treatment of these weeds—several times, if necessary—with a weed killer that does not persist long in soil, such as glyphosate, may be the only way to ensure that they are truly eliminated. Although mature heather gardens can be nearly weed free, because the plants' dense shade will prevent weed seeds from germinating among them, young heathers are no match for existing persistent weeds.

This is the time to improve soil tilth and drainage, to make any adjustments to soil pH needed to grow your chosen heathers, to limb up nearby deciduous trees to allow light to reach the new garden, or to do hill creation as described earlier in this chapter. Whatever effort is put into site preparation will be repaid many times over by the ease of maintenance, health, and beauty of the garden for many years to come.

Layout

Once the soil is prepared and weeds removed, lay out the garden beds and paths. These may be sketched to scale on your garden map and later laid out on the actual site that will become the garden, or you may design the garden beds and paths on site, refining the design as you work.

Whether you are copying the design from your sketch or improvising on site, garden layout is most easily done by using a hose as a guide. Irregularly shaped beds and curved, meandering paths create a natural-looking garden that displays heathers to advantage, and a hose can be easily bent and adjusted until it assumes a shape that pleases you. Let the hose serve as one edge of a path or the boundary of a garden bed. Sprinkle flour along it to make a temporary, biodegradable design on the ground. Then measure out the width of the paths you will need, and mark the other edges the same way.

Three feet (1 m) is the absolute minimum for a garden path except for "working paths," which will be discussed later in this chapter. Main paths that would allow two people to walk side by side need to be at least 5 ft. (1.5 m) wide. When deciding how wide to make your garden paths, remember to allow for plant sprawl. If you intend to soften path edges with plants spilling over them, make the paths about 12 in. (30 cm) wider than these minima.

Paths may be closely mown lawn, chopped bark, pine needles, tree rounds, gravel, flat stones, brick or concrete pavers, or a combination of these paving materials—

Both lawn and bark paths are used in the heather garden at The Bannut, Herefordshire, England. Photo by Daphne Everett.

such as tree rounds or stones set into chopped bark or gravel. Bark and pine needles provide the most natural-looking surfaces, but they break down within a few years and will need to be replenished frequently. Gravel is the next most natural-looking paving material. It will make a firm, long lasting, walking surface if well laid upon an underlay of sharp sand.

Where the heather garden abuts lawn, such as with the "island beds" popular in some countries, it is logical to have the lawn extended as paths through the garden. Lawn paths will be the highest maintenance paths because of their constant need for mowing and for trimming of the path edges to keep grass from invading the heather beds.

Whatever paving material you choose, try to use it throughout the garden. However, if your garden is to be formal near the house and naturalistic at a distance, your paths may reflect this change. For example, stone pavers near the house may give way to stone pavers set into gravel, which in turn are replaced by all gravel in the part of the garden farthest from the house.

Choice of paving material depends primarily upon the style of the garden and the pocketbook of the gardener. Whatever your paving choice, prepare the appropriate foundation for the kind of surfacing material to be used. Unless the paving material is to be poured concrete or macadam (not recommended except in gardens where wheelchair accessibility is required), be sure to line the path with landscape cloth to prevent weeds from rooting in the path. As with soil preparation, proper path preparation can help to ensure an attractive garden and can prevent additional labor and expense for path maintenance for many years.

Plan to use low-growing heather cultivars along paths, and be sure to place the plants far enough back from the path to allow for many years of growth, so that you

The restrained growth of *Calluna vulgaris* 'Snowflake' makes it an excellent choice for edging paths.

are not constantly fighting the plants for walking room. A small amount of spillover can soften the lines of the path and add to the natural appearance of the garden, but aggressive, vigorous cultivars are not the best edging plants.

An occasional grouping of taller plants placed near a path can break up the monotony of uniformly low edging. Again, be sure that these are far enough back from the path to avoid their sprawling halfway across it as they mature. An effective design trick is to plant a curving line of plants of a single tall cultivar, perhaps only one plant wide, that begins at a path and wanders through the garden to emerge at another part of the path or is replaced in the middle of the bed by a different cultivar.

Garden paths should invite leisurely strolling, reflection, and observation, never racing. This means that the paths are sufficiently wide for easy walking—but not too wide, the path edges have been well defined, the surface is firm and free of obstacles that could trip a walker who is busy looking at plants, changes in elevation are gradual or steps are clearly visible, and curves are not too sharp. If the garden's paths have been well designed and surfaced, the garden will give promise of its future beauty even before the plants are in the ground.

Once you have laid out the beds and paths, go back to your original map and sketch in where the *actual* boundaries of beds and paths are. You are then ready to decide which plants will suit your garden, taking into consideration what heathers will grow well in your particular climate, soil type, and exposure.

Growth Potential and Spacing of Plants

When calculating how many heather plants you need for a bed, first consider the tree heaths and conifers, grasses, or other suitable companion plants that will add height and architectural interest to the garden. Estimate the planting area for heathers by deducting one square yard (m^2) for each architectural plant included in the design. Then multiply by five per square yard (m^2) to obtain the number of heathers required. This assumes that the heathers will be planted an average distance of 18 in. (45 cm) between plants. Actual spacing will, of course, vary depending upon the cultivars used.

Knowledge of the growth potential of the many heather cultivars and companion plants is essential for the design of a garden that is intended to last many years. Unless the rate of growth, mature plant shape and size of each cultivar are factored into the design, it will have a very limited life, with the more vigorous cultivars shoving aside their weaker cousins.

The number of plants of a cultivar will need to vary with the size of the cultivar and the growing conditions in the garden. The usual recommendation for a garden in the naturalistic style is to plant in odd numbers to avoid the appearance of symmetry: three, five, seven, or fifteen per grouping. Actually, once you get past seven, even or odd matters little, as the eye and brain are probably not going to register more than the overall impact of the group, particularly if the outline of the group is irregular.

More important is how the heathers are spaced. For large plantings, staggered rows evenly spaced (with slight adjustments made for curved beds) produce the most even coverage after a few years' growth. Although this kind of spacing initially may appear regimented, hence formal, the plants are merely dots in a pointillist painting. What color is put where determines the shape the viewer sees when the painting is finished (that is, the plants have grown together).

When balancing cultivars of different growth propensities, you may need to use three plants of a large cultivar, widely spaced, and seven plants of a smaller one spaced closer to each other. When a very large cultivar is being used in a small garden, one plant may suffice. However, a garden composed of many cultivars but only one plant per cultivar is usually just a jumbled mess with little or no design apparent. Placing several plants of each cultivar together will give stronger visual impact.

Remember that all plants will grow larger than the dimensions given in catalog descriptions, although some have the potential to be much larger than others. Instead of splitting the difference in size when you calculate how far apart to put plants of different cultivars, put small plants at least as far away from large plants as you would put the large plants from each other. This lessens the risk that the larger will overwhelm the smaller.

To avoid serious competition problems, choose adjacent cultivars that do not differ greatly in vigor. This does not mean that you cannot achieve an abrupt drop in height from one cultivar to its neighbor if that is the look you want. Height does not always equal vigor. Two low-growing cultivars such as *Erica cinerea* 'Celebration' and *Calluna vulgaris* 'Soay' may be nearly as unequal in vigor as are *C. vulgaris* 'Kerstin' and 'The Pygmy'. *Erica cinerea* 'Celebration' and *C. vulgaris* 'Kerstin' would be compatible neighbors of similar vigor but different growth habit. The slowly creeping *C. vulgaris*

Slow-growing *Calluna vulgaris* 'Humpty Dumpty', bright green all year, occasionally has a few white flowers. It needs equally slow-growing neighbors.

'Soay' is somewhat more vigorous than bun-shaped 'The Pygmy' but is restrained enough to make a good companion for it.

There is such a thing as leaving too much space between plants. Although with care a heather plant can live 30 years or longer, if you allow space for even 10 years' growth, you will be seeing the ground between plants for many years. Some landscapers, hardly deserving of the name, plant heathers 36 or 48 in. (90 or 120 cm) apart and depart, never to return. The property owner must then cope with the inevitable weeds that will have plenty of time to settle in before the heathers are remotely close to covering the ground. What is saved in the initial cost of plants will be more than made up for in the labor of weeding and the unattractiveness of a garden planted in this manner. Close planting followed by thinning is infinitely preferable.

Design Ideas

The Winter Garden

Winter is a season not normally associated with gardens and garden visiting. Yet a garden can be designed to be at its most inviting during winter, and heathers are often valuable components of winter gardens.

Take a lesson from a famous winter garden. For example, in England, one might visit the Cambridge University Botanic Garden or the RHS Garden Rosemoor in Devon, both of which have gardens dedicated to plants with winter interest. In North America, the Horticulture Centre of the Pacific, Victoria, British Columbia, and the JC Raulston Arboretum of the North Carolina State University in Raleigh both have winter gardens, although the hot, humid summers of the southeastern United States severely limit the selection of heathers growing in the latter. All of these gardens offer an opportunity to see heathers used in the landscape in combination with other plants, and each has its own unique design, as well as features and plants shared with other winter gardens.

The winter garden at the Cambridge University Botanic Garden opened in 1979. The level site was landscaped to provide a shallow valley through which the main path runs. The site is open to the south to let in maximum winter light. All plants in the garden have been selected for their winter interest: bark, berries, flowers, and foliage. Heathers form the understory and ground cover in several parts of the garden, accompanying witch hazels (*Hamamelis*), barberries (*Berberis*), and red osier dogwood (*Cornus* species) among other trees and shrubs. Most of the heathers in this winter garden are winter bloomers: *Erica carnea*, *E.* ×*darleyensis*, *E. erigena*.

The winter garden at the Horticulture Centre of the Pacific, cleverly located adjacent to the heather garden, makes use of *Calluna* cultivars with winter-red or year-round golden foliage, although it, too, has many winter-flowering ericas. As befits a Pacific Northwest garden, it has a dark backdrop of tall conifers; but within the winter garden proper, as in Cambridge, witch hazels are the tree of choice. These vase-shaped, small, deciduous trees throw little shade and can flower any time between November and April, making them ideal for brightening gray days without significantly interfering with the growth of sun-loving plants near them. Winter-flowering heathers and witch hazels are a combination repeated in many winter gardens, but it is a winning combination that is never boring.

At the Horticulture Centre of the Pacific in Victoria, British Columbia, winter-blooming ericas carpet the earth, while witch hazel flowers draw the eye above ground level. Ancient conifers serve as backdrop for both.

Many variations are possible on the theme, depending upon which cultivars are chosen—and there are many excellent cultivars of both witch hazels and heathers. The orange-flowered *Hamamelis* ×*intermedia* 'Jelena', stunning when backlit, goes well with the very dark-leaved *Erica erigena* 'Irish Dusk', with its salmon-pink flowers. The witch-hazel flowers harmonize even better with the distinctly orange-bronze winter foliage tones of *E. carnea* 'Ann Sparkes' or 'Bell's Extra Special', a color combination that will be repeated in autumn when the leaves of the witch hazel turn golden orange before falling. The deep magenta flowers of *E.* ×*darleyensis* 'Kramer's Rote' or *E. carnea* 'Nathalie', on the other hand, provide sharp contrast with the light yellow flowers of *H.* ×*intermedia* 'Pallida', which could also be set off by the orange-red winter foliage of *Calluna vulgaris* 'Firefly' or *E. cinerea* 'Golden Drop', whose colors will be most intense when they are placed on the sunny side of the trees.

The big advantage of using colored-foliage heathers in the winter garden is that they have lovely foliage for the summer garden, as well. A carefully planned "winter garden" will be attractive all year.

Height in the Heather Garden

All gardens benefit from having interest raised above ground level. In heather specialty gardens, an arbor, pergola, or tuteur that can host a climbing plant is a welcome addition where the shade from large trees or buildings would be too great for successful heather cultivation. The major consideration when choosing plants to clothe structures added to give the garden height is that they not be so vigorous as to overgrow their support and proceed to romp over nearby heathers. Avoid rampant vines such as wisteria, honeysuckle, ivy, and some species of *Clematis*. The versatile cultivars and hybrids of *Clematis viticella* and *C. texensis* are well-behaved vines that have historically been grown to good effect with heathers.

Another way to add height to a heather garden is with "lollipop trees," naturally small trees that have been grown as standards with all branches removed on the lower trunk and the top kept trimmed to a small ball or tuft of foliage. These are another way to bring interest up off the ground without substantially preventing light from reaching the heathers around them, although they may not be to everyone's taste. They are used very effectively in Tuinachtertop, the private garden of Jos Flecken, president of Ericultura, the Dutch heather society. This garden of 900 heather cultivars has several such standards of different species, including a beautiful variegated *Acer campestre*, interspersed among the heathers along with dwarf conifers (Flecken 2006).

Of course, the most obvious way to add height to a heather garden is with tree heaths, where they are hardy. Unfortunately, most tree heaths are native to southern Europe so are among the less cold-tolerant European heather species. In general, gardeners living in Zone 7 and warmer should be able to grow at least some tree heaths.

Many "tree" heaths are really just large shrubs, but in favorable climates, *Erica*

Tree heaths line the wall at the rear of the Plumridge garden, County Durham, England. The lilac-pink heath in the center is *Erica australis* 'Riverslea', which is separated by golden-foliaged cultivars of *E. arborea* and *E. lusitanica* from the slightly darker *E. australis* 'Holehird', rear.

arborea and *E. scoparia* achieve true tree stature. Among the advantages of planting tree heaths, in addition to their being happy with the same soil and exposure as other heathers, is their spring blooming season. With the exception of summer-blooming *E. terminalis*, the tree heaths are ideal for bridging the gap between winter- and summer-flowering heathers.

Erica australis 'Riverslea' and a trellis laden with *Clematis montana* add height and help to keep the national heather collection at Cherrybank Gardens, Perth, Scotland, colorful in late spring.

Heather in the Formal Garden

Must all heather gardens be naturalistic in style? No. Some heathers are good choices for the formal landscape. Formality is about control or the *appearance* of being controlled. It is about straight lines, regimentation and symmetry, making things line up with each other, and clean outlines. Such an appearance can be achieved through the use of plants that grow naturally in the desired form, or it can be created through pruning and training.

Both *Erica erigena* 'Irish Dusk' and the taller but relatively narrow 'Brian Proudley' can be used as low hedges either with or without hard pruning. 'Maxima' is valuable as a large, stand-alone specimen, a pair, or a row of identically clipped shrubs. The other *E. erigena* cultivars can also serve these functions, with differing flower colors and slightly different growth habits.

Erica erigena has passed on its tolerance for pruning to its hybrid offspring *E.* ×*darleyensis*, which is also easily shaped, although not into strongly vertical forms. With the exception of widely spreading cultivars such as 'Springwood White', *E. carnea* plants will retain fairly tight, compact form even when in bloom if they are sheared annually after flowering. Many *Calluna* cultivars, in contrast, become quite loose and graceful when they throw out their long flowering stems. Although they may be planted in a formal geometric pattern, they will soften its edges, blur the lines, when they bloom.

Erica ×*darleyensis* 'Arthur Johnson' edges the *Laburnum* walk at The Bannut, Herefordshire, England. A grouping of old farm staddle stones may be glimpsed at the end of the walk. Photo by Daphne Everett.

A few selected *Calluna* cultivars never flower or give only a sprinkling of flowers and need little pruning. They remain tight mounds of foliage, although some may eventually reach 2 ft. (60 cm) in diameter after many growing seasons. *Calluna vulgaris* 'Californian Midge' and 'Foxii' are examples of heathers with this growth habit. These are easily used in formal gardens because of their self-restraint.

At the opposite extreme are the heather species with profuse flowering and vigorous growth that are amenable to very hard pruning, even into old wood with no green showing. These may be trained into low hedges and may be substituted for boxwood (*Buxus*) as the frames of garden beds. *Erica* ×*griffithsii* 'Valerie Griffiths' is superb for this function, and its yellow foliage makes an interesting alternative to the dark green of other hedging plants. It will, however, scorch in hot, sunny locations. In hot summer climates, this cultivar is best situated where it gets only morning sun or dappled shade.

Both parents of the hybrid *Erica* ×*griffithsii* recover well from hard pruning. Cultivars of the more compact parent, *E. vagans*, are suited to use in formal situations and may be kept to a desired size for many years if pruned regularly. The much larger *E. manipuliflora* makes such long flowering stems that trying to restrict most of its cultivars to tight hedge form would be an insult to the species. However, the neat, erect-growing cultivar *E. manipuliflora* 'Aldeburgh' is suitable for low hedging.

Erica tetralix is normally compact and fairly stiff in growth habit, qualities that make the species useful for edging formal beds. The gray-tinted foliage of many *E. tetralix* cultivars increases their utility in formal landscapes, for example, in knot gardens, although the species is not as amenable to hard pruning as are some others that might be better choices where very hard pruning is required.

The Knot Garden

Some heathers lend themselves both through growth habit and acceptance of hard pruning to the ultimate in controlled design: the knot garden. Knot gardens have been known in Europe since at least the sixteenth century and were frequently made of box or of culinary herb plants clipped into intricate, interwoven designs (Johnson 1999).

Erica erigena was the heather of choice for Daphne Everett (1994) when she created a Celtic-themed knot garden at The Bannut in Herefordshire, England. The compact, tidy 'W. T. Rackliff' and its equally compact golden sport, 'Golden Lady', are the interweaving strands of the "knot." In between them are plants of 'Irish Dusk' trimmed into cones so that they resemble little Christmas trees. The ground cover between the heather hedges is another Irish cultivar, the prostrate *Calluna vulgaris* 'Clare Carpet'. When this garden was first planted, the *E. erigena* plants required pruning several times a year. Now that it has matured, it is pruned once annually, with a strimmer (Everett, personal communication).

Twenty miles (32 km) from The Bannut, in the garden of The Laskett, another Herefordshire residence, box blight attacked most of the *Buxus* plants in the parterre directly in front of the house (Young 2006). Owner Sir Roy Strong, who had seen the knot garden at The Bannut shortly after it was planted (Everett, personal communica-

The knot garden at The Bannut utilizes *Erica erigena* cultivars of Irish origin. Photo by Maurice Everett.

tion), replaced the blighted box in that parterre with *Erica erigena* 'W. T. Rackliff' and 'Golden Lady', successfully maintaining the pattern of the original box.

Combining the Formal with the Informal

One interesting approach to designing with heathers is that of Edith and Clark Davis in the creation of their Fort Bragg, California, garden. There, the heathers are grouped in a unique manner, each grouping consisting of a single specimen of a large cultivar and several plants each of several smaller cultivars (Hall 2004). This arrangement ensures that there will be the constant visual challenge of changing elevation and color as the eye travels across this small, carefully tended garden.

The irregular groupings of large and small heathers, with paths winding among them and accentuated by the occasional large rock or small conifer, contrast with the precisely pruned, almost tailored appearance of the individual plants. This unusual combination of formal and informal elements blends into a seamless whole of great beauty.

The Davis garden in Fort Bragg, California, blends informal design with careful attention to pruning.

Viewpoints

A seating alcove can be cut into the hillside and surrounded with fragrant cultivars, for example, the sweetly fragrant *Calluna vulgaris* 'Con Brio' or the delicious *Erica* ×*griffithsii* 'Heaven Scent'. Tall cultivars behind the bench can give way along the sides to shorter ones selected for flower or foliage interest. Here they would be nearly at eye level with someone sitting on the bench. This is just the spot for *Daboecia cantabrica* 'Bicolor', where its unusual flowers—sometimes white, sometimes purple, sometimes striped—can be appreciated up close. If the hillside already has a rockery or retaining walls, a seat of the same type stone can be built right into the hill. Alternatively, a curved-back wooden bench, such as those designed by Monet for his garden at Giverny, can snuggle into a similarly curved alcove. Rather than looking down upon the garden, if possible the view from the bench should be across the garden or toward "borrowed scenery" such as mountains or ocean.

This bench in the Thompson Garden, Manchester, California, commands a view across the garden's billows of heather.

The one situation that calls for the viewer looking down onto a heather garden is where the garden has been designed specifically for viewing from that vantage point. The immense, geometrically designed heather plantings at the heather park in Schneverdingen, Germany, reminiscent of traditional "bedding out" schemes of public parks of a century ago, may best be seen from a special viewing platform in the garden that also allows one to look across the garden to the adjacent Lüneberg Heath, with its myriad wild heathers. The contrast between the park plantings of vivid color blocks, each composed of a single cultivar, and the apparently uniform mauve of the distant heathland demonstrates what can be done with horticultural selection and plant breeding.

Heathers in the formal garden can form the plantings in parterres (descendants of knot gardens), also designed to be viewed from above, in this case from the terrace or upper floors of a grand house. Col. and Mrs. Thompson used an interesting variation on this design style in their otherwise naturalistic garden. Immediately in front of the modest house and visible from the house is a small garden that is a mirror image of the front windows of the house. Each "window pane" is a different heather cultivar.

The geometrically designed heather park in Schneverdingen, Germany, photographed from the viewing platform in late summer.

Each "pane" of the front yard "window" garden that mirrors the front window of the Thompson house in Manchester, California, is planted with a different heather cultivar. The lumpy green cultivar is *Calluna vulgaris* 'Velvet Dome', which rarely flowers.

Mimicry

Mimicking Nature

One of the more effective ways of designing with heathers takes advantage of the great variation available in height and foliage color. Try planting a "river" of low-growing silver- or golden-foliaged heathers flowing between "banks" of taller green plants. If you do not have the real thing, you can plant a "cascade" of *Erica tetralix* 'Alba Mollis' tumbling down a rocky hillside. The cultivar's white flowers and silvery green foliage can substitute for white water, and butterflies love them.

The imitation river design trick has been used effectively in displaying the national heather collection at the RHS Garden, Wisley, in Surrey, England. It is also used at the heather park in Schneverdingen. Even that otherwise highly structured garden has in one area a river of one color heather flowing gracefully through other colors, although at Schneverdingen it is done on a very large scale using hundreds of plants for the river.

A green "river" of *Erica* foliage runs through a flowering *Calluna* planting in the heather park at Schneverdingen, Germany, in late summer. In winter and early spring, the color pattern is reversed, with dark green *Calluna* foliage as the "banks" and *Erica* flowers forming the "river."

A variation on the river idea involves using stones instead of plants: the dry streambed. Dry streambeds are used in many gardens where the soothing effect of flowing water is desired but year-round water is not available. They suggest the presence of water to the mind of the beholder.

In the heather garden, construction of a dry streambed can solve the problem of poorly drained or seasonally wet parts of the garden where heathers would not thrive. They can even be constructed to channel water through and out of the garden during downpours, turning a practical drainage ditch into a beautiful garden asset.

Mimicking natural streams through the careful placement of boulders and water-rounded rocks of various sizes, a properly constructed dry streambed can be a lovely focal point of the garden or a place for growing plants with contrasting foliage that could not normally coexist with heathers. For example, moisture-loving irises and sedges could be planted within the streambed itself. Heathers can be planted along the "banks" of the "stream." When choosing heather cultivars for stream banks, use the same selection criteria as you would for paths: place low-growing cultivars nearest the stream and taller ones farther away. Be sure that the plants are far enough from the edge that they will not overhang and obscure the stream when they mature.

Mimicking Other Art Forms

Among the most pleasing heather gardens are those designed to give the illusion of an ancient tapestry or an intricate Oriental carpet. In such gardens, the various cultivars are interwoven gracefully in flowing curves rather than planted in chunky blocks of color as at Schneverdingen. Flower and foliage color are carefully coordinated so that the design works in all seasons.

The varying heights of the cultivars can contribute texture to the design. They can step up or down gradually, as cultivars with only slightly different heights are placed in ascending or descending order. The height may also change abruptly from one cultivar to the next, much as some carpets are sculpted. Differing growth habits will also contribute to the texture of the overall garden as, for instance, the plants change from prostrate to gently mounding to arching to stiffly upright.

Island Beds

The island bed style of garden popularized by Alan Bloom at Bressingham Gardens, Norfolk, England, is a highly artificial design that nevertheless feels natural to garden visitors and is an excellent showcase for heathers. In an island bed garden, planting beds are of irregularly curving shapes, usually somewhat mounded so that one cannot see completely across the larger beds. Each bed is a small garden unto itself, with low, medium, and tall-growing plants of various forms artfully arranged, with the taller plants toward the center of the bed, allowing all plants to be seen as one walks around the bed.

At Bressingham and most other large gardens that feature island beds, the ground between beds is planted to lawn. In a smaller scale garden with less space between them, the beds could be surrounded by chopped conifer bark, as they are in the Davis garden in California. Careful attention to proportion is needed when designing an island bed garden. If the beds are too small, they will be lost in the lawn and look ridiculous. If they are very large, they will be difficult to maintain unless working paths are created within the beds.

When designing an island bed garden for heathers, once you have determined how the beds should relate to each other in size and shape, treat each bed individually. Include within it the various design elements that produce a satisfying garden, including architectural plants and changes in elevation. In a large garden, the lawn between beds will be sufficient to mediate between any clashing colors in different beds, so as you design each bed, you need consider only the colors to be used within that bed.

Working Paths

Although heather gardens are relatively low-maintenance gardens, they are not no-maintenance gardens. When designing a heather garden, one needs to provide access to all plants in the garden for annual pruning, weeding, and mulching of young plantings, and the digging and dividing or pruning required periodically by some companion plants. If a garden bed is so wide that the gardener cannot reach its interior from the edge of the bed, then working paths are needed.

Unlike other garden paths, working paths need be only wide enough for the gardener to pass between plants without stepping on them. Ideally, working paths should not be part of the garden picture but should be nearly imperceptible. They may be as narrow as 16 in. (40 cm) if they are paved with stepping stones that will guide the gardener, even a gardener carrying an armload of weeds or prunings. Wider working paths, such as those that will accommodate a wheelbarrow, need to be treated as part of the design, for they will inevitably be visible unless at a higher elevation than any potential viewer. Tall heathers planted immediately downhill of a working path that follows the contour of a hillside can be used to blend a wide working path into a landscape designed to be viewed from below.

A working path may extend completely across an island bed, or it may end before reaching the other side of the island. Such a path is much less noticeable if it curves, winding among heathers that are at least as tall as the path is wide.

Although a working path's primary raison d'être is to provide the gardener with access to the center of a wide bed, it may also be designed with no attempt at concealment but as an integral part of the garden, accessible to all. Such a path could be gently curved or even straight, with a bench, small pool, or statue at its interior terminus to justify the path's existence.

Designing with Color

There are numerous approaches to designing with color in the garden. Because heathers are so well endowed with a broad and changeable color palette in their flowers, foliage, and new growth, keeping track of color combinations in a heather garden is more complicated than it is when working with other groups of plants. Heathers are unique in this regard. Consider two popular kinds of plant often grown in collectors' gardens: conifers and rhododendrons.

Conifers show many of the same foliage colors other than green as do heathers: silver, gold, and variegated, as well as a steely blue unavailable in heathers. Some conifers even have foliage color that changes from summer to winter, although it has a more limited range—mainly to dull purple or dull rust—and is not nearly as striking as the vibrant winter colors of many heathers. A few have showy cones. What they do not have are showy flowers in an array of colors.

Rhododendron foliage is, with a few exceptions, mostly in shades of green, although the species with indumentum have colorful orange or silver new spring growth and leaf undersides. Rhododendrons *always* need to have their flower colors considered when they are to be included in a garden—especially when they are to be planted

Flower Color

When designing with heathers, first consider the flower colors of all the cultivars whose bloom season will overlap. Although many heather flowers are essentially purple, simply in lighter or darker shades thereof, some have enough other tones, such as orange or red, to make their colors clash rather than blend with the purple line. Such non-blending colors can be separated by heathers that will bloom in a different season, or by cultivars with white flowers. The white-flowered cultivars that also have grayish green or silver foliage are particularly good as color referees and also contribute to foliage color interest when they are not in bloom.

There are several ways to handle planting heather by flower color. One would be to plant next to each other only contrasting colors, such as pale pink and deep purple, so that each cultivar is totally distinct, easily recognized. Unfortunately, if there is room for only a few plants of each cultivar, such an approach can lead to a very spotty looking garden if there is no color blending. In a larger garden that allows the use of more plants of each cultivar, instead of the color spots that are almost inevitable if only three of each cultivar can be planted, cultivars can be arranged in interesting, uneven shapes and interweaving colors. When done well, this is the most effective way of designing a heather garden by flower color.

The gray-green foliage of *Calluna vulgaris* 'Angela Wain' (background), shown here with *Erica cinerea* 'Coccinea', is a good referee between potentially clashing flower colors.

Heathers with strongly contrasting flower colors can work well together, such as pale pink *Erica* ×*watsonii* 'Cherry Turpin' planted next to the very dark *E. cinerea* 'Atropurpurea'.

Another way to design by flower color involves the planting of a color gradient, a continuum from white through pale pink, through mauve to the darkest purple. This is the kind of "artistic" layout that might have been favored by Gertrude Jekyll, were she designing a heather garden as she did her famous perennial borders.

Yet another approach is for heather collectors who want the maximum number of cultivars but also want to have great color impact. In this case, the garden is designed in large swathes of color, but a number of different cultivars with the same flower color are planted within each swath. A garden planted in this way will be impressive when viewed from a distance. Up close, the differing growth habits of the cultivars will be apparent and should be considered in the layout so that they form their own small textural patterns within the larger pattern based upon color.

Except in the coldest climates, where the heather garden will be covered by either snow or protective mulch for the winter months, planning for flower color will be necessary for each season. When designing by flower color, it is better not to choose specific cultivars initially but just the desired color effect of the heathers when they are in bloom. This allows you to add foliage, height, and growth habit variables to the picture as you proceed through the design process.

Erica cinerea 'Providence' requires careful choice of companions because of its intense ruby red color.

Foliage Color

Once flower color has been dealt with, foliage color should be considered. Of course, you could use only heathers with green foliage, but that would be wasting a great asset in planting heathers: the addition of silvers and various shades of yellow, gold, orange, and nearly red to the garden palette.

The appearance of the garden when the heathers are not blooming can be nearly as colorful as when they are, if cultivars with interesting foliage are chosen. The foliage of the grayish green or silver cultivars remains nearly the same shade throughout the year, so these essentially neutral colors may be used with impunity throughout the garden. One could actually plant an entire heather garden with grayish and silvery foliage, although it would be more interesting if the grays were mixed with true greens. Silver and gray foliage cannot be overdone. Fortunately, it is available in combination with both white and pink or mauve flowers on plants of differing heights and shapes.

When deciding which cultivars to plant where, consider not just adjacent plants but also those that the eye will register at the same time. For example, the red-flowered *Erica cinerea* 'Coccinea' may have been carefully sited next to a gray-foliaged cultivar with white flowers. From a color standpoint, these are companionable neighbors. However, if there is not a wide enough expanse of that gray-foliaged cultivar, the amethyst-colored flowers of 'Golden Sport' planted behind it will be seen at the same time as the carmine-red flowers of 'Coccinea', a decidedly jarring effect for some people's sensibilities.

It is important to consider how the garden will be viewed from all angles. This makes garden planning complicated, particularly if planting island beds where some plants may be seen from nearly every point on the compass, but the result will be worth the effort.

It is the heathers with yellow and golden foliage that add real zing to a garden and also complicate designing with color. Cultivars with yellow foliage and white flowers are fairly easy to accommodate. Like the grays, they remain essentially the same color through every season, varying only in intensity. When using these, the designer needs to consider only personal color preferences and, depending upon the climate, particular cultivars' need for some shading in hot sunny weather.

Changing Foliage Color

The placement of cultivars whose golden foliage changes to bright orange, rust, or nearly fire-engine red in winter needs to be carefully considered. *Erica cinerea* 'Golden Drop' next to *E. carnea* 'Nathalie' may not be to everyone's taste. In summer, the two would be fine companions: an insignificant sprinkling of mauve flowers over a plant with reddish gold foliage next to a plant with dark green foliage. Autumn color would be fine, too: bright orange next to that dark green. In winter, trouble begins, as the orange changes to red and the green is smothered with magenta flowers. The challenge continues through spring, as 'Golden Drop' foliage changes back to orange and 'Nathalie' flowers intensify to purple. Christopher Lloyd, well known for his adventurous garden color combinations, might have appreciated this pairing, but it is not for the faint-hearted.

Sometimes the color challenge can occur on the same plant. Not everyone likes pink flowers over golden foliage (witness the advice sometimes offered in gardening magazines to cut off the pink flowers of *Spiraea japonica* 'Goldflame' so that they do not spoil the appearance of the plant, which is grown for its foliage color), but some people are willing to overlook the appearance of a cultivar while it is in flower in order to have the benefit of its striking foliage color for the remainder of the year. Fortunately, the golden-foliaged heather cultivars that turn orange or red in the winter come in an assortment of flower colors. There is one for every taste, from pale pink through magenta.

The summer combination of pink flowers and golden foliage on *Calluna vulgaris* 'Foya' may not appeal to everyone, but its red winter foliage color is outstanding.

Calluna vulgaris 'Highland Rose' bears deep rose-pink flowers above golden-bronze foliage in late summer.

A few of the winter "red" heathers, including *Erica cinerea* 'Golden Drop' and the very popular *Calluna vulgaris* 'Firefly', never lose the red tint to their foliage, so that in summer they appear from a distance to be almost apricot or terra cotta. This can add to color excitement in the garden, with yet another shade to be considered through the seasons.

The big design danger with heathers is to get carried away with colored foliage, particularly the golds and the reds. Too much yellow and red in a garden can be very tiring. After the initial dazzle wears off, a garden composed entirely of yellow and red foliage (which would be mostly yellow or golden in summer) would be unsettling; it would not invite lingering. Grays and greens, on the other hand, are restful for the eyes. Despite the siren call of the golden cultivars, they should probably make up no more than a third of the heather garden.

In the two-year-old heather garden of the community hospital in Cottage Grove, Oregon, orange and yellow foliage glows in the late-afternoon autumn light.

Some heathers whose green foliage is perfectly acceptable in the summer, especially when the plants are flowering, may darken so much in winter—due to increased production of anthocyanin pigment—as to appear gloomy if they are present in abundance. The brighter greens of white-flowered cultivars, lacking anthocyanin, will not deepen in winter, so these cultivars, along with those having gray foliage, may be judiciously blended with the darker colored ones to brighten the gloom.

The flip side of this coin occurs when the white cultivars flower, making color selection a balancing act if both foliage and flower color are to be considered. Too large a patch of unrelieved white in the garden can be overpowering, because the eye is automatically drawn to white.

In summer, the bright green foliage of *Erica carnea* 'Springwood White' in this British Columbia garden provides welcome visual relief from the intense flower colors nearby.

In early spring, when *Erica carnea* 'Springwood White' is in full bloom in the same garden, viewed from the opposite vantage point, its mass of white flowers dominates the garden.

Nearly as distracting as a large white patch are white plants scattered like polka dots throughout the garden. White-flowered cultivars are best used in winding bands to separate colors that would clash if planted side by side.

Spring Tip Color

The final foliage color challenge is offered by cultivars with spring tips. These tips may be almost white, yellow, orange, or pink to nearly red, depending upon the cultivar. Those with very strong spring tip color may appear to be in bloom, with the color sprinkled evenly over the plants, just as flowers would be. They have fooled many heather garden visitors not familiar with the phenomenon.

Spring tips are a definite asset, as they can give a second season of "bloom" to a plant. They must be considered during garden planning, just as you would consider flower color or winter foliage color. A plant whose foliage is plain green most of the year, for instance *Erica* ×*stuartii* 'Irish Orange', may suddenly be covered with beautiful orange dots in the spring. You might not want to plant 'Irish Orange' next to *E. carnea* 'Nathalie' any more than you would want to plant *E. cinerea* 'Golden Drop' next to *E. carnea* 'Nathalie'. The spring tip season of *E.* ×*stuartii* 'Irish Orange' overlaps the spring bloom of *E. carnea* 'Nathalie': orange and purple again.

Color Design Tool

If all this talk of designing with a multitude of heather colors that can change throughout the year has your head spinning, do not despair. The Heather Society's web site

Left: The Heather Society web site's design program offers gardeners a preview of how their gardens will look at different times of the year. Here is the program's virtual heather garden in late winter.

Right: The same virtual garden seen as it will appear in late summer.

has a wonderful do-it-yourself (DIY) design program for coping with color changes. You may input specific cultivar names, or you may input color specifications to see how your garden would look in different seasons. The program also offers elevations, so that you can see how the garden will appear in a particular season when viewed from above and from various directions. A click of your computer mouse will change aspect or season.

Go to The Heather Society web site, choose "DIY Design" from the topics bar on home page, and follow the instructions for using the program. The program takes a little getting used to, but it can be lots of fun and can give you a general idea of how your planned garden will change color with the seasons. Not every heather cultivar is included within the program, but with more than 1000 cultivars to choose from, if your chosen cultivar is not listed, you can probably find a substitute with similar attributes to plug into the program for design purposes. See Alexander (2005) for a step-by-step guide to using this program.

Companion Plant Color

Once you have determined which heather cultivars will be color compatible with which other heather cultivars, you still need to consider how the colors of companion plants might be assets to your garden. Unfortunately, the DIY program does not allow for companion plant input, so you are on your own with this.

Conifers such as this *Picea pungens* at Bloom River Gardens in Walterville, Oregon, can add steel blue to the heather garden palette.

Use the colors of companion plants as color echoes for heather flower or foliage color. For example, companion plants that contain yellow in either their flowers or foliage might echo the foliage of the yellow heathers. *Kniphofia* species and hybrids with yellow flowers are excellent for this purpose, and the yellow varies from pale to deep gold verging on the orange tones for which the "red hot pokers" are better known.

Likewise, some grasses and sedges have golden or golden-variegated foliage that can be used advantageously in small quantity, for example, *Carex elata* 'Aurea' or *Molinia caerulea* subsp. *caerulea* 'Variegata'. These may scorch in the full sun of hot summer climates, but they can be quite lovely for a shady edge of the garden or under the canopy of a small deciduous tree within the garden.

In her small Zone 6 garden in Saint John's, Newfoundland, Linda Smith made very effective use of both color contrast and color echo. She planted a golden-foliaged *Calluna* cultivar at the front of a border. Behind it is a purple-leaved ninebark (*Physocarpus*) that is in turn backed by a golden-leaved elderberry (*Sambucus*). The color combination is smashing, and the layered effect achieved by combining shrubs of varying heights enhances the color composition. The differing leaf textures of the three shrubs provide the finishing touches to this very appealing design.

One of the best uses for companion plants is to add a color to the heather garden that is not found in heather flowers or foliage: blue. Although at first blue might seem out of place in a garden dominated by mauves and purples, it can be surprisingly attractive against those purple tones if the right shade of blue is used in the right place.

Campanulas and conifers add very different blues to the garden, and both are effective companions in a heather garden (not necessarily next to each other). The relatively small *Campanula* flowers are often rich, intense blues and blue-purples. Steely conifer blue contrasts beautifully with the golden foliage of heathers and other conifers and is wonderful with heather flowers of every hue. If you are adding conifers to the garden, either as backdrop or as architectural plants among the heathers, be sure that some of them are blue. There are many from which to choose.

5 Companion Plants

The appeal of a garden featuring heather can be increased by the addition of carefully chosen companion plants, which should be selected during the planning of the garden, not as afterthoughts. Compatibility and complementarity of the plants are essential to successful heather garden design. Companion plants should be chosen not only because they complement and contrast with the heathers, but because they will grow well under similar cultural conditions: light, soil type, and watering regimen.

If two of the three conditions are met, sometimes the third can be compensated for with a bit of special treatment. For instance, a heather companion that prefers shade could be sited near a wall, building, or trees that would shade it while sunlight reached nearby heathers planted farther from the source of shade. Companions that need more nutrients than do heathers can have long-lasting fertilizers added to their planting holes and sprinkled around them occasionally when that is exhausted. If companion plants need more or less water than heathers require, the individualized watering provided by drip irrigation systems can solve the problem.

Companion plants are particularly useful for heather gardens in cold climates, where there is a distinct bloom gap of a month or two between the end of the winter to spring heather-flowering season and the beginning of summer heather bloom. Even

A roadside heather garden in Scotland demonstrates how carefully chosen heathers and companion plants can keep a garden colorful even in late spring, when most heathers are not flowering.

in mild climates where a great many heather species can be grown, the number of cultivars blooming in late spring and early summer is relatively few as compared with the number blooming during the remainder of the year. Fortunately, many other shrubs and herbaceous perennials flower during this heather bloom gap, including some with additional attributes that recommend them as potential heather companions. (Flowering time should be only one criterion used in selecting companion plants.)

The choice of heather companions is wide, but there are a number of parameters that limit their selection in addition to the considerations mentioned above. Foremost is the requirement that the companion plant not be detrimental to the heathers. If it will shade or crowd out the heather plants, it obviously should not be planted with them. Next is the reverse situation: the heathers should not take over the companion plants. Companion plants should be hardy for the climate of the heather garden. This is not the place to practice zonal denial. If your carefully considered design is ruined because the companion plants did not survive their first winter (or summer), the resulting disappointment will be accompanied by additional design and installation work that could easily have been avoided early in the design process by knowing the needs of all plants to be used. Finally, if your primary reason for making a heather garden is because deer are garden pests in your area, be sure that the companion plants you choose are not deer favorites. Many plants discussed in this chapter will, unfortunately, attract deer into a heather garden.

If culture requirements are compatible, so that neither heather nor potential companion threatens the other plant, then the choice of heather companions is left to the pleasure of the garden owner. Discussed in this chapter will be a representative sample of the many plants that could be grown with heathers.

Trees

Because large trees are good sun blockers, they generally do not make suitable companion plants for the sun-loving heathers. A few garden designers have assumed that birch trees (*Betula* species) are good heather companions, since birch trees occur naturally in some of the same places as do heathers, such as in the Scottish Highlands and on Germany's Lüneberg Heath. Nevertheless, a careful examination of these habitats will reveal that the heather plants growing among the birches flower poorly in comparison with those growing nearby on the open moors and heathlands.

Trees as Backdrops

Large trees can be used effectively as backdrops for a heather garden, framing the picture to focus attention upon the garden's stars, as long as the trees are sited where they will not prevent sunlight from reaching the heathers. Remnant native Douglas fir (*Pseudotsuga menziesii*) forest in Colton, Oregon, provides a wonderful background

Although birch trees may be found on the edges of moorland, such as here on Tulloch Moor, Scotland, heathers bloom much better away from the shade and root competition of trees.

for the display garden designed by owner Cleo Hall for her Green Mountain Heather nursery. The garden was placed to take maximum advantage of available sunlight. A similar effect could be achieved elsewhere by situating tall conifers where they will block unwanted views but not the light that heathers need for good flowering.

Deciduous non-coniferous trees can also serve as backdrops for a heather garden, adding needed height to the garden picture. Although they usually cannot provide for complete screening of an unwanted view during the winter, they have several advantages over their evergreen counterparts.

The garden of Cleo Hall, Colton, Oregon, in early spring, with native Douglas firs and a planted understory of ornamental deciduous trees as backdrop for the heathers.

Because they drop their leaves in winter, deciduous trees allow much more light to reach adjacent heathers then. This feature is particularly advantageous in mild-winter climates, where heathers remain in active photosynthesis during the winter.

The shade thrown by non-coniferous trees is usually less dense than that of conifers, and their lower branches can be removed without the trees appearing unbalanced. This allows early morning and late afternoon sunlight to reach heathers planted near the trees.

Some of the golden-foliaged heathers that would scorch in full sun exposures benefit from being partially shaded during the hottest summer days. In regions where very high summer daytime temperatures combine with very low humidity and low rainfall, such as in the Great Basin of western North America, the dappled shade cast by limbed-up deciduous trees may actually be essential to heather survival.

Trees within the Heather Garden

Trees to be planted *within* a heather garden should be few, far apart, and very carefully chosen. They can be beautiful assets, or they can develop into sun and water hogs that crowd or starve the heathers.

Conifers

Evergreen conifers, especially dwarf conifers, have long been considered ideal heather companions, so inextricably entwined with them in the public consciousness that the two groups have come into and gone out of garden fashion together. Gardeners should consider three important factors when seeking heather-compatible conifers: rate of growth, ultimate size, and shape.

Dwarf conifers are an important component of the garden created by Rita and David Plumridge in Durham, England. Several of these conifers, already rather large when this late summer photograph was taken, have been removed because they outgrew their allotted spaces.

Most "dwarf" conifers have the potential to become large trees or shrubs. They simply take longer to get there than do their "standard" counterparts. If you want a heather garden that will not need to have its conifers removed and replaced regularly because they have outgrown their allotted spaces and are crowding and shading out the heathers, pay particular attention to the purported growth rate of the many conifer cultivars. It varies considerably. Some cultivars appear to differ from each other only in how long it takes them to achieve their mature dimensions. Unless your heather garden is truly huge, choose conifers with very slow growth rates.

The American Conifer Society has set arbitrary standards for the size classes of cultivars. These simplify the selection process considerably. For plants with the slowest growth, least likely to outgrow their garden space during the gardener's lifetime, choose cultivars designated "miniature." These grow no more than an inch (2.5 cm) per year and are particularly useful in container gardens. The next-slowest-growing conifers, labelled "dwarf," can put on from 1 to 6 in. (3 to 15 cm) of new growth in a year. Anything larger than these is probably too large for a heather garden, except as part of a background planting.

Because the majority of heathers, with the exception of tree heaths, are of low, mounding form, it is better to avoid interplanting with small-needled conifers of similar shape (for example, *Picea abies* 'Little Gem'). Nothing is gained from such a combination. An exception to this rule immediately comes to mind: the planting of a steely blue spruce, such as *P. pungens* 'Blue Pearl', that introduces a foliage color unmatched in its blue tones by any of the silvery heathers. Such a planting can be a definite asset, for this cultivar's full-sized needles counterbalance the very short leaves of the heathers.

Although most conifers of low, mounding shape do little to add variety to the heather garden, *Picea pungens* 'Blue Pearl' is welcomed because of its steely blue color and full-sized needles. The very low-growing *Calluna vulgaris* 'Gold Kup', shown here in its autumn foliage color, is an appropriate companion for this spruce.

Erica ×darleyensis 'Furzey' blooms at the base of columnar *Taxus baccata* 'Standishii' in the Plumridge garden.

Slow-growing conifers of conical or columnar habit (for example, *Picea glauca* 'Jean's Dilly' or *Juniperus communis* 'Compressa', respectively), introduce to the heather garden much-needed variation in plant shape. Think of them as exclamation points, and use them as judiciously in the garden as you would exclamations in a dialogue. Too many ruin the effect.

Deciduous Trees

A visit to the winter garden of a famous botanic garden, such as that of Cambridge University, is instructive in how to choose and use trees and shrubs in combination with heathers while balancing the competing needs of the various garden components. *Hamamelis* cultivars are mainstays of such winter gardens and provide a second season of interest when their leaves change color in the autumn.

Magnolia stellata can be a useful small tree or large shrub for the heather garden. In the March 2006 issue of the RHS monthly magazine, *The Garden*, it is illustrated keeping company with *Erica arborea*. This combination makes an excellent garden screen with a long season of flower interest, the magnolia starting the spring show, followed by the longer blooming tree heath. Both are highly fragrant but with very different fragrances, so it is just as well that there is little, if any, overlap in their bloom times. The much larger leaves and flowers of the small, early-blooming magnolia provide good contrast to the tiny leaves and buds of the erica. As added benefit, deciduous *M. stellata* has large, fuzzy flower buds for winter interest.

Most deciduous trees, even relatively small ones such as *Magnolia stellata* and witch hazels, are considerably larger than dwarf conifers and must be very carefully placed, with the direction and extent of their shadows at different times of the year always being the prime consideration. Two other things must also be considered when heathers are grown with or near trees.

Fallen leaves should not be allowed to smother the heathers. Unless the garden is buried under snow all winter or leaves and cut conifer branches are being used to give the heathers winter protection, leaves should be raked out of the plants. Otherwise, the foliage of the heathers covered by decomposing leaves will die, leaving unsightly bare spots in the plants. Leaves used as winter protection should be gradually removed with the arrival of settled warm temperatures in the spring, before the heathers begin active growth.

In all cases of planting heathers near trees, the heathers will benefit from frequent watering during dry spells, since wide-ranging thirsty tree roots greatly reduce the amount of water in the soil that would otherwise be available to the more shallow-rooted heathers. The extent to which the roots of nearby trees will penetrate the heather garden should always be considered.

Shrubs and Vines

Like trees, shrubs may form a backdrop to the heather garden or be incorporated into the garden. Other shrubs used with heathers may be of size and shape similar to an average heather plant, blending into the heathers. They may also be of strikingly different size, form, texture, and color: useful for contrast. Like trees, but usually to a lesser extent, shrubs and vines compete with heathers for nourishment. Large shrubs and vigorous vines can shade or crowd out the heathers. Where they are planted in relation to heathers is very important.

Ericaceous Shrubs

Among the best companions for heather are other plants of the Ericaceae. Many appreciate the same soil and watering regimen as do heathers but offer contrasts in height, leaf size and shape, and flower color. Some have ornamental fruit, as well. These are only a few of the many ericaceous plants that could be planted to advantage with heather.

Andromeda

Bog rosemary is one of the best heather relatives for growing with heathers if deer are not an issue. It shares their preference for acidic soils and sunny locations, although it prefers wetter (but not saturated) conditions than do heathers. There are only two species in the genus, *Andromeda glaucophylla* and *A. polifolia*, both evergreen shrubs of low, mounding form from cool temperate regions in the Northern Hemisphere.

Although these plants produce clusters of attractive bell-shaped pink or pinkish white flowers in spring, they are grown primarily for their handsome foliage. *Andromeda polifolia* 'Macrophylla' has broad, dark green leaves. 'Compacta' and the larger 'Nikko', with large, clear pink flowers, both have glaucous green foliage. The foliage of the well-named 'Blue Ice' has made it a popular plant for adding blue tones to the garden.

Empetrum (crowberry)

The two Northern Hemisphere species of crowberry are especially good heather companions, associating with heather in its native habitat and favoring the same sandy or peaty soil. When they are not in flower or fruit, crowberry plants may easily be mistaken for heathers.

Empetrum nigrum, with purplish black fruits (edible, though not palatable when raw), forms low mats and is particularly suited to cultivating in rock gardens, where it appears much at home. Its various foliage selections are also useful for mixing with heathers in container plantings. A number of cultivars have been selected based upon the color of their evergreen leaves, which are normally dark green, turning brownish in winter. *Empetrum nigrum* cultivars 'Lucia', 'Bernstein', 'Zitronella', and "Kramer

Yellow 1" (the last bred by Kurt Kramer from 'Bernstein' and 'Zitronella' [Kramer, personal communication]) have yellow-gold foliage. The green foliage of 'Compass Harbor' turns golden and red in the autumn. *Empetrum nigrum* cultivars remaining green in winter include 'Smaragd' (sold as EMERALD) and 'Irland'. *Empetrum eamesii*, the purple crowberry, offers attractive pink-red berries but is still rare in the nursery trade.

Kalmia

The mountain laurel, *Kalmia latifolia*, is the showiest and most widely available *Kalmia* species. This tall shrub with long, elliptical, evergreen leaves is an inhabitant of forest edges in the northeastern United States and southeastern Canada. Consequently, the species appreciates dappled sunlight and will be happy on the shady side of a building, although it will not flower well if the shade is too deep. This versatile plant will tolerate considerable sunlight if given adequate water. It is suitable as a backdrop or screen on the shady side of a heather garden and is ideal as an understory plant along the edge of a woods, as it would grow in its native habitat.

Mountain laurel blooms for about two weeks in late spring and early summer, which makes it a plant of value to the heather garden for flower interest during the bloom gap between the winter and summer-flowering heathers, especially in the cooler climates where it thrives. There are many selected cultivars, with flowers in white through pink shades, often with plum-colored markings. Several dwarf cultivars are available, including *Kalmia latifolia* 'Minuet', which grows to about 3 ft. (1 m) tall in 10 years.

Pieris

For compatible companions that add height, are good screening plants, and can serve as a backdrop for the heather garden, the larger *Pieris* selections are excellent. Most are large shrubs; but the spectacular, rather cold-tender *P. formosa* var. *forrestii* is nearly tree-sized, with showy white flowers and bright red new growth. This species has been hybridized with some of the hardy smaller species, such as *P. floribunda*, to produce a range of mid-sized, moderately hardy hybrids that are still large by heather garden standards.

Much more compatible in size but offering interesting contrasts in foliage and flowers, thus useful for planting within the heather garden, are the variegated *Pieris japonica* 'Little Heath', only 18 to 24 in. (45 to 60 cm) tall but sending out stolons to form broad mats up to 48 in. (120 cm) wide, and the slightly more compact 'Little Heath Green'. Both have deep red new growth.

A number of other *Pieris* cultivars are also of relatively small stature and would combine well with heather. *Pieris* will thrive in either full sun or partial shade and have dangling racemes of fragrant white or pink bell-shaped flowers in early to midspring.

Rhododendron

For variation in plant size, leaf texture, and flower color, the genus *Rhododendron* is hard to surpass. However, many rhododendrons are not suitable for cold climates, among them the spectacular large-leaved tree species. Many also will not take full sun and would need to be used on the shady side of the heather garden. The larger rhododendrons are most useful when massed as an evergreen backdrop for heather plantings.

Among the smaller rhododendrons are many that are compatible with heathers, including some that tolerate full sun. In the Boston, Massachusetts area on the border between Zones 6 and 5, garden designer Priscilla Williams (personal communication) planted a bank of ericaceous plants, starting near the top of the bank with Wilson rhododendrons (*Rhododendron* ×*laetevirens*, grown primarily for their attractive evergreen foliage) and 'Delaware Valley White', a showy, white-flowered, *R. mucronatum*-hybrid azalea that blooms in mid- to late spring. Below these rhododendrons are callunas, then an edging of *Iberis sempervirens*, a subshrub in the Brassicaceae that also produces abundant white flowers in mid- to late spring. The heathers are given a heavy winter mulch of pine needles, which would also benefit *I. sempervirens* in very cold climates.

Some rhododendrons that will take sun and are excellent planted within a heather garden are *Rhododendron* 'Ramapo' and 'Maricee'. The very hardy 'Ramapo', about 24 in. (60 cm) tall at 10 years of age, bears pale violet flowers during the late spring lull in heather bloom and has dusty blue new growth that matures to attractive, small,

Rhododendrons form the background of a heather bank at Thompson's Nursery, Waldport, Oregon.

Erica ×*darleyensis* 'Kramer's Rote' (left foreground) is still showing color in late spring when *Rhododendron* 'Cosmopolitan' blooms in the Plumridge garden, County Durham, England.

bluish green leaves. *Rhododendron* 'Maricee', of about the same stature as 'Ramapo', is hardy to Zone 6, has small, aromatic leaves, and bears trusses of interestingly shaped small white or pinkish white flowers.

At Sherwood, a private estate in Devon, England, there is a long bank of heathers and dwarf rhododendrons. Among the heathers is a plant of *Erica* ×*darleyensis* that is more than 80 years old. Its sun-tolerant companions include *Rhododendron calostrotum*, *R. campylogynum*, and *R. myrtifolium* (Lacey 2006).

When choosing rhododendrons as heather companions, in addition to considering their hardiness and sun tolerance, keep in mind that most will bloom for only about two weeks each year. Their foliage will be their primary asset and should be chosen accordingly. Visit a rhododendron display garden when the plants are not in bloom, so that your selections accurately reflect how the plants will look in the garden most of the year. Once you have determined which plants will be interesting when not in bloom, then consider whether their flower colors will harmonize with heather foliage colors and any flowers that may be blooming simultaneously with the rhododendrons.

Vaccinium

Many *Vaccinium* species are ornamental, and most are happy in full sun situations, although they will tolerate light shade. Unlike most other high-bush blueberries (*V. corymbosum* and its hybrids), which are a bit gangly and usually grown for their delicious fruit, *V. corymbosum* 'Sunshine Blue' is grown primarily as an ornamental. This deciduous plant has good, deep red, autumn leaf color and reddish winter bark, as well as pinkish white spring flowers that mature to edible blueberries.

Grown purely for ornament is deciduous *Vaccinium glaucoalbum*, with soft pink flowers and oval leaves that are bluish beneath. Its size is similar to that of some of the larger heathers, about 18 × 24 in. (45 × 60 cm), larger in favorable climates.

The American native cranberry, *Vaccinium macrocarpon*, is a good, very low evergreen creeper for the heather garden, tolerating wetter soils than does heather. 'Hamilton' is an ornamental selection of this species, chosen for its very compact growth habit and attractive red fruit.

The lingonberry (*Vaccinium vitis-idaea*) is another evergreen ericaceous groundcover that has edible fruit. Some of its cultivars can be aggressive and therefore demand careful placement and watching. *Vaccinium vitis-idaea* Koralle Group is particularly attractive, with a heavy crop of bright red fruit.

Non-ericaceous Shrubs and Vines

When considering planting non-ericaceous shrubs and vines as heather companions, one might do well to heed the advice of Graham Stuart Thomas (1995). "Their neighbors should be small shrubs with small leaves such as species roses, not modern roses and hearty perennials or overweening large shrubs." Modern garden designers often favor the opposite approach, with the emphasis placed upon contrast. Either style can be effective if done well.

Caryopteris

The shrubs in this genus, hardy in Zones 5 to 9 (depending upon the species), behave more like herbaceous perennials than woody shrubs, often dying back to the roots in cold climates. *Caryopteris* may be treated as a perennial, because it blooms on new wood. If hard pruned in spring, these plants will sprout from the roots to make low, mounded shrubs. Most kinds are deciduous in cold winter climates and average between 3 and 6 ft. (1 and 2 m) in height.

Many *Caryopteris* cultivars are excellent planted behind the lower-growing heathers or intermingled with tree heaths in a mixed border. Their preference for full sun and well-drained soil of low fertility makes them natural heather companions, and the late-summer blue or blue-purple flowers of most cultivars blend or contrast pleasingly with heather flower and foliage colors. The commonly available hybrid *Caryopteris* ×*clandonensis* has silvery foliage and good cold hardiness. The striking *Caryopteris incana* 'Jason', with golden foliage and deep blue flowers, is also worth investigating.

Clematis

Clematis texensis, *C. viticella*, and their hybrids are good choices as climbers in a heather garden, for they are well behaved enough to be allowed to scramble over winter-flowering heathers, so long as the clematis vines are pruned back to nearly ground level in late autumn (Evison 1987). Partially shaded by the clematis in summer, the heathers will be somewhat less vigorous and floriferous than if growing unencumbered; but heather and vine can coexist amicably and together provide more garden interest than either grown alone. The combination will have flowers both summer and winter.

At Mount Stewart in Northern Ireland, *Erica arborea* is "crowned" with the purple *Clematis* 'Jackmanii' (Thornton-Wood 1995) to form the centerpiece in the sunken garden. Clematis can also profitably be trained over the various cultivars of *E. erigena*, although none reaches the impressive stature of *E. arborea*.

Back close to ground level, a particularly arresting combination would be a golden-foliaged *Erica carnea* cultivar such as 'Golden Starlet' or 'Westwood Yellow' setting off the deep purple flowers of *Clematis* 'Black Prince', *C. viticella* 'Etoile Violette', 'Royal Velours', or 'Venosa Violacea'. More subtle but still eye-catching, is the use of a background of dark green heather foliage to enhance the mauve-pink and white flowers of *C. viticella* 'Minuet' or *C.* 'Pagoda'.

Allow heathers to become established for a year or two before planting clematis among them, lest the clematis overwhelm the young heathers. Dig a spacious hole for each clematis when the heathers are planted. Fill a plastic pot with the soil removed from the hole, and put the soil-filled pot into the hole to hold the space free of heather roots. The pot and its soil can be mulched just as is the surrounding soil. When it is time to plant the clematis, simply remove the soil-filled pot, and you will be able to plant the vine without disturbing adjacent heathers.

Clematis will be happy in the soil of a well-amended heather bed but prefer a richer diet than do heathers. When planting the vines, add some well-composted manure to the bottoms of their planting holes, and mix bone meal in with the soil that will be returned to the holes around the clematis roots.

When it is necessary to prune winter-flowering heathers that are interplanted with clematis, prune the heathers carefully as soon as their flowers begin to turn brown, so that you do not accidentally also prune the new growth off of the clematis.

Cotinus coggygria 'Royal Purple' (purple smoke bush)
Dark red-purple leaves and purplish pink "smoky" flowers in midsummer.

Plant these to either the east or west of a grouping of golden-foliaged heathers with colored flowers, so that the leaves of the smoke bush can be appreciated when backlit by the sun but the heathers are not significantly shaded by the shrub. Prune back hard in early spring, both to keep this potentially large shrub in scale with the heathers and for the best foliage production.

Daphne
Daphnes, like heathers, prefer well-drained soil and do not like to be disturbed once established. Some of the smaller evergreen daphnes make fine companions for heather.

Daphne ×*medfordensis* 'Lawrence Crocker', the popular hybrid between *D. arbuscula* and *D. sericea* Collina Group, has a long blooming season, beginning in late spring and continuing all summer, into autumn in mild climates. The deep purplish pink flowers blend well with those of the summer-blooming heathers. This outstanding plant grows slowly to form tight mounds about 12 in. (30 cm) wide. No pruning is required (or wanted).

The somewhat taller *Daphne retusa* (correctly *D. tangutica* Retusa Group) has a dense round habit, to 30 in. (75 cm) tall and wide. The late spring to early summer flowers are purple and white (giving the overall impression of light purple) and are followed by red berries. This daphne will tolerate pruning.

Hebe
The whipcord *Hebe* species are not so much heather companions as heather impersonators. More than a few heather enthusiasts have been fooled by these sometime look-alikes planted amongst the heathers. They are a wonderful choice for garden pranksters.

When not in bloom, members of this group of hebes appear remarkably similar to heathers—until you look closely at them and notice the cruciform arrangement of the tiny leaves. Some give themselves away by a slight olive tint to the foliage, a shade that is found in few heathers. Whipcord *Hebe ochracea* 'James Stirling' is one of these. Another is *H. salicornioides*.

A lovely whipcord hebe actually described in nursery catalogs as being "heather-like" has been sold under the names *Hebe mckeanii*, *H*. 'McKeanii', *H*. ×*mckeanii*, and *H*. 'Emerald Gem'. Under whatever name you can find this plant, it is a winner, with insignificant, white summer flowers but beautiful, bright green, tiny leaves and a very compact habit, to about 12 × 24 in. (30 × 60 cm). *Hebe* 'Christabel' is similar, and the superficial resemblance of 'Pluto' to a large calluna is uncanny. Plant one of these among your heathers and see how many garden visitors realize that it is *not* a heather.

Hebe cupressoides, growing to about 48 in. (120 cm) tall, resembles a tree heath as well as the conifer for which it is named. The cultivar 'Boughton Dome' is much more compact, only about 12 in. (30 cm) tall. Other whipcords to consider are *H. subsimilis* var. *astonii* and *H. tetragona*.

Like heathers, hebes prefer to grow in full sun, with good drainage but constant moisture. Unfortunately, many hebes are not cold tolerant. Dwarf hebes are usually hardier than larger hebes and may make good companions for the hardy heathers. However, not all are heather impersonators like the whipcord hebes.

Some dwarf hebes worth investigating are *Hebe albicans* 'Sussex Carpet'; *H*. 'Baby Marie'; *H*. 'Maori Gem'; *H. pinguifolia* 'Pagei', an excellent heather companion that makes a low, tight mat of rounded gray foliage and has tiny white flowers in late spring; *H*. 'Pinocchio'; and *H*. 'Silver Beads'. Thomas (1995) recommends threading silver-foliaged hebes through drifts of pink *Erica carnea* and *E*. ×*darleyensis*.

The silvery foliage of *Hebe pinguifolia* 'Pagei' mingles with the golden foliage of *Erica carnea* 'Foxhollow' in the Plumridge garden. The hebe opens its flowers in late spring just as the flowers of the erica are finishing their long blooming season.

Congenial companions *Erica carnea* and *Hebe topiaria* grow together in the garden of Greg Bennett, Corvallis, Oregon. Late summer photo.

Lavandula

Heathers and lavenders were among the favorite plants of the outstanding American landscape architect Beatrix Jones Farrand, who used them together to good effect in her own private gardens at Reef Point and Garland Farm in Bar Harbor, Maine. In her 2004 article about Garland Farm, Jane Lamb described lavender as being "worked in amid a collection of her [Farrand's] signature heaths and heathers." It is worth noting that the heathers at Garland Farm in the best condition after a recent disastrous open winter were those growing in among the old lavenders.

In the garden of Kathy Lewis, Milwaukie, Oregon, the golden early summer foliage of *Calluna* 'Robert Chapman' is a bright foil for the flowers of English lavender (*Lavandula angustifolia*).

Like heathers, lavenders benefit from annual pruning to remove the spent flowers and control plant size. Although they prefer alkaline soil, they tolerate the lean, acidic soils preferred by heathers; and once established, they are highly drought tolerant.

The most commonly grown lavenders are cultivars of hardy English lavender (*Lavandula angustifolia*), which range in size from dwarf mounds of about 12 in. (30 cm) or less to more than 36 in. (90 cm) tall and wide. Less winter hardy, and less suited to the average heather garden, is Spanish lavender, *L. stoechas*.

Rosa

At first glance, roses are unlikely heather companions. The highly bred, pampered tea roses that epitomize the modern rose for many people have nothing to add to a heather garden, with their large, ungainly growth habits and need for fertilizing and preventative treatment for leaf diseases. Many of the larger shrub roses, while more graceful and not as demanding as hybrid teas, are simply too large for any but the largest heather gardens. Other classes of rose are more promising.

Consider first the miniatures. Except for their deciduous nature (a drawback that may be disregarded in cold-winter climates, where both roses and heathers need winter protection), many of these are quite compatible with heathers, in both shape and stature. Both miniature and microminiature classes, with their small stature and equally small leaves, have promising cultivars for intermingling with heathers. They are far more graceful in shape than their larger relatives and can easily be kept to manageable size.

Among the miniatures, good choices are *Rosa* 'MEIfovett' (sold as BABY PARADISE—lavender-pink), 'MICmist' (HEATHER MIST), 'MINimerr' (MERRY GLO—a perfect match for heathers), 'MORchari' (SWEET CHARIOT—red to pink, turning purplish, excellent scent), and 'MORvi' (VI'S VIOLET, which has excellent hips, too).

The following microminiature cultivars will either blend well with or complement heather colors: *Rosa* 'Baby Garnette' (hot pink), 'Misty Dawn' (white), 'MINnco' (PINK CARPET), and 'MORelfire' (PINK ELF).

Graham Stuart Thomas (1994) was firmly convinced that heathers were best treated in the garden as if they were in their wild surroundings. Consequently, he recommended planting them with other dwarf shrubs such as dwarf junipers, dwarf brooms, and, of course, dwarf roses. He recommended two colonizing rose species, in particular, as "ideal for the heather garden": *Rosa nitida* and *R. pendulina* 'Nana', both of which grow to only about 18 in. (45 cm) tall. He recommended several taller colonizing species, as well. We disagree with Thomas about the suitability of these roses for planting among heathers, for he was honest enough to follow his recommendation with the statement that "if you plant these roses you must be prepared for the nuisance of running roots." In addition, his word portrait of *R. pendulina* 'Nana' describes it as "invasive." If a gardener has chosen to plant heathers because of their relatively low-maintenance requirements, planting invasive companions for them defeats the purpose!

A species far better suited to the heather garden is *Rosa glauca* (synonym *R. rubrifolia*). Although it can grow up to 98 in. (245 cm) tall and wide, the growth habit of this handsome rose is upright and arching, so that it has great presence but with careful pruning can have a relatively small footprint. This species is usually grown for its beautiful deciduous foliage, which may be gray-green in shade but takes on "coppery mauve" tones (Thomas 1994) when grown in the full sun that it prefers, the perfect color to combine with heather. The rather insignificant pink flowers borne in early summer mature to attractive brownish red hips that persist through winter.

Rosa glauca makes a good specimen plant, adding both height and movement to the garden. If the winter display of hips is unimportant, this shrub may be pruned to the ground in early spring to keep it small. To keep the plant relatively small but still allow it to produce flowers (that mature to those desirable hips), which are borne on old wood, each spring prune out canes that are more than two or three years old.

Thymus

The creeping thymes are very useful for growing between young heathers. The flower colors of most thymes are compatible with the flower colors of most heathers, so that those whose bloom season overlaps that of the summer-flowering heathers will blend well with them. Quite a few thymes will flower in early summer before the majority of heathers, thus extending the season of color within the garden.

Unlike heathers, most creeping thymes can cover quite a lot of ground in their first season. Care must be taken to choose very compact, tight-growing thymes that will not grow up into the heather plants and overwhelm them.

Some of the *Thymus serpyllum* selections are well suited to this purpose, especially

An early blooming thyme brightens midspring in the Wulff garden while most heathers, with the exception of yellow *Calluna vulgaris* 'Christina' and orange *C. vulgaris* 'Wickwar Flame', are still wearing their dark winter foliage colors. *Carex testacea* (center) provides movement and orange tones to the garden all year.

'Minimalist'. *Thymus* 'Hartington Silver' (sold as HIGHLAND CREAM) is another very well-behaved thyme. However, some thymes that look harmless in their small nursery pots, for example, *T. serpyllum* 'Goldstream', are much too vigorous and will climb up into and over the heather plants.

When choosing thymes as heather companions, you would be well advised to visit a garden in which they have been growing for several years, so that you can estimate their vigor. You want them to carpet the ground around the heathers, not choke the heathers. If you do not have access to a thyme garden, only to potted thymes in a garden center, pay careful attention to the distance between leaf nodes. If the thyme leaves are very tiny and have virtually no stem showing between them, they will probably remain compact enough for planting among heathers. Thymes advertised as good trough plants are also likely to stay compact enough for the heather garden.

Grasses and Grasslike Plants

"*Ohne Gräser kein Heidegarten.*" (Without grasses, no heather garden.) So begins an article by Jürgen Schröder (2005b) in *Der Heidegarten*. This is a slight overstatement, reflecting the great popularity of ornamental grasses in Germany, but it emphasizes the importance of these grasses to successful garden design. Plants with grassy foliage contrast in texture and shape with heather plants, and many offer color contrast, as well.

The waving foliage and flowers of grasses and grasslike plants give needed movement to a garden. The only drawback to this movement is that those plants whose leaves touch the ground will scour away mulch as their leaf tips move in the wind. If these plants are grown in a breezy area, the mulch around them will need to be replenished several times a year.

True Grasses (Poaceae)

When selecting ornamental grasses for planting with heathers, select clump-forming rather than rhizomatous kinds, and perennial rather than annual grasses. They should also be cultivars that will not make pests of themselves by seeding all over the garden. Choose grasses that will stay where they are planted, increasing in size slowly.

Most true grasses grown as garden ornamentals are hardy in cold climates. For mild climates where they are hardy, evergreen grasses are more desirable for the heather garden than are deciduous kinds.

Avoid planting members of the best-known ornamental grass genus, *Miscanthus*, in heather gardens. Although they can be spectacular, most *Miscanthus* species have overwhelming mass and garden presence, too much for the average home garden. They can also be quite invasive when conditions are to their liking.

Mid-sized or small grasses are appropriate choices for the average home garden.

Most large grasses are suitable for use *within* a heather garden only in large public or estate gardens where they can be balanced by huge drifts of heather, as can be seen in some German parks. Large grasses can, however, be used as backdrops for a small heather garden, as you would use trees or large shrubs.

The nearly sterile hybrid *Calamagrostis* ×*acutiflora* 'Karl Foerster' is a particularly impressive large grass with upright, showy flower panicles. It is an excellent choice for a large heather garden, as it is much less likely to sprawl over the heathers than some other grasses. *Calamagrostis* ×*acutiflora* 'Overdam', a variegated cultivar of the hybrid, is also a fine accent plant of upright habit. It is somewhat smaller and less vigorous than 'Karl Foerster' and appreciates light afternoon shade in hot-summer climates.

Another useful, large, clump-forming grass, of columnar form, is *Panicum virgatum*. Unlike the above hybrids, *P. virgatum* produces considerable seed and may naturalize through either seed or rhizomes, although it is not considered invasive. This, too, is for the large garden.

Festuca glauca (synonyms *F. cinerea* and *F. ovina*) is a wild companion for heathers, growing intermingled with them on the hillsides of Scotland. It is also a fitting companion for heathers in gardens, where cultivars selected for their bluish foliage add contrasting form and color to the garden.

Seedlings of this tightly clumping grass species, with blades only about 6 to 8 in. (15 to 20 cm) tall and flower stalks not quite doubling that height, are perfectly good choices for planting throughout the heather garden, but selected cultivars are more predictable in form. *Festuca glauca* 'Blausilber' is stiffly upright. 'Elijah Blue' is often considered the best cultivar. It is sturdy and comparatively long-lived, but it, too, is somewhat stiff. 'Meerblau' is more relaxed in appearance. Choose a cultivar that has graceful form, especially when it is in bloom and the waving flower stalks add greatly to the garden's ambiance.

Festuca glauca seeds about a bit but not to the point of becoming a nuisance. Young plants in the wrong place are easily removed. A sprinkling of these rather small grasses scattered among the heathers will add welcome movement to the late summer garden when they flower.

Two other *Festuca* species are candidates for the small heather garden. Both *Festuca amethystina* and *F. idahoensis* are similar to *F. glauca* but are slightly larger, and both can provide similar blue-toned foliage.

Helictotrichon sempervirens, blue oat grass, is a medium-sized architectural plant useful as a garden accent. Considerably larger than *Festuca glauca*, with blades 12 to 18 in. (30 to 45 cm) tall and bloom stalks 12 to 24 in. (30 to 60 cm) above the blades, it is similar in color to the selected bluish cultivars of *Festuca*. It, too, likes the good drainage that heathers prefer. A few of these spiky grasses can add excitement to the garden, especially if they are used as silver-blue foils for heathers with magenta, crimson, or ruby flowers. It is for the beautiful leaves that this species should be chosen, as the seed heads are not particularly ornamental.

The delightfully wispy Mexican feather grass (*Nassella tenuissima*, synonym *Stipa tenuissima*) is a moderate seeder, but the seedlings are easily removed. It is of medium size and, like blue oat grass, needs to be "combed" in the spring to remove the previous year's dead leaves.

Many ornamental grasses benefit from being cut close to the ground annually in late winter. They also do better when divided and replanted every few years. When grasses are to be included in the heather garden, plan for this maintenance activity during the designing of the garden. You will want easy access to the grasses without having to tromp across the heathers or disturb heather roots.

Some grasses are quite architectural and will make a big statement in the garden. They may be planted as single specimens but may be more effective if several are spaced at irregular intervals throughout the garden, for continuity. The smaller grasses, such as *Festuca glauca*, can be effectively grouped close together, in odd numbers as you would group heather cultivars.

Sedges (Cyperaceae)

Many people think of sedges as grasses. They are often grouped with the true grasses in garden books and are sold as grasses in garden centers. There are nearly 1000 species in the genus *Carex* alone, most found in temperate, moist habitats and of diverse appearances and growing requirements. Several are good candidates for the heather garden. As with the true grasses, choose sedges of clump-forming rather than rhizomatous habit.

The brown-leaved New Zealand sedges can be extremely attractive when grown among heathers. *Carex buchananii* is the best known of the group, but there is some confusion of this species in the horticultural trade with the more lax growing *C. flagellifera*. Whereas the upright growing *C. buchananii* is useful as a vertical accent, the flowing fountain form of *C. flagellifera* is extremely graceful. Several of these grouped together among the heathers, with one or two plants placed farther away from the group to help unify the garden, are an impressive sight, with each plant averaging more than a yard across, slightly less in height.

Heathers line the garden walk that leads to a *Carex flagellifera* "tree" at the display garden of Northwest Garden Nursery in Eugene, Oregon. Garden design by Marietta and Ernie O'Byrne.

Carex testacea has a lot of green and copper mixed with the brown and blends very well with the foliage of *Calluna vulgaris* 'Fort Bragg', *Erica carnea* 'Ann Sparkes', *E. carnea* 'Bell's Extra Special', *E. cinerea* 'Golden Sport', and other heathers with foliage that is a mixture of green, gold, and red. Its very long, thin inflorescences trail across adjoining heathers but are easily tugged loose from the plants when they mature. This sedge is not as large as the others described above. Its form is neither erect nor fountain-shaped but intermediate between the two. It is a plant for scattering randomly about the heather garden, excellent where its graceful foliage can blend with the colors of adjoining heathers.

The swirling, silvery green *Carex albula*, commonly called "Frosty Curls" and sometimes incorrectly sold as *C. comans* 'Frosty Curls', is a slightly shorter plant than the sedges described above and looks good planted where it can trail over a wall or large rock. According to Rick Darke (1999), this is more drought tolerant than the brown sedges, which need moist but well-drained situations.

Another useful sedge is *Carex oshimensis*, from Japan, a tuft former about 16 in. (40 cm) tall. Its beautiful variegated cultivar, 'Evergold', is highly ornamental, good for echoing the foliage colors of golden heather cultivars while contrasting with them in form and texture. Like the golden heathers, it benefits from light shade in hot-summer climates.

All of the above species are "evergreen," needing to be cut to the ground in spring only once every few years to remove the accumulation of dead foliage at the bottom of the plant. For fun, try planting one deciduous *Carex* species (which will require the annual spring removal of dead foliage and flower stems). *Carex grayi*, with green leaves and erect growth to about 3 ft. (1 m), is a plant for the wetter part of the garden, as it requires constant moisture. Its conspicuous seed heads look just like medieval maces.

Eriophorum latifolium, *E. vaginatum*, and *E. virginicum* are clump-forming sedges for the large garden with constant moisture available. The first two prefer cool climates and may be found living near heathers in northern European sphagnum bogs; unlike heathers, they do not mind wet feet. The last species, also a wetland plant, is found in North America as far west as Manitoba and as far south as Florida. Darke describes it as much more tolerant of heat and humidity than the other species. The fluffy white seed heads that give these sedges the common name "cotton grass" are highly ornamental.

Grasslike Plants from Other Families

Although technically "herbaceous perennials," plants in this section are grouped with the grasses because of their similar form and value to the heather garden.

Acorus

Grasslike *Acorus gramineus*, a member of the Araceae, is lovely in the heather garden, especially the golden-variegated cultivar 'Ogon'. Although it will grow in normal garden soils, it is actually a bog plant, preferring to stay constantly moist. This makes it useful for planting in damp "problem spots" where heathers would not prosper.

Iris

The little irises of the *Iris* Reticulata Group are among the ephemeral spring bulbs that are charming additions to the heather garden. They have the advantage of being taller than some of the other small bulbous plants, so they can be planted among somewhat taller, but still low-growing, heather cultivars. If a little bone meal is mixed into the soil at the bottoms of their planting holes, irises in this group will increase gradually for many years without needing to be lifted and divided. Their fine, grasslike foliage is unobtrusive as it matures and dies.

Most irises have showy flowers but a blooming season of only a few weeks. Their primary value in a heather garden is to provide foliage interest, the larger, blade-like iris leaves contrasting strongly with the tiny leaves of the heathers. Many irises can be good heather companions, especially the beardless species and their hybrids, whose foliage usually remains in good condition from the time it emerges in spring until the onset of winter, when it dies back to the ground.

Among the commonly available kinds of beardless iris, the Siberian irises (hybrids within the *Iris sibirica* complex) excel in retaining their foliage in good condition throughout the growing season if they receive adequate summer water. They thrive in acidic, humus-rich soil, and some Siberians rebloom after the main late-spring flowering season. Flower colors are usually shades of blue and purple, with a few pinks, pale yellows, and whites: perfect for blending with heather flower and foliage colors. They may be planted as single specimens or in small groups within heather beds, any place where they may be easily reached for removal of their dead leaves in winter.

Iris (Reticulata Group) 'George' blooming among plants of *Calluna vulgaris* 'Lemon Gem' in early spring, with *Erica arborea* 'Estrella Gold' in the background.

The so-called Pacific Coast irises, for example, *Iris douglasiana* and *I. tenax* and their hybrids, can do nicely in heather gardens. Their foliage is finer than that of the bearded irises and many other beardless irises, and their spring flowers are relatively large for the short statures of the plants. Some species are evergreen; others are summer dormant. Where they are hardy, they coexist happily with heathers. Despite being adapted to summer drought in their native habitats, some Pacific Coast irises, for example, *I. innominata*, will tolerate, and may even do better with, summer watering.

Tall bearded irises are not suitable for the heather garden. Choose, instead, miniature and standard dwarf bearded irises, which bloom in early to midspring. These are much more amenable to having their rhizomes covered with mulch than are tall bearded irises, which need a summer baking, and their leaves stay in good condition much longer than those of their taller relatives. They also are not as fussy about soil type. Most are good increasers, although there is wide variation among cultivars in the rate of increase, those with a slower rate being preferable for planting among heathers.

Because of their very short stature, miniature dwarf bearded irises are best situated at the edge of the garden, along a path, or in the rock garden. A few, such as *Iris* 'Grapelet', rebloom. Standard dwarf bearded irises may be interspersed among the shorter heathers, where their wide leaves provide welcome contrast of form.

Kniphofia

Commonly called torch lilies or red-hot pokers, *Kniphofia* species (Asphodelaceae) have both grassy foliage and showy, erect flower spikes that contrast strongly with heather forms, foliage and flower colors. Like heathers, they want good drainage but also need summer moisture. These are not plants for the dry garden. Their far-ranging, strong roots can take in moisture to the detriment of surrounding heathers if the garden receives insufficient water. In their native southern African habitats, most *Kniphofia* species grow in hillside seepage areas. Where they are hardy, probably not colder than Zone 7 without winter protection, torch lilies are beautiful garden accents.

Kniphofia 'Percy's Pride' provides an excellent color echo for the foliage of *Erica carnea* 'Golden Starlet', its flowers passing from chartreuse to yellow to white as they age, just as the erica's foliage may be either chartreuse or yellow depending upon the season and its light exposure. An elegant torch lily that is a wonderful heather companion when it is young, within a few years its large fountain of foliage can spread to more than 60 in. (150 cm) wide, sprawling across everything planted near it. This magnificent plant, which flowers all summer, is best reserved for large gardens.

There are other kniphofias along the same color lines as *Kniphofia* 'Percy's Pride' that are more proportional in size to the average home garden, among them 'Little Maid', 'Primrose Beauty', and 'Vanilla'. When choosing from among *Kniphofia* cultivars at the nursery or garden center, you can generally find the smaller growing cultivars by comparing the width of their leaves. Those with very narrow leaves when young are likely to stay a manageable size, growing neither too tall nor too wide.

The daring can experiment with the diminutive but orange-red-flowering *Kniphofia* 'Bressingham Comet'. Try this with *Calluna vulgaris* 'Wickwar Flame', the earliest of the foliage cultivars to change color for the winter. The kniphofia may still be blooming when the heather's foliage turns to orange.

A companionable trio that recalls a Drakensberg meadow landscape seen in South Africa's Royal Natal National Park consists of yellow-flowered kniphofias, moderate-sized ornamental grasses such as *Nassella tenuissima*, and upright, magenta-flowered ericas such as *Erica cinerea* 'Knap Hill Pink', with the grasses mediating between the kniphofias and the ericas. Although this combination can be effective in a small garden, using only a few of each kind of plant, it would be wonderful if carried out on an entire hillside, with the scattering of a few small, blue-flowered agapanthus to enhance the picture.

Ophiopogon planiscapus var. *nigrescens*

Black mondo grass, formerly considered to be a member of the lily family but now assigned by taxonomists to the Ruscaceae, can add drama to the garden. A low grower, to only about 6 in. (15 cm) tall, it looks good all year, is hardy in a wide range of climates, and prefers the acidic, moist but well-drained soils in which heathers thrive. This plant grows well in shade or sun but will have the darkest foliage color if grown in full sunlight. It is rhizomatous in habit but spreads very slowly and is easily managed.

The deep purple, nearly black foliage of this *Ophiopogon* cultivar will complement any color heather flowers or foliage, and its summer racemes of pale pink, bell-shaped

Black mondo grass and a golden-foliaged *Calluna* are exciting garden partners.

flowers are attractive in their own right. Plant this at the front of the garden or along a path, and add a sprinkling of *Galanthus* bulbs to the planting for extra spring interest.

Phormium

The statuesque members of the Southern Hemispheric genus *Phormium* (Hemerocallidaceae), commonly called New Zealand flax, have become very popular specimen plants for the perennial garden because of their garden presence and the beautiful leaf color variations they exhibit. Cultivars range from green and bronze through pink and red to yellow, many vertically striped in two or more colors. Most are hardy to Zone 8 or 9 and can provide useful structural and color contrast in the heather garden. Some grow exceedingly large and would overpower all except the largest heather gardens, but there are also small cultivars more in scale with the average garden, for example, *P. tenax* 'Jack Spratt', 'Tiny Tiger', or *P.* 'Tom Thumb'. As with selecting *Kniphofia* plants, consider the leaf width of young *Phormium* plants when looking for the smaller cultivars, those with comparatively narrow leaves as young plants generally maturing into smaller sized adults. Cultivar names can be misleading: *Phormium tenax* 'Bronze Baby' is full-sized, not small as one might assume from its name.

Herbaceous Perennials

A number of herbaceous perennials other than those with grasslike foliage may profitably be grown near or among heathers. In a cold climate where the garden will be covered by snow or mulch during the winter, the tendency of many perennials to die back to the roots in cold weather will not be a drawback.

As with other companion plants, perennials are best planted at the same time as the heathers. Some self-seeding perennials may later plant themselves and can be left where they are growing if they have chosen their spots well. Those in the "wrong" place should be removed while they are still small.

Bergenia

Plant bergenias with heathers for the wonderful contrast provided by their ovoid to nearly circular, large, often shiny, semi-evergreen leaves. They work well as companions to *Erica carnea* and *E.* ×*darleyensis* where winter interest is desired (Anderton 2007). In winter, the leaves of many bergenias take on purple tints that echo the pink to magenta colors of winter *Erica* flowers, as well as complementing their own striking pink to purple spring flower clusters borne on stalks that rise a foot (30 cm) or more above the basal leaves. *Bergenia purpurascens*, *B.* 'Beethoven', and 'Bressingham Ruby' develop especially strong winter leaf color.

Bergenias are widely tolerant of soil and light conditions but benefit from dappled shade and moist soil in hot climates. Although most bergenias are hardy from Zones 4 to 10, they will die back to the ground in the colder zones and so should be chosen for winter interest use only in Zone 7 and warmer. They earn their keep as heather companions the rest of the year because their beautiful broad leaves play so well off the fine texture of heather foliage. In cold climates, plant these on the western edge of the heather garden, where their frost-tender young leaves will receive some protection from early morning sunlight.

Campanula

To bring a bright bit of blue into the heather garden, plant campanulas, but be cautious which you plant from this large genus of diverse plant habits. The species sold for use in rock gardens and as front-of-the-border plants are best suited for heather garden use. Most will be happy in full sun or partial shade as long as they have moist, well-drained soil. Among these are several rampant spreaders that should be avoided. Most campanula species are generous seed producers. If you plant them, be prepared to remove unwanted self-sown seedlings.

Among the better campanulas for the heather garden are *Campanula portenschlagiana* (synonym *C. muralis*), especially 'Resholdt's Variety'; *C. cochlearifolia* (synonyms *C. pusilla* and *C. bellardii*); and *C. rotundifolia*. The first species, only about 8 in. (20 cm) tall, is best planted along a path or where it can trail over the edge of a wall. This is a creeper, albeit not nearly as invasive as the similar *C. poscharskyana* and *C.* 'Camgood', and it will eventually cover all unoccupied ground. Do not plant this with low or slow-growing heathers. When planted with vigorous, taller heather cultivars, it is valuable for its abundant, deep blue-purple flowers borne from late spring (time of most abundant bloom) until autumn.

The well-named fairy bells (*Campanula cochlearifolia*) reaches its vaunted 6 in. (15 cm) height only when it flowers in midsummer. The rest of the year, this tiny treasure slowly creeps, with its leaves barely getting above ground level. The little flower bells are never as intensely blue as the flowers of *C. portenschlagiana*, but they are blue, and this species may safely be planted among the most compact heathers. It never becomes a pest. Tuck it around heathers in the rock garden, where it can creep into crevices.

Campanula rotundifolia, with too many synonyms to list and considerable variation in height, is widely distributed in the Northern Hemisphere, especially at high latitudes and altitudes. A natural heather companion, it may comfortably be planted wherever its delicate stems, topped with blue, bell-shaped flowers, can pop up among heathers as they do in the wild.

Coreopsis

Try adding *Coreopsis verticillata* 'Moonbeam' in front of or among the heathers for a touch of light yellow. This low-growing, tried and true perennial survives with minimal watering and is not aggressive enough to crowd out heathers, although individual plants will gradually increase in width. The abundant, small yellow flowers echo the foliage color of the white-flowered heathers with yellow foliage and combine well with them. Other selections of *C. verticillata* have golden flowers, but some cultivars can get considerably taller than 'Moonbeam'. These would flop over the heathers and for that reason should be avoided.

For a plant with the same feathery foliage, abundant small flowers, and tolerance of neglect as *Coreopsis verticillata* 'Moonbeam', but with pink instead of yellow flowers, plant *C. rosea*. This delicate beauty can be planted among the vivid pinks and near reds of *Erica cinerea* cultivars for blending flower color but contrast in height and texture.

Cut off the dead foliage of both *Coreopsis rosea* and *C. verticillata* either in late autumn or before new growth emerges in early spring. This is the only maintenance required for these plants, although they may occasionally be divided when they outgrow their allotted space or more plants are needed.

Other species in the genus *Coreopsis* can be quite aggressive, especially the annual species that produce enormous quantities of seed. For this reason, they are not recommended for the heather garden.

Dianthus

Many of the smaller *Dianthus* species and cultivars would be at home in the heather garden, although the tiniest should not be planted near vigorous heathers, lest they be overwhelmed by them. In general, *Dianthus* considered suitable for the rock garden would also like the well-drained soil and sunny aspect of the ideal heather garden. Consider planting *D. alpinus*, which forms tight mounds of foliage to about 6 × 10 in. (15 × 25 cm) from which rise attractive white, pink, or red flowers (or some combination thereof) in early summer.

Some *Dianthus* cultivars have silver-gray or bluish gray foliage that contrasts pleasingly with heather foliage, even gray heather foliage, because the plant form and leaf shape is so different. *Dianthus* species with small flowers on relatively short stems are the most attractive companions for heathers.

Geranium

Many hardy geraniums grow far too large or spread far too aggressively to qualify for planting in the heather garden, but a number of the more refined species make good heather companions with long summer-into-autumn blooming seasons. A good rule of thumb for choosing suitable *Geranium* cultivars for the heather garden, as for choosing suitable *Campanula* and *Dianthus*, is that the cultivar be appropriate for planting in a rock garden. If it is well behaved enough for a rock garden, it is worth trying in a heather garden.

Some species have already proven their worth in the heather garden, as reported by Arnold Stow (2004) in his response to a Heather Society questionnaire. Arnold recommended these deciduous geraniums, that "have never interfered with the flowering of the heathers," and grow only 4 to 12 in. (10 to 30 cm) tall: *Geranium* (Cinereum Group) 'Ballerina', dainty purplish pink with darker veins, and 'Laurence Flatman', similar but more vigorous; *Geranium dalmaticum* in both its pink- and white-flowered forms; *Geranium renardii*, valued more for its softly felted gray-green leaves than for its delicate, purple-veined white flowers, and *G. renardii* 'Whiteknights', with lilac flowers; and selected cultivars of *G. sanguineum*, of which there are many, some far better suited to rock or heather garden than others. Arnold recommends *G. sanguineum* 'Shepherd's Warning', which has a compact growth habit and magenta-pink flowers, and *G. sanguineum* var. *striatum*, with white flowers striped pink and a very compact growth habit.

All of the above form low mats or small mounds that pretty much stay put, though *Geranium dalmaticum* is suitable for planting as an easily managed ground cover. Stow's final suggestion, not a compact grower like the others, is a trailer: *Geranium wallichianum* 'Buxton's Variety', which in summer "threads its way through the heather to display sky blue flowers with a large white centerpiece enhanced by black stamens."

Two *Geranium procurrens* hybrids have a similar trailing habit (without that species' invasive tendency to root at every node), attractive, yellow-marked young foliage, and purple flowers with darker centers. Plant *G.* 'Ann Folkard' and 'Salome' where they can scramble up some of the taller yellow-foliaged heathers, such as *Erica cinerea* 'Golden Hue' or *E.* ×*griffithsii* 'Valerie Griffiths', with the dark geranium flowers ('Ann Folkard' is the darker hybrid, but 'Salome' has larger flowers) popping out here and there.

Penstemon

Penstemon pinifolius, an evergreen species native to the American Southwest that is far less demanding in its cultural requirements than many others in its genus, is another heather impersonator. The needle-like leaves that give the species its name contribute to its heather resemblance. Of course, all doubt as to its identity vanishes when it flowers, adding bright orange-red to the heather garden palette after the winter-red foliage heathers have already changed back to gold. Use care in choosing this plant's heather companions so as to avoid unpleasant color associations. Heathers with yellow foliage combine well with the flowers of *P. pinifolius* where a bold color combination is desired. A heather cultivar with gray-green foliage, on the other hand, is a soothing companion that lets the penstemon star in the garden show.

There are two yellow-flowered cultivars: *Penstemon pinifolius* 'Magdalena Sunshine' and 'Mersea Yellow'. Both of these are average size for the species, with foliage only 8 in. (20 cm) tall but 24-inch (60-cm) bloom spikes. There is also a dwarf cultivar with the typical orange-red flowers, 'Compactum', that is only 10 in. (25 cm) tall in bloom.

Penstemon pinifolius is a good choice to add color to the heather garden in late spring, when few heathers flower. It likes full sun or afternoon shade, good air circulation, and well-drained soil, preferably sandy or gritty—growing conditions also favored by heathers. Although the species is drought tolerant, it can stand higher humidity than can most penstemons and is hardy to Zone 4.

Succulents

Sempervivums and sedums can be used either within the heather garden or as edging along paths.

Sempervivum

Commonly called hen-and-chicks or house leeks, *Sempervivum* species combine well with heathers and seem to be available in as many cultivars. In many *Sempervivum* cultivars, the evergreen succulent foliage shares the orange, red, and purple tints that many of the heathers take on in winter. They can be persuaded to retain some of this lovely foliage color in summer by planting them in very lean soil and full sun.

They are more drought tolerant than heathers and therefore can be planted on the edges of the garden farther from irrigation sources than the heathers, although they are happier with a regular water supply as long as they have good drainage. The rosette shapes and "cobwebbing" of some species provide good contrast with the needle-like foliage of heathers.

Sedum

The smaller-growing kinds of *Sedum* are also suitable as heather companions. However, care must be taken to choose cultivars that are not aggressive. Practically any *Sempervivum* could be grown with heathers without fear of its overwhelming the vast majority of heather cultivars (a few of the very compact, slow-growing *Calluna* cultivars being the primary exception to this statement). Not so with sedums. Some sedums, for example, *Sedum* 'Acre', are garden thugs capable of ruling the world if given half a chance. Do not be fooled by their beauty into planting them, unless you want a garden exclusively of sedums, not heathers.

Some sedums that would be good choices to grow companionably with heather are *Sedum cauticola*, *S. dasyphyllum*, and *S. spathulifolium*. The drought tolerance of these succulents makes them candidates for planting in the drier parts of the heather garden, although they will tolerate wetter situations if given sharp drainage.

Spring-Flowering "Bulbous" Plants

Daffodils and Tulips

Daffodils (*Narcissus*) and tulips (*Tulipa*) are usually out of place when planted within the heather garden, although they may be planted behind *Erica carnea* to good effect. Because heather roots should not be disturbed once the plants are established, bulbs that need to be replaced frequently do not make good heather companions. Most large daffodils and tulips are useful in the heather garden only until the heather plants have met each other, by which time most daffodils and tulips will be in need of lifting and dividing and should, instead, be sacrificed for the good of the heathers.

Narcissus

Some of the more graceful large daffodils, especially those with white perianths and pink trumpets, can look good when planted within large patches of *Erica carnea*. For instance, try interplanting *Narcissus* 'French Prairie' with *E. carnea* 'King George'. If you do plant and hope to maintain large *Narcissus* cultivars, be prepared to tolerate their ripening coarse foliage, which can be unattractive for weeks.

Small-flowered *Narcissus* species, not as commonly grown as are larger kinds, are more appropriate for the heather garden. Many of these are not only shorter than their larger cousins, but they have much finer foliage that is less conspicuous as it is ripening—a crucial attribute for interplanting with heathers. The tiny hoop petticoat daffodils (*N. bulbocodium* and related species), with thread-like grassy foliage, are so diminutive that they should be planted with only the most prostrate of heathers, for instance with *Calluna vulgaris* 'Soay' or 'Clare Carpet'. Other small daffodil species, such as *N. rupestris* and *N. willkommii*, have similarly fine leaves, but their delicate flowers are on taller stems, making them suitable for interplanting among a much larger selection of low-growing heathers. Many of the smaller daffodils will naturalize and survive for many years without attention.

When choosing daffodils to plant with heathers, flower size is not an adequate guide. Even such small-flowered daffodils as *Narcissus* 'Segovia', an American Daffodil Society–recognized miniature, can have foliage that is too coarse to make them appropriate heather companions. However, the hybrid 'Hawera' has fine enough foliage to make it suitable for the heather garden, and others with fine foliage can be found with a little sleuthing.

Tulipa

Tulips have the advantage over daffodils as heather companions in that their foliage, though broad, usually takes less time to ripen. Among the tall classes of tulip, the lily-flowered cultivars have the graceful carriage compatible with a heather garden and can be planted in small groupings of a single color judiciously placed within the garden, such as next to a large rock. The very tall *Tulipa* 'White Triumphator' is an excellent choice for such planting, provided that the adjoining heathers, preferably *Calluna* cultivars of upright habit, are also fairly tall and vigorous. Plant these bulbs very deep (up to 10 in. [25 cm]) and give each a generous helping of bone meal to encourage persistent flowering.

Extremely large-flowered, formal tulips such as the Darwin hybrids should be avoided. Long-lived species such as *Tulipa tarda* (synonym *T. dasystemon*) or *T. turkestanica* are a much better choice but need to be planted at the edge of the garden or among prostrate heather cultivars because of their short stature.

The Minor Bulbs

Many of the so-called minor bulbs, ephemeral beauties such as *Chionodoxa*, *Crocus*, *Galanthus*, and *Scilla*, can be planted with heathers. Most of these flower in early spring and have very fine, almost grasslike, foliage that lasts only a short time after the flowers fade, drying up to nearly nothing.

Because so many of these little beauties are short, they are suitable for planting among only very low-growing heathers or on the edge of the garden in front of the heathers. Try, for example, planting *Muscari azureum* among plants of *Calluna*

This shallow bowl planted with several *Erica carnea* cultivars and an assortment of minor bulbs gives colorful flowers from winter through late spring. Now in their second season after planting, the ericas are outgrowing their container and bloom from the bulbs (which had finished flowering before this late spring photograph was taken) has diminished.

vulgaris 'Snowflake'. The true blue of *Chionodoxa sardensis* is perfect with *Erica carnea* 'Schneekuppe'. For a very rich look, plant these with the deep red *E. carnea* 'Rotes Juwel'. Consider a drift of *Scilla siberica* planted among winter heaths with yellow foliage, such as *E. carnea* 'Golden Starlet' or 'Westwood Yellow'. *Crocus tommasinianus* can be scattered and allowed to naturalize anywhere among the shorter heathers.

Chionodoxa forbesii is able to push its way through the low-growing golden foliage of *Erica cinerea* 'Celebration'.

On a slightly larger scale, but still with thin, unobtrusive foliage, is *Fritillaria meleagris*. Its checkered plum-purple flowers look entrancing pushing up through *Erica erigena* 'Irish Dusk'. The new hybrid *E.* ×*darleyensis* cultivars 'Irish Treasure' and 'Phoebe', shorter than their *E. erigena* parent but with the same flower color, are a better size match for the fritillary.

It is a good idea to plant bulbs between heather plants when you plant the heathers, or at least during the heathers' first autumn in the ground. This will minimize the possibility of damaging heather roots when you plant the bulbs. In loose, friable soil, heather roots can travel far beyond the width of the plants.

A few of the smaller bulbs have the unfortunate habit of sending up their foliage in autumn, well in advance of the spring flowers. *Ipheion* and some species of *Muscari*, for example, *M. armeniacum*, are plants that often produce leaves many months before they bloom. These kinds are best avoided, so as not to have their foliage sprawl over that of the heathers for a long time.

Nectaroscordum

Not your ordinary onion, *Nectaroscordum siculum* subsp. *bulgaricum* (synonyms *Allium siculum* and *A. bulgaricum*) has been the subject of taxonomic battles and several name changes. Whatever its name, this plant is guaranteed to bring more questions from garden visitors than any heather will.

Nectaroscordum siculum is a bulbous onion that flowers on 48 in. (120 cm) stems in late spring and early summer, with clusters of showy, bell-shaped flowers in muted shades of dark red, green and white. The flowers are turned up within the bud cluster, face downward on long pedicels as they open, then turn upward again when they are pollinated. Although the basal rosette of foliage is unattractive for a short time as the leaves die down shortly after the flowers are pollinated, the bare flower stalk with its conspicuous seedpods remains standing throughout the summer. A grouping of these can serve the same function as garden sculpture, and the bulbs can easily be tucked between heathers when the heathers are planted. Unlike some onions, this does not become a garden pest.

Heathers in the Mixed Border

In the "mixed border," carefully selected perennials, shrubs, and trees are planted together to provide garden interest throughout the year. The peak of heather bloom occurs in late summer, a time when few other shrubs flower and when many herbaceous perennials are long past their prime. The winter-flowering heather species fill another seasonal gap, often blooming long before other shrubs and trees. Heathers thus can be valuable components of a mixed border, as long as their cultural needs are met.

In the Berkshire Mountains of western Massachusetts, USA, Geoffrey Charlesworth (1996) worked plants of *Calluna vulgaris*, *Erica carnea*, *E. spiculifolia*, and *E. tetralix* into raised beds, perennial borders, and rock gardens. Against the advice of most heather "experts," Charlesworth frequently plants heathers as single plants, where they act as fillers among other kinds of plants, their evergreen foliage serving as background when the other plants bloom.

The idea of planting single heathers evolved from his desire to know how the various cultivars would perform in his garden. By planting only one heather among other kinds of plants, he can easily observe the unique form of each cultivar and also minimize detraction from the garden's design should a particular cultivar not prove hardy in the Berkshires' rigorous climate. Geoffrey also goes against standard pruning advice. He does not shear his plants but allows them to assume the form they would take in the wild. They bloom "well enough" this way, and his approach certainly cuts down on garden maintenance.

On the other side of North America, in Olympia, Washington, Gary Schuldt (personal communication) and Bryant Russell incorporated heathers into their decidedly mixed garden. A plant addict like Geoffrey Charlesworth, Gary also uses only one plant of each heather or perennial cultivar, along with a generous sprinkling of other shrubs and trees of various sizes. His effort to crowd as many different plants as possible into their limited garden space (which caused much head shaking by Russell, a professionally trained horticulturist) breaks many rules of garden design. The result, however, is wonderful and has been featured on many garden tours.

Schuldt and Russell's deft touch with color makes the most unlikely plant companions into congenial neighbors. One of their more successful combinations (there are many) is a threesome: *Calluna vulgaris* 'Firefly' sandwiched between *Geranium pratense* Midnight Reiter Strain and *Persicaria virginiana* 'Painter's Palette'. The color blend in this combination is outstanding, especially when the heather is blooming. The dark purple geranium leaves beautifully complement the deep mauve heather flowers, while the heather foliage accentuates flecks of color in the leaves of the *Persicaria*. In winter, when the perennials die back to ground level, the heather's outstanding, brick-red foliage helps nearby dwarf conifers maintain color in the garden.

Calluna vulgaris 'Firefly' blooms between a plant of *Geranium pratense* Midnight Reiter Strain (foreground) and *Persicaria virginiana* 'Painter's Palette'. Photo by Gary Schuldt.

Although one might expect the perennials, both vigorous spreaders, to overwhelm the heather, *Calluna vulgaris* 'Firefly' is holding its own—with a little help. *Persicaria* 'Painter's Palette' is a threat only for the summer months; and a large, strategically placed piece of basalt keeps it from creeping into the heather. The local deer frequently crop the geranium to the ground while ignoring *C. vulgaris* 'Firefly'. This combination just may last awhile. Meanwhile, Gary Schuldt cannot resist acquiring more heathers and experimenting with new associations.

Annuals

Annuals can help fill the spaces between heathers while the garden is young. Some of them are very effective in this role. In selecting annuals to grow with heathers, the primary consideration is that the annuals not be so tall and vigorous as to overwhelm the young heathers. They should also, of course, be amenable to the same soils and exposure as the heathers among which they are to be planted. These are only a few of the many annual plants that could be grown among young heathers.

Consider first some "annuals" that may be biennial or perennial plants in some gardens, particularly gardens in regions with mild winters and cool summers: pansies (*Viola* hybrids) and snapdragons (*Antirrhinum majus* selections). Where the plants themselves do not overwinter, they may persist in the garden through their seedlings. These will carry the heather garden through its first few summers while there is plenty of empty space between plants.

Viola

The large-flowered pansies are widely available, in just about every flower color and color combination, including blues and oranges: there is one for every taste. All remain low, compact, and no threat to young heathers. Their main drawback is that they will not tolerate full sun conditions where summers are hot. They also require deadheading to encourage continuous flower production.

The exuberant small-flowered *Viola tricolor*, commonly known as Johnny-jump-up, can grow in full sun or in shade and actually produces taller vegetative growth than its overbred pansy cousins. The species is a generous self-seeder needing some restraint and may persist in a garden for generations if a few seedlings are allowed to remain each year. A nearly black seed strain that comes true to color is *V*. 'Bowles Black', also sold under the species synonyms *V. cornuta* and *V. nigra*. It provides excellent color contrast with golden-foliaged heathers, the tiny golden "eye" in each *Viola* flower picking up the gold of the heather foliage, while the rest of the flower, such a dark purple as to appear black, is in stark contrast to the gold.

Antirrhinum

Snapdragons are available in a range of sizes from about 6 in. (15 cm) tall to more than 40 in. (1 m). Choose the shorter strains for planting among young heathers. Massachusetts garden designer Katherine Udall (personal communication), who works primarily on Cape Cod (Zones 6 and 7), finds that the myriad bright colors of these self-seeders combine very well with those heathers having silver foliage.

Portulaca

Katherine Udall also recommends sowing *Portulaca* seeds among the heathers. These drought-tolerant annuals are primarily available in bright, mixed colors, but some

In the newly renovated heather garden at Fort Tryon in New York City, *Portulaca* adds a touch of red to the predominantly "blue" and yellow tapestry created by the interweaving of annual *Nirembergia* and *Salvia* cultivars with golden foliaged callunas.

single color strains can be found. There is little risk that these very low-growing plants would overpower young heathers. They are quick to flower from seed and will bloom profusely in sunny situations until cut down by winter cold.

Lobelia

Another commonly grown annual that may be perennial where winters are mild is a source of true blue for the heather garden. Dwarf edging lobelia (*Lobelia erinus*) cultivars, most under 6 in. (15 cm) tall, are available in white and many shades of blue—and pink—and in mounding or trailing forms. These are usually in bloom by the time the small plants appear in garden centers, so choosing a cultivar with the preferred color is easy. This lobelia will grow in sun or light shade and will be happy with the constantly moist soil needed by young heathers in a new planting.

Ageratum

Dwarf ageratums (*Ageratum* species) are also good choices for summer and autumn flowers planted between young heathers. Their flowers come in white and in various shades of pastel blue and lavender, so they combine well with most colors of heather flowers and foliage.

Petunia

David Wilson created a superb garden of annual flowering plants with heather during one summer at the Heather Farm in Sardis, British Columbia. He used two effective heather and petunia combinations. He planted a border of soft yellow petunias

Yellow-flowered petunias harmonize with a planting of yellow-foliaged heathers: *Calluna vulgaris* 'Lime Glade' (left) and 'Firefly' (right).

(*Petunia* ×*hybrida* ALADDIN YELLOW) along the driveway, with *Calluna vulgaris* 'Lime Glade', 'Firefly', and 'Sesam' behind them. The yellow foliage of the heather cultivars blended beautifully with the color of the yellow petunias.

Farther along the driveway, David widely spaced plants of the vibrant, cerise-flowered *Erica* ×*griffithsii* 'Jacqueline' and surrounded them with a harmonizing mixture of pink petunias. In this monochromatic planting, interest was achieved with both the difference in texture and the difference in height between the low-growing petunias and the much taller heathers.

Use caution when planting annuals among heathers that are more than a year old. A two-year-old heather planting may still have enough soil free of heather roots to accommodate inter-filling with small annuals, but if you attempt to dig between older heathers in order to add new plants, you run the risk of damaging heather roots. Small gaps are best left open but well mulched.

If you positively cannot abide the look of bare ground, fill any remaining gaps with planted containers, small statuary, or interesting rock specimens. These can be moved elsewhere when the heathers increase in size, and their presence on top of the soil will help to provide a cool root run for the heathers.

A pair of worn-out hiking boots planted with *Sempervivum* cultivars fills a gap among three-year-old heathers in the Wulff garden. When these heathers grow together, the boots can be moved easily to another part of the garden. *Calluna vulgaris* 'Annemarie' and 'Crinkly Tuft' bloom behind and to the right of the boots, respectively.

Heathers as Companions or Foils for Other Plants

Rosa

Use *Erica carnea* in the rose garden, to weave around the rose bushes and provide flower color at the time tea roses are looking their worst: late winter and early spring, when they have been pruned to nothing but a few stubs. Choose *Erica* foliage color to complement or contrast with the color of the rose flowers. *Erica carnea* is probably the least demanding heather as to soil type. If the roses are happy, it will be, too.

Daphne

Erica carnea is useful for planting at the base of the hardy, but rather gawky, deciduous *Daphne mezereum*, treasured for its intensely fragrant winter flowers. Winter heath will tolerate the light shade that this daphne prefers, and many *E. carnea* cultivars will be in flower at the same time as the daphne, in colors that harmonize with its purple flowers. One could also have a white-themed winter garden (best appreciated where snow is rare) by using *D. mezereum* f. *alba* underplanted with a white-flowering *E. carnea*, for example, 'Isabell'. Purple daphne flowers mature to red berries; *D. mezereum* f. *alba* has berries of a rich golden color. There is little, if any, overlap between the *E. carnea* flowering season and the time the daphne berries start to color, although some old berries may hang on the plants until the following winter.

Where they are hardy, daboecias are an even better choice for planting around *Daphne mezereum* than *Erica carnea*. A combined planting of *Daphne mezereum* and either *Daboecia cantabrica* or *Daboecia* ×*scotica* can have flowers for at least eight months of the year in Zones 7 or 8, for the daphne begins to flower in early winter at about the time many *Daboecia* cultivars finish blooming. Because these heathers flower when the daphne is in fruit, careful selection of both heather and daphne cultivars is important. The intense cerise, magenta, or purple of some daboecia flowers would look much better near the golden berries of *D. mezereum* f. *alba* than next to the red berries of plants with purple flowers.

Rhododendron

One of the best uses for *Daboecia* cultivars is along the edge of a rhododendron garden, where they can bridge the boundary between sunny situations and the shade that most rhododendrons prefer. They begin flowering at about the time that the rhododendron garden is at its late spring peak of bloom (so when planning for this use, consider the flower color of both daboecias and nearby *Rhododendron* cultivars) and continue the flower show long after most rhododendrons are finished for the year.

Daboecias, especially tall cultivars such as *Daboecia cantabrica* 'Hookstone Purple' and 'Rainbow', are superb for camouflaging the "bare legs" of medium-to-large rhododendrons that have lost their lower leaves. Their ability to tolerate, or even perform better in, light shade suits them admirably to this purpose. Although many ericas and callunas, especially large cultivars of erect habit, are good for edging the sunny side of a rhododendron bed, daboecias come into their own as edgers for the shady sides of rhododendrons. Even if there is too much shade for them to flower well, their handsome foliage, the broadest among the heathers (although admittedly still tiny compared to that of most rhododendrons), makes daboecias good rhododendron companions. The leaves of many daboecias have glossy upper surfaces and whitish under surfaces that echo, in miniature, the leaf surfaces of some rhododendrons. Where there is enough sun for them to flower, daboecias can brighten an otherwise green rhododendron planting during the summer and autumn.

In Saint John's, Newfoundland, Linda Smith skilfully combined small conifers with heathers and other plants in a dooryard container planting.

Conifers

As dwarf conifers are good companion plants for heathers, so are heathers good companions for conifers. If sufficient sun is available for them, heathers may be used as groundcover in the conifer garden, particularly a garden that features specimen plants spaced far enough apart for the individual characteristics of each conifer cultivar to be fully appreciated. Drifts of heather among the conifers in this kind of garden do much to enliven what could otherwise be a rather static planting.

Both heather flowers and heather foliage offer colors unavailable in conifer foliage, such as pink, magenta, and red. Heathers also offer more seasonal contrast than conifers can. Some conifer foliage does change color from summer to winter, but the change is usually more subtle (such as from dark green to purplish green) in conifers than in heathers, where the color change can be from one primary color (yellow) to another primary color (red). There is a good reason, in addition to Adrian Bloom's popular book about them (1986), why heathers and conifers became such a popular combination in the 1980s. The combination, if well done, is flattering to both kinds of plant and can even, with carefully selected cultivars, be extended to container gardens.

Winning Combinations

Gardeners new to growing heather are often overwhelmed by the choice of cultivars and ask for help in choosing which to plant next to each other. Below are some suggested combinations of heather cultivars that work well with each other or with other kinds of plants. If a specified cultivar is not available, substitute one with similar attributes. The number of possible winning combinations is nearly infinite.

Heathers with Other Heathers

Calluna vulgaris 'Highland Rose' (foreground) and *Erica cinerea* 'Knap Hill Pink' are a winning combination in summer, as shown here, and also in winter.

Calluna vulgaris 'Beoley Gold' next to *Erica cinerea* 'Purple Beauty': opposites on the color wheel. See photograph of this combination in Bloom (1975).

Calluna vulgaris 'Foya' planted so that its golden-orange summer foliage pokes up through *Erica cinerea* 'Velvet Night', in striking contrast with the erica's beetroot-red flowers (David Wilson, personal communication). In winter, the combination changes to red and green.

Calluna vulgaris 'Sesam' next to *Erica cinerea* 'C. D. Eason'. The golden summer foliage of the calluna acts as a foil for the magenta flowers of the erica. In winter, the dark green erica foliage sets off the bright orange calluna foliage.

Yet another variation on this theme combines *Calluna vulgaris* 'Highland Rose' with *Erica cinerea* 'Knap Hill Pink'. In cold-winter climates where *E. cinerea* is not hardy, substitute for it a *Calluna* cultivar with long spikes of deeply colored flowers, for example, *C. vulgaris* 'Arabella', 'Carmen', or 'Mazurka'.

Calluna vulgaris 'Silver Queen' with 'Wickwar Flame' (Lortz 2002b).

Calluna vulgaris 'Velvet Fascination' with *Erica cinerea* 'P. S. Patrick' in a random checkerboard pattern of silver and purple (Wilson, personal communication).

Daboecia cantabrica cultivars, purple and white plants intermingled. For example, *D. cantabrica* f. *alba* with *D. cantabrica* 'Atropurpurea' or 'Hookstone Purple'. This interplanting is more effective in the landscape than a large planting of a single cultivar that bears purple and white flowers on the same plant, such as 'Bicolor' or 'Harlequin'.

Erica carnea 'Golden Starlet' with 'Rotes Juwel' for spring excitement.

Erica cinerea 'Iberian Beauty' creeps into a planting of the taller but less vigorous *E. ciliaris* 'White Wings', whose russet-toned spent flowers give additional color to this early autumn picture.

The flower buds of *Erica carnea* 'Wintersonne' blend beautifully with the nearly red winter foliage of *Calluna vulgaris* 'Firefly' and its sport, 'Punch's Dessert'. The magenta-colored *Erica* flowers clash gloriously with the *Calluna* foliage, but the buds are on the *Erica* longer than are the open flowers.

Erica cinerea 'Celebration' mixed randomly with 'P. S. Patrick' (Wilson, personal communication).

Erica cinerea 'Coccinea' with any silver-foliaged *Calluna* cultivar that has white flowers.

Erica cinerea 'Iberian Beauty' intermingled with *E. ciliaris* 'White Wings'. Some restraining pruning may be necessary to keep this duo in balance, but they look lovely when blended together in a side-by-side planting.

Magenta-flowered *Erica cinerea* 'Knap Hill Pink' intermingled with crimson-flowered *Calluna vulgaris* 'Carmen'. These cultivars are of similar height and vigor and should be allowed to mix freely when grown in a climate that favors both species.

Heathers with Other Plants or Garden Features

Allium cernuum, dark colored cultivars interplanted among low-growing, gray-foliaged *Calluna* cultivars such as *Calluna vulgaris* 'Glendoick Silver' or *C. vulgaris* 'Jan Dekker' (Stefani McRae-Dickey, personal communication).

Calluna vulgaris 'Christina' or 'Marion Blum' (or other upright yellow-foliaged *Calluna*) underplanted with *Thymus* 'Hartington Silver'.

Calluna vulgaris 'Corbett's Red' with *Hebe pinguifolia* 'Pagei' (Crooks 2006).

Calluna vulgaris 'Durford Wood' with *Sempervivum* 'Packardian' (Wick 2004).

Calluna vulgaris 'Long White', 'My Dream', or other late-blooming white heather in front of any blue-flowering cultivar of *Caryopteris* ×*clandonensis*, for a striking blue and white color combination that can be a strong component of the late-season mixed border (Udall, personal communication).

Calluna vulgaris 'Redbud' or 'Peter Sparkes' behind a planting of *Ophiopogon planiscapus* var. *nigrescens* mixed with *Galanthus nivalis* for stunning two-season contrast.

Daboecia cantabrica 'Waley's Red' in front of *Rhododendron* 'Hachmann's Charmant'. The color of the daboecia flowers matches the color of the picotee edging on the rhododendron flowers.

Erica carnea 'Ann Sparkes' with a rock. This cultivar looks particularly good against granite.

Erica carnea 'Golden Starlet' underplanted with *Scilla siberica*.

Daboecia cantabrica 'Waley's Red' is a perfect color match for the flowers of *Rhododendron* 'Hachmann's Charmant'.

The pink flowers of *Erica* ×*watsonii* 'Cherry Turpin' are complemented by the bluish foliage of *Festuca glauca* and *Thymus doerfleri* 'Bressingham'. The thyme flowers are the same color as the *Erica* flowers.

Erica carnea 'Rosantha' with *Crocus* 'Ruby Giant' and *Iris* 'Harmony'.

Erica cinerea 'Celebration' underplanted with blue *Chionodoxa forbesii*. (Well-developed bulbs are strong enough to push their foliage and flowers up through the foliage of the erica.)

Erica ×*watsonii* 'Cherry Turpin', *Festuca glauca*, and *Thymus doerfleri* 'Bressingham'.

Fritillaria meleagris with plum-purple flowers, planted among *Erica erigena* 'Irish Dusk' or the similarly colored new introductions *E.* ×*darleyensis* 'Irish Treasure' and 'Phoebe', so that the fritillary flower stems stretch up through the *Erica* foliage. A wonderful color blend.

Heathers, especially long-stemmed *Calluna vulgaris* and *Erica cinerea* cultivars, intermixed with blue-violet lavender cultivars, such as *Lavandula angustifolia* 'Hidcote Blue'. Alternatively, especially in cold-winter climates, plant *Erica carnea* where it can creep under and around the lavenders.

Nandina domestica, shorter growing cultivars, planted with *Calluna* cultivars whose foliage turns orange-red in winter. For example, plant the splendid dwarf *N. domestica* 'Fire Power' near *Calluna vulgaris* 'Firefly', 'Foya', or 'Robert Chapman', for a double display of fireworks.

6 Heather Breeding

Few plant breeders have worked with the hardy heathers until recently. The small size of the individual flowers makes such work tedious, and the few attempts to produce hardy heather hybrids met with even fewer successes.

Little deliberate breeding of *Calluna*, *Daboecia*, and the hardy European *Erica* species has been done since heather cultivation began, although artificial hybridizing of South African *Erica* species started more than 200 years ago (Nelson and Oliver 2004). Many hybrid Cape heaths were in cultivation during the heyday of their popularity, before 1900.

Because so many variations in flower and foliage color and plant habit have been discovered in European heathers, the artificial breeding of these heathers may have appeared to be unnecessary. A high proportion of cultivars selected from their native European heathlands, along with others found as mutations or chance seedlings in gardens, remain in cultivation.

During the early part of the twentieth century, the prolific German nurseryman and hybridizer Georg Arends, best known for his work with the genus *Astilbe*, turned his attention toward heather hybridizing. His 1951 autobiography describes how he crossed *Erica terminalis* (then known as *E. stricta*) with *E. cinerea*. We shall never know if the resulting seedlings were, indeed, hybrids between these species, because they fell victim to a very severe winter before any of them had flowered.

Anne Parris (1976) of Usk, Wales, had the first recorded success in deliberately making a hybrid between European *Erica* species. In 1972, she tied freshly cut sprigs of flowering *Erica carnea* onto branches of *E. erigena* and enclosed both within plastic bags, tapping the bags every few days to help release pollen from the *E. carnea*. Her crude experiment was a success. The *E. erigena* produced seed, and several of the resulting seedlings proved to be the true *E.* ×*darleyensis*, a natural hybrid found in gardens but not in the wild, where the ranges of the parent species do not overlap.

Years later, Hamburg plant breeder Lothar Denkewitz put pollen from *Erica cinerea* 'Pink Ice' onto *E. tetralix* 'Tina'. His pollination efforts were not successful in producing the desired hybrid between these species. Instead, two excellent *E. tetralix* cultivars resulted—'Samtpfötchen' and 'Riko', both introduced in 1991.

Serious efforts currently are under way to improve the selection of heathers through deliberate breeding. The commercial market potential for new heather introductions in continental Europe is huge, with a number of active breeders in the Netherlands and Germany vying for market share. In Germany alone, some 90 million *Calluna* and 20 million *Erica* plants are sold annually. This commercial market potential has led European heather breeders to seek legal protection for many recent cultivar introductions.

Rights and Patents

For many gardeners, propagating their own plants rather than buying plants that someone else has propagated is one of the challenges that keep their avocation interesting. Who can resist peeping to see if anything has sprouted from the seed so carefully sown? How many rose bushes have been raised from the remnants of a cherished bouquet that were carefully tucked into the ground under empty mayonnaise jars? A gardener with the urge to propagate who lives in a populous country with a viable nursery trade sooner or later will run up against the restrictions upon propagation conferred by plant patents or plant breeders' rights.

Plant breeders' rights, also known as plant variety rights, are *intellectual property rights*, as are patents. (Plants covered by such rights will be referred to in this explanation as "patented.") They give the holder of such rights control over the propagation and sale of the protected plant, but *only in countries where it is under patent protection*. Persons who live in those countries and wish to propagate the plant must obtain the permission of the patent holder and, if required, pay a royalty for *each* plant propagated.

The process of obtaining plant breeders' rights is very expensive and time-consuming and varies from country to country. Because of the effort and expense involved in securing breeders' rights in each country, plant breeders usually patent their creations only in countries where there is a potentially large enough market to produce more in royalties than the cost of the patent process *and the cost of defending the patent*.

In the European Union, regulations concerning plant breeders' rights are proposed by the International Union for the Protection of New Varieties of Plants (UPOV) and controlled by the Community Plant Variety Office (CPVO). A breeder may apply for plant breeders' rights for a single country (national plant variety rights) or for the entire European Union (community plant variety rights). After the application fee is paid, the breeder must deliver 30 plants of the new variety to be tested to the appropriate agency within the member country. For example, in Germany, the plants should be delivered to the German Office for Plant Protection (*Bundessortenamt*) in Hanover. The trial lasts one or two years.

Of the hundreds of *Calluna* cultivars that have been proposed for plant breeders' rights at the *Bundessortenamt*, some could not be distinguished from existing cultivars and were denied protection. About one quarter of those proposed have been accepted for protection within Germany, and about half of those also have been granted common European Union protection. Of course, many cultivars are still being tested (Kramer, personal communication).

After CPVO protection is granted, it exists as long as the holder of the rights pays the required annual fees, up to 25 years. If a sport (mutation) is found on a CPVO-protected plant, the holder of the variety right is the person entitled to register the sport as a new, protected cultivar in its own right. (DNA analysis can be, and has been, used to prove the parentage of a legally contested cultivar.)

In the United States, the process of protecting plant breeders' rights is considerably different from that of the European Union. At the time UPOV was established, the United States already had in place a process to offer intellectual property rights protection for plants propagated *asexually*. This protection is granted through the United States Patent and Trademark Office, a part of the Department of Commerce. It is based upon a picture and thorough botanical description of the plant to be patented, without the actual living plant being submitted for trial. Patent protection in the United States lasts 20 years, after which the variety passes into the public domain. After the initial fees are paid, there is usually no annual fee unless very specific, complex protection is sought. A sport or mutant of a United States patented plant would not be covered by the plant patent to the parent plant but would be eligible for separate patenting itself.

"Plant breeders' rights," or "plant variety protection," in the United States refers to *sexually* reproduced lines of plants, usually open pollinated, that breed true to type from seed. This protection is offered through the United States Department of Agriculture Plant Variety Protection Office in the form of a Plant Variety Protection Act (PVPA) Certificate and should not be confused with plant patents, which in the United States are analogous to European plant variety rights for asexually propagated plants.

Although patented plants may not be asexually propagated without permission, the use of patented plants in breeding programs to produce new varieties is allowed. Only when the repeated use of the plant as a parent is needed to maintain a hybrid variety in cultivation (as it is with some annual flowers and vegetables) is such breeding prohibited without permission from the patent holder.

There is one very important way in which European plant variety rights differ from United States plant patents. European plant variety rights law specifically exempts "acts done privately for non-commercial purposes." This contrasts with the way private use is treated under United States patent law.

Unlike United States copyright law, which allows duplication of copyrighted material for *personal* use by its purchaser, there is no concept of "fair use rights" for someone who has purchased a plant patented in the United States. No cuttings (or other asexual propagations) may be made from that plant without permission, even for personal use. In other words, if you buy one patented plant, you may not use it to make the five or ten more plants of the cultivar that you want for your own garden. You must obtain permission and pay the licensing fee for each additional plant that you propagate.

Three Outstanding Modern Heather Breeders

Without a doubt, the differences in the commercial markets for heathers in Great Britain, Europe, and North America have played a role in determining the directions taken by the pre-eminent heather breeders of today: John Griffiths (England), Kurt Kramer (Germany), and David Wilson (Canada).

The German market is driven by the use of heathers as throwaway plants for grave decoration on All Saints and All Souls Day (early November) and in seasonal container gardens. Inevitably, German breeders emphasize the production of colorful heathers that will be at the peak of pot-plant attractiveness in late October. The great surge of interest in the bud-blooming *Calluna* cultivars and extra-early-flowering *Erica carnea* and *E.* ×*darleyensis* is directly traceable to this use.

For years, there has been in Great Britain a steady market for heather plants for the home garden, but it is much smaller than the German market. In North America, the great utility of heathers in the landscape has only recently begun to be recognized. In both North America and Great Britain, heathers purchased for use in permanent garden plantings compete with many other plants for the interest of gardeners. This gives British and North American breeders less commercial incentive for their breeding, but it also gives them the greater flexibility of working with whatever species catch their interest, no matter when the species bloom.

Gourds and chestnuts add autumnal touches to this dish garden of bud-blooming callunas and grasses photographed in Rostrup, Germany.

John Griffiths

John Griffiths is strictly a "hobby breeder," but the picture that calls to mind, an amateur gardener doing a bit of tinkering with plants in his spare time, is seriously misleading. He brings to his hybridizing efforts the focus, meticulousness, and precision of a trained scientist. (In real life, John is a professor of dye chemistry at the University of Leeds.) For him, heather breeding combines his love of plants with the challenge of scientific experimentation, especially when he is trying to determine if it is possible to achieve viable hybrids between particular species.

John came to his interest in heather breeding through a circuitous route. The son of a greengrocer, he spent his early years in a large city, where his exposure to nature and gardening was limited to playing in the local park or watching his father tend the family allotment. The family eventually moved to a house in the suburbs with a modest-sized garden where John played. There, his interest in plants and natural history increased. However, his father's obsession with dahlias, roses, and bedding plants—and the resulting formal appearance of the flower beds and high maintenance that such plants required—gave John a life-long aversion to them. He prefers, instead, the informality of grasses, herbaceous perennials, and shrubs.

Gardening of any kind was forgotten during John's university days, as he concentrated on getting his degree and settling into his chosen career as a chemist. Not until he was married and looking to buy his first house did he realize that he wanted a property with room for a large garden. He and his wife, Valerie, finally found a house with about ⅓ acre (0.14 ha) of relatively flat garden with, by pure chance, acidic soil.

John set about designing and planting the garden to be both informal in appearance and labor saving. He also wanted long-lived plants that could grow old with him. (The Griffiths still live in the same house after nearly 40 years.) After much reading and research, John concluded that heathers could provide everything he wanted in a plant, and they became his favorites in a garden that also includes conifers, rhododendrons, and a mixture of hardy perennials, alpines, and bulbs. Many of the original heather plants are still going strong after 30 years.

When John Griffiths decided to plant heathers in his garden, he also decided that he should learn more about them, so he joined The Heather Society. He soon became fascinated by the descriptions in the *Yearbook of The Heather Society* (1976, 1977, 1978, and 1980) of the breeding work with *Erica carnea* and *E. erigena* being carried out by Anne Parris. John wondered how many other heather hybrids were known. Research revealed that there were few, which naturally pricked his scientific curiosity. He decided to see if he could extend this number.

When John Griffiths began his hybridization experiments in early 1981, the only heathers flowering in his garden were *Erica carnea* and *E. erigena*, so he decided to repeat the *E.* ×*darleyensis* cross, using *E. carnea* 'Myretoun Ruby' as seed parent and *E. erigena* 'W. T. Rackliff' as pollen parent. He wanted to determine if *E. erigena* could be the pollen parent. Anne Parris's experiments had not defined this point. He also crossed *E. carnea* 'Myretoun Ruby' with *E. erigena* 'Irish Dusk'. Neither cross produced viable seed. He then changed tactics, the next year using *E. carnea* 'Foxhollow' pollen applied to *E. erigena* 'Irish Dusk'. By using a plant with golden foliage as the male parent, if some seedlings were golden, he'd know that the cross had been successful without having to wait for the seedlings to mature and flower. This strategy worked, with a batch of healthy seedlings as the result, some of them golden.

There was considerable variation in foliage color and form, the seedlings clearly being *Erica* ×*darleyensis*, larger and less prostrate than pure *E. carnea* at a similar stage of growth. Unfortunately, none was an improvement over known golden-foliaged hybrids such as *E.* ×*darleyensis* 'Jack H. Brummage' or 'Mary Helen', so none was selected for asexual propagation or further breeding.

Once John had proven to himself that he could remake the hybrid *Erica* ×*darleyensis*, curiosity led him to attempt numerous other *Erica* crosses. Eighteen European species of *Erica* were recognized when he began his breeding attempts. He set up a matrix of all the possible hybrids that might occur between different species: there were 153 possible crosses. Since each cross could be carried out in two directions, depending upon which species was used as the seed parent and which the pollen parent, the number of possible crosses doubled to 306. Yet in 1981, only five interspecific hybrids were known, and in no case was the direction of the cross defined.

This lack of information was a direct challenge to the scientist. Between 1981 and 1986, John Griffiths made about 360 attempts to hybridize *Erica* species. After 1986, the rate slowed considerably, and he now makes only a few crosses a year. Challenges still remain, and John expects to become more active again in hybridizing after he retires from the university.

To date, John Griffiths has attempted only about 60 interspecific crosses, but he has tried many of them several times, using different cultivars of the parent species. He was able to duplicate four of the five known hybrids (never getting around to attempting the fifth). He also produced three "new" interspecific crosses: *Erica* ×*griffithsii* (*E. manipuliflora* × *E. vagans*, named after John by David McClintock, past-president of The Heather Society) in both directions; *Erica* ×*garforthensis* (*E. manipuliflora* × *E. tetralix*); and *E. carnea* × *E. tetralix*.

After an unsuccessful first attempt at crossing *Erica manipuliflora* and *E. vagans*, on the second try John produced several seedlings, which turned out not to be new hybrids after all. An example of the hybrid had existed for years, being referred to erroneously as *E. verticillata* (the real *E. verticillata* is a Cape heath) or as the "Maxwell and Beale clone." Once John's known hybrids were available for comparison, the mystery heather was assigned to the hybrid *E.* ×*griffithsii* and given the cultivar name 'Heaven Scent'. Many of John's hybrid seedlings appear indistinguishable from 'Heaven Scent'.

Erica ×*garforthensis*, named by David McClintock after the town where it was originally bred, can produce good garden plants. One of John's seedlings from the cross, a tidy gray-foliaged plant now 3 ft. (1 m) tall, is going strong after 22 years in his garden. It has been given the cultivar name 'Craig', after John's first grandson.

The *Erica carnea* × *E. tetralix* cross was the most challenging. John made numerous unsuccessful attempts, using stored pollen from *E. carnea* because the parent species do not normally flower at the same time. Several attempts resulted in seedlings that survived for only a few weeks. Finally, 17 reasonably healthy seedlings were obtained from *E. tetralix* 'Bartinney' and nine healthy seedlings from *E. tetralix* 'Alba Mollis', both pollinated by *E. carnea* 'Foxhollow' so that successful hybrids would be identifiable through their reduced amount of chlorophyll. Unfortunately, the hybrids were weak growers with very brittle stems. All died within three years of germination, none having flowered.

In addition to hybridizing among the European species, John Griffiths has made many attempts to produce hybrids between the hardy European species and selected South African heaths, all without success. He has also crossed various cultivars of the same species in order to produce plants with special characteristics. Some of his objectives were: a white-flowering *Erica* ×*watsonii* (unsuccessful); a dark-flowered *E.* ×*watsonii* (successful, with a deep magenta-pink seedling registered in 2006 as

Erica ×*williamsii* 'Gold Button', growing in the northern California garden of Katie Griffiths (no relation to John), is a successful product of John Griffiths's hybridizing program.

John and Valerie Griffiths stand next to the planting of *Erica* ×*griffithsii* 'Valerie Griffiths' at Cherrybank Gardens, Perth, Scotland, during the Second International Heather Conference, early autumn 2004. Photo by Glennda Couch-Carlberg.

E. 'Claire Elise'); a floriferous golden-foliaged *E. cinerea* with very dark flowers (unsuccessful); and a golden-foliaged form of *E.* ×*williamsii*, beautifully realized in the dwarf cultivar 'Gold Button'.

It was never John's goal to produce heather hybrids for the trade, but several of his plants have proven worthy of introduction after being observed for three to five years (at least two flowering seasons). His early hybrids were introduced through The Heather Society, being distributed among the members. One of those was the versatile yellow-foliaged *Erica* ×*griffithsii* cultivar named after John's wife. *Erica* ×*griffithsii* 'Valerie Griffiths' has proven to be immensely popular and would earn John a place in the pantheon of heather hybridizers had he produced nothing else of merit.

Even today, John Griffiths collaborates only informally with a commercial propagator to introduce worthy new cultivars resulting from his breeding. He is an amateur in the true sense of the word: one who hybridizes for the love of hybridizing. Although *Erica* ×*griffithsii* 'Valerie Griffiths' has been his most popular cultivar, what pleases John is that he was able to demonstrate that the cross would work both ways, as it is much more difficult when *E. vagans* is used as the seed parent. The cross between *E. vagans* 'Valerie Proudley' and *E. manipuliflora* 'Aldeburgh' also produced *E.* ×*griffithsii* 'Ashlea Gold', which performs better in John's garden than does 'Valerie Griffiths'.

A surprising result of the cross between *Erica vagans* and *E. manipuliflora* was that about two-thirds of the seedlings were always tall and vigorous like *E.* ×*griffithsii* 'Heaven Scent', while the remaining seedlings were dwarf and too delicate to survive long in the garden. None were intermediate between the extremes.

John keeps returning to certain challenges, such as producing a hardy, yellow-

Erica ×*griffithsii* 'Ashlea Gold' performs better in the Griffiths' garden, shown here in late spring, than does the more widely grown *E.* ×*griffithsii* 'Valerie Griffiths'. Photo by John Griffiths.

flowering heather (using genes from the Cape heaths to get the yellow). He continues to work with the *Erica carnea* × *E. tetralix* cross in search of a garden-worthy cultivar. He thinks that a brightly colored, compact *E. cinerea* with the rock-clinging habit of the closely related but tender *E. maderensis* would be wonderful for rockery enthusiasts and that a golden-foliaged form of *E. vagans* f. *viridula* would be stunning. Let us hope that John Griffiths's persistence in pursuing these goals will be rewarded. We shall all be the beneficiaries.

Kurt Kramer

In contrast to John Griffiths, Kurt Kramer spent his early life working with plants and animals on his parents' small farm in northwestern Germany. His preference for plants led to his having his own bed in the vegetable and flower garden. Upon finishing school at age 14, he became a hothouse gardener and later a landscaper and graveyard gardener.

During Kurt's service in the German army, he took part in a training course in northern Scotland, where he saw his first white *Calluna* in nature. Later, he worked in nurseries near Oldenburg, Germany, including the famous Jeddeloh nursery.

At the time, these nurseries sold a variety of field-grown shrubs, so the quality of heathers (*Calluna vulgaris* and *Erica carnea*) was not as high as it was to become later with specialized pot-plant production. While he worked for the German nurseries, Kurt also became acquainted with heather specialist nurseries in the Netherlands, such as Zwijnenburg, that offered many cultivars.

In 1970, Kurt Kramer began to grow heathers on his parents' farmland, aiming to produce the best cultivars in better quality plants than other growers were producing.

He succeeded in this goal and was able to sell all his plants. He also got to know Hermann Westermann, who passed along to Kurt the newest English cultivars. A piece of luck was Kurt's discovery in 1973 of the very vigorous sport *Calluna vulgaris* 'Annemarie' on the late-flowering double 'Peter Sparkes'. Introduced by Kurt in 1977, its similarly late flowers and very long bloom spikes made it easy to sell during the autumn flowering period.

Kurt's early heather breeding work was between different cultivars within a species, rather than an effort to produce hybrids between species. In an attempt to get more late-flowering cultivars, Kurt made his first heather cross in 1974, between the reddest *Calluna* cultivar of that era, 'Darkness', and the latest blooming one, 'Johnson's Variety'. Unfortunately, out of the 200 resulting seedlings, no better plants emerged, so Kurt turned his attention to the winter-flowering *Erica carnea*, and, later, to *E. erigena*.

The selection of seedlings from *Erica carnea* breeding takes longer than from breeding with other species. Seedlings from the crossing of 'Myretoun Ruby' with other *E. carnea* cultivars in 1980 flowered for the first time in 1984. The best of these were cloned every year and compared. By 1990, Kurt was able to propose plant breeders' rights in Germany for the deepest red, 'Nathalie', and introduce it to market. Several other 'Myretoun Ruby' seedlings were also worthy of introduction, including the compact, dark red 'Rotes Juwel' and bright pink 'Rosalie'.

The highly successful *Erica* ×*darleyensis* 'Kramer's Rote' resulted from Kurt Kramer's 1981 crossing of *E. carnea* 'Myretoun Ruby' with *E. erigena* 'Brightness'. The improved white *E. carnea* 'Isabell' came from his 1983 crossing of 'Springwood White' with 'Snow Queen'. Several other fine white cultivars also were selected for introduction from the 113 seedlings of that cross.

Not all of Kurt Kramer's crosses were made with a particular goal in mind. As did

Erica carnea 'Rotes Juwel' is one of several superb 'Myretoun Ruby' offspring bred by Kurt Kramer.

John Griffiths, Kurt crossed some *Erica* species just to see if the cross could produce viable hybrids. Although many of the new interspecific crosses produced no results, some were pleasant surprises, especially those using *Erica spiculifolia* as a parent. The early *E. spiculifolia* hybrids were so promising that Kurt began crossing it with many other species.

The hybrid of *Erica spiculifolia* with *E. carnea* was the first big surprise. Named *E.* ×*krameri* by David McClintock in honor of Kurt, this useful hybrid has a very long blooming season (midspring to midautumn), with flowers like those of *E. spiculifolia* and orange-red spring tips.

When Kurt pollinated *Erica spiculifolia* with the South African heath *E. bergiana*, several interesting seedlings resulted, but these did not appear to be intermediate between the parents, as most hybrids are. The flowers closely resemble the *E. spiculifolia* parent, but they are produced on a much larger, more vigorous plant. Two of these seedlings with garden value have been named and registered (as 'Edewecht Belle' and 'Edewecht Blush'), and the hybrid has been named *E.* ×*gaudificans* (E. C. Nelson and Wulff 2007). The more widely distributed cultivar, 'Edewecht Blush', can bloom nearly all year when given favorable cultural conditions.

The bud-blooming *Calluna vulgaris* 'Marleen' had been shown by 1980 to be a durable, valuable cultivar, so Kurt decided to use it in an attempt to produce a white bud bloomer. In 1984, he made a cross with 'Marleen' that produced about 20 white bud-blooming seedlings. One of these became the well-known 'Melanie', Kurt's most financially successful cross, itself the parent of several other bud bloomers.

Bred by Kurt Kramer from *Erica spiculifolia* and a Cape heath, *E.* ×*gaudificans* 'Edewecht Blush' is a fine garden plant that can bloom nearly all year in moderate climates when grown in sunny locations. It is shown here in the Wulff garden in late autumn.

Other experiments were done with the tree heath *Erica arborea*, which has long been considered the connecting link between the European and the South African heaths. Kurt successfully crossed *E. arborea* with *E. baccans*, producing *E.* ×*afroeuropaea*. He also crossed *E. arborea* with *E. carnea*, making the fine *E.* ×*oldenburgensis*, whose growth habits definitely incline toward those of its tree heath parent.

By 1994, Kurt Kramer's interest in hybridizing had become so consuming that he stopped raising flowering heather plants for market in order to concentrate all his energy on breeding. Instead of making about 20 crosses a year while at the same time producing 350,000 plants for market, as he did in 1990, he now makes 40 to 50 crosses each year, with up to 5000 seedlings.

Kurt repeated the crossing of *Erica cinerea* with *E. terminalis* that Georg Arends had made in 1951, using *E. terminalis* as the seed parent. In 2000, he successfully raised seedlings from the cross. The hybrid, currently thriving in a garden in central England, has recently been described by Charles Nelson and given the name *E.* ×*arendsiana* to honor the original maker of the cross (E. C. Nelson 2007a).

Most groups of hybrid seedlings contain some unusual plants that are selected for further observation and may be used as parents in more crossings. Kurt discovered that if *Calluna* seedlings receive supplemental winter lighting, they may be induced to flower within a year of the crossing. With extra winter light, *Erica* species will flower in two to three years. This shortened maturation time speeds up the breeding work considerably, allowing several generations to be produced in the time normally required for one.

There are no established standards for heathers, so breeders set their own goals. Kurt Kramer's current work emphasis is upon the bud-blooming *Calluna* cultivars, striving for bright colors, upright habit, late development for that all-important October sales period, and resistance to fungal diseases. He is also continuing to work with *Erica carnea*, with the aim of producing earlier flowering cultivars (maybe even into October in Germany) and bright flower colors without any hint of blue, a color currently found only in *E. carnea* 'Treasure Trove'.

Despite Kurt's devoting most of his efforts toward heather breeding, he still takes the time to go out walking on the heath, ever alert for the odd heather that differs from the normal wild type. After all, it was an earlier observer of wild heather who first discovered a bud bloomer.

Kurt's innovations and intense focus upon breeding have led to his position as the acknowledged world leader in heather hybridizing, with many fine introductions, plant patents, and awards to his credit. His most longed-for goal is the same as that of John Griffiths—a hardy, yellow-flowering *Erica*. Great minds really do run in the same direction.

David Wilson

David Wilson seems to have followed a natural inclination toward heather breeding. His father, Kenneth Wilson, had a small nursery business in Yorkshire, England, where David was born. The family moved to Canada when David was young, and his father continued to work in horticulture.

When David Wilson was 19, he began an apprentice gardener program with the Vancouver Parks in British Columbia. Later, during the early 1970s, he worked in an English nursery that specialized in dwarf conifers. Because heathers were becoming popular then, the owner began growing his own heather stock, and David went with him to local nurseries to buy plants. He was able to visit some of the most prominent heather growers of the time. David also spent his spare hours cycling in the heathlands of England and Wales, where he developed a special attachment to heathers in their natural habitat.

In 1973, David returned to Vancouver, where he worked for a small nursery while making plans to start his own. Ken Wilson was then working as supervisor of the University of British Columbia Botanical Gardens, for which he was collecting heathers. Together, David and Ken built a small heather propagation bench in Ken's basement.

When David eventually was able to buy and move onto a small property in Chilliwack, British Columbia, he brought with him 4000 rooted heather cuttings as the basis for his nursery. On weekends, Ken would visit and help him with the heather growing. During the first five or six years, they planted cuttings into the ground in the spring and dug them in the fall. Eventually, they switched to year-round container growing.

After he married, David's wife, Irene, joined him in the business. Now, on a larger property not far from the original nursery, they produce about 400,000 heathers annually, mostly in 4 in. (10 cm) pots. They also grow about 40,000 potted miniature roses for spring sales.

A friend encouraged David to start collecting seedlings from under heather plants, mostly *Calluna* and *Erica*. During winters on the west coast of North America, the climate can be continuously damp. It is easy to find seed germinating under heathers—not in soil, but in the spent flowers lying near or on the ground. The old flowers are sometimes found intact, with a number of seedlings emerging from the brown husk. It is easy to transfer these onto the surface of a tray filled with a mixture of sand, peat, and perlite and cover the roots lightly. As long as the plants are not allowed to dry out or be exposed to bright sunlight until they establish, they will do well.

David collected these seedlings from the stock beds in his garden, although only the *Calluna* seeds that were germinating in the winter wet were easy to find. *Erica carnea* seeds germinate in the early part of summer, when harsh summer conditions would limit their survival. However, it was easy for David to find large numbers of *Erica* seedlings growing on the surface of potted plants in his nursery. He would sometimes sacrifice the potted plant, cut it off at soil level, and grow the seedlings undisturbed until they were large enough to transplant. He learned that golden-foliaged plants produce large numbers of colored-foliaged seedlings, and that darker-flowering plants produce darker-than-average seedlings, and so on; but he found little of lasting interest. None of the seedlings turned out to be new forms of garden merit. David realized that if he were seeking something new and worthwhile, he would need to make deliberate, carefully considered crosses.

When David Wilson began hybridizing heathers, few high quality cultivars of the wild hybrid *Erica* ×*watsonii* (*E. ciliaris* × *E. tetralix*) had been found. *Erica* ×*watsonii* 'Dawn', valued for its colorful spring tips, was the only one that the Wilson nursery sold in any quantity.

David chose to begin his breeding work with *Erica* ×*watsonii*, because the flowers of the parent species are relatively large and easy to handle and because they bloom in the fall, when he had a bit of time to spare from other nursery work. He made the cross in both directions, using the two or three cultivars in bloom in the nursery at the time. *Erica ciliaris* did not produce viable seed, so all resulting seedlings were from *E. tetralix* as the seed parent. From 500 seedlings, he kept 50 beyond the first flowering. From these, two selections with unusual flower colors and beautiful spring tips, *Erica* ×*watsonii* 'Pearly Pink' and 'Pink Pacific', were introduced to the trade and have proven worthy garden plants. A third, unnamed, cultivar still grows in David's garden.

Since 1985, when these first *Erica* ×*watsonii* crosses were made, David Wilson has worked with different cultivars within 10 species, occasionally working with 30 plants at a time, sometimes with only two or three. Some plants might have 50 fertilized flowers per plant, producing an average of 10 seeds per capsule; others might have only a few. Because they are easier to handle, David works only with small plants in 4-inch (10-cm) pots as the seed parents; but pollen may be from any source, the more pollen the better.

Seven of the ten species crossed produced seedlings, and three produced seedlings that are being used in further breeding. His other registered cultivars are grown in small numbers but without any significant impact on the trade.

When David's early breeding experiments yielded abundant seedlings, he attempted to grow on as many as possible from each cross. For example, he crossed the fine *Erica mackayana* 'Shining Light' with several different cultivars of *E. tetralix* in an attempt to produce superior cultivars of the natural hybrid *E.* ×*stuartii*. So much seed was produced, about 10,000 seeds, that David made the mistake of sowing it too thickly in the seed trays, about 2000 seeds per tray. The resulting overcrowded seedlings had to be transplanted in clumps instead of individually into seedling pots. He made cuttings of any seedling that managed to show an interesting flower and eventually planted out about 200 seedlings in the garden. After two years, they had grown into lovely flowering plants about 12 in. (30 cm) across, but not one was an improvement on existing cultivars. The whole lot was dug in. David did not repeat the cross and decided that, in the future, he would work with fewer seeds so as not to be overwhelmed by quantity.

David Wilson began to experiment with making *Erica* ×*williamsii* because it was so rare in the wild. He delighted in having more plants, and in throwing out more, than had ever been found in the wild.

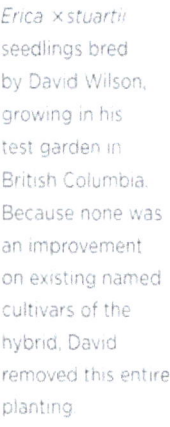

Erica ×*stuartii* seedlings bred by David Wilson, growing in his test garden in British Columbia. Because none was an improvement on existing named cultivars of the hybrid, David removed this entire planting.

At first, David used a number of pink *Erica tetralix* cultivars as seed parents but only the very brightly colored *E. vagans* 'Mrs D. F. Maxwell' as the pollen parent. He was not surprised to produce better colors in the resulting seedlings than had been found in the wild. He sent cuttings of several to Denbeigh nursery in England, where David Small selected an offspring of *E. tetralix* 'Hookstone Pink' that he felt had the strongest color and largest blooms of the lot. That cultivar was named after Ken Wilson in honor of his role in the creation in 1977 of the North American Heather Society. *Erica* ×*williamsii* 'Ken Wilson' is a fine plant with good flower color, although David Wilson feels that it should have more colorful spring tips and more handsome foliage to be really good.

David Wilson considers his greatest achievement to be the development of a white-flowering form of *Erica* ×*williamsii*. He used *E. tetralix* 'Alba Mollis' as the seed parent and *E. vagans* 'Lyonesse' as the pollen parent. It took many attempts to get enough seed, and the seedlings of this rare natural hybrid are painfully slow growing. About 50 seedlings resulted from the cross, but there was only one pure white.

This unique white seedling has been registered as *Erica* ×*williamsii* 'Phantom'. The Wilsons' nursery maintains a small stock of the cultivar, and it also is in cultivation in Britain (E. C. Nelson 2007b). David McClintock (1998b) noted this seedling (under incorrect parentage, unfortunately) in his book *Heathers of the Lizard* (Peninsula, Cornwall, England, where the wild hybrid occurs).

In recent years, David Wilson has become much more selective in his breeding efforts, no longer making crosses that are just speculative. He now keeps his most interesting seedlings for use as breeding stock. He is working only with these, mating them with some of the high quality introductions from Germany. He has also learned the importance of testing new cultivars thoroughly. David's potential introductions are now being sent to Germany to join Kurt Kramer's heather trials.

The focus of David Wilson's commercial work with heathers is pot plant production. For him, making crosses and watching the progress of his own seedlings, especially when they flower, is just pure fun—an interesting sideline but not vital to his nursery business. His current breeding "play" is focused upon *Erica carnea* and *E.* ×*darleyensis*, trying to improve foliage forms and flower size. It has already paid off with the introduction of two new *E.* ×*darleyensis* cultivars: 'Irish Treasure' and 'Goldrush'.

Erica ×*darleyensis* 'Irish Treasure' resulted from crossing the lovely salmon-colored *E. erigena* 'Irish Dusk' with the equally lovely salmon-colored *E. carnea* 'Treasure Trove'. This is one cross that achieved its

Erica ×*williamsii* 'Ken Wilson'.

Erica ×*darleyensis* 'Goldrush' is a vigorous cultivar with golden summer foliage that takes on reddish tones in winter, as shown here.

goal: a salmon-colored *E.* ×*darleyensis*. *Erica* ×*darleyensis* 'Irish Treasure' inherited from both parents their compact growth habit and their unique flower color, rare in heathers. Its very long blooming season, beginning as early as midautumn in western Oregon, makes it a treasure, indeed.

Erica ×*darleyensis* 'Goldrush' is another successful result of David's "playing" with *E. carnea* and *E. erigena*, this time using different parental cultivars in an attempt to expand the very small number of *E.* ×*darleyensis* cultivars grown for their foliage color. The lilac-pink flowers are inconsequential compared to the beautiful reddish tones that the golden foliage takes on during cold winter weather.

To achieve such results as these, David Wilson obviously has had to learn many lessons about heathers and their patterns of inheritance. We look forward to the release of his newest "toy."

The Direction of Future Heather Breeding

When comparing the work of John Griffiths, Kurt Kramer, and David Wilson, what appears most striking is the amount of overlap in both their established work and their breeding goals, which were uncoordinated until quite recently. Although David Wilson now sends his promising seedlings to Kurt Kramer for further testing and evaluation for commercial potential, all three breeders began hybridizing and worked independently for many years.

Gardeners always long for the flower that does not exist in nature: the truly black orchid, the blue rose, or the hardy red delphinium. Both John Griffiths and Kurt Kramer seek the Holy Grail of heathers, a hardy plant with yellow flowers. No European heathers have yellow flowers, but there are several very beautiful yellow *Erica* species living in the milder climate of South Africa. The breeders' challenge is to combine the cold hardiness of the European species with the color of the South African. Both breeders have tried repeatedly to mate European species with South Africans. Only Kurt has been successful so far, with the hybrids mentioned earlier in this chapter. With more than 750 species of *Erica* occurring in South Africa, the hybridizing possibilities in this direction appear to be nearly infinite.

David Wilson has repeated some of the crosses first pursued by John Griffiths. When he began crossing *Erica tetralix* with *E. manipuliflora*, David was unaware that John had already achieved this hybrid, because at that time John had not had a high enough regard for the one seedling he kept to name and introduce it. David crossed *E. tetralix* 'Melbury White' with *E. manipuliflora* 'Korčula'. Nine seedlings resulted from the crossing and were carefully planted into his garden for observation. One of compact growth, heavy flower production, and a very long blooming season was clearly worthy of introduction. Only after David Wilson took steps to introduce the cultivar did he learn that he was not the first to make the hybrid, and only then did

Erica cerinthoides is among both the showier and the hardier Cape heaths, making it a highly desirable candidate for crossing with European heather species.

David McClintock give a name to the hybrid that had been produced more than a decade earlier by John Griffiths. *Erica* ×*garforthensis* 'Tracy Wilson' remains the only commercial cultivar of the hybrid. David also attained a goal that had eluded John, the white-flowering *E.* ×*williamsii* mentioned earlier.

All three breeders continue to work with *Erica carnea*. Both Kurt and David are working with bud-blooming *Calluna* cultivars, as are a number of other breeders. The market for the bud bloomers is too lucrative to ignore, so bud bloomers probably will soon be available in every existing *Calluna* foliage and flower color and growth habit.

Now that breeders have finally turned their attention to heathers, the plants are beginning to undergo the kinds of changes that occurred years ago in other ornamentals, such as roses and daylilies, when plant breeders took notice of them. Flowers are becoming larger, flower colors are being pushed beyond the limits seen in nature (Kurt Kramer is working with a *Daboecia* breeding line of brilliant red flowers), and plants are becoming both more compact and more floriferous. While many of the old, wild-collected cultivars and their selected sports are excellent, tried-and-true garden plants, it is worth paying attention to new introductions, which are occurring at an ever-accelerating rate. Maybe soon we even shall see that elusive, yellow-flowering hardy *Erica*.

The Holy Grail of heather breeders is a hardy plant with yellow flowers, such as those of *Erica* 'Gengold', photographed at Caledon Fynbos Nursery, South Africa. 'Gengold' is a hybrid between the Cape heaths *E. nana* and *E. patersonia*, both of which are easily grown as potted plants but are cold tender.

Basic Genetics for Plant Breeders

The original heading for this section was "Simple Genetics for Plant Breeders." Genetics is not, however, a simple subject. Characteristics of most living organisms, such as people and heathers, are passed from one generation to the next through a highly complex system of inheritance whose mysteries are gradually being unravelled by scientists. This system is based upon genes, molecules that influence the building and functioning of an organism through a series of chemical reactions that produce other molecules. Each organism inherits genes that affect what kind of organism it becomes. This is a very brief introduction to genetics, with a few specifics applicable to plant hybridizing.

Most organisms inherit two copies of each gene, one from each parent. When we say "gene," we are usually referring loosely to a *pair* of genes. In genetic terminology, each gene in a pair is called an allele. In a population of organisms, many alleles (variations) may exist for a given gene; but normally, only two of these occur per individual. Usually, either allele of the pair can do the work of the gene, which is to direct a chemical reaction.

A few characteristics of living organisms are determined by the action of a single gene. Once you have identified the variations of a characteristic that different alleles of a gene, acting alone, may produce, it is fairly easy to predict whether a particular hybrid will have the desired characteristic. Usually, several genes are involved in producing a characteristic (and may be inherited separately), making the prediction of the characteristics they control difficult.

A characteristic such as flower color will vary from individual to individual, depending upon which alleles of a gene have been inherited and which allele is doing the directing. The classic nineteenth-century experiments of the Austrian monk Gregor Mendel showed that one allele of a gene can dominate another allele. In first generation crosses between unlike individuals, all the seedlings appear to be identical to the parent that is dominant for the characteristic directed by a particular gene pair. In this situation, only one allele from each gene pair is actually directing (dominant). The other is silent (recessive).

In the second generation (when two plants from the first generation are crossed with each other), if the original parental alleles were different, both parental types will show up in the offspring in the ratio of 3:1 dominant to recessive. This occurs because a quarter of the second-generation seedlings have inherited no dominant alleles, so the allele that was "silent" when paired with a dominant allele can now control the characteristic. In the language of genetics, the recessive trait will be "expressed" when a gene pair consists of identical recessive alleles.

In some cases, neither allele is dominant. Instead of one gene working while the other rests, both genes of the pair are working simultaneously. When Mendel crossed white and red petunias, he got all pink flowers. (When he bred these pink flowers together, the second generation offspring were red, pink, and white in a 1:2:1 ratio.) This kind of result is sometimes called incomplete dominance, but in the case of genes that direct the production of some pigments, there can be an *additive* effect. Full color saturation ("red") would depend upon both genes working at the same time. If one gene of the pair produces no pigment ("white") while the other produces as much as it can, the flower will be "half red" (pink).

Both of the above examples from Mendel's experiments demonstrate simple inheritance involving a single gene pair controlling a characteristic. If that gene directs the production of a particular chemical and there is no additive effect operating, only one functioning allele of a pair is necessary for the plant to make that chemical. If one of the pair does not work properly, no matter; the other can do the job.

Most characteristics, for example, skin color in humans, are controlled by multiple genes. In plants, flower color can be the result of the production of several different pigments, each of which requires more than one gene to direct the chemical manufacturing process whose end product is the pigment. Anthocyanin is a plant pigment that produces red, blue and purple colors. In many flowers, although by no means all, white is the recessive (non-dominant) color resulting from the blockage of anthocyanin production. Plants with pure white flowers will also have bright green or yellowish green leaves, because there is no anthocyanin being produced anywhere in the plant to blend with or hide other pigments, such as chlorophyll.

According to simple Mendelian genetics, since white is usually recessive, if one crosses two white flowers, all resulting seedlings should be white. If a functioning gene for the production of anthocyanin were present in the plant, there would be at least some pink in the flower. However, it turns out that more than one gene pair is needed to direct anthocyanin production. In this case, the inheritance of the characteristic is no longer "simple."

At the beginning of the twentieth century, orchid breeders were puzzled when they crossed two white-flowered *Cattleya* cultivars and came up with all purple-flowered offspring. English geneticist Charles Chamberlain Hurst postulated in 1925 that in the white cultivars, production of anthocyanin was being interrupted at different points in the chemical pathway that led to the pigment. One white orchid had a pair of non-functioning genes directing one stage of anthocyanin production, thus stopping pigment production at that stage. The other white orchid had a pair of non-functioning genes directing a different stage of production, also stopping production of anthocyanin but at a different stage.

When the different white-flowered orchids were bred with each other, each plant could contribute a functioning gene for the stage of anthocyanin production that was non-functioning in the other parent. Because the hybrid seedlings received a functioning gene for every stage of the process, they could make anthocyanin even though neither of their parents could make the pigment.

Hurst's postulate explains how *Erica* ×*darleyensis* 'Goldrush' can have lilac-pink flowers although both of its parents (*E. carnea* 'Golden Starlet' and *E. erigena* 'Brian Proudley') have white flowers. It also explains why a white-flowering hybrid can be so elusive.

Few plant breeders are interested in only one plant characteristic; and breeding for a change in one characteristic while keeping all others the same is nearly impossible. Sexual reproduction ensures that genes will be scrambled from one generation to the next. Long hidden recessive characteristics (either beneficial or detrimental) may suddenly appear, such as red hair on a baby whose relatives cannot remember anyone else in the family having had that hair color.

This is what makes hybridizing a challenge, sometimes discouraging and sometimes thrilling. It is never boring!

Guide for Novice Heather Breeders

Here are the steps John Griffiths followed to produce his first hybrid heather seedlings, with additional helpful hints from Kurt Kramer and David Wilson.

Begin by choosing plants that are in good flower. On a dry day, insert the flowering stems of the chosen male parent into the neck of a small glass vial or jar. Use a large needle to agitate the flowers until pollen is deposited on the bottom of the vial. On the plant chosen as female (seed) parent, select flowers that are about to open. Working with the aid of a magnifying glass or an optical visor (a watchmaker magnifier with 5× enlargement is helpful), force *Calluna* flowers open with a needle, or split open the flowers of those species with fused corollas, and apply pollen to the sticky tip of each stigma.

By splitting the unopened flowers of *Calluna* and *Daboecia* and the species of *Erica* that do not have exserted stigmas, it is usually possible to avoid having a potential cross polluted by self-pollination, as the pollen is not yet ripe when the stigma is receptive. *Erica cinerea* appears to be the exception to this rule. It is the most difficult species to work with. Manually split bells of *E. cinerea* often have pollen already on the stigma. Thus many seedlings from crosses using it as the seed parent turn out to be selfings, not hybrids.

When working with bud-blooming callunas—always as the seed parent, because bud bloomers do not usually have male parts—you will need to remove the sepals of the bud very carefully in order not to damage the style and stigma. This can be done with tweezers. Alternatively, by using a specialized pair of small tissue forceps that is part scalpel, you can cut and remove the cut-off parts at the same time.

Some cultivars may be used only as seed parents, others only as pollen parents. For example, John Griffiths has observed that the white-flowered *Erica tetralix* cultivars 'Alba Mollis' and 'Bartinney' do not appear to produce pollen. They must be used as seed parents.

The optimum time for making a particular cross is the most difficult to determine variable in the process. To overcome this quandary, make several attempts during the blooming season; at least one may be successful. Pollen will remain viable for several months when stored in the refrigerator, making sequential crosses possible.

For transferring pollen to a stigma, John made a pointed rod out of black plastic so that he could easily see the pollen on it. He rubbed the rod over his woolen sweater to produce a static electric charge on the rod. When he inserted the rod into the pollen, the charge would cause pollen grains to stick to the rod, which could then be wiped over the end of each stigma. He repeated the process until the end was covered in pollen. This was deliberately overdone in the hope that a good coverage of pollen would reduce the risk of any self-pollination. The hand-pollinated flower stems were then enclosed in small, fine mesh, nylon net bags secured to the stems with plastic ties, with labels noting the date the cross was made and the parents. Valerie Griffiths made the bags from old net curtains stretched over cardboard tubes and sprayed with hair lacquer, producing semi-rigid cages.

Successful fertilization of *Calluna vulgaris* is easy to recognize. The style turns brown and collapses. The sepals of fertilized flowers will be retained (except in bud bloomers, where they have been removed for access to the stigma) and look healthy even as the corolla browns and collapses. Eventually, you will be able to feel the hard swelling of the seed within the ovary.

John inspects the flowers periodically for seed development by gently squeezing them at their bases to see if the ovaries are swelling. From a cross made in March, out of 20 flowers on three stems, six showed good capsule swelling after three months. By the end of July, some of the capsules, now brown, were opening and about to shed their seeds. John collected all six flowers, opened the capsules, and shook out the seed onto a sheet of paper.

It is best to harvest pods as soon as they show signs of opening. Dry them in an envelope or on paper, because they can open quickly and valuable seed could be lost. The seed can be cleaned by rolling it off of one piece of paper and onto another, leaving the husks behind.

If for some reason seeds cannot be sown immediately after they ripen, they can be stored safely for a year or two in a cool, dry location. John sowed the 23 seeds he obtained onto a mixture of finely sieved peat, soil, and perlite in a plastic margarine carton. He then sealed the carton with clear plastic and kept it in diffuse daylight in an unheated greenhouse. The first germination became apparent in March, a year after the cross was made, after a very cold winter in which the greenhouse temperatures fell well below freezing. Eventually, John had about 15 seedlings, which he transplanted into trays in the greenhouse. A year later, in August, he planted them in the ground in an open cold frame.

Once the seedlings were large enough for planting in the ground, John inspected them regularly. He discarded any obvious selfings, or plants showing no interesting features, until only a few of the more promising seedlings remained. These he then re-spaced as appropriate for their size and grew them on for further observation. The best were eventually planted in the garden. This winnowing process, repeated with all his crosses, has allowed John to utilize his rather limited growing space to maximum advantage.

How to Register a Heather Name

Why register a heather name? If you are fortunate enough to have discovered or bred a unique heather with excellent garden qualities, consider naming it before giving away or selling any asexual propagations from your new plant. By registering the name of your new heather with The Heather Society, you greatly decrease the possibility that someone else will distribute a different heather with the same name as yours.

Registering the name will help to ensure that it is recognized internationally. What it will not do is offer the protection of intellectual property rights on the new cultivar, nor will it offer trademark protection on the name itself. Cultivar names are available for all to use, and plants should always be distributed under their proper cultivar names.

Should you register a heather name? There are a few factors to consider before registering a name for a new heather cultivar. First, is it truly a *new* cultivar? If you grew it from seed, there can be no question of this. There is such genetic diversity among the various heather species that no two seedlings will be genetically identical. If, however, you have found a small plant in your heather garden that you think may be a seedling, think again. Such small plants can originate from pieces of existing cultivars that were accidentally broken off the parent plant and have taken root. Gardens in moist climates are especially likely to have "new" heathers arise in this manner. If you grow a heather plant found this way for several years, you will be able to observe it sufficiently to know if it is different from all others in your garden.

Second, is it *stable*? If your new plant is a sport on an existing cultivar, for instance a propagation from a yellow-foliaged branch on a cultivar that normally has green foliage, have you grown the sport long enough to be certain that the sport is genetic and not a cultural anomaly? Mutations on existing cultivars should be propagated and grown for several years before registering them as new cultivars and releasing them to the public. This helps ensure that they are genetically different from the parent plant and will not revert back to it.

Third, is your new heather worthy of introduction? Is it *different* enough from similar cultivars to justify naming it? You cannot possibly see all other cultivars of the species, especially of the highly variable *Calluna vulgaris*, but you should be sure that you have visited enough gardens and nurseries (and their web sites) and read enough descriptive heather literature to understand the existing variability within the species in question. If you have not seen many of the existing cultivars of the species, send a

Some mutations (sports) are unstable, such as these white callunas reverting to mauve at the heather park in Schneverdingen, Germany.

sample (flowers and foliage) and some good photographs of your heather to someone who does have the experience to make this judgment.

Last, is your new heather a good grower and an improvement upon similar cultivars? No matter how different your heather may be from other cultivars, if it is weak and requires excessive pampering to survive, it is probably not worth bothering with. There are enough good cultivars available to fill many gardens. Only if your new plant is *healthy* and unique should you register it.

Some of these self-sown seedlings snuggled against a rock in the Wulff garden have colorful spring tips like those of *Calluna vulgaris* 'Kerstin', their probable parent, which is growing above the rock. They will be transplanted and watched for several years to see if any is worth introducing, although the garden value of 'Kerstin' would be very difficult to surpass.

The Registration Process

Registering a heather name is a simple process and can be done either on-line or by post to the International Registrar. Visit the web site of The Heather Society and click on "Naming Heathers" on the left side of home page. The page that pops up is titled "International Cultivar Registration Authority for Heathers" and contains a registration form that you can fill out on-line. There is also a list of names currently being used within the four genera under the supervision of THS as registration authority, so that you can be sure that the name you have chosen is not already taken. This web page will give you all the information you need to register your new cultivar.

There are established rules to follow in choosing a name. These rules, found in the *International Code of Nomenclature for Cultivated Plants* (*ICNCP*, Brickell et al. 2004), include:

- **New names must be unique**. In other words, they may not have been used before in that genus. (Compare your chosen name with The Heather Society's web site list of existing names.)
- **New names must not include the common (vernacular) name, in any language, of the genus to which the plant belongs**. This means that names including the words heather, heath, *Heide*, and so on, may no longer be used.
- **They may not be in Latin form**. Older cultivar names in Latin form, such as 'Alba', are allowed to remain; but no new names may be Latinized.
- **They may not be capable of confusion, whether written or spoken, with any other cultivar name within the genus**.
- **They may not include more than 30 characters**, excluding spaces and the single quotation marks that enclose every cultivar name. Shorter is better.
- **They may not be made up only of simple descriptive words**, for example, 'Tallest Purple'.
- **Your new name should not be liable to interpretation as exaggerating the merits of the cultivar** nor liable to become confusing through later introductions of cultivars with comparable attributes. For example, there is a cultivar of *Erica carnea* named 'December Red' that would be a great disappointment to Northern Hemisphere gardeners who were hoping for red winter flowers when they purchased that cultivar. Its flowers vary from pink to heliotrope as the blooming season progresses, but they could not at any time accurately be described as red nor be guaranteed to be flowering in December.
- If you are not the raiser or breeder of the new heather, **be sure that you have approval from the raiser or breeder before you name the cultivar**.
- Also, if you decide that you would like to name your new heather after a living person, **make sure that this person gives permission for your use of his or her name**.

The registration authority will probably accept your chosen name if you have followed the above guidelines. When you register your heather name, you should also, if possible, donate pressed samples of the heather—including both flowers and foliage—to several well-known herbaria, such as the one at the Royal Horticultural Society Garden, Wisley, England, or the Liberty Hyde Bailey Hortorum of Cornell University in Ithaca, New York.

These samples will serve for future comparison should there ever be any question about the identity of the cultivar or the validity of the species name of your heather. Include with the plant material a complete description and photographs of the plant that show its unique properties. These can then be preserved as the *Nomenclatural Standard*, as defined in the *ICNCP*. (Unfortunately, very few nomenclatural standards have been designated for heather cultivars, although the herbarium of David McClintock [also known as The Heather Society herbarium] contains many voucher specimens for cultivars named before 2000.)

There is one final requirement that must be met before your new heather name is secured. The name must be *published*, accompanied by a description, in a journal, book, or catalog that is *dated*. Merely using the name on plant labels or on a web site is not sufficient. The newsletters and yearbooks of the various heather societies provide excellent vehicles for establishing your new heather name through publication.

7 The Cultivated Hardy Heathers

About 1100 heather cultivars are available, although most can be obtained only from specialist nurseries. The heathers described here are a representative selection that includes old favorites and recent introductions. Many other cultivars have garden value; some are mentioned briefly or pictured elsewhere in this book. For sources of the more unusual cultivars, consult the most recent edition of *The Heather Society's Handy Guide to Heathers* by David and Anne Small, which gives brief descriptions of a large number of commercially available cultivars, with sources specific to each cultivar. The *International Register of Heather Names: Volume 1 Hardy Cultivars and European Species* (Nelson and Small 2000), with addenda produced annually by The Heather Society, lists all published hardy species, forms, and cultivar names.

The cultivar dimensions given throughout the book are typical for a plant, grown from a cutting, that is three to five years old and has been pruned annually. The first dimension specifies height; the second specifies width. Plants will, of course, grow taller and wider than the given dimensions if they are not pruned. They will also live, and continue to grow, for many more than five years if well situated.

Calluna Salisbury
heather, ling, Scotch heather

A monospecific genus of evergreen shrubs found from northernmost Norway to southern Spain and Morocco, being especially frequent on the seaboard of western Europe. The genus extends eastwards into central Siberia.

Calluna is recorded in North America and Australasia only as an introduced plant, usually a garden escape. It is otherwise absent from America, Australasia, and most of Asia. In New Zealand, where *Calluna* has become a serious threat to native plants, its sale is currently banned. The Australian government is considering whether a similar ban is warranted there.

The name *Calluna* derives from the Greek word *kalluno*, which means to sweep clean, so-called because of its frequent use in the construction of brooms. The plant is widely called ling in England and *lyng* in Scandinavia. (For the derivation of these common names, see "Heather for Shelter" in chapter 1).

Heather Bloom Chart

Soil pH	mid-winter	late winter	early spring	mid-spring	late spring	early summer	mid-summer	late summer	early autumn	mid-autumn	late autumn	early winter
Must have acidic soil, pH 5.5 to 6.5				Erica australis				Calluna vulgaris				
				Erica arborea		Erica spiculifolia						
								Erica ciliaris				
							Erica cinerea					
					Erica ×krameri							
						Erica mackayana						
						Erica ×stuartii						
					Erica tetralix							
						Erica watsonii						
	Erica ×gaudificans							Erica ×gaudificans				
Partially lime tolerant								Daboecia azorica				
								Daboecia cantabrica				
						Daboecia ×scotica						
				Erica scoparia			Erica vagans					
							Erica ×williamsii					
Lime tolerant	Erica carnea										Erica carnea	
	Erica ×darleyensis										Erica ×darleyensis	
	Erica ×oldenburgensis											
	Erica erigena										Erica erigena	
				Erica ×veitchii				Erica ×griffithsii				
								Erica manipuliflora				
	Erica lusitanica										Erica lusitanica	
				Erica umbellata			Erica terminalis					

This chart gives the average bloom seasons and soil pH preferences of most hardy European heather species and their hybrids.

Calluna vulgaris (Linnaeus) Hull

The only species in the genus, *Calluna vulgaris* has leathery, triangular leaves in opposite and closely overlapping pairs resembling scales. The species as represented in gardens is very variable, as would be expected from its very large geographic range, with habits ranging from prostrate to erect and from 2 in. (5 cm) to 40 in. (1 m) tall. The tiny leaves vary in color from dark green to bright green, gray, yellow, orange, and red, often changing color in the winter. They can be glabrous or hairy. In addition, some cultivars develop cream to red tips on their new spring growth.

The white to crimson persistent flowers may be held in panicles or, more commonly, one-sided racemes, and are normally single, with the corolla composed of four

Primary area of natural distribution of *Calluna vulgaris*.

oblong petals divided almost to their base. A calyx of four similar sepals about 1/8 in. (3 mm) long, the same size and color as the petals, overlaps the corolla.

The flowering time varies between early summer and early winter. In the wild, the first plants to flower are those at the northern end of their range (early summer). Those from the southern part of the range do not start flowering until late autumn.

Calluna vulgaris prefers either sandy or peaty acidic soils in an open, sunny situation. Those cultivars exhibiting seasonal foliage color variations will show to best advantage in such a situation. There are at least 700 cultivars, including double and bud-blooming forms. Suitable for Zone 5 (or colder with reliable snow cover).

'Alexandra' 12 × 16 in. (30 × 40 cm)
Dark green foliage serves as a foil for bicolored white-crimson buds in late summer. The buds darken with age to deep crimson but never open, thus giving a good show of color through to early winter. Ideal for window boxes as well as gardens.

'Alicia' 12 × 16 in. (30 × 40 cm)
Ideal companion for 'Alexandra'. Bright green foliage and masses of white buds that fail to open, resulting in a long "flowering" period—from late summer to early winter. Excellent, compact, upright habit.

'Allegro' 20 × 24 in. (50 × 60 cm)
Dark green foliage on a vigorous, but neat, plant. This seedling from 'Alportii Praecox', raised in the Netherlands by P. Bakhuyzen & Zonen, puts on an outstanding display of ruby flowers in late summer. Distinctive.

Calluna vulgaris 'Anette'.

'Anette' 14 × 16 in. (35 × 40 cm)
The long, upright spikes of this bud bloomer are ideal for flower arranging and hold their clear pink color well when dried. This outstanding introduction, a sport from 'Melanie', is well suited for late autumn and early winter window box or tub decoration, along with 'Alexandra' and 'Alicia'. Compact habit and medium-green foliage that does not darken in winter.

'Angela Wain' 10 × 14 in. (25 × 35 cm)
A medium-sized plant with abundant white flowers in late summer and early autumn and soft gray-green foliage. It has a semi-prostrate habit and gently curling stems. This attractive cultivar deserves to be more widely grown.

'**Annemarie**'   20 × 24 in. (50 × 60 cm)
A beautiful heather that makes a fountain of long sprays of double rose-pink flowers in late summer and early autumn on dark green foliage. The flower color is pale in mild climates, more intense in harsh climates.

'**Anthony Davis**'   18 × 20 in. (45 × 50 cm)
The gray-green foliage makes a good setting for the long, upright sprays of white flowers in late summer. An ideal plant for flower arrangers.

'**Arabella**'   12 × 16 in. (30 × 40 cm)
Brilliant, blood-red flowers in profusion in late summer make this Kurt Kramer introduction a garden standout. Open erect habit and dark green foliage.

'**Arran Gold**'   6 × 10 in. (15 × 25 cm)
Wild-collected on the Isle of Arran, Scotland, this slow-growing, prostrate cultivar bears mauve flowers in midsummer. The foliage is golden in the summer, becoming a beautiful tricolor (green, gold, and red) in the winter.

Calluna vulgaris 'Arabella'.

'**Beoley Gold**'   14 × 18 in. (35 × 45 cm)
One of the best heathers grown primarily for foliage effects, this seedling from 'Gold Haze' has bright golden foliage throughout the year on an upright plant enhanced by white flowers in late summer. Justifiably a long-time garden favorite. Beoley is a village in Worcestershire, England, near Beechwood Nursery, where the seedling was found.

'**Cairnwell**'   4 × 10 in. (10 × 25 cm)
The few lilac-pink flowers in late summer do not detract from the foliage of this unusual, wild-collected cultivar from Scotland. The golden summer leaves, tinted red in winter sun, are carried on stems that are sometimes flat, sometimes curved, or briefly ascending, producing a unique knobbed appearance resembling a miniature forest all in one plant.

'**Caleb Threlkeld**'   2 × 18 in. (5 × 45 cm)
This extremely prostrate plant, collected by Charles Nelson in County Clare, Ireland, and named for the author of the first Irish flora, bears lavender flowers in late summer on very dark green foliage. It is valuable as a ground cover, particularly for weaving around the bases of taller plants such as tree heaths. The stems self-layer readily, making this cultivar useful for stabilizing the soil on slopes.

Calluna vulgaris 'Cairnwell' has a growth habit unlike that of all other cultivars.

Calluna vulgaris 'Carmen'.

'Carmen' 12 × 22 in. (30 × 55 cm)
A vigorous plant of slightly open, spreading habit, with dark green foliage and abundant crimson flowers in late summer. Makes a wonderful color splash in the garden.

'Cottswood Gold' 12 × 18 in. (30 × 45 cm)
White flowers in late summer are produced on erect stems of bright yellow foliage that retains its color throughout the year. Spreading habit. A seedling found by P. G. Turpin in his garden at Cottswood, Surrey, England.

'County Wicklow' 10 × 14 in. (25 × 35 cm)
This is one of the best compact double-flowered cultivars, bearing masses of beautiful pale shell-pink flowers in late summer on dark green foliage. It was found at Lough Dan, County Wicklow, Ireland.

Calluna vulgaris 'Dark Beauty'.

'Dark Beauty' 10 × 14 in. (25 × 35 cm)
Dutch grower H. Hoekert discovered this outstanding cultivar as a sport on a plant of 'Darkness' that had received x-ray treatment. In late summer, the compact plant of tight, upright habit and dark green foliage bears semi-double flowers that open cerise and deepen to ruby. This cultivar has a tendency to revert to the slightly lighter shade of its parent, 'Darkness'. Such reversions should be cut out as soon as they are detected.

'Darkness' 14 × 14 in. (35 × 35 cm)
Masses of attractive, dark crimson flowers are borne on dense spikes in late summer. A plant of neat, compact, upright habit with dark green foliage, this was a seedling raised at the University of Liverpool Botanic Gardens, Ness, England, hence its name.

'Dark Star' 8 × 14 in. (20 × 35 cm)
Another sport of 'Darkness', 'Dark Star' is much showier than 'Darkness', with brighter, redder flowers, though not so red as those of 'Dark Beauty'. Semi-double, crimson flowers and dark green foliage, with a neat, compact plant habit similar to that of 'Darkness'.

'Devon' 8 × 14 in. (20 × 35 cm)
The very long blooming season, from midsummer through autumn, makes this cultivar a must for every heather garden. It bears deep pink, double flowers on dark green foliage, with new flowers being produced as the season progresses. A sport on

the old favorite 'Tib', with a similar open spreading growth habit, it was named after the elder daughter of Canadian nurseryman David Wilson, who introduced it.

'Elsie Purnell' 20 × 30 in. (50 × 75 cm)
Ideal for flower arranging, this outstanding sport from 'H. E. Beale' has very long, spreading stems of fully double lavender-pink flowers in late summer. The gray-green foliage, unfortunately, turns rather drab in winter.

'Emerald Jock' 6 × 12 in. (15 × 30 cm)
The first *Calluna* to bloom each year in the Wulff garden in Oregon, 'Emerald Jock' is in full bloom there at the summer solstice and usually finishes blooming by the time other *Calluna* cultivars begin to open their flowers. One of the Saint Kilda heathers (see chapter 9), this very hardy plant has white flowers produced in very low arching sprays. The foliage remains bright green all year.

Calluna vulgaris 'Emerald Jock'.

'Firefly' 18 × 20 in. (45 × 50 cm)
A plant of very distinctive, upright habit whose lovely terracotta summer foliage turns to a striking brick red in winter. The deep mauve flowers in late summer combine with the foliage color to create a peach effect when the plant is viewed from a distance. Outstanding.

'Fraser's Old Gold' 16 × 24 in. (40 × 60 cm)
Oregon nurseryman Stuart Fraser discovered this seedling growing under a plant of 'Robert Chapman', its probable parent. This distinctive cultivar produces lavender-colored flowers in midsummer on a plant of open erect habit. Its golden summer foliage turns intense orange-red in the winter.

Calluna vulgaris 'Fraser's Old Gold'.

'Gold Haze' 12 × 18 in. (30 × 45 cm)
White flowers in late summer on a plant of upright habit with pale yellow foliage throughout the year. An old stand-by.

'H. E. Beale' 12 × 20 in. (30 × 50 cm)
Valuable for its long, tapering racemes of double shell-pink flowers in late summer and autumn on a plant of upright habit. The dark green summer foliage turns a drab green-brown in winter. Found in the New Forest, Hampshire, England, in 1925, this deservedly popular cultivar was named after the director of the then-famous Maxwell & Beale nursery.

Plant *Calluna vulgaris* 'Heidezwerg' where it can trail over a rock.

Calluna vulgaris 'Kerstin'.

'Heidezwerg' 4 × 12 in. (10 × 30 cm) or longer
Heliotrope flowers in late summer are borne on a plant of trailing habit ideal for hanging baskets, tubs, and troughs. This heather is particularly lovely when planted where it can dangle over the face of a rock or wall.

'J. H. Hamilton' 6 × 10 in. (15 × 25 cm)
Double, deep pink flowers in late summer on a dwarf plant with dark green foliage. Ideal for the smaller garden or for growing in tubs. Wild-collected near Moughton, north of Settle, Yorkshire, England.

'Jimmy Dyce' 8 × 12 in. (20 × 30 cm)
Very long-lasting, double lilac-pink flowers in autumn. A much underrated, spreading plant with dark green foliage that turns bronze in winter, this is a very good double, more disease-resistant than most other double pink *Calluna* cultivars. Found by J. W. Dyce on Winterton Dunes, Norfolk, England.

'Joy Vanstone' 12 × 20 in. (30 × 50 cm)
A very beautiful heather, having lavender flowers in late summer, with straw-colored summer foliage that turns orange in winter. Erect habit.

'Kerstin' 12 × 18 in. (30 × 45 cm)
A very hardy, vigorous, upright plant with a unique combination of foliage colors. The colorful tips of pale yellow and red on spring new growth eventually turn to downy deep lilac-gray. Mauve flowers in late summer. Bred by Brita Johansson of Vargön, Sweden, and named after her daughter, this heather is a must-have for cold climate gardens.

'Kinlochruel' 10 × 16 in. (25 × 40 cm)
This spectacular double, pure white heather blooms in late summer on neat dark green foliage. A sport on 'County Wicklow', found by Brigadier and Mrs. E. J. Montgomery and named for their house in Argyll, Scotland.

A scattering of dried alder leaves emphasizes the dramatic white of *Calluna vulgaris* 'Kinlochruel'.

'Larissa' 12 × 18 in. (30 × 45 cm)
One of the more spectacular bud bloomers, 'Larissa' has rich, brick-red buds from August through November that gradually fade to silver. A sport on 'Alexandra', it has dark green foliage and an upright, bushy habit.

'Lime Glade' 12 × 18 in. (30 × 45 cm)
This upright grower has white flowers in late summer on lime-green foliage that is less likely to scorch than that of the more golden cultivars. The new growth in spring is almost white. Combines well with many other plants.

Calluna vulgaris 'Larissa'.

'Lyndon Proudley' 6 × 12 in. (15 × 30 cm)
This little heather shines because of its multitude of lavender flowers borne on branched inflorescences in late summer. It has a very compact growth habit and a delightful fragrance.

'Mair's Variety' 16 × 20 in. (40 × 50 cm)
A very good, vigorous plant with mid-green foliage all year. Its long, upright racemes of single white flowers in late summer are excellent for cutting.

'Marleen' 12 × 20 in. (30 × 50 cm)
A reliable plant of good garden presence, bearing white buds tipped with purple in late summer and autumn on dark green foliage. A seedling collected on Ginkel Heath near Arnhem, Netherlands, and used by Kurt Kramer to produce the famous 'Melanie'. Erect habit.

'Martha Hermann' 8 × 12 in. (20 × 30 cm)
A hardy, compact plant of American garden origin whose white summer flowers are shaded lilac. This cultivar is particularly valuable for its bright green foliage that remains a beautiful emerald green all winter.

'Melanie' 14 × 16 in. (35 × 40 cm)
A distinctive plant bred by Kurt Kramer, with long sprays of white buds that fail to open, showing white from late summer through early winter on a mid-green plant of erect habit. Ideal for flower arrangers.

Calluna vulgaris 'Melanie'.
Photo by Kurt Kramer.

'Mullion' 8 × 20 in. (20 × 50 cm)
Lilac-pink flowers are borne in late summer on a dark green plant with low, upright habit. Named after the village on the Lizard Peninsula, Cornwall, England, where it was found.

'Orange Queen' 12 × 20 in. (30 × 50 cm)
The foliage on this erect plant is gold in summer, bronze in autumn, and orange in winter. It bears lavender flowers in late summer.

'Oxshott Common' 20 × 32 in. (50 × 80 cm)
Lavender flowers in late summer and early autumn on a vigorous plant collected on Oxshott Common, Surrey, England. An impressive cultivar with downy, gray-green foliage, highly recommended.

'Peter Sparkes' 16 × 22 in. (40 × 55 cm)
Another late-blooming sport from 'H. E. Beale', valuable for its superb, long spikes of double, rose-pink flowers in early autumn. The flower color is intensified by harsh climates. Dark green foliage.

The winter foliage of *Calluna vulgaris* 'Punch's Dessert' is fiery red like that of *C. vulgaris* 'Firefly', of which it is a sport.

'Punch's Dessert' 18 × 20 in. (45 × 50 cm)
This cultivar has the same strongly upright growth habit, golden summer foliage and fiery red winter foliage as 'Firefly', of which it is a sport, with the bonus of magenta flowers in late summer and early autumn. According to the introducer, Nigel Willis (1998), Punch was a dog belonging to Kathleen Gorie, the finder of the sport. Punch accompanied her on her weekly shopping trip and was left in the car with the groceries and some of the as-yet-unnamed new heather plants while Kathleen and her husband did more shopping. The dog helped himself to the groceries and, having had his fill, started in on the heathers. "Hence was born *Calluna vulgaris* 'Punch's Dessert'!"

'Radnor' 10 × 18 in. (25 × 45 cm)
The best compact double pink. The shell-pink flowers are borne in late summer and early autumn on an erect plant with bright green foliage. Discovered near Radnor, Wales.

'Red Fred' 14 × 18 in. (35 × 45 cm)
An upright plant with brilliant red new growth that persists well into summer, gradually changing to mid-green. The tips are much redder than those of 'Fred J. Chapple', near which it was found, hence its name. Lilac-pink flowers in late summer.

'Reini' 18 × 24 in. (45 × 60 cm)

One of the best *Calluna* cultivars for spring foliage color, this seedling, found by T. Huisman of Hattem, Netherlands, and named after his wife, carries long racemes of white flowers in late summer. The downy gray foliage begins as yellow new growth in spring and early summer. A vigorous plant of very erect habit.

'Robert Chapman' 10 × 26 in. (25 × 65 cm)

A very popular plant that never fails to attract attention, with striking golden-orange foliage in summer that turns flame red in winter. Lavender flowers in late summer on a plant of rounded, compact habit.

'Roland Haagen' 6 × 14 in. (15 × 35 cm)

A plant of neat, compact habit whose golden-yellow summer foliage turns bright orange in winter, with deeper colored tips. Mauve flowers in late summer. This was collected as a sport on a wild plant in County Waterford, Ireland.

'Ruby Slinger' 14 × 16 in. (35 × 40 cm)

White flowers in late summer and early autumn on a plant of excellent upright growth habit. Beautiful yellow tips on bright green spring foliage that gradually darkens to a medium green as the season progresses.

'Serlei Aurea' 12 × 16 in. (30 × 40 cm)

A plant of stout habit that bears white flowers in late summer and early autumn. The yellow-green foliage has yellow tips in summer and autumn.

'Sesam' 12 × 18 in. (30 × 45 cm)

A very hardy plant of Swedish origin, whose name derives from the tale of "Ali Baba and the Forty Thieves." The lilac-pink flowers are carried on narrow, erect racemes. This is a popular winter color selection, the yellow summer foliage turning a beautiful orange-red from autumn into spring.

'Silver Knight' 16 × 20 in. (40 × 50 cm)

The downy gray foliage, deepening in winter to purple-gray, sets off to advantage the lavender flowers in late summer. This neat but vigorous plant, a garden classic, gets its name from the color of the foliage and because it stands straight up like a knight in armour.

'Silver Queen' 16 × 22 in. (40 × 55 cm)

Outstanding, downy, silver-gray foliage in summer that turns dark gray in winter. The broadly spreading plant has lavender flowers in late summer.

Calluna vulgaris 'Silver Queen'.

'Silver Rose' 16 × 20 in. (40 × 50 cm)
This is the best of the grays for flowers, although its blooming season is relatively short for a *Calluna*. The upright plant carries its lilac-pink flowers on delicate stems of silver-gray in late summer.

'Sir John Charrington' 8 × 16 in. (20 × 40 cm)
A plant of broad, upright habit grown for its long, graceful spikes of pale gold foliage, tipped orange in summer and scarlet in autumn. Red winter foliage gives way to bronze in the spring. Lilac-pink flowers in late summer are a bonus.

'Sirsson' 12 × 20 in. (30 × 50 cm)
This is a spectacular plant for cold open aspects, with gold foliage in summer that turns bright orange-red in winter. It has pink flowers in late summer. Don Richards found this chance seedling in his garden in Eskdale, Cumbria, England, about 1978. The odd and witty name arose because 'Sirsson' is thought to be a seedling from 'Sir John Charrington'—thus "Sir's Son."

'Sister Anne' 4 × 10 in. (10 × 25 cm)
A wonderful, semi-prostrate, compact plant for draping over rocks. Mauve flowers in late summer on downy, gray-green foliage that turns bronze-gray in winter. A poor choice for growing where the foliage will remain wet during extended spells of very cold weather. Wild-collected on the Lizard Peninsula, Cornwall, England, by Anne Moseley, who was a nurse and also was called "Sister" by her own sister.

'Spring Cream' 14 × 18 in. (35 × 45 cm)
A plant of compact habit with white flowers in late summer and early autumn on mid-green foliage. The foliage is tipped yellow in autumn and winter and cream in the spring.

'Spring Torch' 16 × 24 in. (40 × 60 cm)
This bushy plant has long set the standard for colorful spring tips. The mid-green foliage has pink and red tips in winter and spring, cream and pink tips in summer. Mauve flowers are borne in late summer and early autumn.

'Sunset' 8 × 18 in. (20 × 45 cm)
The changeable foliage of this spreading cultivar is gold in summer, red in autumn and winter, and bronzes slightly in spring. Lilac-pink flowers in late summer.

'The Pygmy' 2 × 8 in. (5 × 20 cm)
Only a few mauve flowers occasionally appear on this tight little bun of a plant grown for its form, not its bloom. One of the few cultivars that can stand some

trampling, it is a good candidate for planting in a heather lawn or between paving stones.

'Tib' 12 × 16 in. (30 × 40 cm)
A distinctive plant of rather open, spreading habit with double heliotrope flowers, 'Tib' is valuable for its very long blooming season, from early summer to early autumn. An excellent show bench plant, this cultivar frequently won awards when exhibited at English horticultural shows (C. Nelson 2005).

'Velvet Fascination' 20 × 28 in. (50 × 70 cm)
White flowers in late summer and striking silver-gray foliage make this plant of erect habit outstanding. The downy foliage, that turns gray-green in winter, just begs to be stroked.

Calluna vulgaris 'Velvet Fascination'. Photo courtesy of British Heather Growers Association.

'White Coral' 8 × 16 in. (20 × 40 cm)
Spectacular double white flowers in late summer on a compact plant with bright green foliage that stays bright green all through the winter. A sport on 'Kinlochruel'.

'White Lawn' 2 × 16 in. (5 × 40 cm)
Once described as appearing to have been run over by a steamroller, this white-flowered *Calluna* has a distinctive growth habit. The stems grow briefly upward, then make a 90-degree bend and carry their long flower spikes parallel to the ground. Fragrant, late-summer flowers and clear green foliage.

'Wickwar Flame' 20 × 26 in. (50 × 65 cm)
The first of the winter foliage heathers to change color in autumn. The golden summer foliage turns superb shades of orange, then red in exposed conditions in winter. A plant of vigorous habit with mauve flowers in late summer and early autumn. Named after a village in Gloucestershire, England. The plant bearing this name in North America may not be the same cultivar as the one in Europe. It is equally colorful but not as tall.

Calluna vulgaris 'White Lawn'.

'Winter Chocolate' 8 × 18 in. (20 × 45 cm)
Lavender flowers in late summer on a neat, upright plant with golden foliage and pink tips in summer, turning chocolate red in winter. The new spring growth is salmon-colored.

Daboecia D. Don
Saint Dabeoc's heath

A genus of small evergreen shrubs broader than high, somewhat lax in habit, with small, dark green, lance-shaped to elliptical leaves that are broader than the leaves of other heathers and usually white on the undersides. The dangling flowers are borne in slender racemes, usually with several open at a time. Pistils and stamens are contained within the inflated tubular corollas, which look like little hot-air balloons. Except for double flowers and those of the upward-facing *Daboecia cantabrica* f. *blumii*, the showy corollas, the largest among the hardy heathers, do not persist on the plants after pollination, as do *Calluna* and *Erica* flowers, but are shed while they are still fresh looking. The sepals (four per calyx) and stems are covered with short, glandular hairs that make them sticky to the touch.

Plants of this genus are found in northern Spain, northwestern Portugal, western and southwestern France, and western Ireland, with an isolated population on the Azores that is sufficiently different from the rest to be considered a separate species. The generic name was derived two centuries ago from a misspelling of the Irish vernacular name for this shrub, *fraoch Dabeoc* (E. C. Nelson 2000b).

Natural distribution of *Daboecia*.

Daboecia azorica growing wild on Pico, Azores.

Daboecia azorica Tutin & Warburg

This small evergreen shrub, averaging 8 × 16 in. (20 × 40 cm), is endemic to the Azores, where it lives at elevations between 1600 and 7000 ft. (500 and 2100 m), thriving at the higher elevations. The oval leaves are about 1/5 in. (5 mm) long and wide, dark green above and silver-gray below, becoming slightly bronzed in winter. The dangling, urn-shaped flowers, primarily crimson to ruby but varying in color to include pink and white, are borne above the foliage in early summer, making bright patches among the lichen-covered rocks. This species may be distinguished from *Daboecia cantabrica* by its shorter blooming season, generally much smaller size, the smaller leaves and flowers, and the lack of hairs on the corolla.

It prefers acidic soil and is cold hardy only to Zone 8 (with protection).

'Arthur P. Dome' 6 × 16 in. (15 × 40 cm)
Sweetly fragrant ruby flowers in late spring and early summer for only a few weeks. This cultivar is slow growing, almost prostrate in habit. It can be grown without protection in Zone 8.

Daboecia cantabrica (Hudson) K. Koch
Saint Dabeoc's heath, Irish bell heather

A hardy, evergreen subshrub found in western Ireland, western France, northern Portugal, and northern Spain, from whose Cantabrian Mountains the specific name is derived. It has glossy, dark green, elliptical to oval leaves about ½ in. (13 mm) long and ¼ in. (6 mm) wide, white on the underside.

The species has flowers ⅓ to ½ in. (9 to 13 mm) long, carried in lax racemes averaging 6 to 12 but occasionally up to 15 pendent flowers above the shiny foliage from early summer to late autumn. The flowers range in color from white through lavender to deep purple, the lighter shades predominating. Recent breeding work is beginning to produce near-red flowers.

Daboecia cantabrica can tolerate a little shade and is more resistant to drought than many other heathers. It prefers an acidic soil, although it can be grown reasonably successfully on neutral soils. It is suitable for Zone 6 (with protection) and warmer. Plants whose top growth is cut back to the ground by cold winters often produce new growth from the roots.

f. *alba* (synonym 'Alba') 16 × 28 in. (40 × 70 cm)
White flowers from early summer through autumn on a large plant with mid-green foliage. Several clones are marketed under the name 'Alba'. All are equally valuable where a tall white is wanted.

Daboecia cantabrica 'Arielle'.

'Arielle' 12 × 20 in. (30 × 50 cm)
The flowers of this heather are outstanding—large, glowing magenta with just a hint of salmon, almost fluorescent in their intensity. Of compact, yet robust, upright habit, this cultivar is the result of deliberate breeding by Kurt Kramer, Edewecht, Germany. Blooms from summer until frost.

Daboecia cantabrica 'Bicolor'.

'Bicolor' 14 × 26 in. (35 × 65 cm)
A plant to grow more for its novelty value than its impact in the garden, this unusual *Daboecia* cultivar can produce purple, pink, white, and striped flowers on the same stem. The plant has mid-green foliage and bears flowers throughout the summer and autumn.

'Celtic Star' 12 × 16 in. (30 × 40 cm)
The pale lavender corollas of this unusual cultivar contrast strikingly with its very fleshy, cerise, petaloid sepals. The plant, discovered

Daboecia cantabrica 'Celtic Star'.

on Errislannan Peninsula in County Galway, Ireland, has an open, spreading habit and dark green foliage.

'Charles Nelson' 12 × 18 in. (30 × 45 cm)
This fascinating plant produces single flowers early in the growing season, but the later ones are double and do not drop when faded. The mauve flowers are borne from early summer through early autumn on an open, sprawling plant with mid-green foliage.

'Cinderella' 12 × 14 in. (30 × 35 cm)
Handsome, dark green foliage sets off the abundant large white flowers that shade to delicate pink "mouths," beautiful at a distance and intriguing up close. 'Cinderella' is a sport from 'Bicolor', to which it may occasionally revert. Blooms from early summer until frost.

Daboecia cantabrica 'Cinderella'.

'David Moss' 12 × 18 in. (30 × 45 cm)
A free-flowering cultivar of fairly open habit, with glossy, dark green leaves, 'David Moss' produces white flowers throughout the summer.

'Hookstone Purple' 18 × 34 in. (45 × 85 cm)
A very vigorous, long-flowering plant, useful for tall ground cover. The amethyst flowers are borne from early summer until late autumn on a plant with mid-green foliage.

'Praegerae' 16 × 28 in. (40 × 70 cm)
Lovely, glowing cerise flowers from early summer to early autumn over mid-green foliage.

'Waley's Red' 14 × 20 in. (35 × 50 cm)
F. R. Waley of Sevenoaks, Kent, England, collected this beautiful cultivar in Spain. It has deep, glowing magenta flowers, with a slight trace of blue, over mid-green foliage from early summer to early autumn.

Daboecia cantabrica 'Waley's Red'.

Daboecia ×*scotica* D. C. McClintock

A hybrid of garden origin between *Daboecia azorica* and *D. cantabrica*, described from plants raised in Scotland. It has the compactness of *D. azorica* and the hardiness of *D. cantabrica*. The leaves are glossy dark green but smaller than those of *D. cantabrica*. It is ideal for ground cover in the smaller garden, flowering profusely from early summer to early autumn. Suitable for Zone 6.

'Ellen Norris' 12 × 12 in. (30 × 30 cm)
Unopened buds are a rich velvety red, becoming amethyst as the abundant flowers develop, from early summer until autumn. This recent Canadian introduction, whose name memorializes an important Vancouver Island heather grower, has a stiffly erect, compact habit and mid-green leaves.

Daboecia ×*scotica* 'Jack Drake'.

'Jack Drake' 6 × 12 in. (15 × 30 cm)
This plant has a neat, compact habit and lovely ruby flowers during the summer over dark green foliage. It is from the same batch of seedlings as 'William Buchanan' and was named after the introducer.

'Silverwells' 6 × 16 in. (15 × 40 cm)
A very floriferous plant, with white flowers over mid-green foliage from late spring until early autumn. It has a neat, compact habit and was named after the house at the nursery where it was raised.

Daboecia ×*scotica* 'Silverwells'.

'William Buchanan' 14 × 22 in. (35 × 55 cm)
Moderate-sized, deep crimson flowers over dark green foliage on a plant in bloom from late spring until a hard frost. The most vigorous of the original three seedlings given by William Buchanan to Jack Drake, its floriferousness and compact growth make this selection popular wherever it is hardy. It is probably the most widely available *Daboecia* cultivar in North America.

'William Buchanan Gold' 10 × 18 in. (25 × 45 cm)
This sport from 'William Buchanan' differs from it in being slightly less vigorous and in having red and yellow flecks on its dark green foliage throughout the year. A useful novelty.

Daboecia ×*scotica* 'William Buchanan Gold'.

Erica Linnaeus
heath, heather

A genus of about 850 species, ranging from northwestern Europe, through the Mediterranean basin and southwards through east Africa and Madagascar, to South Africa. The vast majority, about 750 species, are confined to the area south of the Limpopo River in South Africa. Most of these South African species cannot tolerate more than a few degrees of frost for short periods.

The genus does not occur naturally on the American continent, in the vast majority of Asia, or in Australasia; but a few hardy European species have become naturalized in parts of Australia, New Zealand, and North America. Some of these have become major weeds.

The name *Erica* is derived from *Ereike*, the ancient Greek name of the heath (probably referring to *Erica arborea*). The hardy species of the genus, and their hybrids, form evergreen shrubs or, in a few species, trees, usually with narrow, needle-like leaves on short petioles. The leaf edges of most *Erica* species are revolute, rolled-back so strongly toward the lower surface that they almost meet in the center, with only a narrow channel showing between them (Schumann et al. 1995). In most European species, the persistent flowers have one bract and two bracteoles, a four-lobed calyx or four free sepals, and a corolla composed of four fused petals.

The hardiness of *Erica* varies considerably from species to species, so details will be found under each species.

Erica ×*afroeuropaea* D. C. McClintock

A plant of tall, erect habit (48 × 28 in. [120 × 70 cm]) with smooth mid-green foliage that bears pale pink flowers about ⅕ in. (5 mm) long irregularly throughout the year, mainly in spring and early summer. This hybrid between *Erica arborea* var. *alpina* and *E. baccans*, the South African berry heath, was produced by Kurt Kramer of Edewecht, Germany.

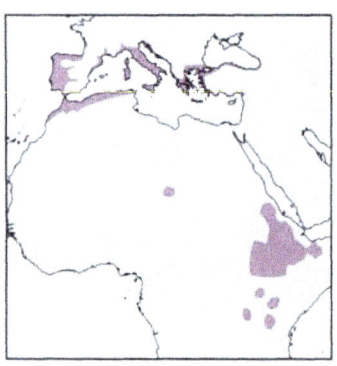

Natural distribution of *Erica arborea*.

Erica arborea Linnaeus
tree heath, briar, brier

A common species of tall, upright, evergreen shrub, typically reaching 6 to 9 ft. (2 to 3 m) tall in cultivation. In the wild, *Erica arborea* is found on Madeira and the Canary Islands; throughout the Mediterranean basin, where it is a conspicuous component of the *maquis* vegetation; and in the highlands of north and east Africa. Measurements from numerous sources, cited by David McClintock (1989b), indicate that this species really can be a tree, growing at least 65 ft. (20 m) tall, with the trunk circumference of some specimens exceeding 6½ ft. (2 m). The bright green leaves, in whorls of three or four, are needle-like, smooth and grooved beneath. Stems on young shoots have numerous branched hairs. The many small, bell-shaped, spring flowers, borne in long cylindrical or pyramidal panicles, are grayish white and honey scented.

It is not as tolerant of lime as commonly supposed, despite growing on dolomitic limestone in the wild, and is best grown in acidic soil. Young plants should be shaped in the early years to avoid untidy growth. They can be damaged by heavy snowfall but will sprout from the base again. If a plant becomes untidy, it can be cut to the ground. Regeneration will take place from the tough, woody roots that are used to make briar pipes, an interesting account of which may be found in the article by Daphne Everett in *The Yearbook of The Heather Society* 2000. "Briar" is an English corruption of the French word for heath, *bruyère*.

Hardiness varies considerably within the species, from being frost tender to surviving in Zone 7.

'Albert's Gold' 70 × 36 in. (180 × 90 cm)
A spectacular tree heath with bright gold foliage in winter that becomes golden-green in summer. The few white flowers are displayed in late spring.

var. *alpina* (synonym 'Alpina') 70 × 36 in. (180 × 90 cm)
This variety has white flowers in late spring in close cylindrical inflorescences with mid-green foliage. It was collected in the Cuenca Mountains of central Spain by Georg Dieck more than 100 years ago. As we are unsure whether he collected one clone or several, it should be considered as variety *alpina*. This requires hard pruning in its early years.

A visitor to the Saint Andrews Botanic Garden gazes up at *Erica arborea* var. *alpina*. To its right is *Hebe cupressoides*.

'Estrella Gold' 48 × 30 in. (120 × 75 cm)
Collected by R. Zwijnenburg in the Estrela Mountains, Portugal, this cultivar has many fine attributes. Branches filled with yellowish flower buds make excellent filler in early spring flower arrangements. In late spring, the buds open to small, sweet-smelling white flowers in profusion, which contrast strikingly with the bright yellow new growth. The new foliage gradually changes to lime-green as the summer progresses. A tree heath of broad, compact habit.

Erica arborea 'Estrella Gold'.

Erica ×*arendsiana* E. C. Nelson

Arends's heath

Kurt Kramer's re-creation of a hybrid between *Erica terminalis* and *E. cinerea* originally claimed (but lost, so not proven) by Georg Arends and named in his honor. It has mid-green foliage on a shrub of upright growth habit, with leaves arranged in whorls of four and the discolored young spring growth typical of hybrid heathers. A mature plant growing in central England has attained 40 × 40 in. (1 m × 1 m) in size after five years.

Although both parent species are summer flowering, the hybrid blooms sporadically between autumn and early spring. Flowers are shell-pink to lavender in color on red pedicels and may be erect or pendulous. They are borne in terminal umbels of up to four or more flowers on short, leafy axillary shoots or in a large umbel at the end of a main shoot. Several umbels are usually ranged toward the end of a main shoot, thus giving it the appearance of a raceme.

Hardy to Zone 7. There are at least two clones in cultivation, but none has been introduced commercially as yet.

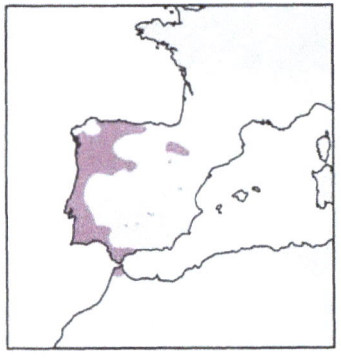

Natural distribution of *Erica australis*.

Erica australis. Photo by Kurt Kramer.

Erica australis 'Mr Robert'.

Erica australis Linnaeus

Spanish heath, southern tree heath

A tall evergreen shrub of rather open habit from western Spain, Portugal and northwestern Africa. The dark green leaves are linear, in whorls of four, and channelled beneath. The fragrant, showy purplish pink or white flowers, ¼ to ⅓ in. (6 to 9 mm) long, are cylindrical and displayed midspring to early summer.

This species requires acidic soil. Although suitable for Zone 8, it is liable to damage by wind or snow.

'Mr Robert' 70 × 36 in. (180 × 90 cm)
This cultivar, the hardiest available, has white flowers in late spring and early summer, with light green foliage. Although of loose upright habit, it is one of the finest of all heathers. The plant was collected at Algeciras, southern Spain, by Lieutenant Robert Williams of Caerhays, Cornwall, England.

'Riverslea' 48 × 34 in. (120 × 85 cm)
An outstanding tree heath with dark green foliage. The late spring to early summer flowers are lilac-pink.

Erica carnea Linnaeus
(synonyms *E. herbacea* and *E. mediterranea*)
winter heath, spring heath

This species of low evergreen shrub is native to the Alps and the Dolomites and extends locally southwards to central Italy and Greece, growing in coniferous woods and on stony slopes (Royal Horticultural Society 2006b). It has very narrow, linear leaves less than ½ in. (13 mm) long, of dark bronze green through apple green to yellow and orange, in whorls of four. The tubular flowers are usually pink in color and about ¼ to ⅓ in. (6 to 9 mm) long, with exserted anthers. The flower pedicels are about as long as the sepals. The flowers, carried on (usually) ascending synflorescences, open in late winter or early spring and may last for months.

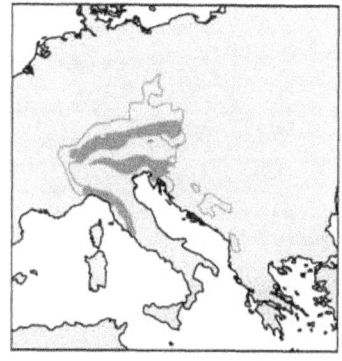

Natural distribution of *Erica carnea*.

The flowering times of *Erica carnea* cultivars vary markedly, plants in milder climates flowering as much as two months earlier than those in colder conditions. In the wild, they flower immediately after snowmelt, having set buds the summer before.

This species grows on limestone in the wild and will succeed in most garden soils. It can tolerate a little shade. All cultivars are low growing and make good ground cover. Care must be taken when pruning, because the new buds are set soon after blooming ends. It is best to prune immediately after the flowers have faded in order not to cut off the new buds and lose a year of flowers.

One of the hardiest of all heaths, it is suitable for Zone 4. Plants covered with snow for weeks on end will still bloom well once the snow has melted. Because of its alpine provenance, *Erica carnea* does not do well in hot climates.

'Adrienne Duncan' 6 × 14 in. (15 × 35 cm)
This superb plant has deep rose-pink flowers in late winter on dark green foliage tinged bronze.

Erica carnea 'Ann Sparkes'.

'Ann Sparkes' 6 × 10 in. (15 × 25 cm)
Rose-pink flowers in late winter deepen to heliotrope by early spring, providing a striking foil to the attractive foliage. The foliage of this plant, which is golden-green with bronze tips during most of the year, turns crimson in very cold weather.

'Aurea' 6 × 14 in. (15 × 35 cm)
This neat, compact plant has golden foliage with bright orange tips in spring, complemented by masses of lilac-pink flowers during late winter and early spring.

'Bell's Extra Special' 6 × 16 in. (15 × 40 cm)
The distinctive whisky-colored foliage flecked with tints of orange and gold has far greater garden impact than the heliotrope flowers that the plant bears in winter and spring. Bred by Kurt Kramer of Edewecht Germany, with 'Myretoun Ruby' as one of its parents, this neat, tidy plant was named after a famous blended whisky, and WHISKY is its trade name.

Erica carnea 'Challenger'.

'Challenger' 6 × 18 in. (15 × 45 cm)
A broad, spreading heath of Dutch origin, 'Challenger' was so named because its dark flower color challenged that of 'Myretoun Ruby'. It has dark bronze-green foliage, and the winter to spring flowers have magenta corollas with crimson sepals.

'Foxhollow' 6 × 16 in. (15 × 40 cm)
The superb yellow and bronze foliage of this cultivar deepens to orange-red in late autumn and winter. It is a vigorous, spreading plant with shell-pink flowers in late winter and early spring.

'Golden Starlet' 6 × 16 in. (15 × 40 cm)
The finest of the golden-foliaged winter heaths, 'Golden Starlet' makes a neat carpet of golden-yellow that turns greenish yellow in spring. The white flowers are borne in late winter and early spring.

'Isabell' 6 × 14 in. (15 × 35 cm)
Out of Kurt Kramer's breeding program using 'Springwood White' as a parent, 'Isabell' displays attractive long spikes of white flowers in late winter and early spring held erect on bright green foliage. Excellent.

'Lake Garda' 6 × 16 in. (15 × 40 cm)
Wild-collected on a hill above Lake Garda by David McClintock, this vigorous,

spreading, dark green plant bears beautiful, pale pink flowers in late winter and spring. Worth seeking.

'Loughrigg' 6 × 20 in. (15 × 50 cm)
A vigorous groundcover, this outstanding plant has rose-pink flowers in late winter and early spring on dark green foliage tinged with bronze.

'March Seedling' 6 × 20 in. (15 × 50 cm)
An excellent, free-flowering plant with grayish pink spring flowers on mid-green foliage.

'Myretoun Ruby' 6 × 18 in. (15 × 45 cm)
The outstanding deep magenta flowers in late winter and early spring, on dark green foliage, make this old favorite an excellent companion to any of the white cultivars.

'Nathalie' 6 × 16 in. (15 × 40 cm)
Superb purple flowers in winter and early spring, against a background of dark green foliage. This neat compact plant, an offspring of 'Myretoun Ruby', has the deepest flower color of all the *Erica carnea* cultivars.

Despite being shaded by a house and two evergreen shrubs, so that it receives no more than an hour or two of direct sunlight each day, this plant of *Erica carnea* 'Myretoun Ruby' growing in northern England manages to survive and even flower. Note how it is clambering into the spruce on the left in its search for light.

Erica carnea 'Nathalie'.

Erica carnea 'Pink Spangles'.

'Pink Spangles' 6 × 18 in. (15 × 45 cm)
Conspicuously lighter sepals held well away from the corolla on the large, shell-pink flowers make this cultivar easy to recognize. An excellent plant with mid-green foliage, flowering in late winter and early spring.

'Praecox Rubra' 6 × 16 in. (15 × 40 cm)

A vigorous, semi-prostrate plant with dark green foliage sometimes tinged brown. Rose-pink flowers in late winter and early spring.

'R. B. Cooke' 6 × 18 in. (15 × 45 cm)

A distinctive plant with masses of bluish pink flowers in winter and early spring on mid-green foliage. It was named after horticulturist Randle Blain Cooke (1881–1973) from Northumberland, England.

'Rosalie' 6 × 14 in. (15 × 35 cm)

Low, upright flowering stems make this cultivar suitable for growing in pots. Bright pink flowers in winter and early spring over bronze-green foliage. Bred by Kurt Kramer, with 'Myretoun Ruby' as one of the parents.

'Rosantha' 6 × 14 in. (15 × 35 cm)

Very attractive rose-pink flowers with little hint of blue, flowering in spring on a plant with mid-green foliage. Another fine 'Myretoun Ruby' seedling from Kurt Kramer.

'Rotes Juwel' 6 × 12 in. (15 × 30 cm)

Yet another 'Myretoun Ruby' offspring from Kurt Kramer, this has the reddest flowers of all the *Erica carnea* cultivars, produced between late fall and spring on a slow-growing plant with dark green foliage. Excellent for use where a winter bloomer with compact growth habit is needed.

'Schneekuppe' 6 × 12 in. (15 × 30 cm)

The very compact growth habit makes this cultivar an improvement over its 'Springwood White' parent. Another product of Kurt Kramer's breeding, 'Schneekuppe' has white flowers in winter and early spring and bright green foliage. It is considered to be the best white cultivar when it reaches five years of age.

Erica carnea 'Schneekuppe'.

Erica carnea 'Treasure Trove' has no blue tones in its pink flowers.

'Springwood White' 6 × 16 in. (15 × 40 cm)
For sheer ability to cover the ground, this cultivar is hard to beat. The vigorous trailing habit makes it ideal for tubs and hanging baskets, and because its stems root where they touch the ground, this cultivar has the potential to increase indefinitely. Masses of white flowers in winter and early spring, and beautiful bright green foliage.

'Treasure Trove' 6 × 16 in. (15 × 40 cm)
The salmon-pink flowers on mid-green foliage in late winter and spring are a very distinctive color break in *Erica carnea*. This is a very compact, slow-growing cultivar.

'Vivellii' 6 × 14 in. (15 × 35 cm)
The dark green foliage with a bronze hue makes this cultivar easy to recognize. In winter and spring, the flowers open heliotrope and darken to magenta as the season progresses. 'Vivellii' was collected in the Engadine Alps, Switzerland, in 1906 by Paul Theoboldt and named after his employer, Adolf Vivell of Olten, Switzerland. Although this plant is still popular, the similar 'Adrienne Duncan' is more reliable.

'Westwood Yellow' 6 × 12 in. (15 × 30 cm)
An excellent, compact plant grown for its foliage, which remains yellow throughout the year. A few shell-pink flowers in late winter and early spring.

'Wintersonne' 6 × 14 in. (15 × 35 cm)
This distinctive plant produces attractively colored, reddish buds in late summer and autumn on bronze foliage that deepens to nearly black in winter. The buds open in late winter to lilac-pink flowers that deepen to magenta in early spring. Kramer introduction.

Erica ciliaris Linnaeus
Dorset heath, ciliated heath

This is a low evergreen shrub of lax, sprawling habit. Its ovate to lanceolate leaves, $1/10$ to $1/4$ in. (2.5 to 6 mm) long and borne in whorls of three, are gray-green or dark green above and white beneath, with gland-tipped hairs. The very attractive, interestingly shaped flowers are borne on terminal, one-sided racemes typically 4 in. (10 cm) long. The corollas, usually lilac-pink and sharply contracted at the mouth, are about $1/3$ to $1/2$ in. (9 to 13 mm) long, with included anthers that do not have spurs. This species has a long blooming season, from midsummer to mid- or even late autumn, and the spent flowers turn an attractive russet brown during the winter.

Erica ciliaris is native to the coastal fringe of western Europe. It ranges from southern Brittany through western France into northern Spain, Portugal, and thence into

Natural distribution of *Erica ciliaris*

The spent flowers of *Erica ciliaris* turn a handsome russet color that adds to winter garden interest.

Erica ciliaris 'Aurea' photographed in midautumn.

southern Spain, crossing into northwestern Africa. In Britain, it is found only in parts of the southwest, in Cornwall, Devon, Somerset, and Dorset. There is also an enigmatic population in western Ireland that may have been deliberately planted. The species occurs naturally in moist, acidic soils in sunny locations. Studies in Brittany of heathland recovery after trampling (Gallet and Roze 2002) affirm this preference for moisture. *Erica ciliaris* is more resilient to summer trampling under wet than under dry conditions. (The reverse is true of *Erica cinerea*.)

This species is suitable for Zone 7. Some cultivars will be killed outright by sudden or prolonged freezes, but others may recover from the roots when freezing kills the foliage. Annual pruning is required to keep the plants shapely.

Erica ciliaris 'Corfe Castle'. Photo by Kurt Kramer.

'Aurea' 10 × 20 in. (25 × 50 cm)

The bright lilac-pink flowers, produced in late summer and autumn, contrast well with the yellow foliage, which deepens to coral in winter and spring. This striking plant needs light shade to prevent sunburn in regions with hot summers. It occasionally throws a stem with green foliage, which should be removed as soon as it is detected.

'Corfe Castle' 8 × 14 in. (20 × 35 cm)

Large, bright rose-pink flowers with no trace of blue are carried on long spikes during late summer on mid-green foliage. A striking cultivar, it was found near Corfe Castle, Dorset, England.

'David McClintock' 12 × 18 in. (30 × 45 cm)
Very distinctive bicolored flowers, white at the base with pale purple tips, in late summer and early autumn on gray-green foliage. This plant has a loose open habit. David McClintock found it at Carnac, Brittany, France, in 1962.

'Mrs C. H. Gill' 8 × 18 in. (20 × 45 cm)
A pretty plant collected near Wareham, Dorset, England, with large crimson bells from midsummer through early autumn. Dark green foliage.

'Stoborough' 10 × 18 in. (25 × 45 cm)
The best white cultivar of *Erica ciliaris*, this plant was found near Stoborough, Dorset, England. The flowers in summer and early autumn are carried on a plant of erect habit with mid-green foliage.

Erica ciliaris 'David McClintock'.

Erica cinerea Linnaeus
bell heather, Scotch heath

An evergreen, compact but usually lax-growing shrub. Typically about 12 in. (30 cm) tall in cultivation, although ranging from 4 in. (10 cm) to 30 in. (75 cm) tall in the wild, this species is found in western Europe from southwestern Norway to southern Portugal and northwestern Italy and also in Algeria. It has naturalized on Nantucket Island, Massachusetts, United States. It is a plant of dry heaths and rocky ground.

Erica cinerea var. *maderensis*, confined to Madeira and not reliably hardy, is recognized by some authorities as sufficiently distinct to be considered a separate species, *Erica maderensis* (Benth.) Bornmueller.

Erica cinerea leaves, 1/5 to 1/3 in. (5 to 9 mm) long, are usually dark, bottle green and linear, with strongly curled-back margins. They are distinctively arranged, as Metheny (1991) described them, "in complicated bundles on short side shoots from the stems below" the synflorescences. The

A drift of *Erica cinerea* 'Atropurpurea' enlivens a steep slope at Bloom River Gardens in Walterville, Oregon.

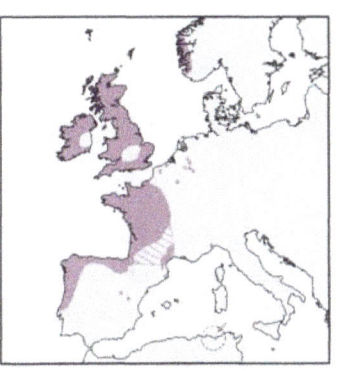

Natural distribution of *Erica cinerea*.

bell-shaped flowers, ⅙ to ⅓ in. (4 to 9 mm) long, can be white, pink, or purple and are borne in profusion from early summer to early autumn. The anthers are included within the corolla, but the stigma is exserted a little.

This is the showiest of the hardy heathers, with clear, bright flower colors of great garden impact. It is also the most demanding in its cultural requirements, being difficult to establish in the garden, although performing well once established. In addition to needing an open, sunny position, it must have acidic, moisture retentive soil. Young plants, in particular, should never be allowed to go dry. At the same time, the species resents overwatering and requires very sharp drainage. Suitable for Zone 7 and warmer, or Zone 6 with protection.

'Alba Minor' 8 × 22 in. (20 × 55 cm)
White flowers in summer and early autumn, with bright green foliage. This cultivar, more than 100 years old, is still one of the best.

'C. D. Eason' 10 × 20 in. (25 × 50 cm)
Bright magenta flowers in mid- to late summer glow against the backdrop of dark green foliage. Wild-collected in 1929 near Broadstone, Dorset, England, by Australian Charles Douglas Eason. Highly recommended.

'Celebration' 8 × 16 in. (20 × 40 cm)
Outstanding for its foliage, consistently the brightest yellow of any heather cultivar, *Erica cinerea* 'Celebration' makes a pool of "sunlight" on the ground at any time of year. Intensely golden in summer and autumn, it turns slightly more lime-green in winter. The few white summer flowers do not spoil the golden effect. This vigorous cultivar appears to tolerate cold temperatures better than do many others of the species.

'Cevennes' 12 × 26 in. (30 × 65 cm)
A very good ground cover of compact, spreading habit. The mauve flowers in late summer and early autumn are borne on mid-green foliage.

'C. G. Best' 12 × 28 in. (30 × 70 cm)
This graceful plant was found by C. G. Best, an employee of the Maxwell & Beale nursery, on Corfe Mullen Heath, Dorset, England. It has rose-pink flowers in summer and early autumn, and mid-green foliage.

'Cindy' 8 × 20 in. (20 × 50 cm)
Purple flowers in summer and autumn, with dark green foliage. Found in Cornwall, England, by Mr. and Mrs. John F. Letts, it was introduced by them and named after one of their dogs.

'Coccinea' 8 × 16 in. (20 × 40 cm)
One of the earliest *Erica cinerea* cultivars to flower, its bright ruby flowers are produced from early summer until early autumn. The abundant flowers are sweetly fragrant, capable of scenting the entire garden during favorable weather conditions.

'Eden Valley' 8 × 20 in. (20 × 50 cm)
A lovely plant with a tidy, prostrate growth habit. The bicolored flowers, midsummer through midautumn, are lavender at the tip, shading to white at the base. Medium-green foliage. Wild-collected near Saint Ives, Cornwall, England, in 1926, on a bank that was later destroyed "to make a cart track" (Small and Small 2001).

'Fiddler's Gold' 10 × 18 in. (25 × 45 cm)
Selected for its yellow-gold foliage, with red tints that deepen through the winter and are at their brightest in spring. The summer flowers are lilac-pink. The name is derived from the garden where it was found, Fiddlestone.

Grown for its fiery red winter foliage, *Erica cinerea* 'Golden Drop' has considerable orange coloring even in summer.

'Golden Drop' 8 × 18 in. (20 × 45 cm)
Sparse mauve flowers in summer. The golden summer foliage turns deep red in winter and is bright orange during spring and autumn. This very popular cultivar was found in Dorset, England, by C. D. Eason of the Maxwell & Beale nursery and named by him because its color reminded him of his favorite jam, made from the Australian plum of the same name.

'Golden Hue' 14 × 28 in. (35 × 70 cm)
The unusually erect growth and pale yellow foliage of this bell heather, tipped orange in winter, makes it easily identifiable from across the garden. Amethyst flowers in summer and early autumn make a pleasing contrast to the foliage color.

'Golden Sport' 6 × 12 in. (15 × 30 cm)
The green-gold foliage of this low-growing cultivar is always tinged with a bit of red, which intensifies considerably during the winter but never as much as that of 'Fiddler's Gold' or 'Golden Drop'. Amethyst flowers from summer into autumn.

'Iberian Beauty' 4 × 18 in. (10 × 45 cm)
A creeper with mid-green foliage and very deep mauve flowers from midsummer to early autumn, this cultivar is useful for ground cover, edgings, and weaving among taller plants.

Erica cinerea 'Golden Hue', winter.

Erica cinerea 'Lime Soda'.

Erica cinerea 'Pentreath'.

'Knap Hill Pink' 12 × 24 in. (30 × 60 cm)
A very long blooming season, from early summer to early autumn, and abundant magenta flowers over dark green foliage make this upright grower a garden standout. It was introduced by Waterer's Knap Hill nursery in Surrey, England.

'Lime Soda' 12 × 22 in. (30 × 55 cm)
Unlike many heather cultivars selected for their foliage color, 'Lime Soda' also has abundant flowers. In summer and early autumn, the soft lavender flowers nearly hide the beautiful lime-green foliage.

'Pentreath' 12 × 22 in. (30 × 55 cm)
The very dark, nearly beetroot red flowers look superb against a light background but disappear against the surrounding soil or dark brown mulch when the plants are young. Collected near the village of Pentreath, Cornwall, England, in 1951, this lovely heather has dark green foliage.

Erica cinerea 'Velvet Night'.

'Pink Ice' 6 × 14 in. (15 × 35 cm)
Another good cultivar for ground cover, 'Pink Ice' has a dwarf bushy habit and dark green foliage. The rose-pink flowers are borne from midsummer until late autumn.

'Stephen Davis' 8 × 18 in. (20 × 45cm)
Intense magenta flowers are produced in profusion throughout the summer on an erect-growing, compact plant with dark green foliage. Wild-collected on Marley Common, Surrey, England, by P. G. Davis.

'Velvet Night' 10 × 22 in. (25 × 55 cm)
A striking combination of beetroot flowers and dark green foliage on a summer-flowering plant of upright habit. The darkest *Erica cinerea* cultivar, the flowers appearing almost black.

'Windlebrooke' 6 × 18 in. (15 × 45 cm)
The golden-yellow foliage in summer turns orange-red in winter. Mauve flowers in summer and early autumn. Found on the Sunningdale Golf Course, Surrey, England, by John F. Letts and named after a brook near his house.

Erica ×darleyensis Bean
Darley Dale heath

A chance hybrid between *Erica carnea* and *E. erigena* was found in a nursery in Darley Dale, Derbyshire, England, and had been introduced by 1900. (Clones of the original plant now carry the cultivar name 'Darley Dale'). These hybrids are typically bushy evergreen shrubs about 24 × 36 in. (60 × 90 cm) and are among the easiest heathers to grow. They are suitable for most soils and are particularly good at smothering weeds.

Erica ×darleyensis 'Arthur Johnson'.

The flowers are similar to those of *Erica carnea* but are usually slightly smaller. Most of these hybrids are sterile and have a long flowering period in winter and spring. An added bonus is the highly colored new spring growth on some cultivars.

Erica ×darleyensis is one of the few heathers tolerant of high summer humidity, and it is winter hardy to Zone 7 (colder with winter protection).

'Arthur Johnson' 24 × 30 in. (60 × 75 cm)
This plant has long stems of slightly scented pink flowers that deepen with age through its late winter and spring blooming season. A tall plant with mid-green foliage tipped cream in spring. Found in his garden at Conwy, North Wales, by A. T. Johnson.

'Furzey' 14 × 24 in. (35 × 60 cm)
An outstanding plant with deep lilac-pink flowers in late winter and spring. The dark green foliage has cream, pink, and red new growth in spring. Found as a seedling at Furzey Gardens, Hampshire, England.

'George Rendall' 12 × 26 in. (30 × 65 cm)
The flowers open pink, darkening to heliotrope through the flowering season of early winter to late spring. The mid-green foliage has red spring tips that fade to pink and cream. The cultivar was named after William George Rendall Eason, son of C. D. Eason.

Erica ×darleyensis 'Furzey'.

'Ghost Hills' 16 × 32 in. (40 × 80 cm)
An attractive plant with pink flowers opening in late autumn and deepening to

heliotrope through the winter and spring blooming season. Cream spring new growth matures to light green foliage. Found and introduced by J. H. Brummage.

'Goldrush'   24 × 36 in. (60 × 90 cm)
Beautiful golden foliage turning deep rust in winter makes this recent introduction from Canadian hybridizer David Wilson a valuable addition to the limited foliage palette of the *Erica* ×*darleyensis* cultivars. Its winter foliage is distinctly darker than that of 'Mary Helen'. Vigorous growth and lilac-pink flowers from early winter until spring.

'Irish Treasure'   14 × 30 in. (35 × 75 cm)
Another valuable new introduction from David Wilson. Salmon-pink flowers inherited from its parents *Erica erigena* 'Irish Dusk' and *E. carnea* 'Treasure Trove', on a compact plant in bloom from autumn through spring. During cold weather, the sepals darken to a deeper tone than the flowers, and the medium green foliage becomes reddish bronze. Much slower growing and less cold hardy than *E.* ×*darleyensis* 'Goldrush'.

'Jack H. Brummage'   12 × 24 in. (30 × 60 cm)
A neat, compact plant with bright yellow foliage in summer that turns to deep gold-tinged rust in winter. Heliotrope flowers from midwinter through spring. Found by Jack Brummage, nurseryman, of Taverham, Norfolk, England, as a seedling growing near *Erica carnea* 'Aurea'.

Erica ×*darleyensis* 'Irish Treasure', photographed in late autumn.

'Jenny Porter'   18 × 24 in. (45 × 60 cm)
Pale lilac flowers in late winter and spring are followed by pronounced cream young growth on mid-green foliage. It was one of a series of hybrids produced by J. W. Porter and was named after one of his sisters.

Erica ×*darleyensis* 'J. W. Porter'.

'J. W. Porter'   10 × 16 in. (25 × 40 cm)
Heliotrope flowers midwinter through spring. The cream and red new foliage in spring gradually changes to dark green. This was a seedling raised by James Walker Porter, Carryduff, County Down, Northern Ireland, selected and named by his wife, Eileen, and introduced by John F. Letts after Porter's death.

'Kramer's Rote'   14 × 24 in. (35 × 60 cm)
Perhaps the most outstanding of all heathers, with magenta flowers displayed all winter and spring (sometimes opening as early as midautumn) on dark bronze-green foliage. Bred by Kurt Kramer, Edewecht, Germany.

'Mary Helen'   10 × 18 in. (25 × 45 cm)

The golden-yellow summer foliage on this popular plant bears bronze tints in winter and displays its pink flowers in spring. It was found by Peter Foley as a seedling at his Holden Clough Nursery in Lancashire, England, and named after his daughter.

'Silberschmelze'   14 × 32 in. (35 × 80 cm)

This cultivar has ashen-white flowers in winter and spring, with mid-green foliage. The cream spring tips are not pronounced. It is a sport on 'Darley Dale' found by Georg Arends of Wuppertal, Germany, and introduced by him in 1937. The name means molten silver.

Erica ×*darleyensis* 'Mary Helen'.

'White Perfection'   16 × 28 in. (40 × 70 cm)

An outstanding, vigorous plant with an erect habit and long-lasting spikes of pure white flowers from early winter through spring. The yellow new growth in spring matures to bright green foliage. A sport on 'Silberschmelze'.

Erica erigena R. Ross
(synonyms *E. hibernica* and *E. mediterranea*)

Irish heath, Mediterranean heath

This erect-stemmed, evergreen shrub inhabits widely separated areas of southwestern France, Spain, and Portugal. It has also become established in western Ireland, where it appears—as determined by analysis of pollen grains preserved in peat deposits—to have existed since no earlier than the fifteenth century, possibly arising from seed inadvertently introduced from Spain during trade or religious pilgrimages (Foss and Doyle 1988). Growing up to about 6 ft. (2 m) tall and considered a "tree heath" by some because of its height and its habit of growing taller than broad, *Erica erigena* is found in moist situations, often growing along stream banks or by lakesides and as a colonizer of disturbed ground.

Erica ×*darleyensis* 'White Perfection'.

Erica erigena has dark green, linear leaves. Its flowers, produced in abundance during the winter and spring, are pale pink, honey-scented bells. The flowers are smaller than the flowers of many *E. carnea* cultivars and usually have flared corolla lobes. The anthers of fully open flowers are not exserted quite as far as are those of *E. carnea*.

Erica erigena can be grown in most soils, and its tight, upright growth makes it very suitable for low hedging or as an "architectural" feature where heavy snowfall is not expected. It is particularly valued as a pollen source by beekeepers (as are the other heathers with winter and early spring flowers,

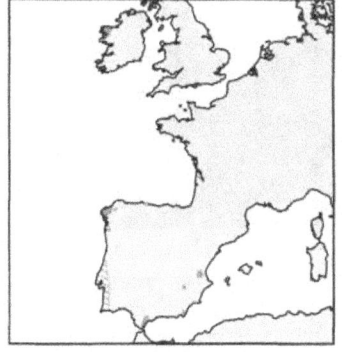

Natural distribution of *Erica erigena*.

Erica erigena 'Brian Proudley'.

E. carnea and *E.* ×*darleyensis*) because it is in flower when few other plants are blooming.

Hardy to Zone 7.

'Brian Proudley'   36 × 16 in. (90 × 40 cm)
White flowers carried in long racemes are freely borne from late autumn to late spring on a vigorous, erect plant with bright green foliage. It is possibly a seedling raised by J. W. Porter that was introduced by Brian Proudley as *Erica erigena* f. *alba*. In 1978, A. W. Jones named this outstanding cultivar after Proudley in recognition of his work with heathers.

'Golden Lady'   30 × 22 in. (75 × 55 cm)
A slow-growing, compact cultivar with outstanding golden foliage throughout the year. White flowers in late spring. Sport on 'W. T. Rackliff'.

'Irish Dusk'   24 × 18 in. (60 × 45 cm)
One of the short cultivars of the species, this very attractive plant has salmon-colored flowers from early winter until late spring. Distinctive dark, gray-green foliage and a bushy, upright habit.

'Maxima'   60 × 36 in. (150 × 90 cm)
A tree heath with dark green foliage and abundant heliotrope spring flowers. The plumply erect habit makes it useful near the back of the garden as a screening plant,

Erica erigena 'Golden Lady'.

Erica erigena 'Irish Dusk'.

Erica erigena 'Maxima'.

or within the garden as a specimen. In the United States, this cultivar sometimes masquerades as 'Superba', which is narrower and has lighter pink flowers.

'Superba' 60 × 20 in. (150 × 50 cm)
This cultivar has shell-pink flowers, deepening with age, in spring and early summer. A plant ideal for producing a flowering hedge with dark green foliage. When grown in this fashion, the hedge should be trimmed immediately after flowering.

'W. T. Rackliff' 30 × 22 in. (75 × 55 cm)
A slow-growing cultivar that makes an attractive, rich green, rounded bush completely covered with white flowers in spring.

Erica erigena 'W. T. Rackliff'.

Erica ×*garforthensis* D. C. McClintock
Garforth heath

A deliberate hybrid between *Erica tetralix* and *E. manipuliflora*, first produced by John Griffiths (Garforth, Leeds, England) in 1983 and subsequently by David Wilson, Chilliwack, British Columbia, Canada. These plants can reach 32 in. (80 cm) tall, with fragrant flowers in dense, branched racemes. Hardy to at least Zone 7, possibly to Zone 6.

'Tracy Wilson' 10 × 18 in. (25 × 45 cm)
Pale pink, slightly fragrant flowers are borne in compact, cylindrical racemes in summer and autumn on a plant of compact, spreading habit. In winter, the orange-tan spent flowers contrast attractively with the light green foliage. Creamy yellow spring tips. Bred by David Wilson and introduced by him in 1999, 'Tracy Wilson' is the only cultivar of the hybrid in commercial production.

Erica ×*garforthensis* 'Tracy Wilson'.

The spent flowers of *Erica* ×*garforthensis* 'Tracy Wilson' contrast with its light green foliage to add winter garden interest.

Erica ×gaudificans E. C. Nelson & E. M. T. Wulff
Edewecht heath

Deliberate hybrid between the European *Erica spiculifolia* and the South African *E. bergiana*, made by Kurt Kramer of Edewecht, Germany. The flowers, borne in clusters on the tips of both main and axillary shoots, strongly resemble those of *E. spiculifolia*, tiny and bell-shaped, with conspicuous, exserted pistils. The stamens are malformed, with the filaments often fused, although the malformations are not consistent from flower to flower. The plants are much larger and more vigorous than those of *E. spiculifolia*, and they have a very long blooming season, from midspring through late autumn, or even longer. There are two clones in cultivation.

'Edewecht Blush' 30 × 30 in. (75 × 75 cm) or larger

The very pale pink flowers (actually bright red immature anthers enclosed within a nearly colorless corolla) can be produced all year when plants are located in full sun situations in mild climates, but it is for the beautiful, light green, feathery foliage that this plant should be grown. Hardy to Zone 7.

Erica ×griffithsii D. C. McClintock
Griffiths's heath

A hybrid between *Erica manipuliflora* and *Erica vagans*. These lime-tolerant hybrids have the vigor of *E. manipuliflora* and the compactness and relatively early flowering of *E. vagans*. Some outstanding cultivars have been produced by deliberate breeding, but some are of chance origin. The hybrid is named after John Griffiths, the first person known to have made the deliberate cross.

Erica ×griffithsii is similar in height to *E. manipuliflora* but slightly more hardy, suitable for Zone 6. These plants make excellent low, decorative hedges that can be kept at any height. This is one of the few heathers that can be cut to the ground and will regenerate from the rootstock, provided that it receives this drastic treatment only once.

Erica ×griffithsii 'Jacqueline'.

'Heaven Scent' 40 × 24 in. (100 × 60 cm)

This plant has strongly scented, lilac-pink flowers in long sprays from midsummer to late autumn. Dark gray-green foliage on a plant of vigorous upright habit. This cultivar was sent in 1949 from the Royal Botanic Gardens, Kew, England, to the Maxwell & Beale nursery, which introduced it under the misapplied name *Erica verticillata* in 1951 (Jones 1997). It was not identified as a hybrid until John Griffiths produced similar plants definitely known to be hybrids.

'Jacqueline' 40 × 24 in. (100 × 60 cm)

A beautiful plant with scented, cerise flowers in long sprays during summer and autumn. Dark gray-green foliage and a vigorous upright habit. This cultivar was a sport on 'Heaven Scent', to which it sometimes reverts. Reversions should be cut out as soon as noticed. First sold un-named in 1998 to a few landscape gardeners by C. Kampa, Chobham, Surrey, England, before coming to the notice of John Hewitt, Summerfield Nursery, Frensham, Surrey, England, who named it after his daughter.

'Valerie Griffiths'   16 × 22 in. (40 × 55 cm)
A tall, bushy plant with yellow summer foliage that deepens to golden-yellow in winter. Pale pink flowers in summer and early autumn. This cultivar is a selection from deliberate hybrids produced by John Griffiths between *Erica manipuliflora* 'Aldeburgh' and *E. vagans* 'Valerie Proudley'. It has proven to be one of the best introductions of the 1990s. It is named after John Griffiths's wife.

Erica ×*krameri* D. C. McClintock
Kramer's heath

Deliberate hybrids between *Erica carnea* and *E. spiculifolia*. They are vigorous plants with a very long flowering period, early summer through late autumn, and tiny flowers similar to those of *E. spiculifolia* (McClintock 1998a). Most exhibit brightly colored new growth in spring. The hybrid is named after Kurt Kramer, Edewecht, Germany, who was the first person to make the cross.

These require an acidic soil and are hardy to Zone 5.

Erica ×*krameri*.
Photo by Kurt Kramer.

'Otto'   8 × 18 in. (20 × 45 cm)
Pink flowers on a plant of broad, spreading habit with medium green foliage. The corollas are cup-shaped, with sides parallel and without noticeable constriction below the lobes. Orange-red spring tips.

'Rudi'   8 × 18 in. (20 × 45 cm)
This cultivar has slightly shorter leaves than 'Otto' but is otherwise similar, with medium green foliage and a broad, spreading habit, with orange-red new growth in spring. The pink flowers have urn-shaped corollas, with a slight constriction below the lobes.

Erica lusitanica Rudolphi (synonym *E. codonodes*)
Portuguese heath, Spanish heath

An elegant, erect, pyramidal, many-branched, evergreen shrub up to 12 ft. (4 m) tall, this species is native to southwestern France; northern, central and southwestern Spain; and Portugal. Jamie Fagúndez and Jesús Izco (2007) recently described a new subspecies based upon morphological and ecological evidence. *Erica lusitanica*

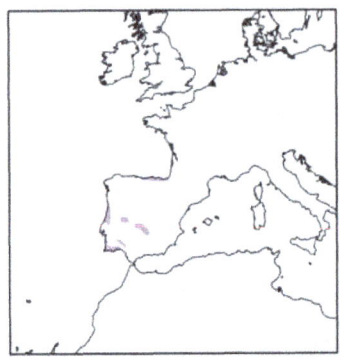

The natural distribution of *Erica lusitanica*.

subsp. *cantabrica* Fagúndez and Izco is found in northern Spain and southwestern France in shrublands and deciduous forests not associated with permanent streams. The type subspecies, *E. lusitanica* subsp. *lusitanica*, from Portugal and central and southwestern Spain, occurs mostly in humid habitats close to streams and is part of the vegetation associated with wet areas such as riparian forest, although it may sometimes be found in shrublands not dependent upon water. Therefore, the species' reputation for drought tolerance may be based upon collections of subspecies *cantabrica*. Clones of the species in cultivation have not yet been assigned to subspecies. Both subspecies prefer acidic soils.

Erica lusitanica (which subspecies has not yet been determined) has naturalized in parts of southwestern England; northern California and south coastal Oregon, United States; New South Wales, Southern Australia, Tasmania, and Victoria, Australia; and in both North Island and South Island, New Zealand. Where growing conditions are favorable, this plant may become invasive, crowding out native vegetation, so careful consideration should be given to its introduction outside its natural distribution area. It is on lists of proscribed invasive aliens and noxious weeds in Humboldt County, California; New Zealand; and Tasmania.

The species has fine, linear, glabrous leaves that give a feathery appearance to the foliage. Stems on young shoots have many simple hairs. It has a very long flowering period in winter and spring, with dense racemes of beautiful pink buds that open to masses of white, slightly fragrant, tubular to bell-shaped flowers $^1/_{10}$ to $^1/_5$ in. (2.5 to 5 mm) long.

Erica lusitanica should be pruned well in its early years to produce a full, shapely shrub. This is best done immediately after the flowers fade. Once established, it is capable of withstanding a considerable amount of drought. Suitable for Zone 8.

'George Hunt' 28 × 18 in. (70 × 45 cm)
The beautiful yellow foliage on this cultivar, lime-green if planted in shady situations, makes it a crowd pleaser at flower shows. Pink winter buds open to white flowers in spring. Found by George Hunt of Lymington, Hampshire, England, in 1959.

Although this can become an outstanding specimen plant, it is tender and should not be attempted where temperatures can drop much below 14°F (−10°C) unless a sheltered but open site can be provided for it. Plants of 'George Hunt' growing in such a favorable site at the Rhododendron Species Foundation Botanical Garden near Seattle, Washington, have survived there for more than a decade and are now taller than 72 in. (180 cm).

Erica lusitanica 'George Hunt'.

Erica mackayana Babington (formerly spelled *mackaiana*)

Mackay's heath

A spreading evergreen shrub found in boggy ground in western Ireland and northern Spain. The northern Spanish plants tend to have a stiffer, more erect habit than the plants from Ireland. *Erica andevalensis* Cabezudo & Rivera, an inhabitant of mine spoils in southwestern Spain and adjacent areas of Portugal (sometimes the *only* plant inhabitant, according to E. C. Nelson [in press]), is sometimes considered to be a subspecies of *E. mackayana*, but determination of its taxonomic status awaits DNA testing.

Natural distribution of *Erica mackayana*.

Erica mackayana has 1/16 to 3/16 in. (2 to 5 mm) long lanceolate, dark green leaves in whorls of four, only slightly revolute, with gland-tipped hairs on the margins, and a white under-surface. According to Hugh McAllister (1996), leaves of this species never have the fine hairs on the upper leaf surfaces that are characteristic of both *E. ciliaris* and *E. tetralix* and their hybrids, with which seedlings of *E. mackayana* could be confused.

The flowers, borne in terminal umbels in summer and early autumn, are usually urn-shaped, contracted at the mouth, and bright pink. The ovary is hairless, which easily distinguishes this species, when in flower, from *Erica tetralix*. Vegetatively, *E. mackayana* may be distinguished from *E. tetralix* by having internodes of approximately equal length, whereas the internodes of *E. tetralix* are longer immediately below the inflorescence than on the remainder of the plant.

Plants of *Erica mackayana* often spread to form large colonies of a single clone, proliferating from the roots (McAllister 1996). It regenerates well from root fragments after soil disturbance, such as peat cutting. This species requires acidic and constantly moist soil. Cultivars of Irish origin are very susceptible to drought and will die quickly if allowed to dry out. Suitable for Zone 8.

'Dr Ronald Gray' 4 × 14 in. (10 × 35 cm)
This broadly spreading cultivar has white flowers in summer and autumn and mid-green foliage. It was found as a sport on 'Lawsoniana' by Dr. Ronald Gray in his garden at Hindhead, Surrey, England.

'Maura' 10 × 14 in. (25 × 35 cm)
Semi-double heliotrope flowers in profusion in summer and early autumn, much more floriferous than 'Plena'. It has eglandular, gray-green foliage and an erect habit. The plant was found near Carna, County Galway, Ireland, by Maura Scannell, a member of staff at the National Botanic Gardens, Glasnevin, Dublin.

Erica mackayana 'Dr Ronald Gray'.

'Plena' 6 × 16 in. (15 × 40 cm)

Collected in County Galway, Ireland, more than 100 years ago, 'Plena' has double magenta flowers in summer and autumn. It has dark green foliage and a neat habit suitable for ground cover.

'Shining Light' 10 × 22 in. (25 × 55 cm)

A superb cultivar, with masses of large white flowers in late summer and early autumn on gray-green foliage. It was collected in Galicia, Spain, by David McClintock, Charles Nelson, and David Small. This is the one to grow if you have room for only one white cultivar of *Erica mackayana*.

Erica mackayana 'Shining Light'.

Erica manipuliflora Salisbury
whorled heath

An evergreen, lime-tolerant shrub from the eastern Mediterranean, with sweetly scented, bell-shaped flowers on (usually) long pedicels in late summer and autumn. The flowers, which vary in color from white to lilac-pink and have exserted stigmas and anthers, are similar to those of *Erica vagans*.

There is considerable variation in foliage, stems, and plant habit. Some plants have brown stems and long leaves, while others have narrow interrupted inflorescences, very short leaves, and whitish stems. A. W. Jones (1989) reported seeing *Erica manipuliflora* in [the former] Yugoslavia ranging from 2 to 90 in. (5 to 225 cm) in height and from tall and erect to prostrate, weeping, and trailing in habit. One plant measured was 68 in. (170 cm) wide, with stems trailing downward for 60 in. (150 cm).

This is a species that can be cut down to the ground and will regenerate from the rootstock. Some cultivars can make good flowering hedges.

Hardy to Zone 8 and probably Zone 7.

Natural distribution of *Erica manipuliflora*.

'Aldeburgh' 36 × 32 in. (90 × 80 cm)

Lilac-pink flowers in late summer and autumn, with light green foliage and white stems. This cultivar has a neat, erect habit that makes it suitable for low hedging in mild climates. It was found by David Small in a garden hedge at Aldeburgh, Suffolk, England.

'Cascades' 12 × 24 in. (30 × 60 cm)
Lilac flowers in late summer and autumn on long trailing stems with mid-green foliage. Its open prostrate habit makes it ideal for trailing over rocks or the sides of a tub. It was collected by Bert Jones and David McClintock in Dalmatia and introduced by Otter's Court Heathers as 'Waterfall'.

'Don Richards' 16 × 24 in. (40 × 60 cm)
A very free-flowering cultivar found on the Greek island of Corfu by Don Richards. This cultivar has a dense, erect habit, light green foliage, and pale pink flowers in summer and autumn.

'Ian Cooper' 16 × 24 in. (40 × 60 cm)
Beautiful shell-pink flowers on a broadly spreading, semi-erect shrub with gray-green foliage. This very floriferous cultivar is among the last to flower of the species, beginning its floral display in late autumn as that of 'Korčula' is ending. Found on Otok Korčula, Croatia, by Albert Small of Eltham, London.

Erica manipuliflora 'Ian Cooper'.

'Korčula' 22 × 44 in. (55 × 110 cm)
An outstanding selection with pale shell-pink flowers in long arching sprays, much larger than normal, in late summer. Mid-green foliage and a broad, rather open habit. Another of Albert Small's introductions, named after the island where it was collected.

Erica multiflora Linnaeus
many-flowered heath, Mediterranean heath

These are large shrubs of erect habit with extensive branching, ranging from 3 to 8 ft. (1 to 2.5 m) tall and about 3 ft. (1 m) wide. The needle-like leaves, about 6/100 × 1/4 to 3/8 in. (1.5 × 6 to 10 mm), have a pale central groove on their undersides and are grouped along the stems in closely spaced whorls of three or five. There is a taproot, from which smaller roots emerge.

According to Metheny (1991), plants in Surrey, England, were flowering in September. Stephen Mifsud (2007) gives a bloom season of early winter to early spring on Malta. The species superficially resembles the closely related *Erica vagans*, with close synflorescences of urn-shaped flowers of similar pink color range. White is uncommon. Unlike in *E. vagans*, all of the flowers may open together and can provide a spectacular display. Also unlike *E. vagans*, the fused corolla is about twice as long as wide, 1/5 × 1/10 in. (5 mm × 2.5 mm), and the four sepals are about half as long as the corolla. The stigma is exserted, and

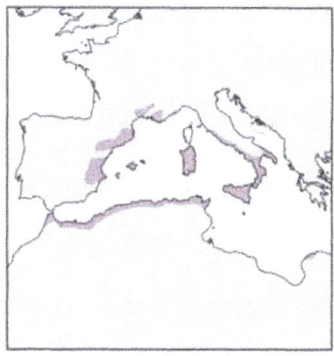

Natural distribution of *Erica multiflora*.

the exserted purple-brown anthers form a ring that superficially appears to be part of the corolla. The flowers are held on very long pedicels that are normally much deeper in color than the corolla.

The species grows in alkaline soils in dry environments (rocky places, dry woods, cliff tops), ranging from the Atlantic coast of Morocco eastward on the Mediterranean islands and near the Mediterranean coasts of Spain, France, and Italy to as far east as the former Yugoslavia. It is quite difficult to root from cuttings, so seed may be the best means of propagating this plant. Not really hardy, these are suitable for Zone 9 and the milder parts of Zone 8.

Erica ×*oldenburgensis* D. C. McClintock
Oldenburg heath

Deliberate hybrids between *Erica arborea* and *E. carnea*, first produced by Kurt Kramer and named after Oldenburg, Germany. The flowers are similar to those of *E. carnea* but are much smaller and are carried in long, plume-like racemes as on *E. arborea*. The plants form small, compact *E. arborea*-like tree heaths and have inherited the extreme hardiness of *E. carnea*. Most have brightly colored, feathery new growth in spring. Lime tolerant and suitable for Zone 5.

Erica ×*oldenburgensis* 'Ammerland' photographed in late autumn.

'Ammerland'   28 × 28 in. (70 × 70 cm)
This very attractive plant with a long blooming season has a compact growth habit. The soft pink flowers are carried on erect spikes during winter and spring. The flowers darken with age, and the mid-green foliage has vivid orange new growth in spring.

'Oldenburg'   28 × 28 in. (70 × 70 cm)
White flowers in spring with relatively long calyx lobes and malformed stamens that may even form a "second corolla" within the flower. Mid-green, *Erica arborea*-like foliage on a plant of broadly spreading habit. This begins flowering considerably later than 'Ammerland'.

Erica scoparia Linnaeus
besom, broom heath

A plant of the western Mediterranean region, being found in France, Spain, Portugal, the coast of northern Africa, and as far east as Italy, plus on the Atlantic islands of Madeira, the Canaries, and the Azores. Infrequently grown in gardens, because its flowers are tiny and generally not showy.

This species was widely used to make brooms (hence the common names) and the harvested shoots, woven together, provide an attractive and long-lived fencing some-

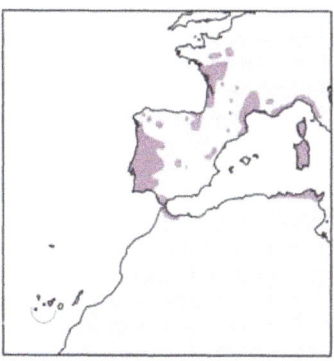

Natural distribution of *Erica scoparia*.

Erica scoparia subsp. *azorica* (synonym *Erica azorica*) forms the dominant vegetation on much of the Azores Archipelago.

Wild *Erica scoparia* in the Azores.

times seen in southern Europe. It is sometimes grown as a low hedge in Great Britain.

The leaves are usually lustrous green, about ¼ in. (6 mm) long but with the margins so curled back that they appear to be less than 4/100 in. (1 mm) wide. They occur in whorls of three or four and stand well out from the stems. The flowers, in the axils of the leaves, are only about 1/10 in. (2.5 mm) long, with the broadly capitate, exserted stigmas typical of wind-pollinated ericas.

Plant size, growth habit, cold tolerance, and flower color vary considerably among the various subspecies. The species requires acidic soil.

subsp. *azorica* (synonym *Erica azorica*)

This subspecies is native to the Azores but is surprisingly tolerant of winter cold. It is sufficiently distinct from the rest of the species to probably deserve species status in its own right and is, in fact, currently treated as *Erica azorica* Hochstetter ex Seubert by a number of botanists. See, for example, Sérvio P. Ribeiro et al. 2003.

It has a neat habit and is more decorative than the other subspecies of *Erica scoparia*, with attractive whorls of foliage and abundant chestnut-colored flowers in early summer. The flowers have smaller calyces and corollas than do the other subspecies. Although in cultivation this may form a low shrub, in the wild it grows naturally much taller and stouter than subspecies *scoparia* and can become a substantial tree (cover photograph by E. C. Nelson for the *Yearbook of The Heather Society* 2003). Suitable for Zones 6 to 9.

subsp. *maderincola*

Found only on Madeira and nearby Porto Santo, this subspecies most closely resembles subspecies *platycodon*. It has a laxer habit, with leaves that are longer, more widely spaced and spreading when mature. The flowers are paler than those of subspecies *platycodon*, a whitish pink, with shorter corollas and calyces and more exserted stigmas. Interestingly, when Jaime Fagúndez and Jesús Izco (2003) analyzed the seeds of all four *Erica scoparia* subspecies, they found that the seeds of subspecies *maderincola* most closely resemble those of subspecies *azorica*. Suitable for Zones 6 to 9.

subsp. *platycodon*

This subspecies from the Canary Islands has larger leaves that are sparser and stand out further from the stem than those of subspecies *scoparia* (McClintock 1989a). It also grows larger than subspecies *scoparia*, reaching tree-like dimensions of 18 ft. (6 m) tall and 6 ft. (2 m) wide. It has brownish red flowers, larger than those of the other subspecies, in late spring and early summer, and light green foliage. The habit is loose, open, and erect. The least hardy of the subspecies, suitable for Zone 7.

subsp. *scoparia*

The most widely distributed subspecies, extending from central and southern France, the Iberian Peninsula, the Balearic Islands, Corsica and Sardinia to as far east as west-central Italy and coastal northern Africa. Of more open habit than the other subspecies, it makes a rather untidy bush with greenish white flowers and can reach 6 ft. (2 m) tall. This subspecies is generally suitable for Zone 7.

Erica spiculifolia Salisbury

Balkan heath, spike heath, Bruckenthalia

This species was formerly known as *Bruckenthalia spiculifolia* but was returned to *Erica* on the basis of new morphological and DNA analysis (Oliver 1996, 2000; Kron et al. 2002; McGuire & Kron 2005). It is the only *Erica* species known at this time to have a haploid chromosome number of 18 (all other European species have a haploid chromosome number of 12), but that characteristic alone is not considered sufficient to warrant placing the species in a separate genus (Oliver 1996).

This evergreen shrublet is found in acidic, sub-alpine regions of the Balkan Peninsula and northern Turkey, between 4000 and 9000 ft. (1220 and 2800 m). Its specific name probably refers to the tiny spikes on the tips of the small, needle-like dark green leaves, that have strongly rolled-back margins and are usually borne in whorls of four.

The tiny flowers, with long exserted styles, are usually clear pink (white and dark pink cultivars also exist) and borne in short dense racemes approximately 4 in. (10 cm) long, held above the plants in early summer.

This dwarf plant is highly recommended for the rock garden or the small heather garden, because its main blooming season is between those of the winter-flowering and early-summer-flowering heathers. Some plants of this species also bloom later in

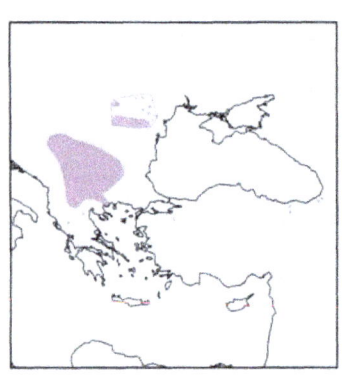

Natural distribution of *Erica spiculifolia*

the summer and early autumn. It requires a lime-free soil and thrives best in full sun. Dorothy Metheny (1991) of Seattle, Washington, found that it did well if planted where its roots could get under a rock.

Hardiness of the different cultivars varies, but it is usually suitable for Zone 6, or Zone 5 with winter protection.

'Balkan Rose' 6 × 12 in. (15 × 30 cm)
This selection is much more attractive than the average plant of the species, with heliotrope flowers in summer, and dark, gray-green foliage. Neat, compact habit.

Erica spiculifolia 'Balkan Rose'.

Erica ×*stuartii* (MacFarlane) Masters (synonym *E.* ×*praegeri*)
Praeger's heath

A naturally occurring hybrid between *Erica mackayana* and *E. tetralix*, requiring moist, acidic soil conditions. The hybrid has been known for some time from several localities in Ireland where the parent species co-exist.

The hybrid can be distinguished from the parents by the few hairs on the ovary: *Erica tetralix* has a woolly ovary, and *E. mackayana* has a hairless ovary. After examining the ovaries of numerous flowers, E. C. Nelson (1989) concluded that a hybrid swarm exists, with intermediates between *E. tetralix* and *E.* ×*stuartii* grading from the typical hairy ovary of the former to an ovary with hardly any hairs, indicating that backcrossing to *E. tetralix* must be occurring. He states (E. C. Nelson 2005) that "*E.* ×*stuartii* invariably accompanies" *E. mackayana* in Ireland.

Erica ×*stuartii* had not, until recently, been discovered in Spain, the only other place where the parent species co-exist. Díaz González and García Rodríguez (1992) reported its existence in Asturias in the wetter heathlands, although the hybrid was absent when the parents co-existed in drier areas. In moist areas, they found a hybrid swarm similar to what Nelson found in Ireland. In 2006, Jaime Fagúndez reported on a solitary *E.* ×*stuartii* plant growing in a peat bog in Galicia.

All cultivars of the hybrid currently in commerce originate from Irish plants and have cultural requirements and growth habits similar to those of the Irish form of *Erica mackayana*. These sterile hybrids exhibit brightly colored spring growth and are suitable for Zone 7.

Erica ×*stuartii* 'Irish Lemon' begins to flower before chlorophyll hides the yellow pigments in the spring new growth.

'Irish Lemon' 10 × 20 in. (25 × 50 cm)
This cultivar has brilliant lemon-yellow new growth in spring that persists until after flowering starts. The large mauve flowers are borne from late spring well into autumn on a plant with medium-green foliage and neat, rounded habit. It was found by David

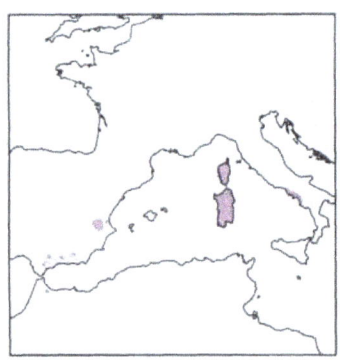

Erica ×*stuartii*
'Irish Orange'.

McClintock on the shores of Lough Nacung, County Donegal, Ireland, in 1965. Outstanding!

'Irish Orange' 10 × 18 in. (25 × 45 cm)
Found by David McClintock at the same time as 'Irish Lemon', also on the shores of Lough Nacung, County Donegal, Ireland. This cultivar is grown primarily for its beautiful, orange spring tips, which gradually change to dark green that becomes even darker in winter. The lilac-pink flowers during summer and autumn usually do not overlap with the spring foliage color.

'Stuart's Original' 10 × 10 in. (25 × 25 cm)
The first cultivar of this hybrid to be discovered, it was found in 1890 in Connemara, Ireland, by Charles Stuart, for whom it is named. (Until recently, this cultivar was known as 'Stuartii'.) This little charmer is best observed close up. The distinctive small flowers, produced from midsummer until autumn, are two-toned, being shell-pink at the base and beetroot at the tip. The gray-green foliage has coral-colored new growth in spring. In 2000, E. C. Nelson (2001) found what appeared to be the same plant, still growing where Charles Stuart had originally observed it more than a century earlier.

Natural distribution of *Erica terminalis*.

Erica terminalis.

Erica terminalis Salisbury (synonym *E. stricta*)
Corsican heath

This erect evergreen shrub, to 100 in. (250 cm) tall, is native to southern Spain, Corsica, Sardinia, and southern Italy, and is naturalized on the Magilligan Dunes in Northern Ireland. It is the only summer-blooming tree heath, with a bloom season from midsummer to early autumn. It bears terminal umbels of lilac-pink, urn-shaped flowers. White-flowered plants have been reported from Corsica but are not known in cultivation at present. The spent flowers provide an attractive russet hue all winter.

Erica terminalis forms a handsome bush of dark olive-green foliage that, if pruned frequently in the early years, assumes a good shape suitable for low hedging and specimen planting. Stems continue to arise from the base throughout the flowering season, so that flowers are borne at different levels on the plant. Branches on older stems quickly assume an erect habit, so that the appearance of the entire shrub is strongly upright yet nearly as wide as tall if not pruned to restrain the width.

Lime tolerant and surprisingly hardy, suitable for Zone 5, although it grows shorter in colder climates and can be damaged by heavy snow loads.

'Thelma Woolner' 26 × 20 in. (65 × 50 cm)
This plant bears deep lilac-pink flowers during summer and autumn on dark green foliage. It is shorter and less reliable than the average plant of the species and was collected in Sardinia by Thelma and Lionel Woolner.

Erica tetralix Linnaeus
cross-leaved heath, bog heather, cat heather

An evergreen shrub widespread throughout western Europe, found from the Arctic Circle to northern Spain and Portugal and as far east as Latvia and central Finland. It has narrow, usually glandular, gray-green leaves up to 1/4 in. (6 mm) long that are white beneath and arranged in whorls. The stems, leaves, and calyces are hairy, giving the plant its grayish appearance.

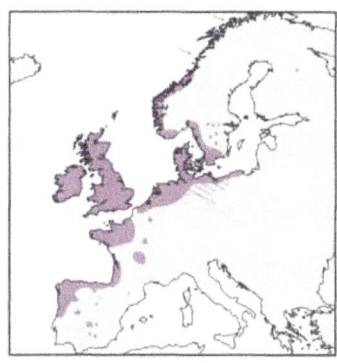

Natural distribution of *Erica tetralix*.

The pink or white urn-shaped flowers are 1/4 to 1/2 in. (6 to 13 mm) long and contracted at the mouth, with included anthers and the stigma only slightly exserted. The flowers are held in drooping terminal umbels of four or more. The blooming season is very long, from early summer until midautumn, so that from midsummer onward, the little bushes will be covered with a mixture of russet-colored spent flowers and brightly colored fresh ones. Some tidy gardeners who do not care for this effect cut off spent umbels throughout the season. Though tedious for the gardener, the practice does no harm to the plants.

Erica tetralix 'Alba Mollis'.

Although often found in boggy areas in the wild, *Erica tetralix* requires well-drained soil in cultivation and is tolerant of somewhat dry conditions when brought into the garden. It requires acidic soil, preferably moist, and is suitable for Zone 4.

'Alba Mollis' 8 × 12 in. (20 × 30 cm)
A compact, upright plant with very attractive gray-green foliage tipped silver-gray. In cultivation for well over a century, this is still

Erica tetralix 'Curled Roundstone'.

Erica tetralix 'Hookstone Pink'.

Erica tetralix 'Pink Star'.

one of the best cultivars of the species, producing bright white flowers in abundance.

'Con Underwood' 10 × 20 in. (25 × 50 cm)
This cultivar has magenta flowers and gray-green foliage. It was collected by Constance Underwood near Aldershot, Surrey, England.

'Curled Roundstone' 4 × 16 in. (10 × 40 cm)
Found by Charles Nelson near Roundstone, County Galway, Ireland, this diminutive heather with pale pink flowers has a prostrate growth habit and irregularly curling stems that make it suitable for ground cover, troughs, window boxes, and hanging baskets. "The name is a punning reference to its origin, and habit of curling round stones!" (E. C. Nelson 2000a).

'George Fraser' 10 × 12 in. (25 × 30 cm)
A popular Canadian introduction, with pale pink flowers from early summer to autumn. Olive-green foliage on a compact plant of erect habit.

'Hookstone Pink' 8 × 14 in. (20 × 35 cm)
The rose-pink flowers of this cultivar combine well with its gray-green foliage. Found on High Curley, Bagshot, Surrey, England, and named after the nursery that introduced it.

'Pink Star' 8 × 14 in. (20 × 35 cm)
Because this attractive cultivar holds its lilac-pink flowers horizontally around the

stem instead of having the terminal umbel pointing downwards in one direction as is typical for the species, this cultivar is classified as *Erica tetralix* f. *stellata*. Gray-green foliage.

'Riko' 8 × 14 in. (20 × 35 cm)
Ruby-colored flowers, the deepest of any *Erica tetralix*, with gray-green foliage on a plant of compact habit. 'Riko' is a seedling of *E. tetralix* 'Tina' that had supposedly been pollinated with *E. cinerea* 'Pink Ice' by Lothar Denkewitz. It is named after his grandson.

'Swedish Yellow' 6 × 12 in. (15 × 30 cm)
This cultivar performs best in exposed and harsh environments, where the green-yellow summer foliage deepens to a rich yellow with reddish tips in winter. Pale rose-pink flowers are borne from midsummer to autumn on a plant of spreading habit. It was found by Brita Johansson as a sport on a wild plant on a peat bog near Vänersborg, Sweden.

Erica umbellata Linnaeus
umbellate heath

An evergreen shrub about 12 to 36 in. (30 to 90 cm) tall, of neat, compact habit. It is native to northwestern Spain, Portugal, and northwestern Africa. The gray-green linear leaves with turned-back edges are arranged in whorls of three. The terminal umbels have two to eight squat, globose, white to rosy purple flowers about 1/12 to 1/10 in. (2 to 2.5 mm) long, with exserted stigma and conspicuous, dark brown exserted anthers that add to the attractiveness of the flowers.

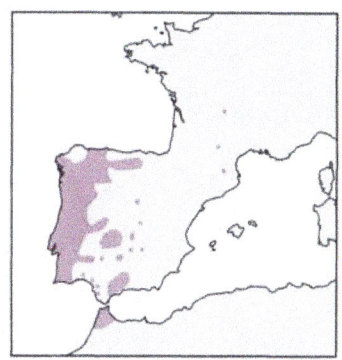

Natural distribution of *Erica umbellata*.

The late-spring blooming season and masses of flowers, when few other heathers are showing color, make this species valuable where it is hardy. Suitable for Zone 8. It requires very well-drained soil that need not be acidic.

'Anne Small' 14 × 18 in. (35 × 45 cm)
White flowers in late spring on a bushy upright shrub with bright green foliage. This cultivar was raised from seed from a white plant that was found by Maria Isabel Fraga Vila in Galicia, Spain, and sent to Denbeigh Heathers, Creeting Saint Mary, England, for germination. It was named after Anne Small, then administrator of The Heather Society, to mark her sustained contribution to the work of the society.

'David Small' 18 × 22 in. (45 × 55 cm)
A bushy, upright shrub with dark green foliage. It bears vivid, very deep helio-

trope flowers in late spring. This cultivar was collected in 1982 at Cabo Villano, La Coruña, Spain, by David McClintock, Charles Nelson, and David Small and was named by The Heather Society in 1999 to honor David Small's outstanding contributions to the society and his endeavours to propagate and promote heathers.

Erica umbellata 'David Small'.

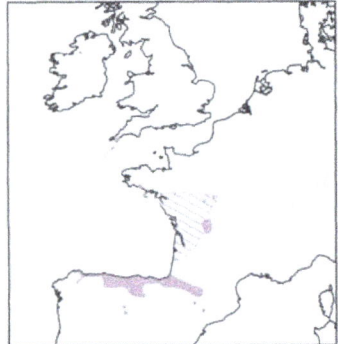

Natural distribution of *Erica vagans*.

Erica vagans 'Birch Glow'.

Erica vagans Linnaeus
Cornish heath

Evergreen shrub native to Cornwall, England; western France from Brittany to the Pyrenees; and northern Spain. There is a colony of white-flowered plants in Northern Ireland. In England, this species is frequently found in areas where the underlying rock is serpentine.

The dense bush, up to 3 ft. (1 m) tall, has linear, dark green leaves and small, bell-shaped pink, mauve, or white flowers with conspicuous, exserted anthers. The flowers are held in cylindrical synflorescences, opening progressively from the bottom to the top, between midsummer and midautumn. They are much loved by butterflies and hover flies.

The species can be successfully grown on any acidic or alkaline soil rich in magnesium and responds well to hard pruning. It is suitable for Zone 5 provided that the dead flowers, which are an attractive russet in winter, are kept on the plant until settled spring weather arrives. *Erica vagans* also tolerates some shading without too much reduction in flowering.

'Birch Glow'   12 × 20 in. (30 × 50 cm)
An outstanding plant with masses of deep rose-pink flowers in late summer and autumn on dark green foliage. It was found as a seedling in a nursery row of 'St Keverne' by W. E. Th. Ingwersen of Birch Farm Nursery, Gravetye, Sussex, England. Growing in the next row were plants of 'Mrs D. F. Maxwell'.

'Cornish Cream'   14 × 26 in. (35 × 65 cm)
This cultivar has off-white flowers in long racemes on bright green foliage, blooming from late summer to late autumn. It was collected on Goonhilly Downs, the Lizard Peninsula, Cornwall, England.

'Fiddlestone'   12 × 24 in. (30 × 60 cm)
Superb deep cerise flowers during late summer and early autumn, with mid-green foliage. Found as a seedling at Fiddlestone Lodge, Burton in the Wirral, Cheshire, England.

'Golden Triumph'   16 × 26 in. (40 × 65 cm)
A very attractive plant with mid-green foliage and bright gold new growth in spring. White flowers in late summer and early autumn. It is a sport from 'Lyonesse'.

Erica vagans 'Golden Triumph' was selected for its bright new spring growth.

'Kevernensis Alba'   10 × 18 in. (25 × 45 cm)
White flowers in late summer and autumn are not as noticeable when faded as in so many other whites, due to the compactness of the inflorescences. Bright green foliage. This cultivar was collected on the Lizard Peninsula, Cornwall, by P. D. Williams of Saint Keverne, Cornwall, England.

'Lyonesse'   16 × 26 in. (40 × 65 cm)
Named after the mythical land said to lie beneath the sea just off Cornwall, England, 'Lyonesse' has abundant white flowers with golden-brown anthers in late summer and autumn and bright green foliage. It was collected by Mr. and Mrs. D. F. Maxwell during their honeymoon on the Lizard Peninsula, Cornwall, England, in 1923.

'Mrs D. F. Maxwell'   14 × 18 in. (35 × 45 cm)
The most widely sold cultivar of *Erica vagans* in North America, this very attractive plant with dark green foliage bears masses of deep rose-pink flowers in late summer and early autumn that justify its popularity. Like 'Lyonesse', it was collected by Mr. and Mrs. D. F. Maxwell during their honeymoon on the Lizard Peninsula, Cornwall, England.

'St Keverne' 8 × 18 in. (20 × 45 cm)

A deservedly popular cultivar with clear pink flowers late summer through midautumn on a plant with dark green foliage. Collected by P. D. Williams in 1909 on the Lizard Peninsula, Cornwall, near the village of the same name.

'Valerie Proudley' 6 × 12 in. (15 × 30 cm)

Bright yellow new growth ages to dull gold foliage that is subject to wind burn, particularly in winter and spring. Raised by Brian Proudley and named after his wife, this cultivar arose as a sport on a normal, green-foliaged plant, to which it sometimes reverts. Reversions should be cut out as soon as they are detected. Sparse white flowers appear in autumn.

'Yellow John' 14 × 18 in. (35 × 45 cm)

Larger and more vigorous than 'Valerie Proudley', this cultivar is also thought to be hardier. The new foliage is bright yellow, but the older growth has a pinkish tinge. The flowers in late summer and autumn are lilac colored. Named after the finder, Jan Dekker, from the Netherlands.

Erica ×*veitchii* Bean
Veitch's heath

A hybrid between *Erica arborea* and *E. lusitanica* that varies in hardiness, depending on the cultivar, from Zones 7 to 8. This hybrid was first exhibited in 1905 by Veitch & Sons nursery, Exeter, England, where it had been found as a chance seedling.

All known cultivars are of garden origin and can be grown in most alkaline soils. The plant can tolerate strong winds but not maritime exposure.

Erica ×*veitchii* 'Gold Tips' grows under a tree at Cherrybank Gardens, Perth, Scotland.

'Exeter' 50 × 26 in. (125 × 65 cm)

A very floriferous cultivar, with light green foliage and sweet-scented, white spring flowers. The least hardy of the hybrids, it is believed to represent the first seedling found and so was named after the city where the Veitch & Sons nursery was established.

'Gold Tips' 26 × 24 in. (65 × 60 cm)

White flowers in late spring and early summer on a plant with bright green foliage. Selected for its yellow new spring growth.

'Pink Joy' 60 × 30 in. (150 × 75 cm)

A beautifully shaped tree heath, with mid-green foliage on fat, round branches that taper at the ends, it is the only cultivar of the hybrid to inherit the pink buds of *Erica lusitanica*. These begin to show color in late winter. The bud stage is almost as lovely as the very fragrant white flowers, which bloom in late spring.

Erica ×*watsonii* Bentham
Watson's heath

A naturally occurring hybrid between *Erica ciliaris* and *E. tetralix*, first found on Carrine Common near Truro, Cornwall, England, in 1831. Most other cultivars of the hybrid were found in the vicinity of Wareham, Dorset, England. It has also been reported from Asturias, Spain (Díaz González and García Rodriguez 1992). The hybrid is intermediate between the parent species, having short appendages on its anthers, whereas *E. ciliaris* has no appendages, and *E. tetralix* has long appendages.

The plant form and habit vary considerably, but there is generally a long flowering period and brightly colored tips on the new growth in spring. *Erica* ×*watsonii* requires acidic soil and is suitable for Zone 7.

'Cherry Turpin' 8 × 18 in. (20 × 45 cm)
Long racemes of pale pink flowers from early summer to autumn on gray-green foliage. It was collected on Carrine Common, Cornwall, England, by Cherry Turpin.

'Dawn' 6 × 14 in. (15 × 35 cm)
The deep pink flowers appear in late summer and early autumn. In spring, the grayish green foliage has red tips that later turn golden. Collected by D. F. Maxwell near Wareham, Dorset, England.

'Dorothy Metheny' 12 × 18 in. (30 × 45 cm)
Pale lilac flowers that deepen with age from early summer to late autumn, and beautiful yellow and pink spring tips. Eglandular, bright green foliage. The name honors the author of *Hardy Heather Species*, from Seattle, Washington. Collected by P. G. Turpin on Hartland Moor, Dorset, England.

'H. Maxwell' 12 × 18 in. (30 × 45 cm)
Mauve flowers from summer to late autumn on mid-green eglandular foliage. The young shoots are orange-bronze in spring, turning yellow later. It was a seedling collected near Wareham, Dorset, England, and named after the finder's father.

Erica ×*watsonii* 'Dorothy Metheny', showing spring tips.

'Mary' 10 × 18 in. (25 × 45 cm)
A fine cultivar with purple flowers from early summer to late autumn, with deep

green eglandular foliage and yellow spring tips. It has a broad, erect habit. The first *Erica* ×*watsonii* to be collected wild in France, it was discovered by Jos Flecken and named after his wife.

'Pearly Pink' 16 × 10 in. (40 × 25 cm)
Clear pink flowers similar in color to those of its sibling 'Pink Pacific', but on a taller, more compact plant. Bred by David Wilson of British Columbia, Canada, and blooming from early summer to autumn, this is a distinctly new color among the *Erica* ×*watsonii* cultivars. Green-gray foliage with striking orange-red new growth in spring.

'Pink Pacific' 10 × 14 in. (25 × 35 cm)
The salmon-pink buds open to clear rose-pink flowers in summer and autumn on a plant of spreading habit. Green-gray foliage and orange-red spring tips. Another selection from the cross of *Erica ciliaris* 'Corfe Castle' and *E. tetralix* 'Hookstone Pink' made by David Wilson.

'Truro' 6 × 16 in. (15 × 40 cm)
Large, pale mauve flowers during summer and autumn, with mid-green foliage. This is supposed to have been propagated from the first-discovered *Erica* ×*watsonii*, which was collected near Truro, Cornwall, England. There is no proof, however, that this cultivar is the same clone.

Erica ×*williamsii* Druce
Williams's heath

A naturally occurring but very rare hybrid between *Erica vagans* and *E. tetralix*, first found on the Lizard Peninsula, Cornwall, England, in 1860 and known from nowhere else. It was not described until 1911, and only individual plants have been found in the wild. The hybrid probably occurs quite frequently, but John Griffiths of Leeds, England, demonstrated by a deliberate breeding program that many seedlings lack vigor and would not survive in the wild.

The plant forms a dense, erect bush, ultimately about 24 in. (60 cm) tall and wider than tall. All forms exhibit, some more than others, bright yellow tips to the spring new growth.

The flowers are small, pale pink, and urn-shaped, intermediate between those of *Erica tetralix* and *E. vagans*. They are displayed in little clusters in summer and early autumn. Suitable for Zone 5 and warmer.

Erica ×*watsonii* 'Mary'.

'Cow-y-Jack' 10 × 18 in. (25 × 45 cm)
This cultivar has the best display of spring tip color of all known *Erica* ×*williamsii*, a brilliant yellow. The flowers in summer and early autumn are pink. The plant, of open, spreading habit, was collected by Andrew Byfield and Marion Hughes at Cow-y-Jack, near Coverack on Goonhilly Downs, the Lizard Peninsula, Cornwall, England.

'Gwavas' 8 × 16 in. (20 × 40 cm)
Shell-pink flowers during summer and autumn on mid gray-green foliage, with the new growth in spring being yellow. Collected on Goonhilly Downs, Cornwall, England, by M. B. G. Waterer of Knap Hill Nursery, while she was staying at Gwavas Farm, near Cadgwith.

'Ken Wilson' 12 × 20 in. (30 × 50 cm)
Blooming in summer and autumn, this lovely cultivar has deep pink flowers without a trace of blue, which eventually fade to shell-pink. A plant of compact spreading habit with mid-green foliage. Having the brightest flower color of the *Erica* ×*williamsii* cultivars, it is the result of deliberate breeding by David Wilson, British Columbia, Canada and is named after his father, a founder of the North American Heather Society.

'P. D. Williams' 10 × 18 in. (25 × 45 cm)
Lilac-pink flowers during summer and autumn on mid-green foliage that is tipped yellow during spring.

Yellow new spring growth of *Erica* ×*williamsii* 'Cow-y-Jack'.

Erica ×*williamsii* 'Gwavas'.

A Caution about Heather Names

Heather specialist nurseries try to ensure that the plants they sell are labelled with their correct cultivar names. Occasionally, however, plants are mixed up in the nursery or the labels fade or are lost. Nursery employees then attempt to guess at the correct name of the plant. Reputable nurseries will usually replace plants sent out under the wrong name when an error is called to their attention.

A plant may be labelled incorrectly because of a spelling error. The name may also have been translated from its original name in a language foreign to the country where the plant is to be sold. Translation is not permitted under the *ICNCP*, but this stricture is frequently ignored. Try searching in a general nursery catalog for the very popular *Erica* ×*darleyensis* 'Kramer's Rote'. You are quite likely to find "Kramer's Red" instead, because someone in marketing decided that the plant would sell better if the customers could pronounce its name easily.

Sometimes the name on the label is incorrect because of nursery shorthand, particularly when the original name has been changed as taxonomists learned more about the plants in question. In North America, nurseries continue to sell many thousands of *Erica* ×*darleyensis* plants under the names "Mediterranean Pink" and "Mediterranean White" or the abbreviations "Med Pink" and "Med White." None of the above is a correct cultivar name, although at one time *E.* ×*darleyensis* was known as *E. mediterranea hybrida*. "Med Pink" is nurseryman shorthand for a pink-flowering *E.* ×*darleyensis*, usually the first to be discovered, 'Darley Dale'. Occasionally, another pink cultivar, such as 'Ghost Hills', may be sold under that name. "Med White" is nurseryman shorthand for a white-flowering *E.* ×*darleyensis*, usually 'Silberschmelze' but sometimes one of several other white cultivars. If you care which cultivar you purchase, do not buy "Med This" or "Med That."

The advent of machines that can produce plant labels by the thousands has not helped the labelling situation. Once a nursery owner has purchased several thousand labels with the wrong name on them, that owner is understandably reluctant to buy new labels with the correct name, even when informed of the error.

There are other ways than through labelling errors or ignorance for plants to be sold under the wrong name. These errors are more difficult to detect and correct. Sometimes seedlings germinate under and grow up through the nursery stock plants from which cuttings are made, and these seedlings may be quite similar to the parent plant through which they are growing. If the grower does not notice the interlopers before taking cuttings from the stock plants, cuttings may be made from the seedlings and sold under the name of the stock plant cultivar. Although the seedlings superficially resemble the parent stock plant, they may differ from it in significant ways, such as in growth habit or blooming period. Eventually, plants propagated from the incorrectly named seedlings may actually supersede the correct cultivar in a particular market.

The Role of National Collections and Herbarium Collections

The only way to determine if a plant is truly the cultivar named on its label (or to find a name for an unnamed heather) is to compare it with living plants that have been asexually propagated (cloned) from the original plant of the cultivar under carefully controlled conditions. National collections of plants in one genus, or a group of closely related genera, such as heathers, are valuable for keeping cultivars true to type. They are carefully maintained to ensure that the original genetic material is preserved intact, not confused through self-sown seedlings or sports, both of which are removed by keepers of the collections as soon as they are detected.

If there is any question about the identity of a plant, the keeper of a national collection may be able to help answer it. There are several national heather collections, and heather specialist nurseries with extensive cultivar collections may help with identification in places far distant from a national collection.

National collections are also valuable as showcases for variation within a species. They are useful for comparing sports or seedlings with well-established cultivars in order to determine if the new plants are an "improvement" on existing cultivars or are sufficiently different from them to warrant introduction to the nursery trade.

A second way to verify that a cultivar is true to name is to compare a specimen from the cultivated, living plant with the pressed specimens preserved in a herbarium. In the case of heathers, reference collections of herbarium specimens are to be found in the RHS Garden, Wisley, and the Bailey Hortorum, New York.

This is the second-best way of identifying cultivars, because herbarium specimens often lose vital identifying characteristics such as flower and foliage colors. However, other characteristics, especially microscopic ones such as the presence or absence of gland-tipped hairs, may provide important clues to identification.

When in doubt, check it out. Whatever you do, please do not make up a new name for a named plant whose label you have lost.

8 Heathers as Cut Flowers

Most heather flowers, with the notable exception of daboecias, remain in good condition for many days if the stems are cut while there are still some unopened buds but before any flowers have wilted. This trait makes heathers valuable for use as cut flowers.

Flower Arrangements

Heathers are, without question, better suited to supporting roles than they are as the focus of floral arrangements. With their abundance of tiny flowers, they are superb when used as "filler" between larger flowers in arrangements and bouquets. Those

A pewter jigger is the perfect container for a midsummer miniature arrangement (8 × 9 in. [20 × 23 cm]) composed exclusively of heathers, orange and golden-green foliage from *Calluna vulgaris* 'Gold Kup' with the flowers of *C. vulgaris* 'Emerald Jock', *Erica ciliaris* 'White Wings', and *E. cinerea* 'Bucklebury Red'.

heathers with long straight stems and long-lasting flowers are the most versatile for cutting, but short-stemmed cultivars can star in miniature arrangements, where their small flowers are in proportion with their containers.

Just as most heather plants appear more at home in naturalistic or informal gardens than they do in formal gardens, so cut heathers are better used in casual rather than in formal flower arrangements. Stems from many different heather cultivars can be mixed together to form delightful arrangements in small vases or baskets. When creating the table decorations for the North American Heather Society Annual Conference held in 2000 in Fort Bragg, California, Edith Davis (2003) and other members of the chapter hosting the conference worked with (mostly) long-stemmed heathers that had been cut the day before from Edith's garden and stored overnight in buckets containing a little water.

They duct-taped wet florist's foam to the bottoms of the vases and baskets and concealed the foam with salal leaves (*Gaultheria shallon*) and huckleberry twigs (*Vaccinium ovatum*). The floral "designers" then inserted sprigs of heather into the foam, mixing and matching colors and occasionally making a foray into the garden to pick another stem that would be just the right color or length for a developing arrangement. Learning what species and colors worked well together as they proceeded, as well as the value of stripping leaves off the bottoms of stems to be inserted into the foam, the committee of inexperienced arrangers had soon created about 30 beautiful and distinctive heather arrangements, which were much admired at the conference banquet.

Ella May Wulff and Alice Knight (center) hold basket arrangements of mixed heathers created by Edith Davis (right) for table decoration at a heather society conference.

These heathers were included in the conference flower arrangements, although not necessarily all kinds in each arrangement.

Calluna vulgaris
   'Applecross'
   'Cuprea'
   'Dark Beauty'
   'Dark Star'
   'Elsie Purnell'
   'Fortyniner Gold'
   'Oxshott Common'
   'Pat's Gold'
   'Peter Sparkes'
   'Velvet Fascination'
Erica arborea 'Estrella Gold'
Erica canaliculata
Erica ciliaris
   'Mawiana'
   'Stoborough'
   'Wych'

Erica cinerea
   'Apple Blossom'
   'Atropurpurea'
   'Atrorubens'
   'Cevennes'
   'Eden Valley'
   'Golden Hue'
   'Golden Sport'
   'G. Osmond'
   'Neptune'
   'P. S. Patrick'
   'Purple Beauty'
Erica ×*stuartii* 'Irish Lemon'
Erica terminalis
Erica vagans
   'Lyonesse'
   'Mrs D. F. Maxwell'
   'St Keverne'

Note the preponderance of double-flowered callunas and of cultivars with very intense colors. Note also that some of these cultivars, for example, *Erica* ×*stuartii* 'Irish Lemon', are not usually recommended for use as cut flowers because of their short stems.

What was amazing about the project was that visitors to the Davis garden the day after the work session never realized that flowers had been cut from the garden. So, go ahead. Cut your heathers to enjoy in the house as well as in the garden. Consider it "pruning."

Winter got you down? Try stuffing a few springs of *Erica carnea* into a water-filled jigger. They'll stay fresh for weeks, and you can enjoy their fragrance more easily when they are in the warm, confined space of a house than outside in the chilly garden.

For a striking early spring arrangement, mix budded stems of *Erica arborea* 'Estrella Gold' with the flowers, buds, and foliage of *Camellia* 'Freedom Bell' or a similar, brightly colored camellia. The pale greenish yellow buds of the tree heath (which will open to bright white flowers later in the season) and its yellow-green winter foliage contrast beautifully with the deep green leaves and red flowers of the camellia.

Later in spring, fill a simple small container with a mixture of cut stems, in full bloom or with only a few tip buds left to open, of *Erica erigena* 'Brian Proudley' and *E. erigena* 'Maxima'. Accent the heather with sprigs of a light-pink-flowered cultivar of *Geranium macrorrhizum* (or if you are bold, go for the knock-out punch of the intensely magenta-flowered *G. macrorrhizum* 'Czakor'). The flowers of the geranium are a good color blend (or contrast) for the *E. erigena* flowers, and the geranium leaves provide excellent contrast in size and shape to the many small heather flowers. Try to select geranium sprigs with small leaves, so that the size contrast is not so great as to unbalance the arrangement. Cut the geraniums when only one flower has opened on each stem, because the individual geranium flowers will not last as long as those of the heaths. The only disadvantage of this combination is that the pungent foliage of the geraniums may overwhelm the sweet scent of the ericas.

A simple spring arrangement of *Erica erigena* 'Brian Proudley' (white) and *E. erigena* 'Maxima' (pink) with the leaves and flowers of *Geranium macrorrhizum*.

The natural garden pairing of heathers with lavenders suggests a similar pairing in summer flower arrangements. Most lavender cultivars have silvery or bluish green foliage that complements their lavender-blue flowers. Continue this theme by using stems of the lovely, downy, silvery foliaged *Calluna vulgaris* 'Velvet Fascination' in an arrangement with *Lavandula* and the mauve flowers of such *Calluna vulgaris* cultivars as 'Kerstin' or 'Spring Torch'. A few small, pink rose buds add the finishing touch to this combination. Alternatively, pair a dark colored lavender such as *Lavandula angustifolia* 'Hidcote' with magenta *Erica cinerea* 'Knap Hill Pink' and roses.

Heathers with golden foliage may be cut for use as arrangement fillers or color accents at any time of year. For autumn arrangements, cultivars whose foliage turns orange or red in cold weather can be combined with similarly colored chrysanthemum flowers and sprigs cut from small-leaved deciduous trees such as *Acer palmatum*.

An early summer centerpiece arrangement of *Erica cinerea* 'Knap Hill Pink' and David Austin English roses is accented with *Lavandula angustifolia* 'Hidcote'.

The suggestions offered here are for making simple heather arrangements for your personal enjoyment. Many other combinations are possible, limited only by the plants you have available for cutting.

Nosegays and Other Bouquets

Heathers are superb for use in boutonnières and nosegays, where their small flower size is an asset. A small sprig of flowering *Erica carnea* or *Calluna vulgaris* makes a satisfactory boutonnière even without a complementary ribbon or the addition of slightly larger flowers or foliage for textural contrast.

The combination of heather, lavender, and rose buds recommended for a summer flower arrangement is also excellent in a summer nosegay. For a fall nosegay, combine *Calluna* flowers with asters or with pom-pom chrysanthemums in blending or contrasting colors.

Most heathers recommended for flower arrangements are also suitable for bouquets, where they again serve as filler among larger flowers. In Scotland, many brides carry white heather in their bridal bouquets "for luck." How the tradition originated is uncertain (see Nelson 2006 for more on this subject), but sprays of white-flowering heather—whether or not they bring good luck—will add grace to any bouquet. *Calluna vulgaris* 'My Dream', with its long stems of double white flowers, is excellent for this purpose.

Drying Heathers

With the exception of daboecias, which drop their flowers quickly, most heather flowers are very easy to dry. In fact, the easiest way to dry them is to arrange cut heather stems in a vase but add no water. In a few weeks, you will have a dried arrangement. For additional interest and contrasting flower form in such an arrangement, mix the cut heathers with cut flower stems of ornamental oreganos such as *Origanum laevigatum* 'Hopleys' or *O. libanoticum*. These dry equally well, and the colors of the dried oregano bracts blend nicely with the colors of most dried heather flowers.

The leaves of dried ericas become brittle and are soon shed. Dried *Calluna* foliage remains on the stem considerably longer, but it, too, will eventually drop. Heather flowers hold much better than heather foliage, especially double callunas and those of *Erica tetralix* and *E.* ×*watsonii* (Oudean 1993a), and can remain on the stems for years if not disturbed. The color of heather flowers deepens several shades as the flowers dry, concentrating the flower pigments.

A light spraying of a dried heather arrangement with either lacquer or hair spray will help to prevent the shedding of flowers and extend the life of the arrangement. In an experiment with *Erica erigena* 'Maxima', application of a commercial spray sold as a dried flower preservative did not seem to reduce the amount of blossom drop as compared with the amount of blossom drop of unsprayed dried heathers.

The dried flowers of *Erica erigena* 'Maxima' are still colorful (slightly darker than when fresh) and fragrant a year after cutting.

Using silica gel desiccant as an aid to drying heathers is unnecessary. The tiny heather flowers and leaves that fall off as stems are removed from the desiccant will merely contaminate the silica gel so that it will be difficult to re-use to dry the large flowers that dry better with such treatment.

Freshly cut heather stems may be bunched, wired together, and formed into wreaths, sprays, or swags, either alone or with other flowers and foliage that dry well, such as many *Helichrysum* and *Artemisia* species. Simply set a freshly made wreath in a warm, dry (and preferably dark) place for several weeks until it has thoroughly dried. A dried wreath of heathers, Silver King *Artemisia* (*Artemisia ludoviciana* subsp. *mexicana* var. *albula*), and small rose buds makes a charming gift. (The much fleshier rose buds may be dried separately and attached to the heather wreath after it has dried.)

Because flowers and foliage shrink in volume as they dry, be sure to make fresh wreaths several times as large as your desired dried wreaths. Likewise, if you are making a simple dried arrangement, overstuff your vase with flowers so that the finished arrangement will not appear skimpy when the flowers have dried. Experiment until you discover how much the different cultivars will shrink upon drying.

Drying can preserve heather fragrance. A year after they were cut, dried flowers of *Erica erigena* 'Maxima' still retained much of the fragrance of fresh blooms.

Preserving Heathers

Various floral preservation methods other than drying may be used to treat heather foliage and those heather flowers that do not hold up well when dried, such as *Erica carnea*, *E.* ×*darleyensis*, and *E. cinerea*. One historically proven way to preserve these flowers is the Victorian wax method, as refined by Karen Oudean.

Victorian Wax Method (Oudean 1993b)
This method was used for flower preservation beginning in the 1840s, when paraffin wax became available as a by-product of petroleum production.

Cut flower stems when lower flowers are fully open and remaining buds are showing color. Foliage stems without flowers may be used at any time. If plant material is cut when the weather is cool, allow it to come to indoor room temperature before preserving. Be sure that material to be preserved is completely dry before treatment. (Gently pat dry with paper towels if necessary.)

Heat paraffin to a temperature of about 135°F (57°C) so that the paraffin is just melted and will coat the plants without cooking them. Remove the paraffin container from the heat source. Firmly holding the base of the stem with your fingers or tongs, dip each cut stem into paraffin just long enough to ensure that all plant surfaces are in contact with the paraffin, remove the stem from the paraffin, and immediately plunge it into cold water. The object is to produce a translucent patina, not a conspicuous wax coating. Lay stems on paper towels to dry. About five stems may be treated before you will need to reheat the paraffin.

Sprays of waxed heather may be used in any way that you would use dried heathers and will last for several years in the open air. If placed under glass as was done in Victorian times, they will keep indefinitely. Some colors may be slightly muted by the paraffin coating.

Freezing
An unlikely but entirely serviceable method for preserving heathers for use out of season, freezing is best attempted with double-flowered callunas. The versatile bud bloomers are potential candidates for this treatment, as well.

Cut heather stems in the morning after any early morning dew has disappeared. There should be no visible water on the flowers, which should all be in good condition, with none wilted or turning brown. Place the cut stems in sturdy polyethylene bags with zipper-locking seals, such as those sold for storing frozen fruits and vegetables. Be sure that the stems are not crowded or bent within the bags.

Put heather-filled bags into the freezer, being careful that nothing else is stored on top of them. They can be taken out of the freezer for use at any time. Once thawed, they will last a few days—long enough for a wedding.

Showing Heathers

Heather shows are a good place to learn about heathers, with many cultivars on exhibit in a relatively small space. Because most heathers entered in shows have been garden grown in full sunlight, their flower and foliage colors demonstrate how the various cultivars can perform. Choosing your favorites from among the cultivars at a show is more reliable than choosing from plants grown for sale in shaded glasshouses or polyethylene tunnels, although seeing the plants actually growing in a garden is the most reliable selection guide. Entering a heather show can be a learning experience and a lot of fun, provided that you do not take the competition too seriously.

Heathers are judged in cut flower arrangements and as either single cut stems or a group of cut stems competing against other cut stems in their class. Different rules pertain to the two types of competition. The classes for arrangements, in particular, can be quite flexible, depending upon the whim of the organization sponsoring the show.

Heathers in Show Arrangements

When other kinds of flowers compete in specialty shows, the show rules usually specify that the featured flower be dominant in all exhibits. However, because heathers have tiny flowers compared to, for example, irises or roses, heather show rules may be less restrictive, requiring only that heathers make up a substantial proportion of each arrangement.

The best way to achieve the appearance of dominance when using heathers in flower arrangements is to group a large number of stems of the same cultivar closely together within the arrangement, using the group as if it were a single, large flower.

Heather flower arrangements entered in the Royal Horticultural Society's London show, August 1983. Photo by Maurice Everett.

The single cultivar group is then repeated for balance throughout the arrangement. This can be a very effective ploy, especially if the chosen cultivar is of a vibrant hue, such as the crimson *Calluna vulgaris* 'Carmen'.

Textural contrast within a heather-emphasis arrangement can be provided through the use of foliage from plants with larger leaves, such as hardy geraniums or some of the smaller hostas. Be careful that the leaves are not proportionally so large that they themselves become dominant in the arrangement. The use of grasses or grass-like plants to add linearity and flow to the design works as well in a heather flower arrangement as it does in a heather garden.

Effective arrangements can be composed exclusively of heather flowers and foliage, and in some heather shows, there may be a "heathers only" class. The use of cultivar groupings works here as well as it does in mixed arrangements, and the pairing of heathers with different flower shapes, such as *Calluna vulgaris* with *Erica cinerea*, increases the visual appeal of the arrangement.

It is difficult to achieve a large arrangement when all plants used must be heathers, but there are enough larger growing heathers that an arrangement of moderate size, such as a table centerpiece, is easy to compose. The beautiful, medium-to-light green, feathery foliage of *Erica* ×*gaudificans* 'Edewecht Blush' may be used to form the framework of large arrangements. Because this plant can have flowers at any time of year, be careful to choose stems that have no spent flowers on them. The foliage of tree heaths also is good as the framework for an arrangement. For color contrast and additional structure, add silver, gold, or red foliage (depending upon the season). When using red winter foliage, remember that the leaves will be red only on the side of the stem that was facing the sun. Consequently, the stems should be turned within the arrangement so that their red sides face outward.

Heathers that bear their flowers in terminal clusters, such as *Erica tetralix* and its hybrids, are useful for adding a downward droop to exclusively heather arrangements. The stems of some cultivars naturally sprawl outward before curving up. When these are placed to drape over the edge of a container, the flowers will face downward.

Classes for miniature arrangements are a natural for heather shows. When you compete in this class, be certain that your arrangement is smaller than the officially specified size limit *in every direction*. Judges will disqualify an arrangement that is well under the limit in height but that sprawls beyond the limit in width.

Choose containers for all arrangements carefully. The container is part of the arrangement and should be sized in proportion to the plant material. Simple containers are best for heather arrangements, as they do not compete for interest with the flowers.

Heathers Judged as Cut Stems

In most shows sponsored by heather societies, cut heather stems are judged either against other entries of the same cultivar or against all cultivars in the same class.

The latter is far more frequent. For example, in a late summer show, there may be a class for bud-blooming *Calluna* cultivars, a class for double-flowered *Calluna* cultivars, a class for single-flowered *Calluna* cultivars, a class for *Erica cinerea*, a class for all other *Erica* species and hybrids (rather unfair, but quite the usual practice), and a class for heathers (of any species) that are grown primarily for their foliage. A late winter or early spring show might have a class for heathers grown primarily for their foliage, a class for *E. carnea*, a class for *E.* ×*darleyensis*, a class for *E. erigena*, and a class for any other heather in bloom.

There usually are no *Daboecia* classes at heather shows. Although the genus boasts the largest flowers among the hardy heathers, it is, unfortunately, not good for showing. Its habit of dropping the showy corollas of spent blossoms, which is a positive attribute in the garden—especially since the plants are continually producing new flushes of flowers throughout the growing season, makes *Daboecia* nearly useless as a source of cut flowers. Cut *Daboecia* stems may hold their flowers for a day or two, but there is no guarantee of this. They are just as likely to drop several corollas the moment you finish arranging them. Enjoy the flowers on the plants, but do not be tempted to use them in arrangements. It will not work.

Calluna vulgaris 'Tib' may hold the record for most prizes at Royal Horticultural Society shows simply because it has the earliest blooming season of the double callunas.

Guidelines for Showing Heathers as Cut Stems

Stems should be long and straight and, except for foliage class entries, well clothed with flowers and buds distributed along the stems in the manner normal for the species being exhibited. No flowers should be turning brown or wilted. Except for the *Calluna* bud bloomers, which do not open their buds, there should be few unopened buds. Bud bloomers should have all buds fully formed and well colored, with none faded. Foliage should be clean, brightly colored, and healthy.

When more than one stem is exhibited per container, the stems should be uniform in length and appearance. Stems of uneven quality will detract from the exhibit. Although several stems usually make a more impressive exhibit than one alone, it is better to show one good stem than one or two good stems combined with others that are not as good.

Cut stems should be representative of the cultivar being judged. For example, a cut stem of *Calluna vulgaris* 'Darkness' that is 6 in. (15 cm) long would be acceptable, but a 6-inch-long cut stem of 'Annemarie' would not be, because 'Annemarie' can produce flowering stems of 10 in. (25 cm) or longer.

Transporting Cut Stems to a Show

Heathers are easily transported to shows when properly packed. If possible, cut stems early in the morning, but be sure that they are not wet. If you must cut from wet plants, very gently pat the flowers and foliage dry with paper towels or a linen tea towel. Put them immediately into a plastic bag containing a small ball of paper towelling that has been moistened and then thoroughly squeezed to remove any excess moisture. This will provide sufficient humidity inside the bag to keep the stems from wilting but not so much that they begin to decay. Zipper-locking polyethylene bags work well for transporting heathers. Pack only one cultivar per bag, and be sure to label the bag with the name of the cultivar.

Do not bend the heather stems within the bags nor crowd them so that the flowers are damaged. If the stems are long, choose a bag large enough to accommodate them. Do not press all the air out of the bags before sealing. The air trapped within the bags is usually sufficient to cushion the cut stems against crushing, but a few plastic foam packing "peanuts" added to each bag will provide additional protection. The bags may be stacked several layers deep in a larger bag or a box and may be carried in airplane hand luggage, as long as heavier items are not placed on top of the heathers. Cut heathers may safely be stored in this manner for several days without losing their freshness.

Cut heathers travel well if packed properly. When *Erica* authority Ted Oliver attended The Heather Society's conference in Dublin in 1995, he brought with him from Cape Town these beautiful South African ericas.

Benching Your Entries

Upon arrival at the show, you will usually be given a water-filled container for each cultivar you are entering, although occasionally the show committee will prepare all entries for exhibit. Arrangement of the stems within the container is as important as transporting them to the show safely. Carelessly stuffing the stems together can ruin an otherwise excellent entry. Make sure that all stems are of even height above the top of the container and that all are facing toward the judges (and the viewing public). Whether or not to remove leaves from the parts of the stems below water level is optional. Sometimes leaves remaining on the lower stems can help to stabilize the cuttings within the container.

If you are allowed to place your own entries on the show benches, be sure that there is adequate space between entries so that adjacent entries do not touch each other and can be easily viewed by both judges and show visitors. Flower show judges usually do not pick up entries, so one entry should not impinge upon or block the judges' view of another entry.

Write the species and cultivar name on each entry label. Be sure that each cultivar is entered in its correct class. Ask for help if you are uncertain which class your cultivar belongs in, because cultivars entered in the wrong class will be disqualified.

After the Judging

If your entries did not win prizes, look carefully at the entries that did. In what ways do they differ from yours? Is your arrangement too crowded or unbalanced? Is it too "busy"? Did your container complement the arrangement or steal the show from it?

If you cannot see any difference in cut stem quality, the difference may be a subjective one. In a class that contains more than one cultivar, sometimes winning or losing may be determined simply by the judges' preference of one flower color over another, particularly in a large class of high quality entries. If possible, offer to clerk for the judges at the next show. During judging, they often explain to the clerks what is good and what is not good about particular entries.

Every time you attend, enter or work at a heather show, you will learn something new about heathers. That is the real value of a show. Any prize you might win is a bonus.

Species and Cultivars for Cutting

Calluna vulgaris 'Long White' is superb for use as a cut flower.

Heathers with long spikes of flowers are the most versatile and easiest to work with in fresh arrangements and bouquets. Double *Calluna* flowers and bud bloomers usually last longer than singles. Because they drop their spent corollas, daboecias are not suitable for use as cut flowers. This list of species and cultivars includes heathers that have proven to be excellent for cutting. It is meant to serve as a starting point for flower arrangers unfamiliar with heathers. Many other cultivars, especially of the listed species, can also be used successfully in bouquets and arrangements.

Calluna vulgaris
- 'Annemarie'
- 'Anette'
- 'Anthony Davis'
- 'Battle of Arnhem'
- 'County Wicklow'
- 'Elsie Purnell'
- 'Fortyniner Gold'
- 'H. E. Beale'
- 'Johnson's Variety'
- 'Long White'
- 'Mair's Variety'
- 'Melanie'
- 'My Dream'
- 'Peter Sparkes'
- 'Reini'
- 'Tib', winner of the highest number of prizes for heathers in RHS shows (C. Nelson 2005)

Erica arborea. These cultivars are especially good when cut in bud in late winter or early spring for use as filler for large arrangements.
- variety *alpina*
- 'Estrella Gold'

Erica australis
Erica carnea
Erica cinerea
Erica erigena
Erica ×gaudificans. The flowers of this hybrid are not particularly showy, but the attractive foliage, with or without flowers, makes excellent arrangement and bouquet filler at any time of year.
Erica ×griffithsii
Erica lusitanica
Erica manipuliflora
- 'Don Richards'
- 'Ian Cooper'
- 'Korčula'

Erica terminalis
Erica vagans
Erica ×veitchii
- 'Exeter'
- 'Pink Joy' in bud or bloom

Heathers for Drying

The heathers listed below are particularly suitable for drying, but many others also will dry satisfactorily.

Calluna vulgaris bud bloomers and double flowers
Erica erigena
Erica ×griffithsii
- 'Heaven Scent'
- 'Jacqueline'

Erica manipuliflora
Erica tetralix
Erica ×watsonii

9 Heathers for Special Uses

This chapter contains lists of heathers with special attributes or those suited to particular uses. Because of the size limitations of this book, most categories contain at least a few cultivars that are not described in chapter 7. Descriptions of these cultivars may be found in the *Handy Guide to Heathers* (Small and Small 2001), the *International Register of Heather Names* (Nelson and Small 2000), and in nursery catalogs.

Some lists are much longer than others. None is exclusive: they are all suggestions based upon the authors' personal experiences, conversations with other heather growers, and accounts in heather literature. These lists can help you to choose cultivars suitable for your garden. As you learn more about heathers, you will undoubtedly find others to add to the lists.

If no cultivars are listed for a species, all cultivars of the species are considered to fall into the category of that list. They may vary considerably in the degree to which they possess the defined attribute.

Alkaline Soil Tolerant

Some heathers cannot survive in alkaline soils, but a few are quite tolerant of them. Others are less tolerant of alkalinity but can survive in neutral or only slightly alkaline soils. This list contains both kinds.

Daboecia
Erica carnea
Erica ×*darleyensis*
Erica erigena
Erica ×*griffithsii*
Erica lusitanica
Erica manipuliflora
Erica multiflora
Erica ×*oldenburgensis*
Erica terminalis
Erica umbellata (requires excellent drainage)
Erica vagans (must have magnesium in soil for good performance)
Erica ×*veitchii*
Erica ×*williamsii*

Amenable to Hard Pruning

These can all be pruned into old wood with no green growth showing, but only *Erica arborea* tolerates being cut all the way to the ground. The others may be killed by such extreme treatment.

Erica arborea
Erica ×*darleyensis*
Erica erigena
Erica ×*griffithsii*
Erica manipuliflora
Erica vagans

Bud Bloomers

Bud bloomers are a group of *Calluna vulgaris* cultivars whose flowers never open properly, remaining "in bud" throughout—and extending—the flowering season. The flowers are effectively sterile, incapable of normal fertilization resulting from pollination by insects. Therefore, they retain their color much longer than do normal *Calluna* flowers. Normal flowers begin to wither soon after they are pollinated and seed development is initiated. Bud bloomers are conspicuous in wild populations because the plants are still colorful in late autumn long after the flowers of most other callunas have withered. During winter, the buds slowly age to pale silver.

Although several different abnormalities in the flowers of *Calluna* can produce the bud-blooming condition, most of the cultivars that are classed as bud bloomers have no corolla and no stamens. Instead, the buds are formed from (usually) eight sepals of similar size and substance. The buds never open, because the corolla and stamens, whose development would force the sepals apart, are absent. Because sepals tend to be more weather resistant than petals, bud bloomers remain colorful and in good condition despite the cold temperatures, wind, and rain of autumn and early winter. They are valuable for their very long "blooming" season, bridging the gap between the late summer and early autumn color peak in the heather garden and the onset of flowering in the winter-blooming *Erica* species.

Since the first reported discovery of a wild bud bloomer, near Brandenburg, Germany, by P. Ruthe in 1903 (Askjaer 1999), numerous others have been found. *Calluna vulgaris* 'David Eason' was introduced to commerce in 1935, and others soon followed. In recent years, there has been a veritable explosion of bud-blooming cultivars (Schröder 2005) as the great garden utility of this group has been recognized. Deliberate breeding for bud bloomers has resulted in the introduction of many more bud colors, bud and foliage color combinations, and growth habits for this class of heathers. The *Calluna* cultivars listed below are but a small sample of those available.

Calluna vulgaris
   'Alexandra'
   'Alicia'
   'Amethyst'
   'Anette'
   'Aphrodite'
   'Athene'
   'Bonita'
   'David Eason'
   'Fritz Kircher'
   'Galaxy'
   'Larissa'
   'Marleen'
   'Melanie'
   'Nelly' (the first trailing bud bloomer)
   'Redbud'
   'Romina'
   'Roodkapje'
   'Roswitha'
   'Sandy'
   'Underwoodii'
   'Venus'
   'Visser's Fancy'

Cape Heaths

Most South African *Erica* species and their hybrids, usually called Cape heaths because the majority of South African species are endemic to that country's Cape Province, are *not* reliably hardy and should be grown in containers that can be moved to a frost-free growing area for the winter. Gardeners in Zones 9 and 10, however, may be able to keep some of these showy ericas alive outdoors for many years in sheltered microclimates. David Robinson, of County Dublin, Ireland, reported in 1995 that a number of South African species had survived growing in the open in his coastal garden since 1986, despite temperatures as low as 23°F (−5°C). The showy *Erica canaliculata*, *E. cruenta*, *E. glandulosa*, and *E. pageana* all thrived in his acidic, well-drained soil (about 25 percent sand), the plants of *E. canaliculata* reaching 98 in. (2.5 m) in height in five years, despite repeated cutting back.

   Gardeners in similarly mild climates are encouraged to experiment with growing Cape heaths in the garden, where they may become substantial specimens. These South African *Erica* species and hybrids will take light freezes (above 21°F/−6°C) of short duration provided that they are protected from wind.

Erica 'African Fanfare'
Erica bauera
Erica caffra
Erica canaliculata
Erica cerinthoides
Erica cruenta
Erica curviflora
Erica glandulosa
Erica mammosa
Erica nana
Erica pageana
Erica speciosa
Erica 'Winter Fire'

Cape heaths thrive best if planted in open ground where they have unrestricted root runs, but they detest being dug up and placed in pots for the winter period. Therefore, most Cape heaths should be pot grown all year in an ericaceous compost. Simon Goodenough (1998) found that many species did better for him when he added a little charcoal to his compost mix. He also recommended watering with rainwater or artificially acidified water in regions where the local water supply is alkaline. Because the plants form large root balls, which must not be allowed to dry out completely at any time, daily watering of potted heaths during the summer may be necessary. Unlike plants grown in the open garden, potted heaths also need regular feeding during the growing season, with a liquid fertilizer formulated for ericaceous plants.

Many Cape heaths are suitable for pot culture. They require very little heat during the winter; it is enough simply to avoid frost. In fact, they prefer cool winter temperatures and consequently are not suited for use as house plants, except in unheated sun rooms. Plants spending the winter in the protection of a glasshouse need good air movement: steamy conditions cause them to wilt. Although they must never be allowed to go completely dry, it is better to keep Cape heaths somewhat drier between late autumn and early spring.

(Gardeners in hot, humid climates may find Cape heaths challenging. According to Satoshi Miwa [2000], the high summer humidity and heavy summer rainfall of southern Japan have tested the ingenuity of commercial potted plant producers there. Although winter temperatures are usually above freezing in that region, commercial growers keep their Cape heaths under cover all year in order to prevent the plants from remaining constantly wet, and thus susceptible to fungal diseases, in the summer.)

Once the plants are finished blooming, usually in late spring, they may be pruned. Prune at the base of the flowering spike. Because most Cape heaths become tall shrubs, young plants, in particular, should have their leading shoots pruned for the first few years to encourage compactness.

Potted heaths may be moved outside when danger of frost has passed. Potting on should be done just before moving the plants outdoors for the summer (Joyner 1979). Pot on regularly, with as little root disturbance as possible, into pots large enough to accommodate the plants' large root systems.

In addition to the hardier Cape heaths listed above, these heaths are suitable for pot culture. Many others of the more than 700 South African *Erica* species may be, as well.

Erica blandfordia
Erica formosa
Erica 'Gengold'
Erica gracilis (Because these are often sold as throwaway seasonal decorations, pot on plants of this species into suitable ericaceous medium immediately after purchase.)
Erica patersonia

Erica quadrangularis
Erica regia
Erica sparsa
Erica ventricosa
Erica versicolor
Erica verticillata
Erica vestita
Erica walkeria

Cold Tolerant

Cold tolerance is only one of several factors that determine the suitability of heather species and cultivars for particular gardens, but it is the first factor to consider when choosing heathers for a high altitude or high latitude garden.

This list contains those species generally considered to be the most cold tolerant. It also includes specific cultivar recommendations for species in which some cultivars are known to tolerate cold winters better than do other cultivars of the same species.

Because *Calluna vulgaris* has such an extensive natural range, from the Arctic to the Mediterranean, there is great variation among its cultivars in their cold tolerance. The ones listed below have been shown to be very cold hardy, but even these may be damaged if subjected to extreme temperature fluctuations. Gardeners in cold climates with short growing seasons have the best chance of succeeding with *Calluna* if they plant cultivars that start to bloom early in the summer and *finish* blooming by the time the majority of cultivars are at their peak of bloom in late summer. These early blooming cultivars appear to be among the hardiest of the species.

Some cultivars of *Erica spiculifolia* are distinctly hardier than others of this generally hardy species, but at this time there is not sufficient hardiness data on which to base specific cultivar recommendations.

Calluna vulgaris
    Cultivars from Saint Kilda
    Cultivars of Swedish origin: 'Brita Elisabeth',
        'Grönsinka', 'Kerstin', 'Matita',
        'Miniöxabäck', 'Peggy', and 'Sesam'
    'Alba Plena'
    'Allegro'
    'Caerketton White'
    'Cairnwell'
    'Caleb Threlkeld'
    'Catherine'
    'Chernobyl'
    'Dunnet Lime'
    'Inshriach Bronze'
    'J. H. Hamilton'
    'Long White'
    'Mair's Variety'
    'Martha Hermann'
    'Mullardoch'
    'Platt's Surprise'
    'Radnor'
    'Radnor Gold'
    'Red Favorit'
    'Reini'
    'Robert Chapman'
    'Silver Knight'
    'Sirsson'
    'Tib'
    'Velvet Fascination'
    'White Knight'
Erica carnea
Erica spiculifolia
Erica tetralix
Erica vagans
    'Birch Glow'
    'Cornish Cream'

Erica vagans 'Birch Glow' and 'Cornish Cream' are known to be among the hardier cultivars of this species. These may be damaged in very cold winters but usually recover from the roots.

Drought Tolerant

Suitable for Mediterranean-type gardens and regions that experience periodic droughts of relatively short duration. All heathers need at least some moisture in the soil at all times. No heather species can stand up to the extended drought conditions that plants specialized to store water, such as cacti, can endure. However, some species are much more drought-tolerant than others and can get by with infrequent watering *once established*. All will need frequent watering during the first year—or two—after planting, and all will benefit greatly if watered deeply once a week during very hot weather (daytime temperatures consistently higher than 85°F [29°C]). Planting heathers in well-drained but water-retentive soils will improve their chances of survival.

These heathers exhibit some drought tolerance. When possible, try to obtain cultivars that originated in the drier parts of a species' range. Note: In general, drought-tolerant heathers are less cold hardy than other heathers.

Calluna vulgaris
   'Fréjus'
   'Hiemalis'
   'Johnson's Variety'
Daboecia
Erica arborea
Erica australis
Erica ×*griffithsii*
Erica lusitanica
Erica manipuliflora
Erica multiflora
Erica scoparia
Erica terminalis
Erica tetralix (when grown where intense summer heat is not a factor)
Erica umbellata
Erica vagans
Erica ×*veitchii*
Erica ×*williamsii*

Early Bloomers among the Summer-Flowering Heathers

Many cultivars of *Erica cinerea* (too many to list) begin blooming in early summer or even late spring. Perhaps equally as many begin to flower in midsummer. Most *Erica tetralix* cultivars begin flowering in early to midsummer except 'Helma' and 'Tina', which delay flowering until late summer. *Erica tetralix* 'Bartinney' begins to flower in late spring.

Calluna vulgaris
    Cultivars from Saint Kilda
    'Caerketton White'
    'Devon'
    'Mullardoch'
    'Tenuis'
    'Tib'
Daboecia
Erica cinerea
Erica ×*krameri*
Erica spiculifolia
Erica ×*stuartii* 'Irish Lemon'
Erica tetralix
Erica ×*watsonii*
    'Cherry Turpin'
    'Dorothy Metheny'
    'Mary'
    'Pearly Pink'
    'Pink Pacific'

Edgers

The cultivars listed here are low growing and easily managed, suitable for planting along paths and near the front of the border. A few also creep or trail.

Calluna vulgaris
    'Cairnwell'
    'Dainty Bess'
    'Dainty Bess Junior' (also sold as "Bess Junior" and "Dainty Bess Minor")
    'Dunnet Lime'
    'Emerald Jock'
    'Gerda'
    'Mrs Ronald Gray'
    'Sister Anne'
    'Snowflake'
    'Soay'
Daboecia ×*scotica*
    'Jack Drake'
    'William Buchanan'
    'William Buchanan Gold'
Erica carnea 'Rotes Juwel'
Erica spiculifolia
Erica tetralix

Fragrant

Fragrance is a means by which plants attract pollinators. Many heathers are fragrant, although some have no scent apparent to humans (who are rarely heather pollinators!), and some have such a faint fragrance that you can detect it only when your nose is very close to the flowers. All the winter-blooming ericas have fragrance, but you may not notice it until you cut a bouquet for the house. Better yet, travel with a few blooming plants in a vehicle with the windows shut.

    Fragrance is especially valuable for cut flowers. The *Calluna* that produces long sprays of white flowers that smell exactly like heather honey—and has golden foliage as a bonus—well deserves its cultivar name *C. vulgaris* 'Fortyniner Gold'. It is a treasure of great worth.

One plant of *Erica arborea* 'Estrella Gold' a few years old can perfume a small garden. A few plants of *E.* ×*griffithsii* 'Jacqueline' will put most late summer garden visitors into a bliss of sniffing. A square yard (m²) of *Calluna vulgaris* 'White Lawn' in full bloom can cause someone who passes the plants to stop, turn around, and inhale deeply. *Erica cinerea* 'Coccinea' can produce the same effect, but with a totally different fragrance. Heathers are as worth exploring for their differing fragrances as they are for their diversity of forms and colors.

Floral fragrance is an on-and-off thing. Plants will be fragrant at some times of day and not at others. They may be fragrant one day and not the next, depending upon the temperature and humidity around them. The timing of fragrant periods is precisely correlated in nature with the conditions when pollinators are likely to be active. A heather plant swarming with insects on a warm, sunny spring day is likely to be fragrant then but not on the next, when the weather has turned cold and gray and the insects wisely choose to remain at home.

As beauty is said to be in the eye of the beholder, so fragrance is in the nose of the inhaler. A heather cultivar that is very fragrant to one person may appear to have no scent to another. The heathers in this list have seemed fragrant to someone, someplace, at some time. Many other heathers are fragrant. Do take the time to visit heather gardens and smell the flowers yourself.

If no cultivar name appears after the name of a species listed below, all cultivars of the species are at least slightly fragrant to humans.

Calluna vulgaris (many but not all)
    'Barnett Anley'
    'Battle of Arnhem'
    'Carmen'
    'Con Brio' (very sweet)
    'Fortyniner Gold'
    'Juno'
    'Lewis Lilac'
    'Long White'
    'Lyndon Proudley'
    'Oxshott Common'
    'Sister Anne'
    'White Lawn'
Daboecia azorica 'Arthur P. Dome'
Erica arborea
Erica australis
Erica carnea
Erica cinerea (many)
    'Bucklebury Red'
    'Coccinea'
    'Iberian Beauty'
    'Knap Hill Pink'
    'Pentreath'
    'Purple Beauty' (Woods 1972)
    'Velvet Night'
Erica ×*darleyensis*
    'Arthur Johnson'
    'George Rendall' (Woods 1972)
Erica erigena
Erica ×*garforthensis* 'Tracy Wilson'
Erica ×*griffithsii*
    'Heaven Scent'
    'Jacqueline'
Erica lusitanica (Turpin 1985)
Erica manipuliflora
    'Ian Cooper'
    'Korčula'
Erica spiculifolia

Erica vagans 'Kevernensis Alba'
Erica ×*veitchii*
Erica ×*williamsii* 'Ken Wilson'

Ground Covers, Low Carpeters, and Heather Lawns

Calluna vulgaris
- 'Alys Sutcliffe'
- 'Anne's Zwerg'
- 'Boreray'
- 'Caleb Threlkeld'
- 'Clare Carpet'
- 'Dart's Flamboyant'
- 'Emerald Jock'
- 'Golden Carpet'
- 'Golden Rivulet'
- 'Heidepracht'
- 'Heideteppich'
- 'Heidezwerg'
- 'Kuphaldtii'
- 'White Lawn'

Daboecia cantabrica
- 'Heather Yates'
- 'Rubra'
- 'White Carpet'

Erica carnea

Erica cinerea
- 'Alba Minor'
- 'Atrorubens'
- 'Carnea'
- 'C. D. Eason'
- 'Celebration'
- 'Cevennes'
- 'Foxhollow Mahogany'
- 'Iberian Beauty'
- 'Pink Ice'
- 'Rock Ruth'
- 'Ruby'
- 'Windlebrooke'

Erica mackayana

Heat Tolerant

Erica arborea
Erica australis
Erica ×*darleyensis*
Erica erigena
Erica lusitanica
Erica manipuliflora
Erica multiflora
Erica scoparia
Erica terminalis
Erica umbellata

Heat and Humidity Tolerant

Few heathers do well in regions that have very hot summers that are also very humid. These heathers have proven tolerant of the combination of high heat with high relative humidity.

Calluna vulgaris 'Multicolor' (Ed
 Chapman and Kay Chapman,
 personal communication)
Erica carnea
 'King George'
'Pink Spangles'
'Springwood Pink'
'Springwood White'
Erica ×*darleyensis*

Hedges

These heathers can grow 2 ft. (60 cm) or higher and tolerate substantial pruning. Although all cultivars of *Erica erigena* are suitable for use as hedges, 'Brian Proudley' is especially valuable for hedging because its width is only about half its height.

Erica ×*darleyensis*
Erica erigena
Erica ×*griffithsii* 'Valerie Griffiths'
Erica manipuliflora
 'Aldeburgh'
 'Don Richards'
Erica terminalis
Erica vagans

Late Bloomers among the Summer-Flowering Heathers

Calluna vulgaris
 bud bloomers
 'Autumn Glow'
 'Battle of Arnhem'
 'Blueness'
 'Bronze Beauty'
 'Christmas Candle'
 'Durford Wood'
 'E. F. Brown'
 'Finale'
 'H. E. Beale'
 'Hibernica'
 'Hiemalis'
 'Jimmy Dyce'
 'Johnson's Variety'
 'Monika'
 'October White'
 'Peace'
 'Peter Sparkes'
 'Red Pimpernel'
 'Saint Nick'
 'Schurig's Sensation'
 'Spring Cream'
 'Spring Glow'
 'Stefanie'
Erica manipuliflora
Erica multiflora

Long Blooming (several months or longer)

Calluna vulgaris
    bud bloomers
    'Devon'
    'Jimmy Dyce'
    'Tib'
Daboecia cantabrica
Daboecia ×*scotica*
Erica cinerea
Erica ×*darleyensis*
Erica ×*garforthensis*
Erica ×*gaudificans*
Erica ×*krameri*
Erica ×*stuartii* 'Irish Lemon'
Erica tetralix

Novelty Flowers with Garden Value

Calluna vulgaris
    bud bloomers
    'Perestrojka'
Daboecia cantabrica
    'Bicolor'
    'Celtic Star'
    'Charles Nelson'
    'Covadonga'
    'Harlequin'
Daboecia cantabrica f. *blumii* (holds flowers facing up instead of the usual drooping)
Erica cinerea
    'Domino'
    'Hutton's Seedling'
    'Yvonne'
Erica ×*stuartii*
    'Stuart's Original'
Erica tetralix 'Pink Pepper'

Rock Gardens, Sinks, and Troughs

This list, by no means comprehensive, includes tight-growing "buns" that rarely produce flowers, very compact low growers, and some trailers that can be used to cascade over rocks or over the sides of sinks and troughs. In general, cultivars of *Erica carnea* and *E. cinerea* will eventually become much wider than plants of the other species listed here.

Troughs are useful for growing plants that are so small and slow growing that they would be overwhelmed by other plants in the garden. They also can house plants that prefer specialized growing conditions difficult to create in a large garden but easy to provide in the microcosm that is the trough garden: for example, a radically different soil pH or very sharp drainage. *Erica umbellata* fits into the latter category (Charles Nelson, personal communication).

Calluna vulgaris
   'Anne's Zwerg'
   'Arran Gold'
   'Baby Ben'
   'Baby Wicklow'
   'Bonsaï'
   'Clare Carpet'
   'Dainty Bess'
   'Dainty Bess Junior' (also sold as "Bess Junior" or "Dainty Bess Minor")
   'Findling'
   'Flatling'
   'Foxii'
   'Foxii Floribunda' (sacrifices bun shape for flower production)
   'Foxii Nana'
   'Glenmorangie'
   'Golden Carpet'
   'Golden Fleece'
   'Grönsinka'
   'Harten's Findling'
   'Heidezwerg'
   'Humpty Dumpty'
   'Miniöxabäck'
   'Miss Muffet'
   'Molecule'
   'Mullardoch'
   'Nelly'
   'Penny Bun'
   'Pygmaea'
   'Soay'
   'The Pygmy'
   'Tom Thumb'
   'Velvet Dome'

Daboecia azorica 'Arthur P. Dome'

Daboecia ×*scotica*
   'Ben'
   'Cora'

Erica carnea
   'Ann Sparkes'
   'Rotes Juwel'
   'Scatterley'

Erica cinerea
   'Eden Valley'
   'Godrevy'
   'Guernsey Lime'
   'Guernsey Purple'
   'Honeymoon'
   'Iberian Beauty'
   'Pink Ice'
   'Rock Ruth'

Erica tetralix
   'Curled Roundstone'
   'Delta'
   'Jos' Creeping'

Erica umbellata

Erica ×*williamsii* 'Gold Button'

Saint Kilda Heathers (*Calluna vulgaris* cultivars)

Saint Kilda is an island group in the North Atlantic 41 mi. (66 km) west of Scotland's Outer Hebrides, between 8 and 9 degrees west longitude and slightly south of 58 degrees north latitude. Most plant life on the islands is dwarfed, a survival response that reduces wind exposure. The plants retain their dwarf growth habits and cold hardiness wherever they are grown. Saint Kilda, abandoned by its human inhabitants in 1930, is now owned by the National Trust for Scotland and has been designated as both a cultural and a natural UNESCO World Heritage Site.

During National Trust working parties in 1966 and 1967 on Hirta, the largest island of the Saint Kilda group, Robert J. Brien took cuttings from more than 70 individuals of *Calluna vulgaris*. He was able to root these and grow them in his garden in Perthshire, Scotland. Plants grown from garden cuttings of the rooted wild-collected specimens were donated to the National Trust for Scotland so that they might be sold to benefit the Saint Kilda Fund.

The Saint Kilda heathers tend to be dwarf, although some are more dwarf than others (Brien 1974). Most have white flowers, because Brien was particularly interested in white-flowering heathers at the time he made the collections.

Calluna vulgaris
   'Alex Warwick'
   'Bob Brien'
   'Boreray'
   'Conachair'
   'Emerald Jock'
   'Floriferous'
   'Isle of Hirta'
   'Minty'
   'Mullach Mor'
   'Oiseval'
   'Soay'

Shade Tolerant

None of these plants will grow well in heavy, dense shade but will bloom with at least a half day of sunlight, preferably morning sun, or dappled shade throughout the day. In shade, the plants will be less compact, and there will be fewer blooms than in full-sun exposures.

Daboecia (the most shade tolerant of the hardy heathers of heathland origin)
Erica carnea
Erica ×*darleyensis*
   These will tolerate some shade but perform much better with full sun exposure.
Erica mackayana

Trailing

These plants are useful for hanging baskets, planters, along the tops of walls, in troughs, and in window boxes.

Calluna vulgaris
   'Anne's Zwerg'
   'Boreray'
   'Caleb Threlkeld'
   'Heidezwerg'
   'Nelly'
   'Prostrata Flagelliformis'
Erica carnea (many cultivars)
Erica manipuliflora 'Cascades'
Erica tetralix 'Curled Roundstone'

Tree Heaths

Heather enthusiasts are, perhaps, overly optimistic in calling a number of European *Erica* species "tree heaths." The term is used in this book to indicate heather species that usually grow more than 3 ft. (1 m) tall, sometimes considerably more, and are taller than—or at least as tall as—wide. Only a few heathers actually qualify as "trees" under the strict botanical definition of that term.

The Azorean subspecies of *Erica scoparia* (synonym *E. azorica*) can become a tree with a substantial trunk, and McClintock (1989b) cites numerous examples of *E. arborea* growing more than 50 ft. (15 m) tall in optimal African habitats. Most other species listed below, and some cultivars of *E. arborea* and *E. scoparia*, are really large shrubs rather than trees. They are suitable for use as accent plants in the heather garden, bringing interest up above ground level.

Heather growers do not all agree upon the inclusion of *Erica erigena* and its hybrids among the tree heaths, citing such cultivars as 'W. T. Rackliff', which grows only slightly taller than a large *Calluna vulgaris*. However, many cultivars of the species grow taller than wide, and at least one old specimen has been reported to reach 12 ft. (4 m) in height (McClintock 1989). For the purposes of this book, *E. erigena* is considered a tree heath.

Tree heaths are not just for heather gardens. They are useful in the mixed border and as backdrop, screening, and specimen plants in many garden settings.

Erica arborea
Erica australis
Erica erigena
Erica lusitanica (Do not plant in northern California or New Zealand, where it is invasive.)
Erica ×*oldenburgensis*
Erica scoparia (Insignificant flowers, more novel than beautiful, but can get very tall. Has considerable weed potential!)
Erica terminalis
Erica ×*veitchii*

Unusual Foliage

Calluna vulgaris
   'Cairnwell'
   'Durford Wood'
   'Goldsworth Crimson Variegated'
   'Kerstin'
   'Matita'
   'Skone' (often sold as NORDLICHT or NORTHERN LIGHTS)
Daboecia cantabrica 'Rainbow'
Daboecia ×*scotica* 'William Buchanan Gold'

Winter Foliage Color

This list includes heathers *not described in chapter 7* whose foliage turns orange or red in winter. Because so many cultivars have been selected for this attribute, this list is purely arbitrary. Many other cultivars also have colorful winter foliage.

Calluna vulgaris
   'Bispingen'
   'Boskoop'
   'Braeriach'
   'Colette'
   'Con Brio'
   'Cuprea'
   'Dart's Flamboyant'
   'Dart's Hedgehog'
   'Desiree'
   'Fire King'
   'Fire Star'
   'Fort Bragg'
   'Foya'
   'Glenlivet'
   'Glenmorangie'
   'Gold Charm'
   'Golden Feather'
   'Highland Rose'
   'Hillbrook Orange'
   'Hoyerhagen'
   'Julia'
   'Red Carpet'
   'Spitfire'
   'Sunrise'
   'Winter Fire'

Erica cinerea
   'Golden Tee'
   'Jos' Golden'

Heather Societies

Belonging to a heather society is an excellent way to learn about heathers and to stay abreast of current trends in heather breeding and cultivar introductions. All societies welcome international members. In addition to producing annual conferences and informative journals, heather societies offer special member benefits that may include nursery discounts and access to hard-to-find cultivars and to private gardens not usually open to the public. The Heather Society and the North American Heather Society have regional affiliates that meet several times a year.

Ericultura
Mevr. T. Velzeboer
Oud Loosdrechtsedijk 64
1231 NB Loosdrecht
Netherlands
pavandijk@hotmail.com
http://ericultura.tuinkrant.com

Gesellschaft der Heidefreunde e. V.
Berner Heerweg 431
22159 Hamburg
Germany
Tel: (0) 40 6448165
http://gdh.heidezuechtung.de

The Heather Society
Tippitiwitchet Cottage
Hall Road, Outwell
Wisbech, Cambridgeshire
United Kingdom PE14 8PE
Tel: (0) 1945 774077 or (0845) 3240580
[local rate in UK]
www.heathersociety.org.uk

North American Heather Society
2299 Wooded Knolls Drive
Philomath, OR 97370
United States
Tel: (541) 929-6272
www.northamericanheathersoc.org

Plant Sources

The nurseries listed here are either heather specialist nurseries or carry significant heather inventories. They sell to the general public either from a nursery shop or by mail order, or both. Most have catalogs or plant lists. Some have display gardens.

Listing does not imply the authors' endorsement of these nurseries nor does it imply criticism of those omitted from the list.

Belgium
Boomkwekerij De Bock LV
Pelikaanstraat 89
9700 Oudenaarde
Tel: (0) 55 30 24 80
www.planten-debock.be
Retail sales.

Boomkwekerij De Bruyn bvba
Vennestraat 6a
3130 Begijnendijk
Tel: (0) 16 56 14 27
info@boomkwekerij-debruyn.com
www.boomkwekerij-debruyn.com
Mail order and retail sales.

Canada
The Heather Farm
Box 2206
Sardis, BC V2R 1A6
Tel: (604) 823-4884
www.theheatherfarm.com
Mail order within Canada. Display garden. No on-site retail sales.

Mason Hogue Gardens
Marjorie Mason
3520 Durham Road #1
R.R. #4, Uxbridge, ON L9P 1R4
Tel: (905) 649-3532
info@masonhogue.com
www.masonhogue.com
Display garden and retail sales.

Pépinière Villeneuve
951, Presqu'île
L'Assomption, QC J5W 3P4
Tel: (450) 589-7158
pepvil@bellnet.ca
www.pepinierevilleneuve.com
Mail order within Canada. Display garden and retail sales.

France
Pépinières Dauguet
La Voisinière
53220 Larchamp
Tel: (0) 243 05 32 20
Retail sales.

Germany
Baumschule H. Hachmann
Brunnenstrasse 68
D-25355 Barmstedt
Holstein
Tel: (0) 41 23 20 55
info@hachmann.de
www.hachmann.de
Mail order, display garden, and retail sales.

Heidböhl-Baumschule Jürgen Krebs
Hauptstrasse 50
27318 Hoyerhagen
Tel: (0) 49 4251 2993
www.baumschule-krebs.de
Mail order and retail sales.

Thomas Witte Heidegärten
Steinkenhöfen 8
29646 Bispingen
Tel: (0) 5194 2378
info@heidegaerten.de
www.heidegaerten.de

Netherlands
Haalboon
Meenkselaan 5
3972 J N Driebergen
Tel: (0) 343-512177
Retail sales.

Heather's Heide (G. and his son
 E. van Hoef)
Esweg 15
3771 PK Barneveld
Tel: (0) 342-751925
info@heathersheide.com
www.heathersheide.com
Mail order and retail sales.

H. Kral & R. Koot
Tuincentrum Vechtweelde b.v.
Herenweg 35
3602 AN Maarssen
Tel: (0) 346 563397
Retail sales.

J. J. Bollaart
Kooiweg 16–18
2771 W J Boskoop

Planten Tuin Esveld
Rijneveld 72
2771 XS Boskoop
Tel: (0) 172 213289
info@esveld.nl
www.esveld.nl
Mail order and retail sales.

Switzerland
Hauenstein AG Baumschulen &
 Garten-Center
Landstrasse 42
CH-8197 Rafz
Tel: (0) 44 879 11 22
www.hauenstein-rafz.ch
*Mail order, display garden, and retail
 sales.*

United Kingdom
Barncroft Nurseries
Dunwood Lane, Longsdon
Stoke on Trent, Staffordshire ST9 9QW
Tel: (0) 1538 384 310
www.barncroftnurseries.com
Mail order and retail sales.

Blundell's Nurseries
68 Southport New Road
Tarleton, Preston
Lancashire PR4 6HY
Tel: (0) 1772 815442
jerplusjeff@aol.com
Retail sales. Open seven days a week.

Bridgemere Nurseries
Bridgemere, Nantwich
Cheshire CW5 7QB
Tel: (0) 1270 521100
info@bridgemere.co.uk
www.bridgemere.co.uk
Display garden. Retail sales.

Galloway Heathers
Carty Port, Newton Stewart
Wigtownshire, Dumfries and Galloway
 DG8 6AY
Tel: (0) 1671 401367
enquiries@gallowayheathers.com
www.gallowayheathers.com

Mail order. Garden center (retail sales) in Holmpark Industrial Estate, Minnigaff, Newton Stewart.

Goscote Nurseries Ltd.
Syston Road, Cossington,
Leicestershire LE7 4UZ
Tel: (0) 1509 812121
sales@goscote.co.uk
www.goscote.co.uk
Retail sales.

Highland Heathers (John and Elaine Davidson)
Muirend, South Crieff Road
Comrie, Perthshire PH6 2JA
Tel: (0) 1764 670440
enquiries@highlandheathers.co.uk
www.highlandheathers.co.uk
Mail order, display garden, and retail sales.

Hillway Nursery
Crawley Down Road, Felbridge
East Grinstead, West Sussex RH19 2PS
Tel: (0) 1342 324950
sales@hillwaynursery.co.uk
www.hillwaynursery.co.uk
Retail sales.

Holden Clough Nursery
Holden, Bolton-by-Bowland
Clitheroe, Lancashire BB7 4PF
Tel: (0) 1200 447615
info@holdencloughnursery.co.uk
www.holdencloughnursery.com
Mail order and retail sales.

Jackson's Nurseries (UK) Ltd.
Thorney Edge Road, Bagnall
Stoke-on-Trent
Staffordshire ST9 9LD
Tel: (0) 1782 502 741
sales@jacksonsnurseries.co.uk
www.jacksonsnurseries.co.uk
Mail order to United Kingdom only. Retail sales.

Plantbase (Graham Blunt)
Sleepers Stile Road, Cousley Wood
Wadhurst, East Sussex TN5 6QX
Tel: (0) 1892 891453
graham@plantbase.freeserve.co.uk
Retail sales, including South African heathers.

Plaxtol Nurseries
Plaxtol
Sevenoaks, Kent TN15 0QR
Tel: (0) 1732 810550
alan@plaxtol-nurseries.co.uk
www.plaxtol-nurseries.co.uk
Mail order and retail sales.

Rumsey Gardens
117 Drift Road, Clanfield
Waterlooville, Hampshire PO8 0PD
Tel: (0) 23 9259 3367
derek.giles@btconnect.com
www.rumsey-gardens.co.uk
Mail order and retail sales. Display garden (please request permission from sales staff before visiting).

Speyside Heather Garden and Visitor Centre
Dulnain Bridge
Inverness-shire PH26 3PA
Tel: (0) 1479 851359
www.heathercentre.com
Mail order to United Kingdom and Europe only. Display garden and retail sales.

Spring Park Nursery
78 Woodland Way
West Wickham, Kent BR4 9LR
Tel: (0) 20 8777 5161
enquiries@springparknursery.co.uk
www.springparknursery.co.uk
Mail order. Retail sales by appointment only.

Swallows Nursery
Mixbury, Brackley
Northamptonshire NN13 5RR
Tel: (0) 1280 847721
Mail order and retail sales.

Triscombe Nurseries
West Bagborough
Near Taunton, Somerset TA4 3HG
Tel: (0) 1984 618267
triscombe.nurseries2000@virgin.net
www.triscombenurseries.co.uk
Mail order to United Kingdom mainland only. Retail sales.

United States

Dayton Nurseries Inc.
3459 Cleveland-Massillon Road
Norton, OH 44203
Tel: (330) 825-3320
info@daytonnursery.com
www.daytonnursery.com
Mail order, display garden, and retail sales.

Glenmar Heather Nursery, Inc.
P.O. Box 479
Bayside, CA 95524
Tel: (707) 268-5560
glenmar@humboldt1.com
Display garden and retail sales most weekdays, weather permitting, and by appointment.

Green Mountain Heather
19610 Green Mountain Road
P.O. Box 172
Colton, OR 97017
Tel: (503) 824-2724
fmsmith@colton.com
Display garden and retail sales by appointment only.

Heaths and Heathers
502 E. Haskell Hill Road
Shelton, WA 98584
Tel: (800) 294-3284 or (360) 427-5318
www.heathsandheathers.com
Mail order. Display garden and retail sales at: 631 E. Pickering Road, Shelton, WA 98584

Hickory Hill Heath and Heather (Paul and Jane Murphy)
2473 Hickory Hill Road
Oxford, PA 19363
Tel: (610) 883-2171
murphy1213@zoominternet.net
Display garden and retail sales.

Highland Heather
8268 S. Gribble Road
Canby, OR 97013
Tel: (503) 263-2428
www.highlandheather.com
Mail order. Retail sales by appointment only.

Log House Herbs Inc., doing business as Log House Heathers
(Art and Judy Pilch)
70 Ajuga Drive
Sylva, NC 28779
Tel: (828) 586-5842
Display gardens and retail sales by appointment only.

Love Ericaceae
P.O. Box 2775
Fort Bragg, CA 95437
Tel: (707) 964-4829
clove@mcn.org
Display garden and retail sales by appointment.

Mo's Nursery
P.O. Box 1122
Molino, OR 97042
Tel: (503) 829-7643
mosnrsry@web-ster.com
Mail order. Display garden and retail sales by appointment only.

Quackin' Grass Nursery
16 Laurel Hill Road
Brooklyn, CT 06234
Tel: (860) 779-1732
qgnursery@earthlink.net
www.quackingrassnursery.com
Display garden and on-site sales. Closes for winter.

Rock Spray Nursery
David and Alissa Krieger-DeWitt
P.O. Box 2035
Truro, MA 02666
Tel: (508) 349-6769
www.rockspray.com
Mail order within the United States, except to California. Display garden and retail sales.

Sylvan Nursery
1028 Horseneck Road
Westport, MA 02790
Tel: (508) 636-4573
sales@sylvannursery.com
www.sylvannursery.com
Mail order and retail sales.

Woodville Nursery
P.O. Box 677
Rogue River, OR 97537
Tel: (541) 582-3338
ladyheather1@earthlink.net
Mail order. On-site sales by appointment only.

Garden Designers

These garden designers are skilled at using heather in the landscape. However, listing does not imply the authors' endorsement of these designers, nor does it imply criticism of those omitted from the list.

Canada
Denis Bernard/Pierre Villeneuve
Pépinière Villeneuve
951 Presqu'Ile
L'Assomption, QC J5W 3P4
Tel: (450) 589-7158
pepvil@bellnet.ca
www.pepinierevilleneuve.com

Germany
Dipl.-Ing. Peter Happe
Garten- und Landschaftsbau
Wollgrasweg 5
26160 Bad Zwischenahn
Tel: (0) 4403 5526

Gartengestaltung Thomas Witte
Steinkenhofen 8
29646 Bispingen
Tel: (0) 5194 2378
info@heidegaerten.de
www.heidegaerten.de

United Kingdom
Highland Heathers
Muirend, South Crieff Road
Comrie, Perthshire PH6 2JA
Tel: (0) 1764 670440
enquiries@highlandheathers.co.uk
www.highlandheathers.co.uk

Karen Platt
35 Longfield Road, Crookes
Sheffield S10 1QW
Tel: (0) 114 268 1700
www.karenplatt.co.uk
www.blackplants.co.uk

Rumsey Gardens
117 Drift Road, Clanfield
Waterlooville, Hampshire PO8 0PD
Tel: (0) 23 9259 3367
derek.giles@btconnect.com
www.rumsey-gardens.co.uk

Speyside Heather Garden and Visitor
    Centre
Dulnain Bridge
Inverness-shire PH26 3PA
Tel: (0) 1479 851359
www.heathercentre.com

Spring Park Nursery Garden Design
78 Woodland Way
West Wickham, Kent BR4 9LR
Tel: (0) 20 8777 5161
enquiries@springparknursery.co.uk
www.springparknursery.co.uk

United States
Barrett Landscape & Design
81518 Lost Creek Road
Dexter, OR 97431
Tel: (541) 937-3780

Stacie Crooks
Crooks Garden Design
17710 14th Avenue Northwest

Seattle, WA 98177
(206) 546-0315
CrooksGardens@aol.com

Derviss Design
1408 Park Avenue
Novato, CA 94945
Tel: (415) 892-3121
dervissdesign@verizon.net
www.dervissdesign.com

Susan Ewalt
2850 Sykes Creek Road
Rogue River, OR 97537
Tel: (541) 582-3338
ladyheather1@earthlink.net

Helen Garcia
P.O. Box 17
Gualala, CA 95445
Tel: (707) 884-4525
garciakoala@hotmail.com

Mary Gearheart
Design-Work
905 H Street
Arcata, CA 95521
(707) 826-7292
msgheart@gmail.com

Lucy Hardiman, Principal
Perennial Partners
1234 SE 18th Avenue
Portland, OR 97214
Tel: (503) 231-0025
lucyflora@comcast.net

Terry Knaus
21601 Forster Lane
Fort Bragg, CA 95437
Tel: (707) 964-0681

Maria Krenek
Glenmar Heather Nursery, Inc.
P.O. Box 479
Bayside, CA 95524
Tel: (707) 268-5560
glenmar@humboldt1.com

North Hill Garden Design, Inc.
North Hill
P.O. Box 178
Readsboro, VT 05350
Tel: (802) 423-5444
www.northhillgarden.com

Gary Ratway
Integrated Designs/Digging Dog
    Nursery
P.O. Box 471
Albion, CA 95410
Tel: (707) 937-1235
gratway@pacific.net

Lily Ricardi
P.O. Box 898
Mendocino, CA 95460
Tel: (707) 937-0920
edges@mcn.org

Katherine H. Udall
TerraDomicile Gardens
35 Keziah's Lane
Orleans, MA 02653-4126
Tel: (508) 255-1663
wkudall@cape.com

Priscilla Hutt Williams
Pumpkin Brook Organic Gardening Inc.
35 Turner Road
Townsend, MA 01469
Tel: (978) 597-3005
phw@seedlingspecialist.com
www.seedlingspecialist.com

Gardens with Heather Interest

The gardens listed below are not all heather gardens, but all have significant heather plantings. Although some are privately owned, most open regularly to the public throughout the year. Please check the gardens' web sites, or telephone, for travel directions and current open hours and admission fees (if any) before visiting.

Australia

Adelaide Botanic Garden
North Terrace
Adelaide, South Australia 5000
Tel: (61 8) 8222 9311
www.environment.sa.gov.au/botanic
 gardens/index.html
Mediterranean Garden

Mount Lofty Botanic Garden
Summit Road *or* Piccadilly Road
Crafers, South Australia 5152
Tel: (61 8) 8370 8370
www.environment.sa.gov.au/botanic
 gardens/index.html

Mount Tomah Botanic Garden
Bells Line of Road via Bilpin
New South Wales 2758
Tel: (02) 4567-2154
www.bluemts.com.au/mounttomah
The extensive Mount Tomah heather collection contains both European and South African heather species.

Wittunga Botanic Garden
Shepherd's Hill Road
Blackwood, South Australia 5051
Tel: (61 8) 8370 8370
www.environment.sa.gov.au/botanic
 gardens/index.html

Canada

Butchart Gardens
800 Benvenuto Avenue
Brentwood Bay, BC V8M 1J8
Tel: (866) 652-4422
www.butchartgardens.com

Dan Cooke Memorial Heather Garden
Cobble Hill Farmer's Institute
Corner of Watson Avenue and Fisher
 Road
Cobble Hill, BC V0R 1L0
Tel: (250) 743-0965
www.bcheathersociety.org
Small, well-designed garden created and maintained by the Vancouver Island Heather Society.

Government House Gardens
1401 Rockland Avenue
Victoria, BC V8S 1V9
Tel: (250) 595-5605
www.ltgov.bc.ca

Horticulture Centre of the Pacific
505 Quayle Road
Victoria, BC V9E 2J7
Tel: (250) 479-6162
www.hcp.bc.ca

Memorial University Botanical Garden
306 Mount Scio Road
Saint John's, NL A1C 5S7
Tel: (709) 737-8590
www.mun.ca/botgarden/home.php

University of British Columbia Botanical Garden
6804 SW Marine Drive
Vancouver, BC V6T 1Z4
Tel: (604) 822-9666
www.ubcbotanicalgarden.org

VanDusen Botanical Garden
5251 Oak Street (at 37th)
Vancouver, BC V6M 4H1
Tel: (604) 878-9274
www.city.vancouver.bc.ca/parks/parks/vandusen/website

France
Les jardins de Callunes
5, chemin de la Prelle
F-88210 Ban de Sapt
Tel: (0) 3 29 58 94 94
www.chateaux-france.com/callunes
Near Saint Die.

Germany
Arboretum Thiensen
Thiensen 17
25373 Ellerhoop
Tel: (0) 4120 2 18
www.ellerhoop.de/html/arboretum.html

Berggarten Hannover
Herrenhäuser Str. 4
30419 Hannover-Herrenhausen
Tel: (0) 511 168-47576
www.berggarten-hannover.de

Botanischer Garten Bremen
Marcusallee 60
28359 Bremen
Tel: (0) 421 361 89 779
www.rhodo.org/park.php

Botanischer Garten Hamburg
Heesten 10
22609 Hamburg
Tel: (0) 40 42 81 60
www.bghamburg.de

Botanischer Garten Rombergpark
Rombergpark 49 b
44225 Dortmund
Tel: (0) 231 50-2 41 64
www.rombergpark.dortmund.de

Gartenkulturzentrum - Park der Gärten
Elmendorfer Strasse 65
26160 Bad Zwischenahn-Rostrup
Tel.: (0) 4403 81 96-0
www.park-der-gaerten.de

Heidegarten Gommern
Am Fuchsberg (über Pretzienerstr.)
39245 Gommern
www.gommern.de

Heidegarten Lüllingen
An de Klus
47608 Geldern-Lüllingen
www.luellingen.de

Heidegarten Schneverdingen
Schaftrift über Overbeckstr.
29640 Schneverdingen
www.schneverdingen.de
Public heather park.

Lausitzer Findlingspark Nochten
02943 Nochten bei Weißwasser
Tel.: (0) 357 74-74711
www.lausitzer-findlingspark-nochten.
   com

Ireland

Barnagh Gardens
Newcastle West
Limerick
Tel: (0) 69 61446

Fernhill Gardens
Enniskery Road
Sandyford, Co. Dublin
Tel: (0) 1 2954257
dihb@eircom.net
www.gardensireland.com/
   fernhill-gardens.html
*Private garden. Bergenias grow with ericas
   on the heather bank.*

Heather Crest
Priorstown
Clonmel, Co. Tipperary
Tel: (0) 52 33329
Open by appointment only.

Ilnacullin
Glengarriff
Bantry, Co. Cork
Tel: (0) 27 63040
www.heritageireland.ie/en/
   ParksandGardens/South

K Gardens
Booleigh
Nurney, Co. Kildare
Tel: (0) 507 26189
www.athyrar.com/local-business.asp
Private garden.

Lakemount Garden
Barnavara Hill
Glanmire, Co. Cork
Tel: (0)21 4821052
www.lakemountgarden.com
Open by appointment only.

National Botanic Gardens, Glasnevin
Near the junction of Botanic Avenue
   and Botanic Road
Glasnevin, Dublin 9
Tel: (0)1 837 7596
www.botanicgardens.ie
Collection includes many Cape heaths.

Netherlands

Heidetuin Driebergen-Rijsenburg
http://www.floraliadriebergen.nl/
   terugblik_20030510.htm
Heather reserve near Utrecht.

Von Gimborn Arboretum
Vossensteinsesteeg 8
3941 BL Doorn
Tel: (0) 30 25 35 455
www.bio.uu.nl/bottuinen

New Zealand

Christchurch Botanic Gardens
Rolleston Avenue, adjacent to Armagh
   Street car park
Christchurch City Council
P.O. Box 237
Christchurch 8015
Tel: (03) 941 7590
www.ccc.govt.nz/Parks/Botanic
   Gardens/

Coehaven Gardens
150 Rangiuru Road
Otaki 5512
Tel: 06 364 7001
ccc@coehaven.co.nz
www.coehaven.biz

Larnach Castle
145 Camp Road
Otago Peninsula
P.O. Box 1350
Dunedin 9054
Tel: (64) 3 476 16 16
www.larnachcastle.co.nz

Norway
Det Norske Arboret
Mildeveien 240
5259 Hjellestad
Tel: 55 98 72 50
www.uib.no/arboretet

Spain
Atlantic Botanical Garden
Avenida del Jardín Botánico s/n
33394 Gijón
Asturias
Tel: 985-185130/185131
jardin.botanico@ayto-gijon.es
www.botanicoatlantico.com

United Kingdom
Abbotswood
Stow-on-the-Wold
Gloucestershire GL54 1EN
Private garden opening to the public through the National Gardens Scheme (The Yellow Book). Good place to view plantings of heathers that tolerate some lime.

Benmore Botanic Garden
Dunoon, Argyll PA23 8QU
Tel: (0) 1369 706 261
www.rbge.org.uk
Administered by RBG Edinburgh.

Branklyn Garden
116 Dundee Road, Perth
Perth and Kinross PH2 7BB
Tel: (0) 1738 625535
www.branklyngarden.org.uk

Cambridge University Botanic Garden
Cory Lodge, Bateman Street
Cambridge CB2 1JF
Tel: (0) 1223 336265
www.botanic.cam.ac.uk

Champs Hill Garden
Waltham Park Road
Coldwaltham
Pulborough, Sussex RH20 1LY
Tel: (0) 1798 831868
www.gardenvisit.com/g/cham.htm

Cherrybank Gardens
Bell's Cherrybank Centre
Necessity Brae, Perth PH2 0PF
Tel: (0) 1738 472800
Holder of the national heather collection.

Cragside Gardens & Estate
Rothbury, Morpeth
Northumberland NE65 7PZ
Tel: (0) 1669 620333/620150
www.nationaltrust.org.uk

Dyffryn Gardens
Saint Nicholas, Cardiff
South Glamorgan CF5 6SU
Tel: (0) 2920 593 328
www.dyffryngardens.org.uk

Exbury Gardens
Exbury, Southampton SO45 1AZ
Tel: (0) 2380 89 1203
www.exbury.co.uk

The Garden at The Bannut
Bringsty, Herefordshire WR6 5TA
Tel: (0) 1885 482 206
www.bannut.co.uk
The heather knot garden here is of special interest. Those who wish to visit this privately owned garden on days when it is not regularly open are urged to telephone for an appointment.

Glasgow Botanic Gardens
730 Great Western Road at Queen Margaret Drive
Glasgow G12 0UE
Tel: (0) 141 334 2422
www.clyde-valley.com/Glasgow/botanic.htm

Golden Acre Park
Otley Road, Bramhope, Leeds
West Yorkshire LS16
Tel: (0) 113 2610374
www.leeds.gov.uk

Harris Garden, University of Reading
Whiteknights, Reading RG6 6AS
Tel: (0) 118 378 8070 (ext. 8070)
www.plantsci.rdg.ac.uk/facilities/harrisgarden.htm

Hill of Tarvit
Cupar, Fife KY15 5PB
Tel: (0) 1334 635127
www.nts.org.uk
Excellent use of Daboecia *cultivars.*

Holehird Gardens
Patterdale Road, Windermere
Cumbria LA23 1NP
Tel: (0) 15394 46008
www.holehirdgardens.org.uk

Mount Stewart
Greyabbey, Newtonwards
Co. Down BT22 2AD
Tel: (0) 2842 788387
www.nationaltrust.org.uk

National Botanic Garden of Wales
Llanarthne
Carmarthenshire SA32 8HG
Tel: (0) 1558 668768
www.gardenofwales.org.uk
Includes Cape heaths.

Ness Botanic Gardens, The University of Liverpool
Ness, Neston
South Wirral CH64 4AY
Tel: (0) 151 353-0123
www.nessgardens.org.uk

Nymans Garden
Handcross
nr Haywards Heath RH17 6EB
Tel: (0) 1444 400321
www.nationaltrust.org.uk/nymans

Penrhyn Castle
Bangor
Gwynedd LL57 4HN
Tel: (0) 1248 353084
www.nationaltrust.org.uk

Raby Castle
Staindrop, Darlington
Co. Durham DL2 3AH
Tel: (0) 1833 660202
www.rabycastle.com

RHS Garden Harlow Carr
Crag Lane, Harrowgate
North Yorkshire HG3 1QB
Tel: (0) 1423 565418
www.rhs.org.uk/whatson/gardens/
   harlowcarr/

RHS Garden Rosemoor
Rosemoor, Great Torrington
North Devon EX38 8PH
Tel: (0) 1805 624067
www.rhs.org.uk/whatson/gardens/
   rosemoor/index.asp

RHS Garden Wisley
Wisley, Woking
Surrey GU23 6QB
Tel: (0) 845 260 9000
www.rhs.org.uk/whatson/gardens/
   wisley/index.asp
Holder of the national heather collection.

Rowallane
Saintfield, Ballynahinch
Co. Down BT24 7LH
Tel: (0) 2897 510131
www.ntni.org.uk

Royal Botanic Garden Edinburgh
20a Inverleith Row
Edinburgh EH3 5LR
Tel: (0) 131 552 7171
www.rbge.org.uk

Saint Andrews Botanic Garden
Canongate
Saint Andrews KY16 8RT
Tel: (0) 1334 476452
www.st-andrews-botanic.org

Sir Harold Hillier Gardens and
   Arboretum
Jermyns Lane, Ampfield
Romsey SO51 0QA
Tel: (0) 1794 368787
www.hilliergardens.org.uk

Threave Garden
Castle Douglas
Dumfries and Galloway DG7 1RX
Tel: (0) 1556 502575
www.nts.org.uk

The Valley Gardens, Windsor Great
   Park
Windsor, Berkshire SL4 2HT
Tel: (0) 1753 743900
www.thamesweb.co.uk/windsor/info/
   valleygdns.html
Naturalistic heather garden set in a quarry.

United States
Berkshire Botanical Garden
Route 102 and Route 183
Stockbridge, MA 01262
Tel: (413) 298-3926
www.berkshirebotanical.org

Brooklyn Botanic Garden
100 Washington Avenue
Brooklyn, NY 11225-1099
Tel: (718) 623-7220
www.bbg.org

Bloom River Gardens
39744 Deerhorn Road
Springfield, OR 97478
Tel: (541) 726-8997
plants@bloomriver.com
www.bloomriver.com
Private garden; open by appointment only.

Cottage Grove Community Hospital
    Heather Garden
1515 Village Drive
Cottage Grove, OR 97424
Tel: (541) 942-0511

Cutler Botanic Garden
840 Front Street
Binghamton, NY 13905
Tel: (607) 772-8953
http://media.cce.cornell.edu/hosts/
    counties/broome/agriculture/CBG

Deep Cut Gardens
352 Red Hill Road
Middletown, NJ 07738
Tel: (732) 671-6050
www.monmouthcountyparks.com

The Fells
Route 103A
Newbury, NH 03255
Tel: (603) 763-4789
www.thefells.org

Fort Tryon Park
741 Fort Washington Avenue
New York, NY 10040
Tel: (212) 795-1388
www.hhoc.org/fftp

Fortuna River Lodge
1800 Riverwalk Drive
Fortuna, CA 95540
Tel: (707) 725-7572
www.fortunariverlodge.com

The Heather Gardens at the Stone
    House Conference Center
University of Southern Maine
642 Wolf Neck Road
Freeport, ME 04032
Tel: (207) 865-3428
stonehouse@usm.maine.edu
Naturalized heathers.

The Holden Arboretum
9500 Sperry Road
Kirtland, OH 44094-5172
Tel: (440) 946-4400
www.holdenarb.org

The JC Raulston Arboretum at North
    Carolina State University
NCSU Horticulture Field Laboratory
4415 Beryl Road
Raleigh, NC 27606-1446
Tel: (919) 515-3132
www.ncsu.edu/jcraulstonarboretum

Leonard J. Buck Garden
11 Layton Road
Far Hills, NJ 07931
Tel: (908) 234-2677
www.somersetcountyparks.org/
    activities/gardens/gardens_Buck.htm

Longwood Gardens
Route 1, P.O. Box 501
Kennett Square, PA 19348-0501
Tel: (610) 388-1000
www.longwoodgardens.org

Mendocino Coast Botanical Gardens
18220 North Highway One
Fort Bragg, CA 95437
Tel: (707) 964-4352
www.gardenbythesea.org

Tower Hill Botanic Garden
Church Street
Boylston, MA 01505
Tel: (508) 869-6111
www.towerhillbg.org

The Oregon Garden
879 W. Main Street
Silverton, OR 97381
Tel: (503) 874-8100
www.oregongarden.org

Rhododendron Species Foundation
    Botanical Garden
2525 South 336th Street
Federal Way, WA 98003
On the campus of the Weyerhaeuser
    Corporation Headquarters
Tel: (253) 838-4646 or 927-6960
www.rhodygarden.org

Rosewood Gardens
3250 Sims Road
Sevierville, TN 37876
Tel: (865) 453-1310
www.rosewoodgardens.com
*Private garden open to the public
    midspring through midautumn.*

University of California, Santa Cruz,
    Arboretum
1156 High Street
Santa Cruz, CA 95064
Tel: (831) 427-2998
www2.ucsc.edu/arboretum
One of the largest collections of Erica
    outside South Africa.

Washington Park Arboretum
Graham Visitors Center
2300 Arboretum Drive East
Seattle, WA 98112
Tel: (206) 543-8800
www.depts.washington.edu/wpa

Washington State University Skagit
    County Extension Discovery Garden
16650 State Route 536 (Memorial
    Highway)
Mount Vernon, WA 98273
Tel: (360) 428-4270
www.skagit.wsu.edu/mg/
    discovery-gardens.htm

Glossary

anther: the apex of the stamen, where the pollen is produced

ascomycete: a fungus whose spores develop within sacs; includes molds, mildews, and morels

aseptic: free from contamination by microorganisms; sterile

asexual propagation: production of new plants from pieces of existing plants; not involving the fusion of gametes; vegetative propagation

awn: a horn-like appendage at or near the base of the anther

axil: the angle between the leaf and the stem on which the leaf is carried

basidiomycete: a fungus whose spores develop within basidia; includes most familiar mushrooms

bract: small, usually leaf-like, organ on the pedicel

calyx: the whorl immediately below the corolla; collective name for the sepals

Cape heath: an erica from the Cape provinces of South Africa; any South African erica

capitate: ending in a distinct head

chimaera: a plant consisting of two or more genetically distinct kinds of cells, the result of a somatic mutation

chromosome: the thread-like structure, found in cell nuclei, that carries the genes

ciliate: edged with hairs

circumboreal: found in the Arctic and temperate regions of Eurasia and North America

clone: a group of identical plants produced by vegetative (asexual) propagation

corolla: collective name for the petals

cross: to mate individuals of different cultivars or species; the result of such mating

dib: to make holes in the ground (for seeds or young plants)

diploid: the number of chromosomes in a cell that contains a set of chromosomes (the haploid number) received from each parent

DNA (deoxyribonucleic acid): complex molecule that contains the genetic instructions for the development and functioning of living organisms

ectomycorrhizae (singular ectomycorrhiza): external mycorrhizae (root and fungal associations) that form a cover on root surfaces, unlike endomycorrhizae (such as ericoid mycorrhizae), where the fungal partner actually enters the root cells of the host plant; ectomycorrhizae are often found on the roots of trees such as oaks and pines

eglandular: without glands

exserted (refers to anthers and stigma): extended beyond the corolla

filament: the stalk of the stamen that supports the anther

garden hybrid: a hybrid between species whose wild ranges do not overlap but which have been brought together in gardens or nurseries

gene: a region of DNA that controls a hereditary characteristic; a unit of inheritance
glabrous: without hairs
glands: secreting organs
glandular: with glands
glaucous: having a powdery appearance
globose: rounded
haploid: the number of chromosomes in the reproductive cell (egg or sperm) of an individual
harden off: to gradually expose to colder, brighter, or less humid conditions
herbarium: a collection of plants dried or otherwise preserved for taxonomic purposes
hortorum: herbarium that specializes in preserving specimens of cultivated varieties
hybrid: the offspring resulting from a mating between parents of different species
hyphae (singular hypha): long, branching filaments that are parts of a fungus
hyphal weft: interwoven mass of hyphae
included (refers to anthers and stigma): within the corolla
inflorescence: a stem bearing (usually) two or more flowers
internode: part of the stem between nodes
interspecific: between species
intraspecific: within a species
lanceolate: shape tapering to a point at both ends
lateral: arising from the side rather than the tip
linear: arranged along a straight line
microclimate: small region that differs in some aspect(s) of climate from the larger area around it
molecule: a group of atoms bonded together; smallest unit of an element or compound
monospecific: consisting of only one species
mutation: change in genetic composition
mutualism: symbiosis that benefits both partners
natural hybrid: a hybrid found in the wild where the parent species grow near each other
node: the point on the stem where the leaves or branches are attached
ovary: the organ of the flower containing ovules which, when fertilized, become the seeds
pedicel: the stalk of an individual flower
petal: a segment of the corolla; usually the showy, colored part of a flower
petaloid: resembling a petal
petiole: the stalk of a leaf
pH: measure of acidity of a solution based upon the concentration of hydrogen ions in the solution

pistil: the female reproductive organ of a flower

raceme: an unbranched flowering stem with the flowers borne in succession along the stem, the lowest opening first

reversion: opposite of sport, with the plant or plant part returning to its original form

revolute: curled or rolled back

sepal: a segment of the calyx

sexual propagation: the production of a new individual through the combination of male and female gametes from different individuals

somatic mutation: a change in the genetic composition of a body cell rather than in a germ (reproductive) cell; genetic change not passed on to offspring through sexual reproduction

spike: flowering stem bearing many flowers attached directly to the stem

sport: somatic mutation resulting in an obviously different growth form (or color)

stamen: the male reproductive organ of a flower

stigma: the apex of the pistil, which receives the pollen

stomata (plural of stomate): tiny pores in the epidermis of a leaf or stem specialized for the controlled exchange of gases between the plant and its environment

style: the section of a pistil above the ovary and ending in the stigma

symbiosis: interaction between two unlike organisms living in close physical association

synflorescence: a compound inflorescence composed of both terminal and lateral-flowering branches

transpiration: the loss of water vapor through open stomata

umbel: flower cluster, usually flat-topped, in which all pedicels arise from the same point on the stem

tetraploid: containing four times the haploid number of chromosomes

xylem: vascular tissue that conducts water and dissolved nutrients upwards from the root; forms part of the wood of shrubs and trees

Bibliography

The books, monographs, and journal articles listed here include references cited in the text, plus additional sources of information about heathers and heathlands. Many heather books are out of print but may be found by diligent searching in shops that specialize in antiquarian and used books. Some are available from one or more of the heather societies.

Alexander, G. 2005. Heather garden design, web-based. *Heather News Quarterly* 28(1): 13–15.

Allaby, M. 2006. *A Dictionary of Plant Sciences*. Revised second edition. Oxford: Oxford University Press.

Alm, T. 1999. Heather (*Calluna vulgaris*) in Norwegian folk tradition. *Yearbook of The Heather Society 1999*: 49–52.

Anderton, S. 2007. Setting the winter garden ablaze. *The Garden: Journal of the Royal Horticultural Society* 132 (2): 86–91.

Arends, G. 1951. *Mein Leben als Gärtner und Züchter*. Stuttgart: Eugen Ulmer Verlag.

Arruda, R. 2005. Humming and feeding on the Pacific Rim. *Heathers* 2: 31–34.

Askjaer, S. A. 1999. Knopblomstrende hedelyng. http://www.kalmiopsis.dk/Papers/knopblomstrende_hedelyng.htm. Accessed 04 April 2006.

Beijerinck, W. 1940. Calluna: *A Monograph on the Scotch Heather*. Amsterdam: Verhandelingen der Koninklijke Nederlandse Akademie van Wetenschapappen, 38.

Bergero, R., S. Perotto, M. Giflanda, G. Vidano, and A. M. Luppi. 2000. Ericoid mycorrhizal fungi are common root associates of a Mediterranean ectomycorrhizal plant (*Quercus ilex*). *Molecular Ecology* 9: 1639–1649.

Bloom, A. 1975. *Adrian Bloom's Guide to Garden Plants: Book 1 Heathers*. Norwich, England: Jarrold Sons.

Bloom, A. 1986. *Conifers and Heathers for a Year Round Garden*. London: Marshall Cavendish Books Ltd. for Aura Books and Floraprint Ltd.

Bloom, A. 1989. *Making the Most of Conifers and Heathers*. Wisbech, England: Burrall Floraprint Ltd.

Brickell, C. D., B. R. Baum, W. L. A. Hetterscheid, A. C. Leslie, J. McNeil, P. Trehane, F. Vrugtman, and J. H. Wiersema, eds. 2004. International Code of Nomenclature for Cultivated Plants. *Acta Horticulturae* 647.

Brien, R. J. 1974. St Kilda Heathers. *Yearbook of The Heather Society* 2 (3): 4–74.

Bunce, R. G. H. 1989. *Heather in England and Wales*. Institute of Terrestrial Ecology Research Publication No. 3. London: Her Majesty's Stationery Office.

Burrill, J. 2003. Myxomatosis: Eradication of a Species? www.burrill.demon.co.uk/meddoc/myxo.html. Accessed 24 March 2006.

Cairney, J. W. G., and R. M. Burke. 1998. Extracellular enzyme activities of the ericoid mycorrhizal endophyte *Hymenoscyphus ericae* (Read) Korf & Kerman: Their likely roles in decomposition of dead plant tissue in soil. *Plant and Soil* 205 (2): 181–192.

Carr, D. 1991. *Heathers and Conifers: Step by Step to Growing Success*. Ramsbury, England: Crowood Press. Reprinted. London: Trafalgar Square Books, 1992.

Chapple, F. J. 1952. *The Heather Garden*. Reprint. London: W. H. & L. Collingridge Ltd., 1960.

Chapple, F. J. 1967. Heather rope. *Yearbook of The Heather Society 1967*: 43.

Charlesworth, G. B. 1996. Growing heathers in western Massachusetts. *Yearbook of The Heather Society 1996*: 17–19.

Community Plant Variety Office. 2006. http://www.cpvo.fr. Accessed 29 March 2006.

Crooks, S. 2006. Fall fireworks. *Fine Gardening* 112: 30–35.

Daneri, D. 1998. The heather sanctuary. *Yearbook of The Heather Society 1998*: 17–22.

Darke, R. 1999. *The Color Encyclopedia of Ornamental Grasses*. Portland, Oregon: Timber Press.

Davis, E. 2003. The Fort Bragg heather arrangements. *Heather News Quarterly* 26 (3): 12–14.

Díaz González, T. E., and A. García Rodriguez. 1992. Comportamiento ecológico y distribución en Asturias de *Erica × praegeri* Ostenf. (*Erica mackaiana × Erica tetralix*). *XII Jornadas de Fitosociologia*, panel 097. *Libro de resúmenes*. Oviedo, 23 al 25 Septiembre de 1992.

Duckett, J. G., and D. J. Read. 1995. Ericoid mycorrhizas and rhizoid-ascomycete associations in liverworts share the same mycobiont: Isolation of the partners and resynthesis of the associations in vitro. *New Phytologist* 129: 439–447.

Edwards, M. 1996. Some bees, wasps and other insects associated with British heathlands. *Yearbook of The Heather Society 1996*: 31–35.

Everett, D. 1996. Ye olde Irish knot garden. *Yearbook of The Heather Society 1994*: 1–4.

Everett, D. 2000a. *Erica arborea*—the pipe smoker's dream. *Yearbook of The Heather Society 2000*: 11–14.

Everett, D. 2000b. *The Heather Society's Guide to Everyone Can Grow Heathers*. The World of Heathers Booklet Series: 1. Creeting Saint Mary: The Heather Society.

Evison, R. J. 1987. *Making the Most of Clematis*. Wisbech: Burrall Floraprint Ltd.

Fagúndez, J. 2006. Two wild hybrids of *Erica* L. (Ericaceae) from northwest Spain. *Botanica Complutensis* 30: 131–135.

Fagúndez, J., and J. Izco. 2003. Seed morphology of *Erica* L. Sect. *Chlorocodon* Bentham. *Acta Botanica Gallica* 150 (4): 401–410.

Fagúndez, J., and J. Izco. 2007. A new European heather: *Erica lusitanica* subsp. *cantabrica* subsp. *nova* (Ericaceae). *Nordic Journal of Botany* 24: 389–394.

Flecken, J. 2006. The Flecken garden in the Netherlands. *Heather News Quarterly* 29 (1): 15, 17.

Foss, P. J., and G. J. Doyle. 1988. Why has *Erica erigena* (the Irish heather) such a markedly disjunct European distribution? *Plants Today* 1(5): 161–168.

Gallet, S., and F. Roze. 2002. Long-term effects of trampling on Atlantic Heathland in Brittany (France): Resilience and tolerance in relation to season and meteorological conditions. *Biological Conservation* 103 (3): 267–275.

Gibson, B. R., and D. T. Mitchell. 2006. Sensitivity of ericoid mycorrhizal fungi and mycorrhizal *Calluna vulgaris* to copper mine spoil from Avoca, County Wicklow. *Biology and Environment: Proceedings of the Royal Irish Academy* Vol. 106B (1): 9–18.

Goodenough, S. 1998. How my life was changed by Lady Shannon: The conversion of an anti-heather person with some easy-to-grow Cape heaths. *Yearbook of The Heather Society 1998*: 27–31.

Gorman, N. R., and M. C. Starrett. 2003. Host range of a select isolate of the ericoid mycorrhizal fungus *Hymenoscyphus ericae*. *HortScience* 38 (6): 1163–1166.

Griffiths, J., 1985. Hybridisation of the Hardy Ericas. *Yearbook of The Heather Society* 3 (2): 17–34.

Hagerup, E., and O. Hagerup. 1953. Thrips pollination of *Erica tetralix*. *New Phytologist* 52: 1–7.

Hall, A. 2005. North American Heather Society Conference August 2004. *Bulletin of The Heather Society* 6 (13): 6–11.

Heather Society, The. 2005. Naming Heathers. http://www.users.zetnet.co.uk/heather. Accessed 1 April 2006.

Honey Health.com. 2005. www.honey-health.com/honey025.shtml. Accessed 11 December 2006.

Howkins, C. 1997. *Heathland Harvest. The Uses of Heathland Plants through the Ages*. Addlestone, Kent, England: Chris Howkins. www.chrishowkins.com.

Howkins, C. 2004. *Heathers and Heathlands*. Addlestone, Kent, England: Chris Howkins. www.chrishowkins.com.

Hurst, C. C. 1925. *Experiments in Genetics*. Cambridge: Cambridge University Press.

International Society for Horticultural Science. 2006. How to name a new cultivar. http://www.ishs.org/sci/icraname.htm. Accessed 13 December 2006.

Jackson, B. L. 2006. Butterflies in the rock garden. *Rock Garden Quarterly* 64 (2): 115–118.

Johansson, B. 2001. Hardiness and heathers—a Swedish view. *Yearbook of The Heather Society 2001*: 22–26.

Johnson, A. T. 1928. *The Hardy Heaths and Some of Their Nearer Allies*. London: The Gardeners' Chronicle, Ltd.

Johnson, A. T. 1952. *The Hardy Heaths and Some of Their Nearer Allies*. London: W. H. & L. Collingridge.

Johnson, A. T. 1956. *The Hardy Heaths and Some of their Nearer Allies*. Rev. ed. London: Blandford Press Ltd.

Johnson, K. 1999. Kirk's Garden. http://www.harborside.com/~rayj/knot.htm. Accessed 28 April 2006.

Jones, A. W. 1989. *Erica manipuliflora* Salisb. in Southern Yugoslavia, October 1988. *Yearbook of The Heather Society* 3 (7): 36–44.

Jones, A. W. 1997. *Erica* 'Heaven Scent'. *Yearbook of The Heather Society 1997*: 38.

Jones, D. 1998. *Step-by-Step Garden Guides: Conifers and Heathers*. London: Aura Books.

Joyner, P. 1979. Have a Go with Cape Heaths. *Yearbook of The Heather Society* 2(8): 21–23.

Knight, F. P. 1972. *Heaths and Heathers*. Wisley Handbook 3. Reprint. London: The Royal Horticultural Society, 1979.

Knight, F. P. 1986. *Heaths and Heathers*. Rev. ed. London: Cassell Educational for the Royal Horticultural Society.

Knight, F. P. 1991. *Heaths and Heathers*. 3d ed. London: Cassell Educational for the Royal Horticultural Society.

Knight, F., R. Pearson, J. Bond, and L. Randall. 1995. *Heathers, Conifers, and the Winter Garden*. Wisley Gardening Companion. London: Cassell Educational Ltd.

Kron, K. A., W. S. Judd, P. F. Stevens, D. M. Crayn, A. A.

Anderberg, P. A. Gadek, C. J. Quinn, and J. L. Luteyn. 2002. A phylogenetic classification of Ericaceae: Molecular and morphological evidence. *Botanical Review* 68: 335–423.

Lacey, S. 2006. Sublime Sherwood. *The Garden: Journal of the Royal Horticultural Society* 131 (5): 330–335.

Lamb, J. 2004. Beatrix Farrand's last Maine masterpiece. *Down East* 51 (2): 57–59, 90.

Lambie, D. 1994. *Introducing Heather*. The Scottish Collection. Reprint. Fort William, Scotland: Firtree Publishing Ltd., 2000.

Lambie, D. A., and B. Lambie. 2001. *Heathers: A Guide to Designing a Heather Garden*. Dulnain Bridge, Scotland: Speyside Heather.

Lange, J. 1999. *Lyngen fortæller*: The lore and use of heather in Denmark, and the origins of the word ling. Trans. B. Johansson. *Yearbook of The Heather Society 1999*: 46–48.

Lerner, A. J. 1947. The Heather on the Hill. In *Brigadoon*. New York: Sam Fox Publishing Company.

Letts, J. F. 1966. *Hardy Heaths and the Heather Garden*. (Handbook of Hardy Heaths and Heathers.) Windlesham, England: John F. Letts.

Lortz, K. 2002a. DNR Study on deer browsing habits. *Cascade Heather Society News* July 2002: 3.

Lortz, K. 2002b. *Heaths & Heathers: Color for All Seasons*. Shelton, Washington: Heaths and Heathers.

Lortz, K. 2004. A woodland heather garden. *Heathers* 1: 1–3.

Lortz, K. 2007a. *Heaths and Heathers with Colorful Foliage*. Choosing Heathers Booklet Series: 1. Shelton, Washington: Heaths and Heathers.

Lortz, K. 2007b. *Heaths and Heathers: The Short Ones*. Choosing Heathers Booklet Series: 2. Shelton, Washington: Heaths and Heathers.

Mackay, D. A. M. 2005a. Setting the heather on fire. *Heather News Quarterly* 28 (1): 2–4.

Mackay, D. A. M. 2005b. *Calluna* versus *Erica*—long term trends. *Heather Notes* 15 (3): 4–5.

Maloof, J. E. 2001. The effects of a bumble bee nectar robber on plant reproductive success and pollinator behavior. *American Journal of Botany* 88: 1960–1965.

Martino, E., S. Perotto, R. Parsons, and G. M. Gadd. 2003. Solubilization of insoluble inorganic zinc compound by ericoid mycorrhizal fungi derived from heavy metal polluted sites. *Soil Biology and Biochemistry* 35 (1): 133–141.

Maxwell, D. F. 1927. *The Low Road: Hardy Heathers and the Heather Garden*. London: Sweet and Maxwell.

Maxwell, D. F., and P. S. Patrick. 1966. *The English Heather Garden*. London: MacDonald & Co.

McAllister, H. 1996. Reproduction in *Erica mackaiana*. *Yearbook of The Heather Society 1996*: 43–46.

McClintock, D. 1969. *A Guide to the Naming of Plants*. London: Straker Brothers Ltd. Reprinted. Leicester: Prontaprint, 1980.

McClintock, D. 1989a. The *Erica scoparia* in Madeira. *Yearbook of The Heather Society* 3 (7): 32–35.

McClintock, D. 1989b. Heather records. *Yearbook of The Heather Society* 3 (7): 54–60.

McClintock, D. 1990. *Erica scoparia* and its variants. *Yearbook of The Heather Society* 3 (8): 53–61.

McClintock, D. 1998a. *Erica* ×*krameri*: The hybrid between *E. carnea* and *E. spiculifolia*. *Yearbook of The Heather Society 1998*: 26.

McClintock, D. 1998b. *Heathers of the Lizard*. Cornwall: Cornwall Garden Society.

McGuire, A. F., and K. A. Kron. 2005. Phylogenetic relationships of European and African Ericas. *International Journal of Plant Science* 166 (2): 311–318.

McNeill et al. 2006. *International Code of Botanical Nomenclature (Vienna Code) adopted by the Seventeenth International Botanical Congress Vienna, Austria, July 2005*. Ruggell, Liechtenstein: Gantner Verlag.

Metheny, D. 1991. *Hardy Heather Species and some related plants*. Seaside, Oregon: Frontier Press.

Mifsud, S. 2007. Wild Plants of Malta and Gozo. http://maltawildplants.com/ERIC/Erica_multiflora.html. Accessed 29 January 2007.

Mikolajski, A. 1997. *Heathers*. The New Plant Library. New York: Anness Publishing Ltd.

Mikolajski, A. 2001. *Heathers*. Reprint. New York: Anness Publishing Ltd. First published 1997 in a larger format by Lorenz Books (Anness).

Miwa, S. 2000. Recent development of pot-flower production of Cape heaths in Japan. *Yearbook of The Heather Society 2000*: 43–46.

Morales, R., M. Pardo de Santayana, B. Álvarez and L. Ramón-Laca. 2003. Religious associations of heathers in Spain. *Yearbook of The Heather Society 2003*: 51–53.

Nelson, C. 2003. Cat heather. *Bulletin of The Heather Society* 6 (9): 7.

Nelson, C. 2005. The most rewarded heathers. *Bulletin of The Heather Society* 6 (15): 5–9.

Nelson, E. C. 1989. Heathers in Ireland. *Botanical Journal of the Linnean Society* 101: 269–277.

Nelson, E. C. 2000a. *A Heritage of Beauty. The Garden Plants of Ireland. An Illustrated Encyclopaedia*. Dublin: Irish Garden Plant Society.

Nelson, E. C. 2000b. A history, mainly nomenclatural, of St Dabeoc's Heath. *Watsonia* 23: 47–58.

Nelson, E. C. 2001. Dr Charles Stuart's heather rediscovered in Connemara, Ireland. *Yearbook of The Heather Society* 2001: 35–37.

Nelson, E. C. 2005. *Erica mackaiana* Bab. and *Erica ×stuartii* (MacFarl.) Mast. (Ericaceae): Two heathers new to south Kerry (V. C. H1), Ireland. *Watsonia* 25: 414–417.

Nelson, E. C. 2006. Lucky white heather: A sesquicentennial review of a Scottish Victorian conceit. *Heathers* 3: 38–46.

Nelson, E. C. 2007a. *Erica ×arendsiana* (*E. terminalis* × *E. cinerea*): A hardy German hybrid re-created. *Heathers* 4: 59–60.

Nelson, E. C. 2007b. Williams's heath: The wild-collected clones. *Heathers* 4: 45–56.

Nelson, E. C. In press. *Hardy heathers from the Northern Hemisphere*. London: RBG Kew.

Nelson, E. C., and E. G. H. Oliver. 2004. Cape heaths in European gardens: The early history of South African *Erica* species in cultivation, their deliberate hybridization and the orthographic bedlam. *Bothalia* 34 (2): 127–140.

Nelson, E. C., and E. M. T. Wulff. 2007. *Erica ×gaudificans* (*E. spiculifolia* × *bergiana*): Kurt Kramer's second north-south hybrid. *Heathers* 4: 57–58.

Nelson, E. C., and D. J. Small, eds. 2000. *International Register of Heather Names: Vol. 1: Hardy Cultivars & European Species*. Creeting Saint Mary: The Heather Society.

Nelson, E. C., and D. J. Small, eds. 2006. *International Register of Heather Names. Vol. 2: African Species and Cultivars*. Creeting Saint Mary: The Heather Society.

Noble, R., and E. Coventry. 2005. Suppression of soil-borne plant diseases with composts: A review. *Biocontrol Science and Technology* 15 (1): 3–20.

Oliver, E. G. H. 1996. The position of *Bruckenthalia* versus *Erica*. *Yearbook of The Heather Society* 1996: 6.

Oliver, E. G. H. 2000. *Systematics of Ericeae (Ericaceae-Ericoideae): Species with indehiscent and partially dehiscent fruits*. Cape Town: Bolus Herbarium, University of Cape Town. Contributions from the Bolus Herbarium Number 19.

Osborne, B. D. 1998. *The Scottish Heather Book*. Belfast: Appletree Press.

Oudean, K. 1993a. Preserving heathers for crafts. *Heather News* 18 (2): 10.

Oudean, K. 1993b. Preserving heathers by the Victorian wax method. *Heather News* 18 (3): 7.

Packham, C. 1989. *Heathlands*. Collins Wild Habitats. London: Collins.

Pardo de Santayana, M., L. Ramón-Laca, and R. Morales. 2002. Traditional uses for heathers in Spain. *Yearbook of The Heather Society* 2002: 47–56.

Parris, A. 1976. Preliminary note on a cross between *Erica erigena* and *E. carnea*. *Yearbook of The Heather Society* 2 (5): 48–49.

Parris, A. 1977. Further note on a cross beween *Erica erigena* and *E. carnea*. *Yearbook of The Heather Society* 2 (6): 10.

Parris, A. 1978. Further notes on the induced *Erica erigena* × *Erica carnea* hybrids. *Yearbook of The Heather Society* 2 (7): 42–43.

Parris, A. 1980. Further notes on *E. ×darleyensis* induced hybrids. *Yearbook of The Heather Society* 2 (9): 67–70.

Parry, J. 2003. *Heathland*. Living Landscapes Series. London: National Trust Enterprises Ltd.

Peterson, P., S. V. Fowler, and P. Barrett. 2004. Is the poor establishment and performance of heather beetle in Tongariro National Park due to the impact of parasitoids, predators or disease? *57th Conference Proceedings of The New Zealand Plant Protection Society Incorporated*.

Phillips, S., and N. Sutherland. 1996. *A Creative Step-by-Step Guide to Heathers and Conifers*. London: Aura Books.

Plant Health Risk Assessment Unit, Canadian Food Inspection Agency. 2003. Hosts of *Phytophthora ramorum* (with notes on geographical distribution and mating types). http://www.cnr.berkeley.edu/comtf/pdf/P.ramorum.hosts.June.2003.pdf. Accessed 11 April 2006.

Poruban, R. 2006. A "new" mycorrhizal fungus. *Heather News Quarterly* 29 (2): 11–13.

Price, E. 2003. *Lowland Grassland and Heathland Habitats*. Routledge Habitat Guides. London: Taylor & Francis Ltd. (Routledge).

Proudley, B., and V. Proudley. 1974. *Heathers in Colour*. London: Blandford Press Ltd.

Pscheidt, J. W. 2005. Diagnosis and Control of *Phytophthora* Diseases. *An Online Guide to Plant Disease Control, Oregon State University Extension*. http://plant-disease.ippc.orst.edu/articles.cfm?article_id=4. Accessed 11 April 2006.

Rackham, O. 2003 (1994). *The Illustrated History of the Countryside*. London: Weidenfeld & Nicolson Ltd.

Read, D. J. 1981. Heathers and Their Mycorrhizas. *Yearbook of The Heather Society* 2 (10): 28–43.

Read, D. J., and J. Pérez-Moreno. 2003. Mycorrhizas and nutrient cycling in ecosystems—a journey towards relevance? *New Phytologist* 157: 475–492.

Rees, S. M. 1996. The flora and fauna of the North York Moors, and the uses of heather and moorland by mankind. *Yearbook of The Heather Society* 1996: 23–30.

Ribeiro, S. P., P. A. V. Borges, and C. Gaspar. 2003. Ecology and evolution of the arborescent *Erica azorica* Hochst (Ericaceae). *Arquipélago* 1 (1): 41–49.

Rizzo, D. M., and M. Garbelotto. 2003. Sudden oak death: Endangering California and Oregon forest ecosystems. *Frontiers in Ecology and the Environment* 1 (5): 197–204.

Robinson, D. 1995. Cape heaths in eastern Ireland. *Yearbook of The Heather Society 1995*: 17–22.

Rogers, C. 2006. Sunburn or frostbite? Observations on the changing colour of some heathers. *Heathers* 3: 9–13.

Rose, R. J., P. Bannister, and S. B. Chapman. 1996. Biological flora of the British Isles: *Erica ciliaris* L. *Journal of Ecology* 84: 617–628.

Royal Horticultural Society. 1966. *RHS Colour Chart*. London: Royal Horticultural Society.

Royal Horticultural Society. 2006a. Advice: Vine Weevil (*Otiorhynchus sulcatus*). http://www.rhs.org.uk/advice/profiles0600/vineweevil.asp. Accessed 10 April 2006.

Royal Horticultural Society 2006b. Harlow Carr Plant of the month: February. http://www.rhs.org.uk/WhatsOn/gardens/harlowcarr/archive/harlowcarrpomfeb.asp. Accessed January, 2007.

Sakai, A., and S. Miwa. 1979. Frost hardiness of Ericoideae. *Journal of the American Society for Horticultural Science*: 104 (1): 26–28.

Scagel, C. F. 2005. Inoculation with ericoid mycorrhizal fungi alters fertilizer use of highbush blueberry cultivars. *HortScience* 40 (3): 786–794.

Schröder, J. 2005a. The explosion of bud-flowerers. *Heathers 2: Yearbook of The Heather Society*: 17–18.

Schröder, J. 2005b. Gräser im Heidegarten. *Der Heidegarten* 58: 16–20.

Schumann, D., G. Kirsten, and E. G. H. Oliver. 1995. *Ericas of South Africa*. Vlaeberg, South Africa: Fernwood Press, 1992. Reprint, Timber Press.

Sellers, B. 1999. Propagation of heathers from seed. *Yearbook of The Heather Society 1999*: 23–29.

Sharpe, J., and A. Julian. 1992. Heathers in Yorkshire. *Yearbook of The Heather Society* 3 (10): 53–57.

Silva, J. S., and F. C. Rego. 2003. Root distribution of a Mediterranean shrubland in Portugal. *Plant and soil* 255 (2): 529–540.

Simmons, I. G. 2003. *Moorlands of England and Wales: An Environmental History 8000 BC to AD 2000*. Edinburgh: Edinburgh University Press Ltd.

Small, D., and A. Small. 2001. *The Heather Society's Handy Guide to Heathers*. Creeting Saint Mary: The Heather Society.

Small, D., and R. Cleevely. 1999. *The Heather Society's Guide to Recommended Heathers*. The World of Heathers Booklet Series: 2. Creeting Saint Mary: The Heather Society.

Small, I., and H. Alanine. 1994. Some speculations on colourful foliage in heathers. *Yearbook of The Heather Society 1994*: 27–34.

Small, I., and K. A. Kron. 2001. Placing heathers on the "Tree of Life." *Yearbook of The Heather Society 2001*: 15–21.

Smout, T. C. 2004. Review of *Moorlands of England and Wales: An Environmental History 8000 BC to AD 2000*, by Ian G. Simmons. *Environmental History* 9 (3): 543.

Soanes, C., and A. Stevenson, eds. 2004. *Concise Oxford English Dictionary*, 11th ed. Oxford: Oxford University Press.

Somer, R. 2005. Hummingbird report. *Heather News Quarterly* 28 (3): 22.

Stow, A. 2004. What to plant with heathers. *Bulletin of The Heather Society* 6 (13): 18–19.

Straker, C. J. 1996. Ericoid mycorrhiza: Ecological and host specificity. *Mycorrhiza* 6: 215–225.

Thomas, G. S. 1994. *The Graham Stuart Thomas Rose Book*. Sagaponack, New York: Sagapress.

Thomas, G. S. 1995. Heathers in the garden. *Yearbook of The Heather Society 1995*: 13–16.

Thompson, D. B. A., A. J. Hester, and M. B. Usher, eds. 1995. *Heaths and Moorland: Cultural Landscapes*. Edinburgh: HMSO.

Thornton-Wood, S. 1995. Heathers in National Trust Gardens. *Yearbook of The Heather Society 1995*: 1–3.

Toogood, A. R. 1986. *Gardening with Conifers and Heathers*. London: Marshall Cavendish Ltd.

Toogood, A. R. 1989a. *Conifers and Heathers*. New York: Smithmark Publishers.

Toogood, A. R. 1989b. *Heathers and Heaths*. Collins Aura Garden Handbooks. London: Collins.

Trudell, S. 2000. Mycorrhizas part 2: A diversity of types. *Mushroom: The Journal of Wild Mushrooming* 18 (4): 12-17.

Turpin, P. 1985. Heather perfume. *Bulletin of The Heather Society* 3 (17): 5.

UK PRA. 2003. CSL Pest Risk Analysis for *Phytophthora ramorum*. http://www.defra.gov.uk/planth/pra/sudd.pdf. Accessed 11 April 2006.

Underhill, T. L. 1972. *Heaths and Heathers:* Calluna, Daboecia and Erica. New York: Drake Publishers Inc.

Underhill, T. L. 1990. *Heaths and Heathers: The Grower's Encyclopedia*. Newton Abbott, England: David & Charles.

United States Department of Agriculture 1990. Plant Hardiness Zone Map. USDA Miscellaneous Publication No.

1475. Also see the United States National Arboretum "Web Version" of the USDA Plant Hardiness Zone Map at http://www.usna.usda.gov/Hardzone/ushzmap.html. Accessed 4 November 2007.

United States Department of Agriculture Plant Variety Protection Office. 2006. http://www.ams.usda.gov/Science/PVPO/PVPindex.htm. Accessed 13 December 2006.

United States Food and Drug Administration, Center for Food Safety and Applied Nutrition. 2006. Foodborne Pathogenic Microorganisms and Natural Toxins Handbook. http://www.cfsan.fda.gov/~mow/chap44.html. Accessed 11 December 2006.

United States Patent and Trademark Office. 2005. http://www.uspto.gov/web/offices/pac/plant/index.html. Accessed 29 March 2006.

University of Pennsylvania (Chan et al). 2002. *Poisonous Plants*. http://cal.vet.upenn.edu/poison/plants/pppieri.htm. Accessed 11 December 2006.

van de Laar, H. 1978. *The Heather Garden: The Plants and Their Cultivation*. Trans. P. Rowe-Dutton. London: Wm. Collins Sons & Co. Ltd.

Villarreal-Ruiz, L., I. C. Anderson, and I. J. Alexander. 2004. Interaction between an isolate from the *Hymenoscyphus ericae* aggregate and roots of *Pinus* and *Vaccinium*. *New Phytologist* 164: 183–192.

Webb, N. R. 1986. *Heathlands: A Natural History of Britain's Lowland Heaths*. The New Naturalist. London: Collins.

Werres, S., R. Marwitz, W. A. Man in't Veld, A. W. A. M. De Cock, P. J. M. Bonants, M. De Weerdt, K. Themann, E. Ilieva, and R. P. Baayen. 2001. *Phytophthora ramorum* sp. nov., a new pathogen on *Rhododendron* and *Viburnum*. *Mycological Research* 105: 1155–1164.

Wick, W. 2004. Heathers in Ontario, Part 2. *Heather News Quarterly* 27 (4): 2–6.

Wick, W. 2005. Heathers in Ontario, Part 3. *Heather News Quarterly* 28 (2): 2–6.

Willis, N. 1998. Punch's Dessert (published excerpt from a letter). *Bulletin of The Heather Society* 5 (14): 11.

Witchner, B. W. 2001. Pruning Heathers and the California Coastal Heather Project. *Heather News* 24 (1): 9–12.

Woods, M. 1972. The Scent of Heaths. *Bulletin of The Heather Society* 1 (17): 6.

Yates, G. 1978. *Pocket Guide to Heather Gardening*. Ambleside, England: Tabramhill Gardens.

Yates, G. 1985. *The Gardener's Book of Heathers*. London: Frederick Warne & Co. Ltd.

Young, C. 2006. Coming of age. *The Garden* 131 (6): 414–419.

Index

Page numbers in *italic* include photographs.

A

Abkhazi Garden, 53, *54*
Acer campestre, 95
Acer negundo, 31
Acer palmatum, 235
Acer saccharum, 31
acetylandromedol. See grayanotoxin.
Acorus gramineus 'Ogon', 132
Adelanthaceae, 38
'Adrienne Duncan' (*Erica carnea*), 195, 199
'African Fanfare' (*Erica*), 247
Agapanthus, 134
Ageratum, 146
'Alba'. See *Daboecia cantabrica* f. *alba*.
'Alba Erecta' (*Calluna vulgaris*), 57
'Alba Minor' (*Erica cinerea*), 202, 253
'Alba Mollis' (*Erica tetralix*), *18*, *44*, 101, 157, 165, 170, 177, *221*
'Alba Plena' (*Calluna vulgaris*), 249
'Albert's Gold' (*Erica arborea*), 193
'Aldeburgh' (*Erica manipuliflora*), 97, 158, 211, 214, 254
'Alexandra' (*Calluna vulgaris*), *24*, 178, 183, 247
'Alex Warwick' (*Calluna vulgaris*), 257
'Alicia' (*Calluna vulgaris*), 178, 247
'Allegro' (*Calluna vulgaris*), 178, 249
Allium bulgaricum. See *Nectaroscordum siculum* subsp. *bulgaricum*.
Allium cernuum, 150
Allium siculum. See *Nectaroscordum siculum*.
'Alpina'. See *Erica arborea* var. *alpina*.
'Alys Sutcliffe' (*Calluna vulgaris*), 253
American Conifer Society, 117
'Amethyst' (*Calluna vulgaris*), 247
'Ammerland' (*Erica* ×*oldenburgensis*), 216
Andrena fuscipes, 19
andromeda. See *Pieris*.
Andromeda, 13, 23, 119
Andromeda glaucophylla, 119
Andromeda polifolia, 119
  'Blue Ice', 119
  'Compacta', 119
  'Macrophylla', 119
  'Nikko', 119

andromedotoxin. See grayanotoxin.
'Anette' (*Calluna vulgaris*), 178, 244, 247
'Angela Wain' (*Calluna vulgaris*), 105, 178
'Annemarie' (*Calluna vulgaris*), *147*, 160, 179, 241, 244
'Anne Small' (*Erica umbellata*), 223
'Anne's Zwerg' (*Calluna vulgaris*), 253, 256–257
'Ann Sparkes' (*Erica carnea*), 94, 131, 150, 196, 256
'Anthony Davis' (*Calluna vulgaris*), 179, 244
Antirrhinum, 145
'Aphrodite' (*Calluna vulgaris*), 247
Apis mellifera, 19
'Apple Blossom' (*Erica cinerea*), 234
'Applecross' (*Calluna vulgaris*), 234
'Arabella' (*Calluna vulgaris*), *149*, 179
Arends, Georg, 152, 161, 194, 207
Arends's heath. See *Erica* ×*arendsii*.
'Arielle' (*Daboecia cantabrica*), 189
'Arran Gold' (*Calluna vulgaris*), 179, 256
Artemesia, 237
Artemisia albula 'Silver King'. See *Artemisia ludoviciana* subsp. *mexicana* var. *albula*.
Artemisia ludoviciana subsp. *mexicana* var. *albula*, 237
'Arthur Johnson' (*Erica* ×*darleyensis*), 97, 205, 252
'Arthur P. Dome' (*Daboecia azorica*), 188, 252, 256
'Ashlea Gold' (*Erica* ×*griffithsii*), 159
'Athene' (*Calluna vulgaris*), 247
'Atropurpurea' (*Daboecia cantabrica*), 149
'Atropurpurea' (*Erica cinerea*), 57, 105, 201, 234
'Atrorubens' (*Erica cinerea*), 234, 253
'Aurea' (*Erica carnea*), *61*, 196, 206
'Aurea' (*Erica ciliaris*), 200
'Autumn Glow' (*Calluna vulgaris*), 254

B

'Baby Ben' (*Calluna vulgaris*), 256
'Baby Wicklow' (*Calluna vulgaris*), 256
Bailey Hortorum, 175, 231
Bakhuyzen, P. & Zonen, 178

'Balkan Rose' (*Erica spiculifolia*), 219
Bannut, The, 89, 97, 98
'Barnett Anley' (*Calluna vulgaris*), 252
'Bartinney' (*Erica tetralix*), 157, 170, 250
'Battle of Arnhem' (*Calluna vulgaris*), 244, 252, 254
Beechwood Nursery, 179
bees. See *Andrena*, *Apis*, *Bombus*, and *Colletes*.
bell heather. See *Erica cinerea*.
'Bell's Extra Special' (*Erica carnea*), *27*, 131, 196
'Ben' (*Daboecia* ×*scotica*), 256
'Beoley Gold' (*Calluna vulgaris*), *149*, 179
Berberis, 93
Bergenia, 136
Bergenia 'Beethoven', 136
Bergenia 'Bressingham Ruby', 136
Bergenia purpurascens, 136
Best, C. G., 202
Betula, 114, *115*
'Bicolor' (*Daboecia cantabrica*), 99, 189, 190, 255
bilberry. See *Vaccinium myrtillus*.
birch. See *Betula*.
Birch Farm Nursery, 225
'Birch Glow' (*Erica vagans*), *224*, 249
Birsay Moor Nature Reserve, *24*
'Bispingen' (*Calluna vulgaris*), 259
Bloom River Gardens, *112*, 201
blueberry. See *Vaccinium corymbosum*.
'Blueness' (*Calluna vulgaris*), 254
'Bob Brien' (*Calluna vulgaris*), 257
bog heather. See *Erica tetralix*.
bog rosemary. See *Andromeda*.
Bombus, 19
'Bonita' (*Calluna vulgaris*), 247
'Bonsaï' (*Calluna vulgaris*), 256
'Boreray' (*Calluna vulgaris*), 253, 257
'Boskoop' (*Calluna vulgaris*), 259
Botrytis cinerea, 47, 67
boxwood. See *Buxus*.
'Bradford' (*Calluna vulgaris*), 50
'Braeriach' (*Calluna vulgaris*), 259
Bressingham Gardens, 103

286 INDEX

'Brian Proudley' (*Erica erigena*), 54, 96, 170, 208, 234, 235, 254
Brien, Robert J., 257
'Brightness' (*Erica erigena*), 160
'Brita Elisabeth' (*Calluna vulgaris*), 249
'Bronze Beauty' (*Calluna vulgaris*), 254
Bruckenthalia. See *Erica spiculifolia*.
Brummage, Jack H., 206
Buchanan, William, 191
'Bucklebury Red' (*Erica cinerea*), 232, 252
bud bloomers, 24, 254–255
bumblebees. See *Bombus*.
Bundessortenamt, 153
butterflies. See *Nymphalis* and *Vanessa*.
Buxus, 97
Byfield, Andrew, 229

C

Cadophora finlandia, 37
'Caerketton White' (*Calluna vulgaris*), 249, 251
'Cairnwell' (*Calluna vulgaris*), 179, 249, 251, 258
Calamagrostis ×*acutiflora* 'Karl Foerster', 130
Calamagrostis ×*acutiflora* 'Overdam', 130
'Caleb Threlkeld' (*Calluna vulgaris*), 179, 249, 253, 257
Caledon Fynbos Nursery, 167
'Californian Midge' (*Calluna vulgaris*), 97
Calluna vulgaris, 12–13, 16, 17, 20–25, 74–75, 79, 82, 102, 155, 170–171, 173, 176–188, 240–242, 244, 246–247
  'Alba Erecta', 57
  'Alba Plena', 249
  'Alexandra', 24, 178, 183, 247
  'Alex Warwick', 257
  'Alicia', 178, 247
  'Allegro', 178, 249
  'Alys Sutcliffe', 253
  'Amethyst', 247
  'Anette', 178, 244, 247
  'Angela Wain', 105, 178
  'Annemarie', 147, 160, 178, 241, 244
  'Anne's Zwerg', 253, 256–257
  'Anthony Davis', 179, 244
  'Aphrodite', 247
  'Applecross', 234
  'Arabella', 149, 179
  'Arran Gold', 179, 256
  'Athene', 247
  'Autumn Glow', 254
  'Baby Ben', 256
  'Baby Wicklow', 256
  'Barnett Anley', 252
  'Battle of Arnhem', 244, 252, 254
  'Beoley Gold', 149, 179
  'Bispingen', 259
  'Blueness', 254
  'Bob Brien', 257
  'Bonita', 247
  'Bonsai', 256
  'Boreray', 253, 257
  'Boskoop', 259
  'Bradford', 50
  'Braeriach', 259
  'Brita Elisabeth', 249
  'Bronze Beauty', 254
  'Caerketton White', 249, 251
  'Cairnwell', 179, 249, 251, 258
  'Caleb Threlkeld', 179, 249, 253, 257
  'Californian Midge', 97
  'Carmen', 149–150, 180, 240, 252
  'Carole Chapman', 30
  'Catherine', 249
  'Chernobyl', 249
  'Christina', 30, 128, 150
  'Christmas Candle', 254
  'Clare Carpet', 98, 140, 256
  'Colette', 259
  'Conachair', 257
  'Con Brio', 99, 252, 259
  'Corbett's Red', 150
  'Cottswood Gold', 180
  'County Wicklow', 57, 180, 182, 244
  'Crinkly Tuft', 147
  'Cuprea', 234, 259
  'Dainty Bess', 251, 256
  'Dainty Bess Junior', 251, 256
  'Dark Beauty', 180, 234
  'Darkness', 160, 180, 241
  'Dark Star', 180, 234
  'Dart's Flamboyant', 253, 259
  'Dart's Hedgehog', 259
  'David Eason', 246–247
  'Desiree', 259
  'Devon', 180, 251, 255
  'Dunnet Lime', 249, 251
  'Durford Wood', 150, 254, 258
  'E. F. Brown', 254
  'Elsie Purnell', 181, 234, 244
  'Emerald Jock', 181, 232, 251, 253, 257
  'Finale', 254
  'Findling', 256
  'Firefly', 30, 94, 109, 144, 146, 147, 150–151, 181, 184
  'Fire King', 30, 259
  'Fire Star', 50, 259
  'Flatling', 256
  'Floriferous', 257
  'Fort Bragg', 131, 259
  'Fortyniner Gold', 234, 244, 251–252
  'Foxii', 97, 256
  'Foxii Floribunda', 256
  'Foxii Nana', 256
  'Foya', 108, 149, 151, 259
  'Fraser's Old Gold', 42, 181
  'Fred J. Chapple', 184
  'Frejus', 259
  'Fritz Kircher', 247
  'Galaxy', 247
  'Gerda', 251
  'Glendoick Silver', 150
  'Glenlivet', 259
  'Glenmorangie', 256, 259
  'Gold Charm', 259
  'Golden Carpet', 253, 256
  'Golden Feather', 259
  'Golden Fleece', 256
  'Golden Rivulet', 253
  'Gold Haze', 27, 181, 179
  'Gold Kup', 117, 232
  'Goldsworth Crimson Variegated', 75, 258
  'Gronsinka', 249, 256
  'Harten's Findling', 256
  'H. E. Beale', 181, 184, 244, 254
  'Heidepracht', 253
  'Heideteppich', 253
  'Heidezwerg', 182, 253, 256–257
  'Hibernica', 254
  'Hiemalis', 250, 254
  'Highland Rose', 84, 108, 149, 259
  'Hillbrook Orange', 259
  'Hoyerhagen', 259
  'Humpty Dumpty', 92, 256
  'Inshriach Bronze', 249
  'Isle of Hirta', 257
  'Jan Dekker', 150
  'J. H. Hamilton', 182, 249
  'Jimmy Dyce', 182, 254–255
  'Johnson's Variety', 160, 244, 250, 254
  'Joy Vanstone', 27, 182
  'Julia', 259

'Juno', 252
'Kerstin', 92, 173, *182*, 235, 249, 258
'Kinlochruel', *182*, 187
'Kuphaldtii', 253
'Larissa', *183*, 247
'Lemon Gem', 30, *133*
'Lewis Lilac', 252
'Lime Glade', 30, *146*, 147, 183
'Long White', 150, *243*, 244, 249, 252
'Lyndon Proudley', 183, 252
'Mair's Variety', 183, 244, 249
'Marion Blum', 30, 150
'Marleen', 161, 183, 247
'Martha Hermann', 183, 249
'Matita', 249, 258
'Mazurka', 149
'Melanie', 161, 178, *183*, 244, 247
'Miniöxabäck', 249, 256
'Minty', 257
'Miss Muffet', 256
'Molecule', 256
'Monika', 254
'Mrs Pat', *25*
'Mrs Ronald Gray', 251
'Mullach Mor', 257
'Mullardoch', 249, 251, 256
'Mullion', 184
'Multicolor', 254
'My Dream', 150, 236, 244
'Nelly', 247, 256–257
'October White', 254
'Oiseval', 257
'Orange Queen', 184
'Oxshott Common', 184, 234, 252
'Pat's Gold', 234
'Peace', 254
'Peggy', 249
'Penny Bun', 256
'Perestrojka', 255
'Peter Sparkes', 150, 160, 184, 234, 244, 254
'Platt's Surprise', 249
'Prostrata Flagelliformis', 257
'Punch's Dessert', 150, *184*
'Pygmaea', 256
'Radnor', 184, 249
'Radnor Gold', 249
'Redbud', 150, 247
'Red Carpet', 259
'Red Favorit', 249
'Red Fred', 184

'Red Pimpernel', 254
'Reini', 185, 244, 249
'Robert Chapman', *126*, 151, 181, 185, 249
'Roland Haagen', 185
'Romina', 247
'Roodkapje', 247
'Roswitha', 247
'Ruby Slinger', 185
'Saint Nick', 254
'Sandy', 247
'Schurig's Sensation', 254
'Serlei Aurea', 185
'Sesam', 147, 149, 185, 249
'Silver Knight', 57, 249
'Silver Queen', 149, *185*
'Silver Rose', 186
'Sir John Charrington', 186
'Sirsson', 186, 249
'Sister Anne', 186, 251, 252
'Skone', *75*, 258
'Snowflake', 90, 141–142, 251
'Soay', 22, 92–93, 140, 251, 256–257
'Spitfire', 259
'Spring Cream', 186, 254
'Spring Glow', 254
'Spring Torch', 51, *70*, 186, 235
'Stefanie', 254
'Sunrise', 259
'Sunset', 186
'Tenuis', 251
'The Pygmy', *52*, 92–93, 186, 256
'Tib', *40*, 187, *241*, 244, 249, 251, 255
'Tom Thumb', *85*, 256
'Underwoodii', 247
'Velvet Dome', *101*, 256
'Velvet Fascination', 149, *187*, 234–235, 249
'Venus', 247
'Visser's Fancy', 247
'White Coral', 187
'White Knight', 249
'White Lawn', *187*, 252, 253
'Wickwar Flame', *128*, 134, 149, 187
'Winter Chocolate', 187
'Winter Fire', 259
Calypogeiaceae, 38
Cambridge University Botanic Garden, 93, 118
Camellia 'Freedom Bell', 234
Campanula, 112, 136–137
Campanula bellardii. See *C. cochlearifolia*.

Campanula 'Camgood', 136
Campanula cochlearifolia, 136–137
Campanula portenschlagiana, 136–137
Campanula portenschlagiana 'Resholdt's Variety', 136
Campanula poscharskyana, 136
Campanula pusilla. See *C. cochlearifolia*.
Campanula rotundifolia, 81, 137
campanulas. See *Campanula*.
Cape heaths, 18, 27, 28, 60, 152, 157, 159, 161, 166–167, 242, 247–248
Carex albula, 133
Carex buchananii, 131
Carex comans 'Frosty Curls'. See *Carex albula*.
Carex elata 'Aurea', 112
Carex flagellifera, 131
Carex grayi, 132
Carex oshimensis, 132
Carex oshimensis 'Evergold', 132
Carex testacea, *128*, 131
'Carmen' (*Calluna vulgaris*), 149–150, *180*, 240, 252
'Carnea' (*Erica cinerea*), 253
'Carole Chapman' (*Calluna vulgaris*), 30
Caryopteris, 123
Caryopteris ×*clandonensis*, 123, 150
Caryopteris incana 'Jason', 123
'Cascades' (*Erica manipuliflora*), 215
Cassiope, 13
cat heather, 12,
'Catherine' (*Calluna vulgaris*), 249
Cattleya, 169
'C. D. Eason' (*Erica cinerea*), 149, 202, 253
'Celebration' (*Erica cinerea*), 92, *142*, 150–151, 202, 253
'Celtic Star' (*Daboecia cantabrica*), 189, *190*, 255
Ceratothrips ericae, 20
Cephaloziaceae, 38
Cephaloziellaceae, 38
'Cevennes' (*Erica cinerea*), 202, 234, 253
'C. G. Best' (*Erica cinerea*), 202
'Challenger' (*Erica carnea*), 196
'Charles Nelson' (*Daboecia cantabrica*), 52, *190*, 255
Charlesworth, Geoffrey, 143
'Chernobyl' (*Calluna vulgaris*), 249
Cherrybank Gardens, 96, *158*, 226
'Cherry Turpin' (*Erica* ×*watsonii*), *105*, 151, 227, 251
Chionodoxa, 141–142
Chionodoxa forbesii, *142*, 151

Chionodoxa gigantea. See *Chinodoxa forbesii*.
Chionodoxa luciliae. See *Chinodoxa forbesii*.
Chionodoxa sardensis, 142
'Christina' (*Calluna vulgaris*), 30, *128*, 150
'Christmas Candle' (*Calluna vulgaris*), 254
'Cinderella' (*Daboecia cantabrica*), 190
'Cindy' (*Erica cinerea*), 202
'Claire Elise' (*Erica ×watsonii*), 157–158
'Clare Carpet' (*Calluna vulgaris*), 98, 140, 256
Clavaria acuta, 37
Clavaria argillacea, 37
Clematis, 123–124
Clematis 'Black Prince', 123
Clematis 'Jackmanii', 123
Clematis montana, 96
Clematis 'Pagoda', 123
Clematis texensis, 95, 123
Clematis viticella, 95, 123
   'Etoile Violette', 123
   'Minuet', 123
   'Royal Velours', 1123
   'Venosa Violacea', 123
'Coccinea' (*Erica cinerea*), 105, 107, 150, 203, 252
'Colette' (*Calluna vulgaris*), 259
Colletes succinctus, 19
Community Plant Variety Office. See CPVO.
'Conachair' (*Calluna vulgaris*), 257
'Con Brio' (*Calluna vulgaris*), 99, 252, 259
conifers, 81, 83–84, 104, 112, 116–118, *148*, 149
'Con Underwood' (*Erica tetralix*), 222
Cooke, Randle Blain, 198
'Cora' (*Daboecia ×scotica*), 256
'Corbett's Red' (*Calluna vulgaris*), 150
Coreopsis, 137
Coreopsis rosea, 137
Coreopsis verticillata 'Moonbeam', 137
'Corfe Castle' (*Erica ciliaris*), 200, 228
'Cornish Cream' (*Erica vagans*), 225, 249
Cornish heath. See *Erica vagans*.
Cornus, 93
Corrigall Farm Museum, *20–21*
Corsican heath. See *Erica terminalis*.
Cotinus coggygria 'Royal Purple', 124
'Cottswood Gold' (*Calluna vulgaris*), 180
'County Wicklow' (*Calluna vulgaris*), 57, 180, *182*, 244
'Covadonga' (*Daboecia cantabrica*), 255
'Cow-y-Jack' (*Erica ×williamsii*), 229

CPVO, 153–154
'Craig' (*Erica ×garforthensis*), 157
cranberry. See *Vaccinium macrocarpon*.
'Crinkly Tuft' (*Calluna vulgaris*), *147*
Crocus, 141–142
Crocus 'Ruby Giant', 151
Crocus tommasinianus, 142
cross-leaved heath. See *Erica tetralix*.
crowberry. See *Empetrum*.
Cuphea hyssopifolia, 13
'Cupido' (*Daboecia cantabrica*), 19
'Cuprea' (*Calluna vulgaris*), 234, 259
'Curled Roundstone' (*Erica tetralix*), 222, 256–257
Cyperaceae, 131–132

D

Daboecia, 12–13, 19–20, 34, 45–46, 52–53, 72, 75, 148, 150, 188–191, 245, 250, 257
Daboecia azorica, 13, 52, 79, 177, 188, 191
Daboecia azorica 'Arthur P. Dome', 188, 252, 256
Daboecia cantabrica, 52, 78–79, 148, 177, 188–191, 255
   'Arielle', *189*
   'Atropurpurea', *149*
   'Bicolor', 99, 189, *190*, 255
   'Celtic Star', 189, *190*, 255
   'Charles Nelson', 52, 190, 255
   'Cinderella', *190*
   'Covadonga', 255
   'Cupido', *19*
   'David Moss', 190
   'Harlequin', 255
   'Heather Yates', 253
   'Hookstone Purple', 148–149, 190
   'Praegerae', 190
   'Rainbow', 148, 258
   'Rubra', 253
   'Waley's Red', 18, 150, *151*, 190
   'White Blum', 52
   'White Carpet', 253
Daboecia cantabrica f. *alba*, 57, 149, 189
Daboecia cantabrica f. *blumii*, 52, 188, 255
Daboecia ×scotica, 52, 148, 177, 191, 255
   'Ben', 256
   'Cora', 256
   'Ellen Norris', 191
   'Jack Drake', *191*, 251
   'Silverwells', 191
   'Tabramhill', 18
   'William Buchanan', 18, 191, 251

'William Buchanan Gold', *191*, 251, 258
daffodils. See *Narcissus*.
'Dainty Bess' (*Calluna vulgaris*), 251, 256
'Dainty Bess Junior' (*Calluna vulgaris*), 251, 256
Dancing Oaks Nursery, 57
Daphne, 124, 147–148
Daphne arbuscula, 124
Daphne sericea Collina Group, 124
Daphne ×medfordensis 'Lawrence Crocker', 124
Daphne mezereum, 147
Daphne mezereum f. *alba*, 147
Daphne retusa. See *Daphne tangutica*.
Daphne ×susannae 'Lawrence Crocker'. See *Daphne ×medfordensis*.
Daphne tangutica Retusa Group 124
'Dark Beauty' (*Calluna vulgaris*), 180, 234
'Darkness' (*Calluna vulgaris*), 160, 180, 241
'Dark Star' (*Calluna vulgaris*), 180, 234
'Darley Dale' (*Erica ×darleyensis*), 205, 230
Darley Dale heath. See *Erica ×darleyensis*.
'Dart's Flamboyant' (*Calluna vulgaris*), 253, 259
'Dart's Hedgehog' (*Calluna vulgaris*), 259
'David Eason' (*Calluna vulgaris*), 246–247
'David McClintock' (*Erica ciliaris*), 201
'David Moss' (*Daboecia cantabrica*), 190
'David Small' (*Erica umbellata*), 18, 223, *224*
Davis, Clark, 99
Davis, Edith, 99, *233*
Davis garden, 99
Davis, P. G., 204
'Dawn' (*Erica ×watsonii*), 163, 227
'December Red' (*Erica carnea*), 174
deer, 60–62
Dekker, Jan, 226
'Delta' (*Erica tetralix*), 256
Denbeigh Heathers, 165, 223
Denkewitz, Lothar, 152, 223
'Desiree' (*Calluna vulgaris*), 259
'Devon' (*Calluna vulgaris*), 180, 251, 255
Dianthus, 137–138
Dianthus alpinus, 137
Dieck, Georg, 193
DIY design, *111*, 112
'Domino' (*Erica cinerea*), 255
'Don Richards' (*Erica manipuliflora*), 215, 244, 254
'Dorothy Metheny' (*Erica ×watsonii*), 227, 251
Douglas fir. See *Pseudotsuga menziesii*.

Drake, Jack, 191
'Dr Ronald Gray' (*Erica mackayana*), 213
'Dunnet Lime' (*Calluna vulgaris*), 249, 251
'Durford Wood' (*Calluna vulgaris*), 150, 254, 258
Dyce, J. W., 182

E

Eason, Charles Douglas, 203, 205
'Eden Valley' (*Erica cinerea*), 203, 234, 256
'Edewecht Belle' (*Erica* ×*gaudificans*), 161
'Edewecht Blush' (*Erica* ×*gaudificans*), 161, 210, 240
Edewecht heath. See *Erica* ×*gaudificans*.
'E. F. Brown' (*Calluna vulgaris*), 254
elderberry. See *Sambucus*.
'Ellen Norris' (*Daboecia* ×*scotica*), 191
'Elsie Purnell' (*Calluna vulgaris*), 181, 234, 244
'Emerald Jock' (*Calluna vulgaris*), 181, 232, 251, 253, 257
Empetrum, 119–120
Empetrum eamesii, 120
Empetrum EMERALD. See *Empetrum nigrum* 'Smaragd'.
Empetrum nigrum, 119–120
    'Bernstein', 119–120
    'Compass Harbor', 120
    'Irland', 120
    "Kramer Yellow 1", 119–120
    'Lucia', 119
    'Smaragd', 120
    'Zitronella', 119–120
Erica, 12–13, 20, 45, 53–57, 94, 102, 148, 152–153, 162–163, 166, 170, 188, 192–230, 247
Erica 'African Fanfare', 247
Erica ×*afroeuropaea*, 161, 192
Erica andevalensis, 213
Erica arborea, 16, 21, 46, 56–57, 79, 96, 161, 177, 192–193, 246, 250, 252–253, 258
    'Albert's Gold', 193
    'Estrella Gold', 18, 56, 57, 133, 193, 234, 244, 252
Erica arborea var. *alpina*, 56, 192, 193, 244
Erica ×*arendsiana*, 161, 194
Erica australis, 21, 23, 57, 79, 177, 194, 195, 244, 250, 252–253, 258
    'Holehird', 83, 95
    'Mr Robert', 194
    'Riverslea', 95–96
Erica azorica. See *Erica scoparia* subsp. *azorica*.

Erica baccans, 161, 192
Erica bauera, 247
Erica bergiana, 161, 210
Erica blandfordia, 248
Erica caffra, 247
Erica canaliculata, 27, 234, 247
Erica carnea, 53, 59–61, 76, 79, 141, 147–148, 165–166, 177, 195–199, 244–245, 249, 252–253, 257
    'Adrienne Duncan', 195, 199
    'Ann Sparkes', 94, 131, 150, 196, 256
    'Aurea', 61, 196, 206
    'Bell's Extra Special', 27, 131, 196
    'Challenger', 196
    'December Red', 174
    'Foxhollow', 125, 156–157, 196
    'Golden Starlet', 30, 123, 134, 142, 150, 170, 196
    'Isabell', 147, 160, 196
    'King George', 140, 254
    'Lake Garda', 196–197
    'Loughrigg', 197
    'March Seedling', 197
    'Myretoun Ruby', 156, 160, 196, 197
    'Nathalie', 94, 107, 111, 160, 197
    'Pink Spangles', 197, 254
    'Praecox Rubra', 198
    'R. B. Cooke', 198
    'Rosalie', 160, 198
    'Rosantha', 150, 198
    'Rotes Juwel', 142, 150, 160, 198, 256
    'Scatterley', 256
    'Schneekuppe', 198
    'Sherwood Creeping', 61
    'Snow Queen', 27, 160
    'Springwood Pink', 254
    'Springwood White', 96, 110, 160, 196, 198–199, 254
    'Treasure Trove', 162, 165, 198, 199, 206
    'Vivellii', 199
    'Westwood Yellow', 30, 123, 142, 199
    'Wintersonne', 150, 199
Ericaceae, 12–13, 32, 36–39, 66, 119
Erica cerinthoides, 27, 167, 247
Erica ciliaris, 19, 45, 55, 74, 77, 79, 163, 177, 199, 200, 201, 213, 227
    'Aurea', 200
    'Corfe Castle', 200, 228
    'David McClintock', 201
    'Mawiana', 234
    'Mrs C. H. Gill', 201
    'Stoborough', 201, 234

    'White Wings', 150, 232
    'Wych', 234
Erica cinerea, 12, 33–34, 46, 55, 79, 151–152, 170, 177, 200–205, 240–241, 244, 250, 255
    'Alba Minor', 202, 253
    'Apple Blossom', 234
    'Atropurpurea', 57, 105, 201, 234
    'Atrorubens', 234, 253
    'Bucklebury Red', 232, 252
    'Carnea', 253
    'C. D. Eason', 149, 202, 253
    'Celebration', 92, 142, 150–151, 202, 253
    'Cevennes', 202, 234, 253
    'C. G. Best', 202
    'Cindy', 202
    'Coccinea', 105, 107, 150, 203, 252
    'Domino', 255
    'Eden Valley', 203, 234, 256
    'Fiddler's Gold', 203
    'Foxhollow Mahogany', 253
    'Godrevy', 256
    'Golden Drop', 94, 107, 109, 111, 203
    'Golden Hue', 55, 203, 234
    'Golden Sport', 107, 131, 203, 234
    'Golden Tee', 259
    'G. Osmond', 234
    'Guernsey Lime', 256
    'Guernsey Purple', 256
    'Honeymoon', 256
    'Hutton's Seedling', 255
    'Iberian Beauty', 76, 150, 203, 252–253, 256
    'Jos' Golden', 259
    'Kerry Cherry', 86
    'Knap Hill Pink', 134, 149, 150, 235, 236, 252
    'Lime Soda', 204
    'Neptune', 234
    'Pentreath', 204, 252
    'Pink Ice', 152, 204, 223, 253, 256
    'Providence', 106
    'P. S. Patrick', 149, 234
    'Purple Beauty', 18, 149, 234, 252
    'Rock Ruth', 253, 256
    'Ruby', 253
    'Stephen Davis', 204
    'Velvet Night', 149, 204, 252
    'Windlebrooke', 205, 253
    'Yvonne', 255
Erica cinerea var. *maderensis*, 159, 201
Erica codonodes. See *E. lusitanica*.

Erica cruenta, 247
Erica curviflora, 247
Erica ×*darleyensis*, 31, 53–54, 77, 155–156, 165–166, 177, 205–208, 230, 238, 241, 245–246, 253–255, 257
  'Arthur Johnson', 97, 205, 252
  'Darley Dale', 205, 230
  'Furzey', 118, 205
  'George Rendall', 205, 252
  'Ghost Hills', 205–206, 230
  'Goldrush', 165, 166, 169, 206
  'Irish Treasure', 142, 151, 165–166, 206
  'Jack H. Brummage', 156, 206
  'Jenny Porter', 206
  'J. W. Porter', 206
  'Kramer's Rote', 41, 94, 206, 230
  'Margaret Porter', 53, 54,
  'Mary Helen', 156, 205, 206
  'Phoebe', 142, 151
  'Silberschmelze', 206, 230
  'Spring Surprise', 54
  'White Perfection', 206
Erica erigena, 20, 53–55, 61, 77, 79, 98, 152, 166, 177, 207–209, 241, 244–246, 252–254, 258
  'Brian Proudley', 54, 96, 170, 208, 234, 235, 254
  'Brightness', 160
  'Golden Lady', 98–99, 208
  'Irish Dusk', 54, 96, 98, 142, 151, 156, 165, 206, 208
  'Maxima', 96, 208, 234, 235, 237
  'Superba', 54, 209
  'W. T. Rackliff', 98–99, 156, 208, 209, 258
Erica erigena f. *alba*. See 'Brian Proudley'.
Erica formosa, 248
Erica ×*garforthensis*, 157, 209, 255
  'Craig', 157
  'Tracy Wilson', 167, 209, 252
Erica ×*gaudificans*, 56, 161, 177, 210, 244, 255
  'Edewecht Belle', 161,
  'Edewecht Blush', 161, 210, 240
Erica 'Gengold', 167, 248
Erica glandulosa, 247
Erica gracilis, 248
Erica ×*griffithsii*, 55, 61, 157, 177, 210–211, 244–246, 250
  'Ashlea Gold', 159
  'Heaven Scent', 99, 157, 210–211, 244
  'Jacqueline', 147, 210, 244, 252
  'Valerie Griffiths', 31, 97, 158, 211, 254

Erica ×*krameri*, 177, 211, 251, 255
  'Otto', 211
  'Rudi', 211
Erica lusitanica, 16, 27, 57, 74, 79, 95, 177, 211–212, 226–227, 244–245, 250, 252–253, 258
  'George Hunt', 74, 212
Erica lusitanica subsp. *cantabrica*, 212
Erica lusitanica subsp. *lusitanica*, 212
Erica mackaiana. See *Erica mackayana*.
Erica mackayana, 32, 46, 55, 77, 79, 177, 213–214, 219, 257
  'Dr Ronald Gray', 213
  'Lawsoniana', 213
  'Maura', 213
  'Plena', 214
  'Shining Light', 29, 78, 164, 214
Erica maderensis. See *Erica cinerea* var. *maderensis*.
Erica mammosa, 247
Erica manipuliflora, 55, 61, 79, 97, 157, 177, 209, 214–215, 244–246, 250, 253–254, 257
  'Aldeburgh', 97, 158, 211, 214, 254
  'Cascades', 215
  'Don Richards', 215, 244, 254
  'Ian Cooper', 215, 244, 252
  'Korčula', 166, 215, 244, 252
Erica mediterranea hybrida, 230. See also *Erica* ×*darleyensis*.
Erica multiflora, 16, 21, 73, 79, 215–216, 245, 250, 253–254
Erica nana, 167, 247
Erica ×*oldenburgensis*, 57, 161, 177, 216, 245, 258
  'Ammerland', 216
  'Oldenburg', 216
Erica pageana, 247
Erica patersonia, 167, 248
Erica ×*praegeri*. See *E.* ×*stuartii*.
Erica quadrangularis, 248
Erica regia, 248
Erica scoparia, 16, 18, 21, 23, 57, 79, 96, 177, 216, 250, 253, 258
Erica scoparia subsp. *azorica*, 13, 217
Erica scoparia subspecies *maderincola*, 217
Erica scoparia subsp. *platycodon*, 217–218
Erica scoparia subsp. *scoparia*, 218
Erica sparsa, 248
Erica speciosa, 27, 247
Erica spiculifolia, 79, 143, 161, 177, 210–211, 218–219, 249, 251–252
  'Balkan Rose', 219

Erica stricta. See *Erica terminalis*.
Erica ×*stuartii*, 55, 164, 177, 219–220, 251
  'Irish Lemon', 219, 234, 255
  'Irish Orange', 111, 220
  'Stuart's Original', 220, 255
Erica terminalis, 18, 57, 79, 152, 161, 177, 194, 220, 221, 234, 244–245, 250, 253–254, 258
  'Thelma Woolner', 221
Erica tetralix, 73–74, 77, 79, 97–98, 163–166, 221–223, 240, 244, 250–251, 255
  'Alba Mollis', 18, 44, 101, 157, 165, 170, 177, 221
  'Bartinney', 157, 170, 250
  'Con Underwood', 222
  'Curled Roundstone', 222, 256–257
  'Delta', 256
  'George Fraser', 222
  'Helma', 250
  'Hookstone Pink', 165, 222, 228
  'Jos' Creeping', 256
  'Melbury White', 166
  'Pink Pepper', 255
  'Pink Star', 222
  'Riko', 152, 223
  'Samtpfötchen', 152
  'Swedish Yellow', 30, 223
  'Tina', 152, 223, 250
Erica umbellata, 21, 56, 79, 177, 223–224, 245, 250, 253, 255–256
  'Anne Small', 223
  'David Small', 18, 223, 224
Erica vagans, 18, 36, 56, 77, 79, 157–158, 177, 224–226, 244–246, 249–250, 254
  'Birch Glow', 224, 249
  'Cornish Cream', 225, 249
  'Fiddlestone', 225
  'Golden Triumph', 225
  'Kevernensis Alba', 226, 253
  'Lyonesse', 165, 226, 234
  'Mrs D. F. Maxwell', 56, 165, 226, 234
  'St Keverne', 225–226, 234
  'Valerie Proudley', 158, 211, 226
  'Yellow John', 226
Erica vagans f. *viridula*, 159
Erica ×*veitchii*, 57, 177, 226–227, 245, 250, 253, 258
  'Exeter', 226, 244
  'Gold Tips', 226
  'Pink Joy', 226, 244
Erica ventricosa, 248
Erica versicolor, 248

Erica verticillata, 157, 248. See also *E.* ×*griffithsii* 'Heaven Scent'.
Erica vestita, 248
Erica walkeria, 248
Erica ×*watsonii*, 55, 157, 163–164, 177, 227–228, 237, 244
   'Cherry Turpin', 105, 151, 227, 251
   'Claire Elise', 157–158
   'Dawn', 163, 227
   'Dorothy Metheny', 227, 251
   'H. Maxwell', 227
   'Mary', 227, 228, 251
   'Pearly Pink', 163, 228, 251
   'Pink Pacific', 163, 228, 251
   'Truro', 228
Erica ×*williamsii*, 55, 77, 164–165, 167, 177, 228–229, 245, 250
   'Cow-y-Jack', 229
   'Gold Button', 158, 256
   'Gwavas', 229
   'Ken Wilson', 165, 253
   'P. D. Williams', 229
   'Phantom', 165
Erica 'Winter Fire', 25, 247
Ericultura, 95
Eriophorum latifolium, 132
Eriophorum vaginatum, 132
Eriophorum virginicum, 132
'Estrella Gold' (*Erica arborea*), 18, 56, 57, 133, 193, 234, 244, 252
'Exeter' (*Erica* ×*veitchii*), 226, 244

F

false heather. See *Cuphea hyssopifolia*.
Farrand, Beatrix Jones, 126
Festuca, 81
Festuca amethystina, 130
Festuca cinerea. See *Festuca glauca*.
Festuca glauca, 130–131, 151
   'Blausilber', 130
   'Elijah Blue', 130
   'Meerblau', 130
Festuca idahoensis, 130
Festuca ovina. See *Festuca glauca*.
'Fiddler's Gold' (*Erica cinerea*), 203
'Fiddlestone' (*Erica vagans*), 225
Fiddlestone Lodge, 203, 225
'Finale' (*Calluna vulgaris*), 254
'Findling' (*Calluna vulgaris*), 256
'Firefly' (*Calluna vulgaris*), 30, 94, 109, 144, 146, 147, 150–151, 181, 184

'Fire King' (*Calluna vulgaris*), 30, 259
'Fire Star' (*Calluna vulgaris*), 50, 259
'Flatling' (*Calluna vulgaris*), 256
Flecken, Jos, 95
'Floriferous' (*Calluna vulgaris*), 257
Foley, Peter, 207
'Fort Bragg' (*Calluna vulgaris*), 131, 259
Fort Tryon, 147
'Fortyniner Gold' (*Calluna vulgaris*), 234, 244, 251–252
'Foxhollow' (*Erica carnea*), 125, 156–157, 196
'Foxhollow Mahogany' (*Erica cinerea*), 253
'Foxii' (*Calluna vulgaris*), 97, 256
'Foxii Floribunda' (*Calluna vulgaris*), 256
'Foxii Nana' (*Calluna vulgaris*), 256
'Foya' (*Calluna vulgaris*), 108, 149, 151, 259
Fraga Vila, Maria Isabel, 223
Fraser, Stuart, 181
'Fraser's Old Gold' (*Calluna vulgaris*), 42, 181
'Fred J. Chapple' (*Calluna vulgaris*), 184
'Fréjus' (*Calluna vulgaris*), 250
Fritillaria meleagris, 142, 151
'Fritz Kircher' (*Calluna vulgaris*), 247
Frosty Curls. See *Carex albula*.
'Furzey' (*Erica* ×*darleyensis*), 118, 205
Furzey Gardens, 205

G

Galanthus, 135, 141
Galanthus nivalis, 150
'Galaxy' (*Calluna vulgaris*), 247
Gardner, Ben, 32
Garland Farm, 126
Garland Nursery, 40
Gaultheria shallon, 233
'Gengold' (*Erica*), 167, 248
'George Fraser' (*Erica tetralix*), 222
'George Hunt' (*Erica lusitanica*), 74, 212
'George Rendall' (*Erica* ×*darleyensis*), 205, 252
Geranium, 138
Geranium 'Ann Folkard', 138
Geranium (Cinereum Group) 'Ballerina', 138
Geranium (Cinereum Group) 'Laurence Flatman', 138
Geranium dalmaticum, 138
Geranium macrorrhizum, 235
Geranium macrorrhizum 'Czakor', 235
Geranium pratense Victor Reiter Junior strain, 144

Geranium procurrens, 138
Geranium renardii, 138
Geranium renardii 'Whiteknights', 138
Geranium 'Salome', 138
Geranium sanguineum, 138
Geranium sanguineum 'Shepherd's Warning', 138
Geranium sanguineum var. *striatum*, 138
Geranium wallichianum 'Buxton's Variety', 138
'Gerda' (*Calluna vulgaris*), 251
German Office for Plant Protection. See Bundessortenamt.
'Ghost Hills' (*Erica* ×*darleyensis*), 205–206, 230
'Glendoick Silver' (*Calluna vulgaris*), 150
'Glenlivet' (*Calluna vulgaris*), 259
'Glenmorangie' (*Calluna vulgaris*), 256, 259
'Godrevy' (*Erica cinerea*), 256
'Gold Button' (*Erica* ×*williamsii*), 158, 256
'Gold Charm' (*Calluna vulgaris*), 259
'Golden Carpet' (*Calluna vulgaris*), 253, 256
'Golden Drop' (*Erica cinerea*), 94, 107, 109, 111, 203
'Golden Feather' (*Calluna vulgaris*), 259
'Golden Fleece' (*Calluna vulgaris*), 256
'Golden Hue' (*Erica cinerea*), 55, 203, 234
'Golden Lady' (*Erica erigena*), 98–99, 208
'Golden Rivulet' (*Calluna vulgaris*), 253
'Golden Sport' (*Erica cinerea*), 107, 131, 203, 234
'Golden Starlet' (*Erica carnea*), 30, 123, 134, 142, 150, 170, 196
'Golden Tee' (*Erica cinerea*), 259
'Golden Triumph' (*Erica vagans*), 225
'Gold Haze' (*Calluna vulgaris*), 27, 181, 179
'Gold Kup' (*Calluna vulgaris*), 117, 232
'Goldrush' (*Erica* ×*darleyensis*), 165, 166, 169, 206
'Goldsworth Crimson Variegated' (*Calluna vulgaris*), 75, 258
'Gold Tips' (*Erica* ×*veitchii*), 226
Gorie, Kathleen, 184
gorse. See *Ulex*.
'G. Osmond' (*Erica cinerea*), 234
grasses, 129–131, 134, 155
Gray, Ronald, 213
grayanotoxin, 22–23
Green Mountain Heather, 115
grey mould. See *Botrytis cinerea*.
Griffiths, John, 155–157, 158, 159, 161–162, 166–167, 170–172, 209–211, 228

Griffiths, Valerie, 156, *158*, 159, 171
Griffiths garden, *159*
Griffiths' heath. See *Erica* ×*griffithsii*.
'Grönsinka' (*Calluna vulgaris*), 249, 256
grouse, 17–18
'Guernsey Lime' (*Erica cinerea*), 256
'Guernsey Purple' (*Erica cinerea*), 256
'Gwavas' (*Erica* ×*williamsii*), 229

H

Hachmann Nursery, *11*
Hall, Cleo, 114–115
Hamamelis, 93, 94, 118
Hamamelis ×*intermedia* 'Jelena', 94
Hamamelis ×*intermedia* 'Pallida', 94
Handy Guide to Heathers, 28, 42, 44, 176, 245
hares, 60
'Harlequin' (*Daboecia cantabrica*), 255
'Harten's Findling' (*Calluna vulgaris*), 256
Hawaiian heather. See *Cuphea hyssopifolia*.
Heather Acres, 68
heather beetle. See *Lochmaea suturalis*.
heather family. See Ericaceae.
Heather Society, The, 13, 111, 156–158, 172, 174–175, 223–224, 242
Heather Society herbarium, 175
'Heather Yates' (*Daboecia cantabrica*), 253
'Heaven Scent' (*Erica* ×*griffithsii*), 99, 157, 210–211, 244
Hebe, 124–126
Hebe albicans 'Sussex Carpet', 125
'H. E. Beale' (*Calluna vulgaris*), 181, 184, 244, 254
Hebe 'Baby Marie', 125
Hebe 'Christabel', 125
Hebe cupressoides, 125, *193*
Hebe cupressoides 'Boughton Dome', 125
Hebe 'Emerald Gem', 125
Hebe 'Maori Gem', 125
Hebe mckeanii. See *Hebe* 'Emerald Gem'.
Hebe ochracea 'James Stirling', 125
Hebe pinguifolia 'Pagei', *125*, 150
Hebe 'Pinocchio', 125
Hebe 'Pluto', 125
Hebe salicornioides, 125
Hebe 'Silver Beads', 125
Hebe subsimilis var. *astonii*, 125
Hebe tetragona, 125
Hebe topiaria, 126
'Heidepracht' (*Calluna vulgaris*), 253

'Heideteppich' (*Calluna vulgaris*), 253
'Heidezwerg' (*Calluna vulgaris*), *182*, 253, 256–257
Helichrysum, 237
Helictotrichon sempervirens, 130
'Helma' (*Erica tetralix*), 250
hens and chicks. See *Sempervivum*.
Hewitt, John, 211
'Hibernica' (*Calluna vulgaris*), 254
'Hiemalis' (*Calluna vulgaris*), 250, 254
'Highland Rose' (*Calluna vulgaris*), 84, *108*, 149, 259
'Hillbrook Orange' (*Calluna vulgaris*), 259
'H. Maxwell' (*Erica* ×*watsonii*), 227
Hoekert, H., 180
Holden Clough Nursery, 207
'Holehird' (*Erica australis*), 83, 95
honeybees. See *Apis*.
'Honeymoon' (*Erica cinerea*), 256
'Hookstone Pink' (*Erica tetralix*), 165, 222, 228
'Hookstone Purple' (*Daboecia cantabrica*), 148–149, 190
Horticulture Centre of the Pacific, 93, 94
hostas, 240
'Hoyerhagen' (*Calluna vulgaris*), 259
huckleberry. See *Vaccinium ovatum*.
Hughes, Marion, 229
Huisman, T., 185
hummingbirds. See Trochilidae. See also *Selasphorus rufus*.
'Humpty Dumpty' (*Calluna vulgaris*), 92, 256
Hunt, George, 212
Hurst, Charles Chamberlain, 169
'Hutton's Seedling' (*Erica cinerea*), 255
Hymenoscyphus ericae, 37–38

I

'Ian Cooper' (*Erica manipuliflora*), 215, 244, 252
'Iberian Beauty' (*Erica cinerea*), 76, 150, 203, 252–253, 256
Iberis sempervirens, 121
ICNCP, 174–175, 230
Ingwersen, W. E. Th., 225
'Inshriach Bronze' (*Calluna vulgaris*), 249
intellectual property rights, 153–154, 172
International Code of Nomenclature for Cultivated Plants. See ICNCP.
International Cultivar Registration Authority, 13, 174

International Register of Heather Names, 28, 176, 245
International Registrar, 174
International Union for the Protection of New Varieties of Plants, The. See UPOV.
Ipheion, 142
Iris, 102, 132–133
Iris douglasiana, 133
Iris 'Grapelet', 133
'Irish Dusk' (*Erica erigena*), 54, 96, 98, 142, 151, 156, 165, 206, 208
'Irish Lemon' (*Erica* ×*stuartii*), 219, 234, 255
'Irish Orange' (*Erica* ×*stuartii*), 111, 220
'Irish Treasure' (*Erica* ×*darleyensis*), 142, 151, 165–166, 206
Iris innominata, 133
Iris Reticulata Group, 132
Iris Reticulata Group 'George', *133*
Iris Reticulata Group 'Harmony', 151
Iris sibirica, 133
Iris tenax, 133
'Isabell' (*Erica carnea*), 147, 160, 196
'Isle of Hirta' (*Calluna vulgaris*), 257

J

'Jack Drake' (*Daboecia* ×*scotica*), 191, 251
'Jack H. Brummage' (*Erica* ×*darleyensis*), 156, 206
'Jacqueline' (*Erica* ×*griffithsii*), 147, 210, 244, 252
'Jan Dekker' (*Calluna vulgaris*), 150
'Jenny Porter' (*Erica* ×*darleyensis*), 206
'J. H. Hamilton' (*Calluna vulgaris*), *182*, 249
'Jimmy Dyce' (*Calluna vulgaris*), *182*, 254–255
Johansson, Brita, *182*, 223
Johnson, Arthur T., 205
'Johnson's Variety' (*Calluna vulgaris*), 160, 244, 250, 254
Jones, Albert, 208, 215
'Jos' Creeping' (*Erica tetralix*), 256
'Jos' Golden' (*Erica cinerea*), 259
'Joy Vanstone' (*Calluna vulgaris*), 27, 182
'Julia' (*Calluna vulgaris*), 259
Juniperus communis 'Compressa', 118
'Juno' (*Calluna vulgaris*), 252
'J. W. Porter' (*Erica* ×*darleyensis*), 206

K

Kalmia, 23, 120
Kalmia latifolia, 120
Kalmia latifolia 'Minuet', 120

Kampa, C., 211
'Ken Wilson' (*Erica* ×*williamsii*), 165, 253
'Kerry Cherry' (*Erica cinerea*), 86
'Kerstin' (*Calluna vulgaris*), 92, 173, 182, 235, 249, 258
'Kevernensis Alba' (*Erica vagans*), 226, 253
'King George' (*Erica carnea*), 140, 254
'Kinlochruel' (*Calluna vulgaris*), 182, 187
Knap Hill nursery, 204, 229
'Knap Hill Pink' (*Erica cinerea*), 134, 149, 150, 235, 236, 252
Knight, Alice, 68, *233*
Kniphofia, 112, 133–135
Kniphofia 'Bressingham Comet', 134
Kniphofia 'Little Maid', 134
Kniphofia 'Percy's Pride', 134
Kniphofia 'Primrose Beauty', 134
Kniphofia 'Vanilla', 134
'Korčula' (*Erica manipuliflora*), 166, 215, 244, 252
Kramer, Kurt, 155, 159–162, 165–167, 170, 183, 192, 194, 196, 198–199, 206, 210–211, 216
Kramer's Red. See *Erica* ×*darleyensis* 'Kramer's Rote'.
'Kramer's Rote' (*Erica* ×*darleyensis*), 41, 94, 206, 230
'Kuphaldtii' (*Calluna vulgaris*), 253

L

Laburnum,
Lagopus lagopus, 18. See also grouse.
'Lake Garda' (*Erica carnea*), 196–197
'Larissa' (*Calluna vulgaris*), 183, 247
Lasiocampa quercus, 18
Lautenschlaeger, Berndt, 57–58, 87
Lavandula, 126–127
Lavandula angustifolia, 126, 151, 235, 236
Lavandula stoechas, 127
lavender. See *Lavandula*.
'Lawsoniana' (*Erica mackayana*), 213
'Lemon Gem' (*Calluna vulgaris*), 30, 133
Lepidoziaceae, 38
Letts, John F., 202, 205–206
Leucothoe, 23
Lewis garden, *126*
'Lewis Lilac' (*Calluna vulgaris*), 252
Liberty Hyde Bailey Hortorum. See Bailey Hortorum.
'Lime Glade' (*Calluna vulgaris*), 30, 146, 147, 183
'Lime Soda' (*Erica cinerea*), 204
ling. See *Calluna vulgaris*.

lingonberry. See *Vaccinium vitis-idaea*.
liverworts, 38
Lobelia erinus, 146
Lochmea suturalis, 62–63
'Long White' (*Calluna vulgaris*), 150, 243, 244, 249, 252
'Loughrigg' (*Erica carnea*), 197
Lüneberg Heath, *14*, 100, 114
'Lyndon Proudley' (*Calluna vulgaris*), 183, 252
lyng. See *Calluna vulgaris*.
'Lyonesse' (*Erica vagans*), 165, 226, 234

M

mad honey disease, 22
Magnolia stellata, 118
'Mair's Variety' (*Calluna vulgaris*), 183, 244, 249
maple. See *Acer*.
'March Seedling' (*Erica carnea*), 197
'Margaret Porter' (*Erica* ×*darleyensis*), 53, *54*,
'Marion Blum' (*Calluna vulgaris*), 30, 150
'Marleen' (*Calluna vulgaris*), 161, 183, 247
'Martha Hermann' (*Calluna vulgaris*), 183, 249
'Mary' (*Erica* ×*watsonii*), 227, 228, 251
'Mary Helen' (*Erica* ×*darleyensis*), 156, 205, 206
'Matita' (*Calluna vulgaris*), 249, 258
'Maura' (*Erica mackayana*), 213
'Mawiana' (*Erica ciliaris*), 234
'Maxima' (*Erica erigena*), 96, 208, 234, 235, 237
Maxwell, Douglas Fyfe and Mrs, 225, 227
Maxwell & Beale nursery, 181, 202–203, 210
'Mazurka' (*Calluna vulgaris*), 149
McClintock, David, 157, 175, 196, 201, 214–215, 219–220, 224
Mediterranean Pink, 230
Mediterranean White, 230
'Melanie' (*Calluna vulgaris*), 161, 178, 183, 244, 247
'Melbury White' (*Erica tetralix*), 166
Mendel, Gregor, 168–169
Mendocino Coast Botanical Gardens, 49
Mendocino Coast Heather Society, 49
Mexican feather grass. See *Nassella*.
Mexican heather. See *Cuphea hyssopifolia*.
mice, 31, 60
Milbert's Tortoiseshell. See *Nymphalis milberti*.

'Miniöxabäck' (*Calluna vulgaris*), 249, 256
'Minty' (*Calluna vulgaris*), 257
Miscanthus, 129
'Miss Muffet' (*Calluna vulgaris*), 256
mist propagation, 73
'Molecule' (*Calluna vulgaris*), 256
Molinia caerulea subsp. *caerulea* 'Variegata', 112
mondo grass. See *Ophiopogon*.
'Monika' (*Calluna vulgaris*), 254
Montgomery, E. J., 182
Moseley, Anne,
mountain heather. See *Calluna* and *Phyllodoce*.
mountain laurel. See *Kalmia latifolia*.
Mount Stewart, 123
mourning cloak. See *Nymphalis antiopa*.
'Mr Robert' (*Erica australis*), 194
'Mrs C. H. Gill' (*Erica ciliaris*), 201
'Mrs D. F. Maxwell' (*Erica vagans*), 56, 165, 226, 234
'Mrs Pat' (*Calluna vulgaris*), 25
'Mrs Ronald Gray' (*Calluna vulgaris*), 251
'Mullach Mor' (*Calluna vulgaris*), 257
'Mullardoch' (*Calluna vulgaris*), 249, 251, 256
'Mullion' (*Calluna vulgaris*), 184
'Multicolor' (*Calluna vulgaris*), 254
Muscari armeniacum, 142
Muscari azureum, 141
mycorrhizae, 33, 36–39
'My Dream' (*Calluna vulgaris*), 150, 236, 244
'Myretoun Ruby' (*Erica carnea*), 156, 160, 196, 197
myxomatosis, 60

N

Nandina domestica 'Fire Power', 151
Narcissus, 140–141
Narcissus bulbocodium, 140
Narcissus 'French Prairie', 140
Narcissus 'Hawera', 140–141
Narcissus rupestris, 140
Narcissus 'Segovia', 140
Narcissus willkommii, 140
Nassella tenuissima, 131, 134
'Nathalie' (*Erica carnea*), 94, 107, 111, 160, 197
National Botanic Gardens, Glasnevin, 213
Nectariniidae, 18

Nectaroscordum siculum subsp. *bulgaricum*, 142–143
'Nelly' (*Calluna vulgaris*), 247, 256–257
Nelson, E. Charles, 161, 179, 214, 222, 224
'Neptune' (*Erica cinerea*), 234
ninebark. See *Physocarpus*.
'Nordlicht'. See *Calluna vulgaris* 'Skone'.
North American Heather Society, 165, 229
'Northern Lights'. See *Calluna vulgaris* 'Skone'.
Northwest Garden Nursery, 131
Nymphalis antiopa, 18
Nymphalis milberti, 18

O

oat grass. See *Helictotrichon*.
'October White' (*Calluna vulgaris*), 254
Oidiodendron maius, 37–38
'Oiseval' (*Calluna vulgaris*), 257
'Oldenburg' (*Erica* ×*oldenburgensis*), 216
Oliver, E. G. H. (Ted), 242
Ophiopogon planiscapus var. *nigrescens*, 62, 134–135, 150
'Orange Queen' (*Calluna vulgaris*), 184
Oregon Heather Society, 49
Origanum laevigatum 'Hopleys', 237
Origanum libanoticum, 237
Otiorhynchus sulcatus, 63–64
Otter's Court Heathers, 215
'Otto' (*Erica* ×*krameri*), 211
Oudean, Karen, 238
'Oxshott Common' (*Calluna vulgaris*), 184, 234, 252

P

Pacific Coast irises, 133
Painted Lady. See *Vanessa*.
Panicum virgatum, 130
pansy. See *Viola*.
Parris, Anne, 152, 156
'Pat's Gold' (*Calluna vulgaris*), 234
'P. D. Williams' (*Erica* ×*williamsii*), 229
'Peace' (*Calluna vulgaris*), 254
'Pearly Pink' (*Erica* ×*watsonii*), 163, 228, 251
'Peggy' (*Calluna vulgaris*), 249
'Penny Bun' (*Calluna vulgaris*), 256
Penstemon pinifolius, 138–139
    'Compactum', 139
    'Magdalena Sunshine', 139
    'Mersea Yellow', 139

'Pentreath' (*Erica cinerea*), 204, 252
'Perestrojka' (*Calluna vulgaris*), 255
Persicaria virginiana 'Painter's Palette', 144
'Peter Sparkes' (*Calluna vulgaris*), 150, 160, 184, 234, 244, 254
Petunia, 146–147
Petunia ×*hybrida* ALADDIN YELLOW, 147
'Phantom' (*Erica* ×*williamsii*), 165
'Phoebe' (*Erica* ×*darleyensis*), 142, 151
Phormium, 135
Phormium tenax
    'Bronze Baby', 135
    'Jack Spratt', 135
    'Tiny Tiger', 135
Phormium 'Tom Thumb', 135
Phyllodoce, 13
Physocarpus, 112
Phytophthora cinnamomi, 47, 65–66
Phytophthora ramorum, 66
Picea abies 'Little Gem', 117
Picea glauca 'Jean's Dilly', 118
Picea pungens, 112
Picea pungens 'Blue Pearl', 117
Pieris, 23, 120
Pieris floribunda, 120
Pieris formosa var. *forrestii*, 120
Pieris japonica 'Little Heath', 120
Pieris japonica 'Little Heath Green', 120
'Pink Ice' (*Erica cinerea*), 152, 204, 223, 253, 256
'Pink Joy' (*Erica* ×*veitchii*), 226, 244
'Pink Pacific' (*Erica* ×*watsonii*), 163, 228, 251
'Pink Pepper', 255
'Pink Spangles' (*Erica carnea*), 197, 254
'Pink Star' (*Erica tetralix*), 222
Pinus sylvestris, 37
'Platt's Surprise' (*Calluna vulgaris*), 249
'Plena' (*Erica mackayana*), 214
Plumridge garden, 95, 116, 118, 121, 125
Poaceae, 129–131
Porter, James Walker, 206, 208
Portulaca, 145, 146
'Praecox Rubra' (*Erica carnea*), 198
'Praegerae' (*Daboecia cantabrica*), 190
Praeger's heath. See *Erica* ×*stuartii*.
'Prostrata Flagelliformis' (*Calluna vulgaris*), 257
Proudley, Brian, 208, 226
'Providence' (*Erica cinerea*), 106
Pseudotsuga menziesii, 114, 115
'P. S. Patrick' (*Erica cinerea*), 149, 234

'Punch's Dessert' (*Calluna vulgaris*), 150, 184
'Purple Beauty' (*Erica cinerea*), 18, 149, 234, 252
'Pygmaea' (*Calluna vulgaris*), 256
Pythium, 65–67

Q

Quercus ilex, 38

R

rabbits, 59–60
'Radnor' (*Calluna vulgaris*), 184, 249
'Radnor Gold' (*Calluna vulgaris*), 249
'Rainbow' (*Daboecia cantabrica*), 148, 258
rats, 60
Raulston, JC, Arboretum, 93
'R. B. Cooke' (*Erica carnea*), 198
'Redbud' (*Calluna vulgaris*), 150, 247
'Red Carpet' (*Calluna vulgaris*), 259
'Red Favorit' (*Calluna vulgaris*), 249
'Red Fred' (*Calluna vulgaris*), 184
red-hot poker. See *Kniphofia*.
'Red Pimpernel' (*Calluna vulgaris*), 254
red spider mite. See *Tetranychus urticae*.
Reef Point, 126
'Reini' (*Calluna vulgaris*), 185, 244, 249
Rhizoctonia solani, 47, 65–66
Rhododendron, 22–23, 83, 104–105, 121, 122, 148
Rhododendron albiflorum, 22
Rhododendron calostrotum, 122
Rhododendron campylogynum, 122
Rhododendron 'Cosmopolitan', 121
Rhododendron 'Delaware Valley White', 121
Rhododendron 'Hachmann's Charmant', 150, 151
Rhododendron ×*laetevirens*, 121
Rhododendron macrophyllum, 22
Rhododendron 'Maricee', 121–122
Rhododendron mucronatum, 121
Rhododendron myrtifolium, 122
Rhododendron occidentale, 22
Rhododendron ponticum, 22
Rhododendron 'Ramapo', 121–122
Rhododendron Species Foundation Botanical Garden, 212
rhodotoxin. See grayanotoxin.
Richards, Don, 186, 215
'Riko' (*Erica tetralix*), 152, 223
Ring of Brodgar, 15

'Riverslea' (*Erica australis*), 95–96
'Robert Chapman' (*Calluna vulgaris*), 126, 151, 181, 185, 249
'Rock Ruth' (*Erica cinerea*), 253, 256
'Roland Haagen' (*Calluna vulgaris*), 185
'Romina' (*Calluna vulgaris*), 247
'Roodkapje' (*Calluna vulgaris*), 247
root rot. See *Phytophthora cinnamomi* and *Pythium*.
Rosa, 127–128, 147, 235, 236, 237
Rosa 'Baby Garnette', 127
Rosa BABY PARADISE. See *R.* 'MElfovett'.
Rosa glauca, 128
Rosa HEATHER MIST. See *R.* 'MICmist'.
'Rosalie' (*Erica carnea*), 160, 198
Rosa 'MElfovett', 127
Rosa MERRY GLO. See *R.* 'MINimerr'.
Rosa 'MICmist', 127
Rosa 'MINimerr', 127
Rosa 'MINnco', 127
Rosa 'Misty Dawn', 127
Rosa 'MORchari', 127
Rosa 'MORelfire', 127
Rosa 'MORvi', 127
Rosa nitida, 127
'Rosantha' (*Erica carnea*), 150, 198
Rosa pendulina 'Nana', 127
Rosa PINK CARPET. See *R.* 'MINnco'.
Rosa PINK ELF. See *R.* 'MORelfire'.
Rosa rubrifolia. See *R. glauca*.
Rosa SWEET CHARIOT. See *R.* 'MORchari'.
Rosa VI'S VIOLET. See *R.* 'MORvi'.
Roses. See *Rosa*.
'Roswitha' (*Calluna vulgaris*), 247
'Rotes Juwel' (*Erica carnea*), 142, 150, 160, 198, 256
Royal Botanic Gardens, Kew, 210
Royal Horticultural Society Colour Chart, 42
Royal Horticultural Society Garden, Rosemoor, 93
Royal Horticultural Society Garden, Wisley, 102, 175, 231
'Rubra' (*Daboecia cantabrica*), 253
'Ruby' (*Erica cinerea*), 253
'Ruby Slinger' (*Calluna vulgaris*), 185
'Rudi' (*Erica* ×*krameri*), 211
Russell, Bryant, 143–144
Ruthe, P., 246

S

Saint Andrews Botanic Garden, 193
Saint Dabeoc's heath. See *Daboecia*.
Saint Kilda heathers, 181, 249, 251, 256–257
'Saint Nick' (*Calluna vulgaris*), 254
salal. See *Gaulteria shallon*.
Sambucus, 112
'Samtpfötchen' (*Erica tetralix*), 152
'Sandy' (*Calluna vulgaris*), 247
Saturnia pavonia, 18
Scannell, Maura, 213
'Scatterley' (*Erica carnea*), 256
'Schneekuppe' (*Erica carnea*), 198
Schneverdingen heather park, 100, 101–102, 103, 173
Schuldt, Gary, 143–144
'Schurig's Sensation' (*Calluna vulgaris*), 254
Scilla, 141–142
Scilla siberica, 142, 150
Scots pine. See *Pinus sylvestris*.
Scottish Highlands, 114
sedges 102, 131–132
Sedum, 139–140
Sedum 'Acre', 140
Sedum cauticola, 140
Sedum dasyphyllum, 140
Sedum spathulifolium, 140
Selasphorus rufus, 18
Sempervivum, 139, 147
Sempervivum 'Packardian', 150
'Serlei Aurea' (*Calluna vulgaris*), 185
'Sesam' (*Calluna vulgaris*), 147, 149, 185, 249
sheep, 17, 18
Sherwood, 122
'Sherwood Creeping' (*Erica carnea*), 61
'Shining Light' (*Erica mackayana*), 29, 78, 164, 214
'Silberschmelze' (*Erica* ×*darleyensis*), 206, 230
'Silver Knight' (*Calluna vulgaris*), 57, 249
'Silver Queen' (*Calluna vulgaris*), 149, 185
'Silver Rose' (*Calluna vulgaris*), 186
'Silverwells' (*Daboecia* ×*scotica*), 191
'Sir John Charrington' (*Calluna vulgaris*), 186
'Sirsson' (*Calluna vulgaris*), 186, 249
'Sister Anne' (*Calluna vulgaris*), 186, 251, 252
'Skone' (*Calluna vulgaris*), 75, 258
Small, Albert, 215
Small, Anne, 223

Small, David, 165, 214, 224
Smith, Linda, 112, 148
snapdragon. See *Antirrhinum*.
'Snowflake' (*Calluna vulgaris*), 90, 141–142, 251
'Snow Queen' (*Erica carnea*), 27, 160
'Soay' (*Calluna vulgaris*), 22, 92–93, 140, 251, 256–257
Spiraea ×*bumalda* 'Goldflame'. See *Spiraea japonica*.
Spiraea japonica 'Goldflame', 108
'Spitfire' (*Calluna vulgaris*), 259
'Spring Cream' (*Calluna vulgaris*), 186, 254
'Spring Glow' (*Calluna vulgaris*), 254
'Spring Surprise' (*Erica* ×*darleyensis*), 54
spring tips, 25
'Spring Torch' (*Calluna vulgaris*), 51, 70, 186, 235
'Springwood Pink' (*Erica carnea*), 254
'Springwood White' (*Erica carnea*), 96, 110, 160, 196, 198–199, 254
spruce. See *Picea*.
'Stefanie' (*Calluna vulgaris*), 254
Steinernema kraussei, 64
'Stephen Davis' (*Erica cinerea*), 204
Stipa tenuissima. See *Nassella tenuissima*.
'St Keverne' (*Erica vagans*), 225–226, 234
'Stoborough' (*Erica ciliaris*), 201, 234
Stow, Arnold, 138
Stuart, Charles, 220
'Stuartii'. See *Erica* ×*stuartii* 'Stuart's Original'.
'Stuart's Original' (*Erica* ×*stuartii*), 220, 255
succulents, 139–140
Summerfield Nursery, 211
sunbirds. See Nectariniidae.
'Sunrise' (*Calluna vulgaris*), 259
'Sunset' (*Calluna vulgaris*), 186
'Superba' (*Erica erigena*), 54, 209
'Swedish Yellow' (*Erica tetralix*), 30, 223

T

'Tabramhill' (*Daboecia* ×*scotica*), 18
Taeniothrips. See *Ceratothrips*.
Taxus baccata 'Standishii', 118
Taylor, Bryan, 53–54
Taylor, Joan, 53, 54
'Tenuis' (*Calluna vulgaris*), 251
Tetranychus urticae, 63
'Thelma Woolner' (*Erica terminalis*), 221
Theoboldt, Paul, 199

'The Pygmy' (*Calluna vulgaris*), 52, 92–93, 186, 256
Thompson, Beverly, 86–87, 100
Thompson, James, 86–88, 100
Thompson garden, 2, 100–101
Thompson's Nursery, 121
thread mould. See *Rhizoctonia solani*.
thrips. See *Ceratothrips*.
Thymus, 81, 128, 129
Thymus doerfleri 'Bressingham', 151
Thymus 'Hartington Silver', 129, 150
Thymus serpyllum, 128
Thymus serpyllum 'Goldstream' 129
Thymus serpyllum 'Minimalist', 129
'Tib' (*Calluna vulgaris*), 40, 187, 241, 244, 249, 251, 255
'Tina' (*Erica tetralix*), 152, 223, 250
'Tom Thumb' (*Calluna vulgaris*), 85, 256
Tongariro National Park, 63
torch lily. See *Kniphofia*.
'Tracy Wilson' (*Erica* ×*garforthensis*), 167, 209, 252
'Treasure Trove' (*Erica carnea*), 162, 165, 198, 199, 206
tree heaths, 11–12, 83, 40, 47, 56–57, 61, 95–96, 258
Trochilidae, 18
'Truro' (*Erica* ×*watsonii*), 228
Tuinachtertop, 95
Tulipa, 141
Tulipa dasystemon. See *Tulipa tarda*.
Tulipa tarda, 141
Tulipa turkestanica, 141
Tulipa 'White Triumphator', 141
tulips. See *Tulipa*.
Tulloch Moor, 115
Turpin, Cherry, 227
Turpin, P. G., 180, 227

U

Udall, Katherine, 145–146
Ulex, 14
Underwood, Constance, 222
'Underwoodii' (*Calluna vulgaris*), 247
United States Department of Agriculture Plant Hardiness Zone Map, 26
University of California at Santa Cruz, 18
University of Liverpool Botanic Gardens, Ness, 180
UPOV, 153–154

V

Vaccinium, 13, 122
Vaccinium corymbosum 'Sunshine Blue', 122
Vaccinium glaucoalbum, 122
Vaccinium macrocarpon, 37
Vaccinium macrocarpon 'Hamilton', 122
Vaccinium myrtillus, 37–38
Vaccinium ovatum, 233
Vaccinium vitis-idaea, 122
Vaccinium vitis-idaea Koralle Group, 122
'Valerie Griffiths' (*Erica* ×*griffithsii*), 31, 97, 158, 211, 254
'Valerie Proudley' (*Erica vagans*), 158, 211, 226
Vanessa, 18
Veitch & Sons nursery, 226
Veitch's heath. See *Erica* ×*veitchii*.
'Velvet Dome' (*Calluna vulgaris*), 101, 256
'Velvet Fascination' (*Calluna vulgaris*), 149, 187, 234–235, 249
'Velvet Night' (*Erica cinerea*), 149, 204, 252
'Venus' (*Calluna vulgaris*), 247
vine weevil. See *Otiorhynchus sulcatus*.
Viola, 145
Viola 'Bowles Black', 145
Viola cornuta. See *Viola tricolor*.
Viola nigra. See *Viola tricolor*.
Viola tricolor, 145
'Visser's Fancy' (*Calluna vulgaris*), 247
Vivell, Adolf, 199
'Vivelli' (*Erica carnea*), 199

W

Waley, F. R., 190
'Waley's Red' (*Daboecia cantabrica*), 18, 150, 151, 190
Waskerley Moor, 17
Waterer, M. B. G., 229
Watsonia, 32
Watson's heath. See *Erica* ×*watsonii*.
'Westwood Yellow' (*Erica carnea*), 30, 123, 142, 199
WHISKY. See 'Bell's Extra Special' (*Erica carnea*).
'White Blum' (*Daboecia cantabrica*), 52
'White Carpet' (*Daboecia cantabrica*), 253
'White Coral' (*Calluna vulgaris*), 187
'White Knight' (*Calluna vulgaris*), 249
'White Lawn' (*Calluna vulgaris*), 187, 252, 253
'White Perfection' (*Erica* ×*darleyensis*), 206
'White Wings' (*Erica ciliaris*), 150, 232

Wick, Willa, 31, 60
'Wickwar Flame' (*Calluna vulgaris*), 128, 134, 149, 187
'William Buchanan' (*Daboecia* ×*scotica*), 18, 191, 251
'William Buchanan Gold' (*Daboecia* ×*scotica*), 191, 251, 258
Williams, P. D., 225–226
Williams, Priscilla, 121
Williams, Robert, 195
Williams heath. See *Erica* ×*williamsii*.
Willis, Nigel, 184
Wilson, David, 146–147, 155, 162–167, 166–167, 170, 206, 209, 228–229
Wilson, Irene, 163
Wilson, Kenneth, 162–163, 165
Wilson rhododendron. See *Rhododendron* ×*laetevirens*.
'Windlebrooke' (*Erica cinerea*), 205, 253
'Winter Chocolate' (*Calluna vulgaris*), 187
'Winter Fire' (*Calluna vulgaris*), 259
'Winter Fire' (*Erica*), 25, 247
'Wintersonne' (*Erica carnea*), 150, 199
witch hazel. See *Hamamelis*.
Woolner, Lionel, 221
Woolner, Thelma, 221
'W. T. Rackliff' (*Erica erigena*), 98–99, 156, 208, 209, 258
Wulff, Ella May, 233
Wulff garden, 33, 34, 35, 44, 128
'Wych' (*Erica ciliaris*), 234

Y

'Yellow John' (*Erica vagans*), 226
yew. See *Taxus*.
'Yvonne' (*Erica cinerea*), 255

Z

Zwijnenburg, R., 193

www.ingramcontent.com/pod-product-compliance
Lightning Source LLC
Chambersburg PA
CBHW081417230426

43668CB00016B/2263